Ford Transit Owners Workshop Manual

I M Coomber

Models covered
All Ford Transit ('Mk 2') models with in-line petrol engines
1599 cc ohv, 1593 cc ohc & 1993 cc ohc

*Does not cover Diesel or V6 petrol engines, non-standard bodywork and fittings,
or Transit '86 models*

ISBN 1 85010 176 0

ABCDE
FGHI.

THE
BOOK

Haynes Publishing Group
Sparkford Nr Yeovil
Somerset BA22 7JJ England

Haynes Publications, Inc
861 Lawrence Drive
Newbury Park
California 91320 USA

British Library Cataloguing in Publication Data
Coomber, Ian
Ford Transit (petrol) owners workshop manual.–
2nd ed.–(Owners Workshop Manuals)
1. Ford Transit truck
I. Title II. Series
629.28'73 TL230.5.F57
ISBN 1–85010–176–0

Acknowledgements

Special thanks are due to the Ford Motor Company for the supply of technical information and certain illustrations. Duckhams Oils provided lubrication data, and the Champion Sparking Plug Company supplied the illustrations showing the various spark plug conditions.

Sykes-Pickavant provided some of the workshop tools. Thanks are due also to the staff at Sparkford who assisted in the production of this manual.

About this manual

Its aim

The aim of this manual is to help you get the best from your car. It can do so in several ways. It can help you decide what work must be done (even should you choose to get it done by a garage), provide information on routine maintenance and servicing, and give a logical course of action and diagnosis when random faults occur. However, it is hoped that you will use the manual by tackling the work yourself. On simpler jobs it may even be quicker than booking the car into a garage and going there twice to leave and collect it. Perhaps most important, a lot of money can be saved by avoiding the costs the garage must charge to cover its labour and overheads.

The manual has drawings and descriptions to show the function of the various components so that their layout can be understood. Then the tasks are described and photographed in a step-by-step sequence so that even a novice can do the work.

Its arrangement

The manual is divided into thirteen Chapters, each covering a logical sub-division of the vehicle. The Chapters are each divided into Sections, numbered with single figures, eg 5; and the Sections into paragraphs (or sub-sections), with decimal numbers following on from the Section they are in, eg 5.1. 5.2 etc.

It is freely illustrated, especially in those parts where there is a detailed sequence of operations to be carried out. There are two forms of illustration: figures and photographs. The figures are numbered in sequence with decimal numbers, according to their position in the Chapter – Fig. 6.4 is the fourth drawing/illustration in Chapter 6. Photographs carry the same number (either individually or in related groups) as the Section or sub-section to which they relate.

There is an alphabetical index at the back of the manual as well as a contents list at the front. Each Chapter is also preceded by its own individual contents list.

References to the 'left' or 'right' of the vehicle are in the sense of a person in the driver's seat facing forwards.

Unless otherwise stated, nuts and bolts are removed by turning anti-clockwise, and tightened by turning clockwise.

Vehicle manufacturers continually make changes to specifications and recommendations, and these, when notified, are incorporated into our manuals at the earliest opportunity.

Whilst every care is taken to ensure that the information in this manual is correct, no liability can be accepted by the authors or publishers for loss, damage or injury caused by any errors in, or omissions from, the information given.

Introduction to the Ford Transit

The 'new' Transit range of vehicles was introduced in 1978 and incorporated many improvements over its predecessor, both mechanical and aesthetic. The restyled front end allows more engine compartment workspace and is better aerodynamically than the earlier model. The dashboard has also been updated and has improved instrumentation and controls.

Various power units are available. Those covered by this manual are the 1.6 litre ohv Kent engine and the 1.6 and 2.0 litre ohc engine variants.

Three transmission systems are available according to vehicle type, these being a four-speed manual gearbox, a four-speed manual gearbox with overdrive and a three-speed automatic transmission. The

manual gearboxes are available with standard or close ratio gears. The rear axle and differential are also variable to suit certain vehicle types.

All models are now fitted with dual circuit servo-assisted brakes with discs at the front and self-adjusting drum brakes at the rear.

Seemingly innumerable variations of body types and styles of Transit are available, from the humble Pick-up to the Caravanette. All body styles and variants are mounted on long or short wheelbase chassis as necessary.

The Transit, given regular maintenance at the specified intervals, will give reliable service over a long period, and is therefore worth looking after.

Contents

Transit 100 Van

General dimensions, weights and capacities

Dimensions
Overall length:
- Short wheelbase .... 192.2 in (4.552 m)
- Long wheelbase .... 208.75 in (5.302 m)

Overall width:
- Short wheelbase .... 77.16 in (1.960 m)
- Long wheelbase .... 81.06 in (2.060 m)

Wheelbase:
- Short wheelbase .... 106 in (2.690 m)
- Long wheelbase .... 118 in (3.000 m)

Weights
Kerb weight (with standard engines, full fuel tank and minimum equipment):
- Transit 80 (SWB) .... 2667 lb (1211 kg)
- Transit 100 (SWB) .... 2689 lb (1221 kg)
- Transit 120 (SWB) .... 2782 lb (1263 kg)
- Transit 100 (LWB) .... 2940 lb (1335 kg)
- Transit 130 (LWB) .... 3152 lb (1431 kg)
- Transit 160 (LWB) .... 3169 lb (1439 kg)
- Transit 175 (LWB) .... 3463 lb (1572 kg)
- Transit 190 (LWB) .... 3260 lb (1480 kg)

Capacities
Engine oil (including filter):
- OHV .... 7.0 pints (4.0 litres)
- OHC .... 6.6 pints (3.75 litres)

Manual transmission oil:
- Standard .... 2.6 pints (1.5 litres)
- Heavy duty .... 3.5 pints (2.0 litres)
- With overdrive .... 4.4 pints (2.5 litres)

Automatic transmission .... 11.25 pints (6.4 litres) including converter

Rear axle:
- Models 80 to 120 .... 4.75 pints (2.7 litres)
- Models 130 to 190 .... 3.25 pints (1.9 litres)

Cooling system (including heater):
- OHV .... 10.6 pints (6.0 litres)
- OHC .... 14.4 pints (8.2 litres)

Fuel tank:
- Models 80 to 120 .... 9.25 gallons (42 litres)
- Models 130 to 190 .... 15.0 gallons (68 litres)

Buying spare parts and vehicle identification numbers

Buying spare parts

Spare parts are available from many sources, for example: Ford garages, other garages and accessory shops, and motor factors. Our advice regarding spare part sources is as follows:

Officially appointed Ford garages – This is the best source of parts which are peculiar to your vehicle and are otherwise not generally available (eg complete cylinder heads, internal gearbox components, badges, interior trim etc). It is also the only place at which you should buy parts if your vehicle is still under warranty – non-Ford components may invalidate the warranty. To be sure of obtaining the correct parts it will always be necessary to give the storeman your vehicle's identification number, and if possible, to take the 'old' part along for positive identification. Remember that many parts are available on a factory exchange scheme – any parts returned should always be clean! It obviously makes good sense to go straight to the specialists on your vehicle for this type of part for they are best equipped to supply you.

Other garages and accessory shops – These are often very good places to buy materials and components needed for the maintenance of your vehicle (eg oil filters, spark plugs, bulbs, drivebelts, oil and greases, touch-up paint, filler paste etc). They also sell general accessories, usually have convenient opening hours, charge lower prices and can often be found not far from home.

Motor factors – Good factors will stock all of the more important components which wear out relatively quickly (eg clutch components, pistons, valves, exhaust systems, brake cylinders/pipes/hoses/seals/shoes and pads etc). Motor factors will often provide new or reconditioned components on a part exchange basis – this can save a considerable amount of money.

Vehicle identification numbers

Although many individual parts, and in some cases sub-assemblies, fit a number of different models, it is dangerous to assume that just because they look the same, they are the same. Differences are not always easy to detect except by serial numbers. Make sure therefore, that the appropriate identity number for the model or sub-assembly is known and quoted when a spart part is ordered.

The vehicle identification plate is located in the cab footwell and lists the vehicle type and axle weight.

The engine number on the ohv engine is located on the left-hand side of the crankcase towards the front.

The engine number on the ohc engine is located on the right-hand side of the crankcase towards the front.

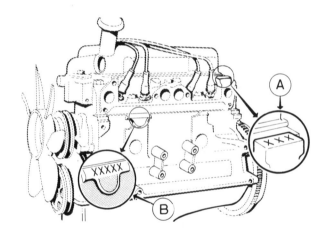

Engine serial number (B) and code number (A) on the ohv engine

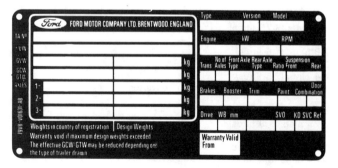

Vehicle identification plate

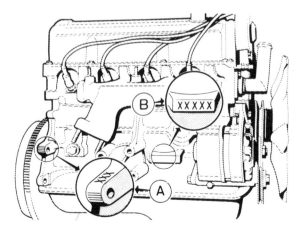

Engine serial number (B) and engine code (A) locations on the ohc engine

Tools and working facilities

Introduction

A selection of good tools is a fundamental requirement for anyone contemplating the maintenance and repair of a motor vehicle. For the owner who does not possess any, their purchase will prove a considerable expense, offsetting some of the savings made by doing-it-yourself. However, provided that the tools purchased are of good quality, they will last for many years and prove an extremely worthwhile investment.

To help the average owner to decide which tools are needed to carry out the various tasks detailed in this manual, we have compiled three lists of tools under the following headings: *Maintenance and minor repair, Repair and overhaul,* and *Special.* The newcomer to practical mechanics should start off with the *Maintenance and minor repair* tool kit and confine himself to the simpler jobs around the vehicle. Then, as his confidence and experience grow, he can undertake more difficult tasks, buying extra tools as, and when, they are needed. In this way, a *Maintenance and minor repair* tool kit can be built-up into a *Repair and overhaul* tool kit over a considerable period of time without any major cash outlays. The experienced do-it-yourselfer will have a tool kit good enough for most repair and overhaul procedures and will add tools from the *Special* category when he feels the expense is justified by the amount of use these tools will be put to.

It is obviously not possible to cover the subject of tools fully here. For those who wish to learn more about tools and their use there is a book entitled *How to Choose and Use Car Tools* available from the publishers of this manual.

Maintenance and minor repair tool kit

The tools given in this list should be considered as a minimum requirement if routine maintenance, servicing and minor repair operations are to be undertaken. We recommend the purchase of combination spanners (ring one end, open-ended the other); although more expensive than open-ended ones, they do give the advantages of both types of spanner.

Combination spanners - 10, 11, 12, 13, 14 & 17 mm
Adjustable spanner - 9 inch
Gearbox/rear axle drain plug key
Spark plug spanner (with rubber insert)
Spark plug gap adjustment tool
Set of feeler gauges
Brake bleed nipple spanner
Screwdriver - 4 in long x $\frac{1}{4}$ in dia (flat blade)
Screwdriver - 4 in long x $\frac{1}{4}$ in dia (cross blade)
Combination pliers - 6 inch
Hacksaw (junior)
Tyre pump
Tyre pressure gauge
Grease gun
Oil can
Fine emery cloth (1 sheet)
Wire brush (small)
Funnel (medium size)

Repair and overhaul tool kit

These tools are virtually essential for anyone undertaking any major repairs to a motor vehicle, and are additional to those given in the *Maintenance and minor repair* list. Included in this list is a comprehensive set of sockets. Although these are expensive they will be found invaluable as they are so versatile - particularly if various drives are included in the set. We recommend the $\frac{1}{2}$ in square-drive type, as this can be used with most proprietary torque spanners. If you cannot afford a socket set, even bought piecemeal, then inexpensive tubular box wrenches are a useful alternative.

The tools in this list will occasionally need to be supplemented by tools from the *Special* list.

Sockets (or box spanners) to cover range in previous list
Reversible ratchet drive (for use with sockets)
Extension piece, 10 inch (for use with sockets)
Universal joint (for use with sockets)
Torque wrench (for use with sockets)
Splined bolt tools (ohc engine — see Chapter 1)
Mole wrench - 8 inch
Ball pein hammer
Soft-faced hammer, plastic or rubber
Screwdriver - 6 in long x $\frac{5}{16}$ in dia (flat blade)
Screwdriver - 2 in long x $\frac{5}{16}$ in square (flat blade)
Screwdriver - 1$\frac{1}{2}$ in long x $\frac{1}{4}$ in dia (cross blade)
Screwdriver - 3 in long x $\frac{1}{8}$ in dia (electricians)
Pliers - electricians side cutters
Pliers - needle nosed
Pliers - circlip (internal and external)
Cold chisel - $\frac{1}{2}$ inch
Scriber
Scraper
Centre punch
Pin punch
Hacksaw
Valve grinding tool
Steel rule/straight-edge
Allen keys
Selection of files
Wire brush (large)
Axle-stands
Jack (strong scissor or hydraulic type)

Special tools

The tools in this list are those which are not used regularly, are expensive to buy, or which need to be used in accordance with their manufacturers' instructions. Unless relatively difficult mechanical jobs are undertaken frequently, it will not be economic to buy many of these tools. Where this is the case, you could consider clubbing together with friends (or joining a motorists' club) to make a joint purchase, or borrowing the tools against a deposit from a local garage or tool hire specialist.

The following list contains only those tools and instruments freely available to the public, and not those special tools produced by the vehicle manufacturer specifically for its dealer network. You will find occasional references to these manufacturers' special tools in the text of this manual. Generally, an alternative method of doing the job without the vehicle manufacturers' special tool is given. However, sometimes, there is no alternative to using them. Where this is the case and the relevant tool cannot be bought or borrowed you will have to entrust the work to a franchised garage.

Valve spring compressor
Piston ring compressor
Balljoint separator
Universal hub/bearing puller
Impact screwdriver
Micrometer and/or vernier gauge
Dial gauge
Stroboscopic timing light
Dwell angle meter/tachometer
Universal electrical multi-meter
Cylinder compression gauge
Lifting tackle
Trolley jack
Light with extension lead

Buying tools

For practically all tools, a tool dealer is the best source since he will have a very comprehensive range compared with the average garage or accessory shop. Having said that, accessory shops often offer excellent quality tools at discount prices, so it pays to shop around.

Remember, you don't have to buy the most expensive items on the shelf, but it is always advisable to steer clear of the very cheap tools. There are plenty of good tools around at reasonable prices, so ask the proprietor or manager of the shop for advice before making a purchase.

Care and maintenance of tools

Having purchased a reasonable tool kit, it is necessary to keep the tools in a clean serviceable condition. After use, always wipe off any dirt, grease and metal particles using a clean, dry cloth, before putting the tools away. Never leave them lying around after they have been used. A simple tool rack on the garage or workshop wall, for items such as screwdrivers and pliers is a good idea. Store all normal wrenches and sockets in a metal box. Any measuring instruments, gauges, meters, etc, must be carefully stored where they cannot be damaged or become rusty.

Take a little care when tools are used. Hammer heads inevitably become marked and screwdrivers lose the keen edge on their blades from time to time. A little timely attention with emery cloth or a file will soon restore items like this to a good serviceable finish.

Working facilities

Not to be forgotten when discussing tools, is the workshop itself. If anything more than routine maintenance is to be carried out, some form of suitable working area becomes essential.

It is appreciated that many an owner mechanic is forced by circumstances to remove an engine or similar item, without the benefit of a garage or workshop. Having done this, any repairs should always be done under the cover of a roof.

Wherever possible, any dismantling should be done on a clean flat workbench or table at a suitable working height.

Any workbench needs a vise: one with a jaw opening of 4 in (100 mm) is suitable for most jobs. As mentioned previously, some clean dry storage space is also required for tools, as well as the lubricants, cleaning fluids, touch-up paints and so on which become necessary.

Another item which may be required, and which has a much more general usage, is an electric drill with a chuck capacity of at least $\frac{5}{16}$ in (8 mm). This, together with a good range of twist drills, is virtually essential for fitting accessories such as wing mirrors and reversing lights.

Last, but not least, always keep a supply of old newspapers and clean, lint-free rags available, and try to keep any working area as clean as possible.

Spanner jaw gap comparison table

Jaw gap (in)	Spanner size
0.250	$\frac{1}{4}$ in AF
0.276	7 mm
0.313	$\frac{5}{16}$ in AF
0.315	8 mm
0.344	$\frac{11}{32}$ in AF; $\frac{1}{8}$ in Whitworth
0.354	9 mm
0.375	$\frac{3}{8}$ in AF
0.394	10 mm
0.433	11 mm
0.438	$\frac{7}{16}$ in AF
0.445	$\frac{3}{16}$ in Whitworth; $\frac{1}{4}$ in BSF
0.472	12 mm
0.500	$\frac{1}{2}$ in AF
0.512	13 mm
0.525	$\frac{1}{4}$ in Whitworth; $\frac{5}{16}$ in BSF
0.551	14 mm
0.563	$\frac{9}{16}$ in AF
0.591	15 mm
0.600	$\frac{5}{16}$ in Whitworth; $\frac{3}{8}$ in BSF
0.625	$\frac{5}{8}$ in AF
0.630	16 mm
0.669	17 mm
0.686	$\frac{11}{16}$ in AF
0.709	18 mm
0.710	$\frac{3}{8}$ in Whitworth; $\frac{7}{16}$ in BSF
0.748	19 mm
0.750	$\frac{3}{4}$ in AF
0.813	$\frac{13}{16}$ in AF
0.820	$\frac{7}{16}$ in Whitworth; $\frac{1}{2}$ in BSF
0.866	22 mm
0.875	$\frac{7}{8}$ in AF
0.920	$\frac{1}{2}$ in Whitworth; $\frac{9}{16}$ in BSF
0.938	$\frac{15}{16}$ in AF
0.945	24 mm
1.000	1 in AF
1.010	$\frac{9}{16}$ in Whitworth; $\frac{5}{8}$ in BSF
1.024	26 mm
1.063	$1\frac{1}{16}$ in AF; 27 mm
1.100	$\frac{5}{8}$ in Whitworth; $\frac{11}{16}$ in BSF
1.125	$1\frac{1}{8}$ in AF
1.181	30 mm
1.200	$\frac{11}{16}$ in Whitworth; $\frac{3}{4}$ in BSF
1.250	$1\frac{1}{4}$ in AF
1.260	32 mm
1.300	$\frac{3}{4}$ in Whitworth; $\frac{7}{8}$ in BSF
1.313	$1\frac{5}{16}$ in AF
1.390	$\frac{13}{16}$ in Whitworth; $\frac{15}{16}$ in BSF
1.417	36 mm
1.438	$1\frac{7}{16}$ in AF
1.480	$\frac{7}{8}$ in Whitworth; 1 in BSF
1.500	$1\frac{1}{2}$ in AF
1.575	40 mm; $\frac{15}{16}$ in Whitworth
1.614	41 mm
1.625	$1\frac{5}{8}$ in AF
1.670	1 in Whitworth; $1\frac{1}{8}$ in BSF
1.688	$1\frac{11}{16}$ in AF
1.811	46 mm
1.813	$1\frac{13}{16}$ in AF
1.860	$1\frac{1}{8}$ in Whitworth; $1\frac{1}{4}$ in BSF
1.875	$1\frac{7}{8}$ in AF
1.969	50 mm
2.000	2 in AF
2.050	$1\frac{1}{4}$ in Whitworth; $1\frac{3}{8}$ in BSF
2.165	55 mm
2.362	60 mm

Jacking and towing

Jacking points

To change a wheel in an emergency, use the jack supplied with the vehicle. Ensure that the roadwheel nuts are released before jacking up the vehicle and make sure that the arm of the jack is fully engaged with the body bracket and that the base of the jack is standing on a firm level surface.

The jack supplied with the vehicle is not suitable for use when raising the vehicle for maintenance or repair operations. For this work, use a trolley or heavy duty bottle jack of suitable capacity. Whenever possible jack up on firm level ground and locate the jack under the front or rear axle as applicable.

If jacking up at the front end, ensure that the handbrake is fully applied, engage a gear and place chocks each side of the rear wheels. If jacking up at the rear, place chocks each side of the front wheels before raising the vehicle. Whenever possible, and especially when attending to major service or repair work under the vehicle, supplement any jack with axle stands.

When changing a wheel on vehicles fitted with six-stud wheels, note that the wheel nuts on the left-hand side of the vehicle have a *left-hand thread*, ie they undo *clockwise*. These nuts and studs are marked with the letter L.

When fitting twin rear wheels, make sure that the wheel mating surfaces are clean.

Towing

If your vehicle is to be towed, attach the tow-rope to the front axle within the leaf spring locations and so that it does not interfere with the steering. Ensure that the steering lock is released!

Where the vehicle is fitted with automatic transmission, the distance towed must not exceed 12 miles (20 km), nor the speed 25 mph (40 kph), otherwise serious damage to the transmission may result. If these limits are likely to be exceeded, or if transmission damage is suspected, disconnect the propeller shaft and remove it as given in Chapter 7.

Remember that if the vehicle is to be towed and the engine is not running, there will be no servo assistance to the brakes and therefore additional pressure will be required to operate them.

If towing another vehicle, attach the tow-rope to the towing eyes where fitted, or around the rear shock absorber mounting bracket.

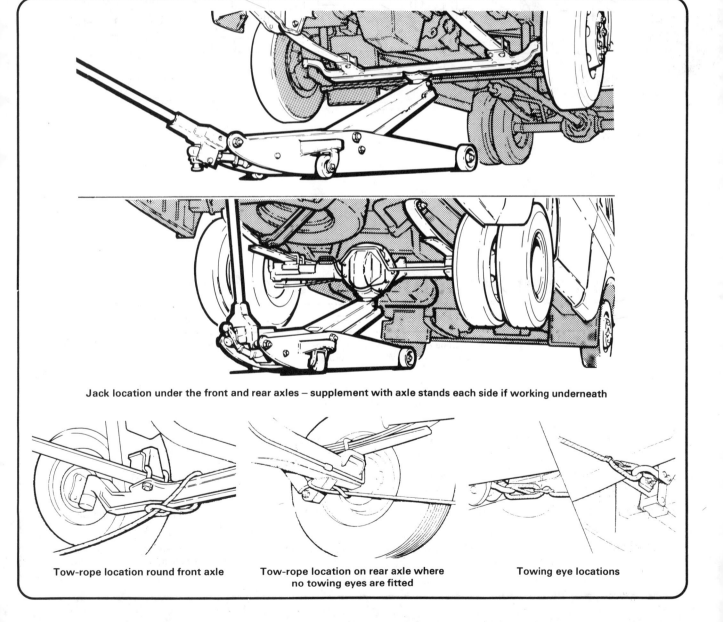

Jack location under the front and rear axles – supplement with axle stands each side if working underneath

Tow-rope location round front axle

Tow-rope location on rear axle where no towing eyes are fitted

Towing eye locations

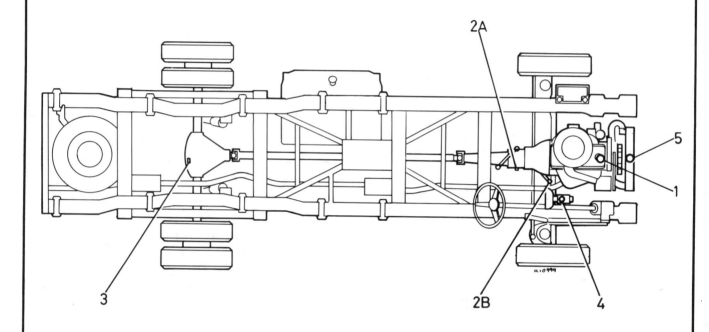

Recommended lubricants and fluids

Component or system	Lubricant type/specification	Duckhams recommendation
1 Engine	Multigrade engine oil, viscosity range SAE 10W/30 to 20W/50, to Ford spec. SSM-2C9001-AA	Duckhams QXR, Hypergrade, or 10W/40 Motor Oil
2A Manual transmission	Hypoid gear oil, viscosity SAE 80EP, to Ford spec. SQM-2C9008-A	Duckhams Hypoid 80
2B Automatic transmission Black dipstick (up to Sept 1980) Red dipstick (from Oct. 1980)	 ATF to Ford spec. SQM-2C-9007-AA ATF to Ford spec. SQM-2C-9010-A	 Duckhams Q-Matic Duckhams D-Matic
3 Rear axle	Hypoid gear oil, viscosity SAE 90EP, to Ford spec. SRM-2C-9102-A	Duckhams Hypoid 90S
4 Braking system	Hydraulic fluid to Ford spec. SAM-6-9103 A (amber)	Duckhams Universal Brake and Clutch Fluid
5 Cooling system	Antifreeze to Ford spec. SSM-97B-9101-A	Duckhams Universal Antifreeze and Summer Coolant

Safety first!

Professional motor mechanics are trained in safe working procedures. However enthusiastic you may be about getting on with the job in hand, do take the time to ensure that your safety is not put at risk. A moment's lack of attention can result in an accident, as can failure to observe certain elementary precautions.

There will always be new ways of having accidents, and the following points do not pretend to be a comprehensive list of all dangers; they are intended rather to make you aware of the risks and to encourage a safety-conscious approach to all work you carry out on your vehicle.

Essential DOs and DON'Ts

DON'T rely on a single jack when working underneath the vehicle. Always use reliable additional means of support, such as axle stands, securely placed under a part of the vehicle that you know will not give way.

DON'T attempt to loosen or tighten high-torque nuts (e.g. wheel hub nuts) while the vehicle is on a jack; it may be pulled off.

DON'T start the engine without first ascertaining that the transmission is in neutral (or 'Park' where applicable) and the parking brake applied.

DON'T suddenly remove the filler cap from a hot cooling system – cover it with a cloth and release the pressure gradually first, or you may get scalded by escaping coolant.

DON'T attempt to drain oil until you are sure it has cooled sufficiently to avoid scalding you.

DON'T grasp any part of the engine, exhaust or catalytic converter without first ascertaining that it is sufficiently cool to avoid burning you.

DON'T allow brake fluid or antifreeze to contact vehicle paintwork.

DON'T syphon toxic liquids such as fuel, brake fluid or antifreeze by mouth, or allow them to remain on your skin.

DON'T inhale dust – it may be injurious to health (see *Asbestos* below).

DON'T allow any spilt oil or grease to remain on the floor – wipe it up straight away, before someone slips on it.

DON'T use ill-fitting spanners or other tools which may slip and cause injury.

DON'T attempt to lift a heavy component which may be beyond your capability – get assistance.

DON'T rush to finish a job, or take unverified short cuts.

DON'T allow children or animals in or around an unattended vehicle.

DO wear eye protection when using power tools such as drill, sander, bench grinder etc, and when working under the vehicle.

DO use a barrier cream on your hands prior to undertaking dirty jobs – it will protect your skin from infection as well as making the dirt easier to remove afterwards; but make sure your hands aren't left slippery. Note that long-term contact with used engine oil can be a health hazard.

DO keep loose clothing (cuffs, tie etc) and long hair well out of the way of moving mechanical parts.

DO remove rings, wristwatch etc, before working on the vehicle – especially the electrical system.

DO ensure that any lifting tackle used has a safe working load rating adequate for the job.

DO keep your work area tidy – it is only too easy to fall over articles left lying around.

DO get someone to check periodically that all is well, when working alone on the vehicle.

DO carry out work in a logical sequence and check that everything is correctly assembled and tightened afterwards.

DO remember that your vehicle's safety affects that of yourself and others. If in doubt on any point, get specialist advice.

IF, in spite of following these precautions, you are unfortunate enough to injure yourself, seek medical attention as soon as possible.

Asbestos

Certain friction, insulating, sealing, and other products – such as brake linings, brake bands, clutch linings, torque converters, gaskets, etc – contain asbestos. *Extreme care must be taken to avoid inhalation of dust from such products since it is hazardous to health.* If in doubt, assume that they *do* contain asbestos.

Fire

Remember at all times that petrol (gasoline) is highly flammable. Never smoke, or have any kind of naked flame around, when working on the vehicle. But the risk does not end there – a spark caused by an electrical short-circuit, by two metal surfaces contacting each other, by careless use of tools, or even by static electricity built up in your body under certain conditions, can ignite petrol vapour, which in a confined space is highly explosive.

Always disconnect the battery earth (ground) terminal before working on any part of the fuel or electrical system, and never risk spilling fuel on to a hot engine or exhaust.

It is recommended that a fire extinguisher of a type suitable for fuel and electrical fires is kept handy in the garage or workplace at all times. Never try to extinguish a fuel or electrical fire with water.

Fumes

Certain fumes are highly toxic and can quickly cause unconsciousness and even death if inhaled to any extent. Petrol (gasoline) vapour comes into this category, as do the vapours from certain solvents such as trichloroethylene. Any draining or pouring of such volatile fluids should be done in a well ventilated area.

When using cleaning fluids and solvents, read the instructions carefully. Never use materials from unmarked containers – they may give off poisonous vapours.

Never run the engine of a motor vehicle in an enclosed space such as a garage. Exhaust fumes contain carbon monoxide which is extremely poisonous; if you need to run the engine, always do so in the open air or at least have the rear of the vehicle outside the workplace.

If you are fortunate enough to have the use of an inspection pit, never drain or pour petrol, and never run the engine, while the vehicle is standing over it; the fumes, being heavier than air, will concentrate in the pit with possibly lethal results.

The battery

Never cause a spark, or allow a naked light, near the vehicle's battery. It will normally be giving off a certain amount of hydrogen gas, which is highly explosive.

Always disconnect the battery earth (ground) terminal before working on the fuel or electrical systems.

If possible, loosen the filler plugs or cover when charging the battery from an external source. Do not charge at an excessive rate or the battery may burst.

Take care when topping up and when carrying the battery. The acid electrolyte, even when diluted, is very corrosive and should not be allowed to contact the eyes or skin.

If you ever need to prepare electrolyte yourself, always add the acid slowly to the water, and never the other way round. Protect against splashes by wearing rubber gloves and goggles.

When jump starting a car using a booster battery, for negative earth (ground) vehicles, connect the jump leads in the following sequence: First connect one jump lead between the positive (+) terminals of the two batteries. Then connect the other jump lead first to the negative (–) terminal of the booster battery, and then to a good earthing (ground) point on the vehicle to be started, at least 18 in (45 cm) from the battery if possible. Ensure that hands and jump leads are clear of any moving parts, and that the two vehicles do not touch. Disconnect the leads in the reverse order.

Mains electricity

When using an electric power tool, inspection light etc, which works from the mains, always ensure that the appliance is correctly connected to its plug and that, where necessary, it is properly earthed (grounded). Do not use such appliances in damp conditions and, again, beware of creating a spark or applying excessive heat in the vicinity of fuel or fuel vapour.

Ignition HT voltage

A severe electric shock can result from touching certain parts of the ignition system, such as the HT leads, when the engine is running or being cranked, particularly if components are damp or the insulation is defective. Where an electronic ignition system is fitted, the HT voltage is much higher and could prove fatal.

Routine maintenance

Maintenance is essential both for safety and for obtaining the best in terms of performance and economy from your vehicle. Over the years, the need for periodic lubrication – oiling, greasing, so on – has been drastically reduced, and this has led some owners to think that the various components either no longer exist or will last forever. This is a serious delusion. It follows, therefore, that the largest initial element of maintenance is visual examination.

The following routine maintenance summary is based on the manufacturer's recommendation, but is supplemented by certain checks which the author feels will add up to improved reliability and an increase of component life. In severe operating conditions, more frequent engine oil changes may be advisable. Consult your Ford dealer if in doubt on this point.

Every 250 miles (400 km) or weekly, whichever is sooner

Engine

Check the engine oil with the vehicle standing on level ground; withdraw dipstick, wipe it clean, re-insert it and withdraw it again to observe the level reading (photo). Oil level must be maintained between the 'MAX' and 'MIN' marks on the dipstick. Top up the oil level if necessary.

Cooling system

Check the level of the coolant by removing the radiator (or expansion tank) filler cap (photo). The cap should only be removed when the engine is cold, but if required it can be removed when hot providing the cap is muffled with a rag and the cap is turned very slowly anti-clockwise to release the pressure in the system. **Do not** completely remove the cap until all pressure is released. The coolant level should be kept between 1.0 and 1.5 in (25 to 35 mm) below the filler neck. Top up if necessary using coolant containing the correct ratio of anti-freeze to maintain its efficiency.

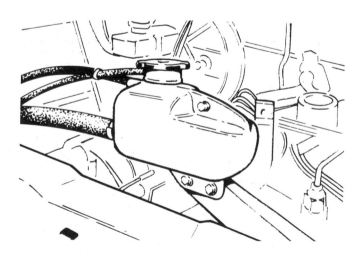

Coolant expansion tank

Brakes

Wipe clean the fluid reservoir and cap(s) and observe the fluid level. The level should be up to the base of the filler neck or the level marking on the reservoir as applicable (photo).
If necessary top up the level, using only the specified fluid type, and avoid spilling fluid onto the paintwork – wash it off at once if you do. If the fluid level suddenly drops by a considerable amount, check the hydraulic circuit and connections for signs of leakage and if necessary renew without delay any defective section, component or seal.

Steering and suspension

Check the tyre pressures and adjust if necessary – refer to Chapter 11 for the specified pressures.
Examine the tyres for signs of excessive wear and damage.
Check the steering for smooth and accurate response.

Electrical

Check the battery electrolyte level and top up as necessary – refer to Chapter 10.
Check the operation of lights, indicators and horn.
Check the windscreen washer reservoir fluid level and top up if required.

Every 6000 miles (10 000 km) or 6 months, whichever comes first

Engine

Renew the engine oil and filter (photo). Drain the oil when the engine is hot into a suitable container. Renew the oil filter as given in Chapter 1. Top up the engine oil level using the recommended grade of oil. Clean the filler cap before refitting (photo).
Check the condition and tension of the alternator drivebelt and adjust or renew if necessary as given in Chapter 2.
Refer to Chapter 1, Section 50 or 115 as applicable, and check/adjust the valve clearances as necessary.
Remove and clean the spark plugs. Adjust the electrode clearances to the specified gap – see Chapter 4.
Check the distributor contact points clearance and adjust as given in Chapter 4 if necessary.
Clean and inspect the distributor cap and leads. Renew if found defective.
Refer to Chapter 4, Section 10, and check the ignition timing – adjust if necessary.
Check the engine idle speed (with the engine at its normal operating temperature) and if necessary adjust the carburettor as given in Chapter 3.
Check the engine for oil and/or coolant leaks. Also inspect the coolant hoses for signs of deterioration. Renew if required.

Electrical

Remove battery and clean the battery terminals and case.

Brakes

Check the front disc pads and the rear drum shoe linings for signs of excessive wear. Refer to Chapter 9 for details and renew if necessary.
Check all brake hydraulic pipes and hoses for damage or deterioration and renew where necessary.

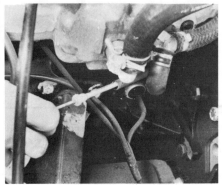

Dipstick location on the OHC engine

Topping up the coolant

Topping up the brake fluid

Topping up the engine oil

Removing the oil filter with special removal wrench which may be necessary if very tight

Gearbox oil level/filler plug (A) and drain plug (B)

Steering and suspension

Check the front and rear spring U-bolts for tightness – refer to Chapter 11 for torque setting of nuts.

Check the respective steering and suspension linkages for signs of excessive wear.

Apply grease to each front axle swivel pin. There is an upper and lower grease nipple on each side.

Check the front wheel toe-in referring to Chapter 11, Section 15 for details.

Check the steering and ball-joint covers for wear or damage.

Transmission

Check the gearbox oil level and top up with the specified grade of oil if necessary through the filler/level plug hole (photo).

Check the automatic transmission fluid level as described in Chapter 6.

Check the rear axle oil level and top up if necessary with the specified grade of oil through the filler/level plug hole.

General checks

Check the exhaust system for damage, corrosion, leaks and/or insecurity. Repair or renew as necessary.

Check the underbody and chassis for signs of severe corrosion or damage.

Check and lubricate if necessary the bonnet lock and safety catch. Where fitted, lubricate the sliding door roller mechanisms.

Check the tightness of the wheel nuts. If wished, interchange the tyre positions to even out wear.

Check and if necessary adjust the clutch as given in Chapter 5.

Every 12 000 miles (20 000 km) or 12 months, whichever comes first

---

Complete the 6000 mile service plus the following:

Remove and renew the air filter element, referring to Chapter 3 if necessary.

Renew the spark plugs. Check the electrode clearances before

fitting and do not overtighten the plugs.

Refer to Chapter 4 and renew the distributor contact points.

Check the automatic choke adjustment (where applicable) as given in Chapter 3.

On automatic transmission models, lubricate the linkages of the control rods and cable. Adjust the front brake band.

On manual transmission models, lubricate the clutch cable ends. Lubricate the handbrake linkage and check its operation. If necessary adjust the cable as given in Chapter 9.

Check that the windscreen wipers, washers and (where fitted) the headlight washers operate in a satisfactory manner. Renew the wiper blades if worn or defective.

Check the operation of the respective instruments, controls and equipment.

Lubricate and check the operation of door locks and hinges.

On models fitted with a load-conscious (apportioning) valve in the brake system, have your Ford dealer check its adjustment.

Every 24 000 miles (40 000 km) or 2 years, whichever comes first

---

Complete the 6000 and 12 000-mile services, plus the following:

Renew the crankcase emission control valve.

Refer to Chapter 3 and check the fast idle speed setting, adjust if necessary.

Refer to Chapter 11 and dismantle the front hub units for lubrication. Adjust on reassembly.

Adjust the steering sector shaft pre-load setting if required, referring to Chapter 11 for details (Section 13).

Drain the cooling system and renew the coolant using new anti-freeze – see Chapter 2.

Every 36 000 miles (60 000 km) or 3 years, whichever comes first

---

Renew all braking system seals and hoses and refill with clean, fresh fluid of the specified type.

Fault diagnosis

Introduction

The vehicle owner who does his or her own maintenance according to the recommended schedules should not have to use this section of the manual very often. Modern component reliability is such that, provided those items subject to wear or deterioration are inspected or renewed at the specified intervals, sudden failure is comparatively rare. Faults do not usually just happen as a result of sudden failure, but develop over a period of time. Major mechanical failures in particular are usually preceded by characteristic symptoms over hundreds or even thousands of miles. Those components which do occasionally fail without warning are often small and easily carried in the vehicle.

With any fault finding, the first step is to decide where to begin investigations. Sometimes this is obvious, but on other occasions a little detective work will be necessary. The owner who makes half a dozen haphazard adjustments or replacements may be successful in curing a fault (or its symptoms), but he will be none the wiser if the fault recurs and he may well have spent more time and money than was necessary. A calm and logical approach will be found to be more satisfactory in the long run. Always take into account any warning signs or abnormalities that may have been noticed in the period preceding the fault – power loss, high or low gauge readings, unusual noises or smells, etc – and remember that failure of components such as fuses or spark plugs may only be pointers to some underlying fault.

The pages which follow here are intended to help in cases of failure to start or breakdown on the road. There is also a Fault Diagnosis Section at the end of each Chapter which should be consulted if the preliminary checks prove unfruitful. Whatever the fault, certain basic principles apply. These are as follows:

Verify the fault. This is simply a matter of being sure that you know what the symptoms are before starting work. This is particularly important if you are investigating a fault for someone else who may not have described it very accurately.

Don't overlook the obvious. For example, if the vehicle won't start, is there petrol in the tank? (Don't take anyone else's word on this particular point, and don't trust the fuel gauge either!) If an electrical fault is indicated, look for loose or broken wires before digging out the test gear.

Cure the disease, not the symptom. Substituting a flat battery with a fully charged one will get you off the hard shoulder, but if the underlying cause is not attended to, the new battery will go the same way. Similarly, changing oil-fouled spark plugs for a new set will get you moving again, but remember that the reason for the fouling (if it wasn't simply an incorrect grade of plug) will have to be established and corrected.

Don't take anything for granted. Particularly, don't forget that a 'new' component may itself be defective (especially if it's been rattling round in the boot for months), and don't leave components out of a fault diagnosis sequence just because they are new or recently fitted. When you do finally diagnose a difficult fault, you'll probably realise that all the evidence was there from the start.

Electrical faults

Electrical faults can be more puzzling than straightforward mechanical failures, but they are no less susceptible to logical analysis if the basic principles of operation are understood. Vehicle electrical wiring exists in extremely unfavourable conditions – heat, vibration and chemical attack – and the first things to look for are loose or corroded

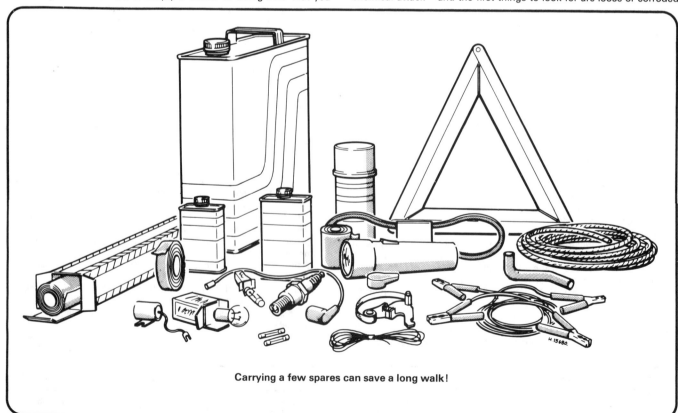

Carrying a few spares can save a long walk!

connections and broken or chafed wires, especially where the wires pass through holes in the bodywork or are subject to vibration.

All metal-bodied vehicles in current production have one pole of the battery 'earthed', ie connected to the vehicle bodywork, and in nearly all modern vehicles it is the negative (–) terminal. The various electrical components' motors, bulb holders etc – are also connected to earth, either by means of a lead or directly by their mountings. Electric current flows through the component and then back to the battery via the vehicle bodywork. If the component mounting is loose or corroded, or if a good path back to the battery is not available, the circuit will be incomplete and malfunction will result. The engine and/or gearbox are also earthed by means of flexible metal straps to the body or subframe; if these straps are loose or missing, starter motor, generator and ignition trouble may result.

Assuming the earth return to be satisfactory, electrical faults will be due either to component malfunction or to defects in the current supply. Individual components are dealt with in Chapter 10. If supply wires are broken or cracked internally this results in an open-circuit, and the easiest way to check for this is to bypass the suspect wire temporarily with a length of wire having a crocodile clip or suitable connector at each end. Alternatively, a 12V test lamp can be used to verify the presence of supply voltage at various points along the wire and the break can be thus isolated.

If a bare portion of a live wire touches the vehicle bodywork or other earthed metal part, the electricity will take the low-resistance path thus formed back to the battery: this is known as a short-circuit. Hopefully a short-circuit will blow a fuse, but otherwise it may cause burning of the insulation (and possibly further short-circuits) or even a fire. This is why it is inadvisable to bypass persistently blowing fuses with silver foil or wire.

Spares and tool kit

Most vehicles are only supplied with sufficient tools for wheel changing; the *Maintenance and minor repair* tool kit detailed in *Tools and working facilities,* with the addition of a hammer, is probably sufficient for those repairs that most motorists would consider attempting at the roadside. In addition a few items which can be fitted without too much trouble in the event of a breakdown should be carried. Experience and available space will modify the list below, but the following may save having to call on professional assistance:

> *Spark plugs, clean and correctly gapped*
> *HT lead and plug cap – long enough to reach the plug furthest from the distributor*
> *Distributor rotor, condenser and contact breaker points*
> *Drivebelt – emergency type may suffice*
> *Spare fuses*
> *Set of principal light bulbs*
> *Tin of radiator sealer and hose bandage*
> *Exhaust bandage*
> *Roll of insulating tape*
> *Length of soft iron wire*
> *Length of electrical flex*
> *Torch or inspection lamp (can double as test lamp)*
> *Battery jump leads*
> *Tow-rope*
> *Ignition waterproofing aerosol*
> *Litre of engine oil*
> *Sealed can of hydraulic fluid*
> *Emergency windscreen*
> *'Jubilee' clips*
> *Tube of filler paste*

If spare fuel is carried, a can designed for the purpose should be used to minimise risks of leakage and collision damage. A first aid kit and a warning triangle, whilst not at present compulsory in the UK, are obviously sensible items to carry in addition to the above.

When touring abroad it may be advisable to carry additional spares which, even if you cannot fit them yourself, could save having to wait while parts are obtained. The items below may be worth considering:

> *Cylinder head gasket*
> *Alternator brushes*
> *Fuel pump*
> *Timing belt (ohc engine)*

One of the motoring organisations will be able to advise on availability of fuel etc in foreign countries.

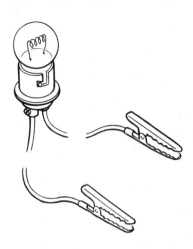

A simple test lamp is useful for diagnosing electrical faults

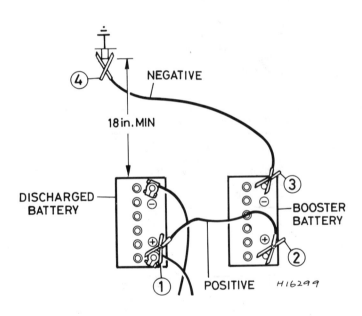

Correct way to connect jump leads. Do not allow car bodies to touch!

Engine will not start

Engine fails to turn when starter operated

Flat battery (recharge, use jump leads, or push start)
Battery terminals loose or corroded
Battery earth to body defective
Engine earth strap loose or broken
Starter motor (or solenoid) wiring loose or broken
Automatic transmission selector in wrong position, or inhibitor switch faulty
Ignition/starter switch faulty
Major mechanical failure (seizure) or long disuse (piston rings rusted to bores)
Starter or solenoid internal fault (see Chapter 10)

Starter motor turns engine slowly

Partially discharged battery (recharge, use jump leads, or push start)
Battery terminals loose or corroded
Battery earth to body defective
Engine earth strap loose
Starter motor (or solenoid) wiring loose
Starter motor internal fault (see Chapter 10)

Starter motor spins without turning engine

Flat battery (inertia starter only)
Starter motor pinion sticking on sleeve (inertia starter only)
Flywheel gear teeth damaged or worn
Starter motor mounting bolts loose

Engine turns normally but fails to start

Damp or dirty HT leads and distributor cap (crank engine and check for spark) (photo)
Dirty or incorrectly gapped contact breaker points
No fuel in tank (check for delivery at carburettor)
Excessive choke (hot engine) or insufficient choke (cold engine)
Fouled or incorrectly gapped spark plugs (remove, clean and regap)
Other ignition system fault (see Chapter 4)
Other fuel system fault (see Chapter 3)
Poor compression (see Chapter 1)
Major mechanical failure (eg camshaft drive)

Engine fires but will not run

Insufficient choke (cold engine)
Air leaks at carburettor or inlet manifold
Fuel starvation (see Chapter 3)
Ballast resistor defective, or other ignition fault (see Chapter 4)

Engine cuts out and will not restart

Engine cuts out suddenly – ignition fault

Loose or disconnected LT wires
Wet HT leads or distributor cap (after transversing water splash)
Coil or condenser failure (check for spark)
Other ignition fault (see Chapter 4)

Engine misfires before cutting out – fuel fault

Fuel tank empty
Fuel pump defective or filter blocked (check for delivery)
Fuel tank filler vent blocked (suction will be evident on releasing cap)
Carburettor needle valve sticking
Other fuel system fault (see Chapter 3)

Engine cuts out – other causes

Serious overheating
Major mechanical failure (eg camshaft drive)

Engine overheats

Ignition (no-charge) warning light illuminated

Slack or broken drivebelt – retension or renew (Chapter 2)

Ignition warning light not illuminated

Coolant loss due to internal or external leakage (see Chapter 2)
Thermostat defective
Low oil level
Brakes binding
Radiator clogged externally or internally
Engine waterways clogged
Ignition timing incorrect or automatic advance malfunctioning
Mixture too weak

Note: *Do not add cold water to an overheated engine or damage may result*

Low engine oil pressure

Gauge reads low or warning light illuminated with engine running

Oil level low or incorrect grade
Defective gauge or sender unit
Wire to sender unit earthed
Engine overheating
Oil filter clogged or bypass valve defective
Oil pressure relief valve defective

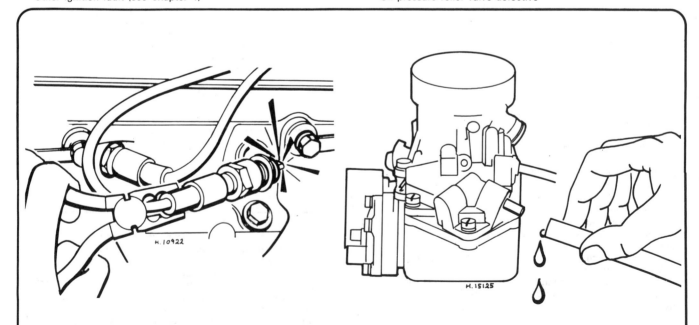

Crank engine and check for spark. Note use of insulated tool

Remove fuel pipe and check for fuel delivery. Disable ignition before cranking engine

Oil pick-up strainer clogged
Oil pump worn or mountings loose
Worn main or big-end bearings
Note: *Low oil pressure in a high-mileage engine at tickover is not ncessarily a cause for concern. Sudden pressure loss at speed is far more significant. In any event, check the gauge or warning light sender before condemning the engine.*

Engine noises

Pre-ignition (pinking) on acceleration
Incorrect grade of fuel
Ignition timing incorrect
Distributor faulty or worn
Worn or maladjusted carburettor
Excessive carbon build-up in engine

Whistling or wheezing noises
Leaking vacuum hose
Leaking carburettor or manifold gasket
Blowing head gasket

Tapping or rattling
Incorrect valve clearances
Worn valve gear
Worn timing chain (ohv)
Broken piston ring (ticking noise)

Knocking or thumping
Unintentional mechanical contact (eg fan blades)
Worn fanbelt
Peripheral component fault (generator, water pump etc)
Worn big-end bearings (regular heavy knocking, perhaps less under load)
Worn main bearings (rumbling and knocking, perhaps worsening under load)
Piston slap (most noticeable when cold)

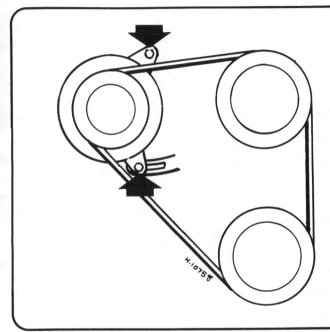

A slack drivebelt may cause overheating and battery charging problems. Slacken bolts (arrowed) to adjust

Chapter 1 Engine

For modifications, and information applicable to later models, see Supplement at end of manual

Contents

Specifications

Part A : OHV engine
General
Engine code designation	L1C
Type	Four-cylinder, in-line, overhead valve
Firing order	1 – 2 – 4 – 3
Bore	3.188 in (80.98 mm)
Stroke	3.056 in (77.62 mm)
Capacity	1599 cc
Compression ratio	8.0 : 1
Compression pressure (at starter speed)	130 to 160 lbf/in^2 (9 to 11 kgf/cm^2)
Idling speed	800 ± 25 rpm
Maximum engine speed (continuous)	5800 rpm
Power output (DIN)	63 bhp at 5000 rpm
Torque (DIN)	81 lbf ft at 2500 rpm

Cylinder block
Number of main bearings	5
Cylinder liner bore	3.311 to 3.313 in (84.112 to 84.138 mm)
Cylinder bore diameter:	
A (standard)	3.1869 to 3.1873 in (80.947 to 80.957 mm)
B	3.1873 to 3.1877 in (80.957 to 80.967 mm)
C	3.1877 to 3.1881 in (80.967 to 80.977 mm)
D	3.1881 to 3.1885 in (80.977 to 80.987 mm)
E	3.1885 to 3.1889 in (80.987 to 80.997 mm)
F	3.1889 to 3.1893 in (80.997 to 81.007 mm)
Main bearing shells (fitted) internal diameter:	
Standard	2.126 to 2.128 in (54.013 to 54.040 mm)
Undersize:	
0.010 in (0.254 mm)	2.116 to 2.118 in (53.759 to 53.786 mm)
0.020 in (0.508 mm)	2.106 to 2.108 in (53.505 to 53.532 mm)
0.030 in (0.762 mm)	2.096 to 2.098 in (53.251 to 53.278 mm)
Main bearing bore in block:	
Standard	2.271 to 2.2715 in (57.683 to 57.696 mm)
Oversize	2.286 to 2.2865 in (58.064 to 58.077 mm)
Camshaft bearing in block:	
Standard	1.6885 to 1.6894 in (42.888 to 42.913 mm)
Oversize	+0.020 in (+0.508 mm)

Crankshaft
Main bearing journal diameter:	
Standard	2.125 to 2.126 in (53.983 to 54.003 mm)
Undersize:	
0.010 in (0.254 mm)	2.115 to 2.116 in (53.729 to 53.749 mm)
0.020 in (0.508 mm)	2.105 to 2.106 in (53.475 to 53.495 mm)
0.030 in (0.762 mm)	2.095 to 2.096 in (53.221 to 53.241 mm)
Crankshaft endfloat	0.003 to 0.011 in (0.075 to 0.280 mm)
Clearance in main bearing shell	0.0004 to 0.0024 in (0.010 to 0.060 mm)
Crankpin diameter:	
Standard	1.937 to 1.938 in (49.195 to 49.215 mm)
Undersize:	
0.010 in (0.25 mm)	1.927 to 1.928 in (48.941 to 48.961 mm)
0.020 in (0.51 mm)	1.917 to 1.918 in (48.687 to 48.707 mm)
0.030 in (0.76 mm)	1.907 to 1.908 in (48.433 to 48.453 mm)
0.040 in (1.02 mm)	1.897 to 1.898 in (48.179 to 48.199 mm)
Thrust washer thickness:	
Standard	0.090 to 0.092 in (2.311 to 2.362 mm)
Oversize	0.098 to 0.100 in (2.502 to 2.553 mm)

Camshaft
Retaining plate thickness	0.175 to 0.178 in (4.470 to 4.521 mm)
Cam lift:	
Inlet	0.2355 in (5.984 mm)
Exhaust	0.2320 in (5.894 mm)
Camshaft bearing diameter	1.560 to 1.561 in (39.616 to 39.637 mm)
Internal diameter of bearing bush	1.561 to 1.562 in (39.662 to 39.675 mm)
Camshaft endfloat	0.002 to 0.008 in (0.06 to 0.2 mm)

Pistons
Piston diameter (standard):	
Grade D	3.1867 to 3.1871 in (80.944 to 80.954 mm)
Grade E	3.1872 to 3.1876 in (80.954 to 80.964 mm)
Grade F	3.1876 to 3.1880 in (80.964 to 80.974 mm)

Piston diameter (oversize):
 +0.0025 in (0.064 mm) .... 3.188 to 3.190 in (80.978 to 81.038 mm)
 +0.014 in (0.38 mm) .... 3.201 to 3.203 in (81.294 to 81.354 mm)
 +0.029 in (0.76 mm) .... 3.216 to 3.218 in (81.674 to 81.734 mm)
Piston to bore clearance .... 0.0009 to 0.0016 in (0.023 to 0.043 mm)
Ring gap (fitted):
 Top .... 0.009 to 0.014 in (0.23 to 0.36 mm)
 Centre .... 0.009 to 0.014 in (0.23 to 0.36 mm)
 Bottom .... 0.016 to 0.055 in (0.4 to 1.40 mm)
Ring gap location:
 Top .... 180° to scraper ring gap
 Centre .... 90° to scraper ring gap
 Bottom (scraper) .... In line with gudgeon pin

Gudgeon pins
Length of pin .... 2.795 to 2.810 in (70.99 to 71.37 mm)
Diameter of pin:
 Grade 1 .... 0.8119 to 0.8120 in (20.622 to 20.625 mm)
 Grade 2 .... 0.8120 to 0.8121 in (20.625 to 20.627 mm)
 Grade 3 .... 0.8121 to 0.8122 in (20.627 to 20.630 mm)
 Grade 4 .... 0.8122 to 0.8123 in (20.630 to 20.632 mm)
Pin interference in piston at 21°C .... 0.0001 to 0.0003 in (0.003 to 0.008 mm)
Clearance in connecting rod at 21°C .... 0.00015 to 0.0004 in (0.004 to 0.010 mm)

Connecting rods
Bore diameter at big-end .... 2.0823 to 2.0831 in (52.89 to 52.91 mm)
Bore diameter at small-end .... 0.8122 to 0.8126 in (20.629 to 20.640 mm)
Standard big-end bore diameter (shells fitted) .... 1.938 to 1.939 in (49.221 to 49.260 mm)
Big-end undersizes .... 0.002, 0.010, 0.020, 0.030 and 0.040 in (0.051, 0.254, 0.508, 0.762 and 1.016 mm)
Clearance of big-end journal to bearing .... 0.0002 to 0.003 in (0.006 to 0.064 mm)

Cylinder head
Valve seat angle .... 44° 30′ to 45°
Valve guide bore:
 Standard .... 0.311 to 0.312 in (7.907 to 7.937 mm)
 Oversize .... 0.326 to 0.328 in (8.288 to 8.319 mm)

Valve clearances (cold)
Inlet .... 0.008 in (0.20 mm)
Exhaust .... 0.022 in (0.55 mm)

Inlet valves
Length .... 4.348 to 4.388 in (110.45 to 111.46 mm)
Head diameter .... 1.496 to 1.507 in (38.02 to 38.28 mm)
Stem diameter:
 Standard .... 0.3097 to 0.3104 in (7.868 to 7.886 mm)
 Oversize .... 0.015 in (0.381 mm)
Clearance of stem to guide .... 0.0008 to 0.0027 in (0.02 to 0.068 mm)

Exhaust valves
Length .... 4.371 to 4.411 in (111.04 to 112.04 mm)
Head diameter .... 1.23 to 1.24 in (31.3 to 31.60 mm)
Stem diameter:
 Standard .... 0.3089 to 0.3096 in (7.846 to 7.863 mm)
 Oversize .... 0.015 in (0.381 mm)
Clearance of stem to guide .... 0.0017 to 0.0036 in (0.043 to 0.091 mm)

Valve timing
Inlet opens .... 21° BTDC
Inlet closes .... 55° ABDC
Exhaust opens .... 70° BBDC
Exhaust closes .... 22° ATDC

Valve springs
Free length:
 Inlet .... 1.48 in (37.6 mm)
 Exhaust .... 1.43 in (36.2 mm)

Lubrication system
Capacity:
 From dry, including filter .... 6.7 pints (3.75 litres)
 Drain and refill, including filter .... 5.7 pints (3.25 litres)
 Drain and refill, less filter .... 5.3 pints (3.0 litres)

Minimum oil pressure (engine hot):
    At 700 rpm .... 8.5 lbf/in² (0.6 kgf/cm²)
    At 2000 rpm .... 21 lbf/in² (1.5 kgf/cm²)
Oil pressure warning light activated at .... 5.7 ± 1.5 lbf/in² (0.4 ± 0.1 kgf/cm²)
Excess pressure valve opens at .... 35 to 40 lbf/in² (2.5 to 2.8 kgf/cm²)

Oil pump clearances:
    Outer rotor to casing .... 0.0055 to 0.0105 in (0.1397 to 0.2667 mm)
    Inner to outer rotor .... 0.002 to 0.005 in (0.0508 to 0.1270 mm)
    End cover to rotors .... 0.001 to 0.003 in (0.0254 to 0.076 mm)
Oil type/specification .... Multigrade engine oil, viscosity range SAE 10W/30 to 20W/50, to Ford spec. SSM-2C9001-AA (Duckhams QXR, Hypergrade, or 10W/40 Motor Oil)

Torque wrench settings – ohv engine

	lbf ft	kgf m
Main bearing caps	55 to 60	7.5 to 8.2
Connecting rod bolts	31 to 35	4.2 to 4.8
Crankshaft belt pulley	24 to 28	3.3 to 3.8
Camshaft chain sprocket	13 to 15	1.7 to 2.1
Rear main bearing sealing ring carrier	13 to 15	1.7 to 2.1
Camshaft thrust plate bolts	2.5 to 3.5	0.4 to 0.5
Flywheel	50 to 56	6.8 to 7.6
Oil pump	13 to 15	1.7 to 2.1
Oil pump inlet pipe	13 to 15	1.7 to 2.1
Oil pump cover	5 to 7	0.7 to 1.0
Rocker shaft	25 to 30	3.5 to 4.1
Cylinder head:		
(1)	5	0.7
(2)	20 to 30	2.7 to 4.0
(3)	50 to 55	6.8 to 7.5
(4) After 10 to 20 minutes wait	65 to 70	8.8 to 9.5
(5) After engine has warmed up (15 minutes at 1000 rpm) retighten to	65 to 70	8.8 to 9.5
Rocker cover	3 to 4	0.4 to 0.5
Sump:		
(1)	3 to 5	0.4 to 0.7
(2)	6 to 8	0.8 to 1.1
Oil drain plug	20 to 25	2.7 to 3.4
Oil pressure switch	10 to 11	1.3 to 1.5
Spark plugs	22 to 29	3.0 to 3.9
Inlet manifold	13 to 15	1.7 to 2.1
Exhaust manifold	15 to 18	2.1 to 2.5
Fuel pump	12 to 15	1.6 to 2.0
Water pump:		
$\frac{1}{4}$ inch bolts	5 to 7	0.7 to 1.0
$\frac{5}{16}$ inch bolts	13 to 15	1.7 to 2.1
Thermostat housing	13 to 15	1.7 to 2.1
Fan to water pump flange	5 to 7	0.7 to 1.0
Timing chain tensioner	5 to 7	0.7 to 1.0

Part B : OHC engine
General

Engine code designation:		
LAT	1.6 litre	
NAT	2.0 litre (Standard)	
NUT	2.0 litre (Economy)	
NAW	2.0 litre (Heavy duty)	
NAX	2.0 litre (Extra cooling)	
NAV	2.0 litre (Automatic transmission)	
Engine type	Four in-line, single overhead camshaft	

	1.6	**2.0**
Engine type	1–3–4–2	1–3–4–2
Firing order		
Bore in (mm)	3.452 (87.67)	3.576 (90.82)
Stroke in (mm)	2.6 (66)	3.03 (76.95)
Cubic capacity (cc) (nominal)	1593	1993
Compression ratio	8.2 : 1	8.2 : 1
Compression pressure at starter speed – lbf/in² (kgf/cm²)	128 to 156 (9 to 11)	142 to 170 (10 to 12)
Engine idle speed	800 ± 50 rpm	800 ± 50 rpm
Maximum continuous engine speed	5800 rpm	5800 rpm
Engine power (DIN) hp at rpm:		
Manual transmission	65 at 4750	78 at 4500
Automatic transmission	–	75 at 4400
Torque (DIN) lbf ft (kg fm) at rpm:		
Manual transmission	84 (11.6) at 2800	108 (15.0) at 2800
Automatic transmission	–	107 (14.8) at 2800

Cylinder block

	1.6		**2.0**	
Cast identification marks	16		20	
Number of main bearings	5		5	
Cylinder bore diameter grades:	inches	mm	inches	mm
Standard grade:				
1	3.4508 to	(87.650 to	3.5748 to	(90.800 to
	3.4512	87.660)	3.5752	90.810)
2	3.4512 to	(87.660 to	3.5752 to	(90.810 to
	3.4516	87.670)	3.5756	90.820)
3	3.4516 to	(87.670 to	3.5756 to	(90.820 to
	3.4520	87.680)	3.5760	90.830)
4	3.4520 to	(87.680 to	3.5760 to	(90.830 to
	3.4524	87.690)	3.5764	90.840)
Oversize A	3.4709 to	(88.160 to	3.5949 to	(91.310 to
	3.4713	88.170)	3.5953	91.320)
Oversize B	3.4713 to	(88.170 to	3.5953 to	(91.320 to
	3.4717	88.180)	3.5957	91.330)
Oversize C	3.4717 to	(88.180 to	3.5957 to	(91.330 to
	3.4720	88.190)	3.5961	91.340)
Standard supplied in service	3.4520 to	(87.680 to	3.5760 to	(90.830 to
	3.4524	87.690)	3.5764	90.840)
Oversize 0.5	3.4717 to	(88.180 to	3.5957 to	(91.330 to
	3.4720	88.190)	3.5961	91.340)
Oversize 1.0	3.4913 to	(88.680 to	3.6154 to	(91.830 to
	3.4917	88.690)	3.6157	91.840)

Main bearings

Centre main bearing width in (mm)	1.070 to 1.072 in (27.17 to 27.22 mm)
Main bearing shells – inside diameter (fitted):	
Standard	2.244 to 2.245 in (57.000 to 57.033 mm)
0.010 in (0.25 mm) undersize	2.234 to 2.235 in (56.750 to 56.788 mm)
0.020 in (0.50 mm) undersize	2.224 to 2.225 in (56.500 to 56.538 mm)
0.030 in (0.75 mm) undersize	2.214 to 2.216 in (56.250 to 56.288 mm)
0.040 in (1.00 mm) undersize	2.204 to 2.206 in (56.000 to 56.038 mm)
Main bearing parent bore diameter:	
Standard	2.386 to 2.387 in (60.620 to 60.640 mm)
0.015 in (0.40 mm) oversize	2.402 to 2.403 in (61.020 to 61.040 mm)

Crankshaft

Endfloat	0.0032 to 0.0110 in (0.08 to 0.28 mm)
Main bearing journal diameter:	
Standard	2.242 to 2.243 in (56.97 to 56.99 mm)
0.010 in (0.25 mm) undersize	2.233 to 2.234 in (56.72 to 56.74 mm)
0.020 in (0.50 mm) undersize	2.223 to 2.224 in (56.47 to 56.49 mm)
0.030 in (0.75 mm) undersize	2.213 to 2.214 in (56.22 to 56.24 mm)
0.040 in (1.00 mm) undersize	2.203 to 2.204 in (55.97 to 55.99 mm)
Thrust washer thickness:	
Standard	0.091 to 0.0925 in (2.3 to 2.35 mm)
Oversize	0.098 to 0.100 in (2.5 to 2.55 mm)
Main bearing running clearance	0.0004 to 0.0025 in (0.010 to 0.064 mm)
Crankpin journal diameter:	
Standard	2.046 to 2.047 in (51.98 to 52.00 mm)
0.010 in (0.25 mm) undersize	2.036 to 2.037 in (51.73 to 51.75 mm)
0.020 in (0.50 mm) undersize	2.026 to 2.027 in (51.48 to 51.50 mm)
0.030 in (0.75 mm) undersize	2.016 to 2.017 in (51.23 to 51.25 mm)
0.040 in (1.00 mm) undersize	2.007 to 2.008 in (50.98 to 51.00 mm)

Camshaft

Drive	Toothed belt
Number of bearings	3
Thrust plate thickness	0.157 to 0.158 in (3.98 to 4.01 mm)
Cam lift (inlet and exhaust):	
1.6	0.234 in (5.9639 mm)
2.0	0.249 in (6.3323 mm)
Camshaft bearing journal diameter:	
Front	1.653 to 1.654 in (41.99 to 42.01 mm)
Centre	1.756 to 1.757 in (44.61 to 44.63 mm)
Rear	1.771 to 1.772 in (44.99 to 45.01 mm)
Bearing inside diameter:	
Front	1.654 to 1.655 in (42.035 to 42.055 mm)
Centre	1.7580 to 1.7588 in (44.655 to 44.675 mm)
Rear	1.7730 to 1.7738 in (45.035 to 45.055 mm)
Camshaft endfloat	0.001 to 0.004 in (0.024 to 0.104 mm)

Auxiliary shaft
Endfloat .... 0.0015 to 0.005 in (0.04 to 0.12 mm)

Pistons

	1.6	2.0
Piston diameter:		
Standard	3.4494 to 3.4497 in (87.615 to 87.625 mm)	3.5734 to 3.5738 in (90.765 to 90.775 mm)
Standard 2	3.4497 to 3.4501 in (87.625 to 87.635 mm)	3.5738 to 3.5742 in (90.775 to 90.785 mm)
Standard 3	3.4501 to 3.4505 in (87.635 to 87.645 mm)	3.5742 to 3.5745 in (90.785 to 90.795 mm)
Standard 4	3.4505 to 3.4509 in (87.645 to 87.655 mm)	3.5745 to 3.5749 in (90.795 to 90.805 mm)
KD standard	3.4499 to 3.4509 in (87.630 to 87.655 mm)	3.5740 to 3.5749 in (90.780 to 90.805 mm)
KD oversize (0.5 mm)	3.4696 to 3.4706 in (88.130 to 88.155 mm)	3.5936 to 3.5946 in (91.280 to 91.305 mm)
KD oversize (1.0 mm)	3.4893 to 3.4903 in (88.630 to 88.655 mm)	3.6133 to 3.6143 in (91.780 to 91.805 mm)

Piston to cylinder bore clearance .... 0.001 to 0.0024 in (0.025 to 0.060 mm)

Piston ring gap (fitted):
Top and centre .... 0.015 to 0.023 in (0.38 to 0.58 mm)
Bottom .... 0.016 to 0.055 in (0.4 to 1.4 mm)
Ring gap position:
Top .... 150° from one side of the helical expander gap
Centre .... 150° from the side opposite the helical expander gap
Top mark towards piston crown
Bottom .... Helical expander; opposite the marked piston front side
Intermediate rings: 1 in (25 mm) each side of helical expander gap

Gudgeon pins
Length .... 2.83 to 2.87 in (72.0 to 72.8 mm)
Diameter .... 0.9446 to 0.9450 in (23.944 to 24.003 mm) in 3 grades
Clearance in piston .... 0.0003 to 0.0005 in (0.008 to 0.014 mm)
Interference in small-end bush .... 0.0007 to 0.0015 in (0.018 to 0.039 mm)

Connecting rods
Big-end bore .... 2.1653 to 2.1661 in (55.00 to 55.02 mm)
Bearing inside diameter (fitted):
Standard .... 2.0474 to 2.0489 in (52.006 to 52.044 mm)
0.25 mm undersize .... 2.0376 to 2.0391 in (51.756 to 51.794 mm)
0.50 mm undersize .... 2.0277 to 2.0292 in (51.506 to 51.544 mm)
0.75 mm undersize .... 2.0179 to 2.0194 in (51.256 to 51.294 mm)
1.00 mm undersize .... 2.0078 to 2.0096 in (51.006 to 51.044 mm)
Big-end bearing running clearance .... 0.0002 to 0.0023 in (0.006 to 0.060 mm)

Cylinder head
Cast identification number:
1.6 6
2.0 0
Valve seat angle .... 44° 30′ to 45°
Valve guide bore:
Standard .... 0.3174 to 0.3184 in (8.063 to 8.088 mm)
0.2 mm oversize .... 0.3253 to 0.3262 in (8.263 to 8.288 mm)
0.4 mm oversize .... 0.3331 to 0.3441 in (8.463 to 8.488 mm)
Camshaft bearing bore:
Front .... 1.774 to 1.775 in (45.072 to 45.102 mm)
Centre .... 1.877 to 1.878 in (47.692 to 47.722 mm)
Rear .... 1.892 to 1.893 in (48.072 to 48.102 mm)

Valve clearances (cold)
Inlet .... 0.008 in (0.20 mm)
Exhaust .... 0.010 in (0.25 mm)

Valve timing

	1.6	2.0
Inlet opens	22° BTDC	24° BTDC
Inlet closes	54° ABDC	64° ABDC
Exhaust opens	64° BBDC	70° BBDC
Exhaust closes	12° ATDC	18° ATDC

Exhaust valves
Valve length:
1.6 .... 4.411 to 4.450 in (112.05 to 113.05 mm)
2.0 .... 4.332 to 4.372 in (110.05 to 111.05 mm)

Valve head diameter:
1.6	1.338 to 1.354 in (34.00 to 34.40 mm)
2.0	1.409 to 1.425 in (35.80 to 36.20 mm)

Valve stem diameter:
Standard	0.3149 to 0.3156 in (7.999 to 8.017 mm)
0.2 mm oversize	0.3227 to 0.3235 in (8.199 to 8.217 mm)
0.4 mm oversize	0.3306 to 0.3313 in (8.399 to 8.417 mm)
0.6 mm oversize	0.3385 to 0.3392 in (8.599 to 8.617 mm)
0.8 mm oversize	0.3464 to 0.3471 in (8.799 to 8.817 mm)
Valve stem to guide clearance	0.0018 to 0.0035 in (0.046 to 0.089 mm)

Valve lift (excluding valve clearance):
1.6	0.3741 in (9.5034 mm)
2.0	0.3984 in (10.121 mm)

Inlet valves

Valve length:
1.6	4.4350 to 4.4744 in (112.65 to 113.65 mm)
2.0	4.3562 to 4.3956 in (110.65 to 111.65 mm)
Valve head diameter	1.645 to 1.661 in (41.80 to 42.20 mm)

Valve stem diameter:
Standard	0.3159 to 0.3166 in (8.025 to 8.043 mm)
0.2 mm oversize	0.3238 to 0.3245 in (8.225 to 8.243 mm)
0.4 mm oversize	0.3316 to 0.3324 in (8.425 to 8.443 mm)
0.6 mm oversize	0.3395 to 0.3402 in (8.625 to 8.643 mm)
0.8 mm oversize	0.3474 to 0.3481 in (8.825 to 8.843 mm)
Valve stem to guide clearance	0.00078 to 0.0024 in (0.020 to 0.063 mm)

Valve lift (excluding valve clearance):
1.6	0.3741 in (9.5034 mm)
2.0	0.3984 in (10.121 mm)

Valve springs

Free length – inlet and exhaust	1.732 in (44.0 mm)

Lubrication system

Oil capacity – with filter	6.6 pints (3.75 litres)
Oil capacity – less filter	5.72 pints (3.25 litres)
Minimum oil pressure at 750 rpm	14 lbf/in^2 (1.0 kgf/cm^2)
Minimum oil pressure at 2000 rpm using SAE 10W-30 oil	36 lbf/in^2 (2.5 kgf/cm^2)
Relief valve opening pressure	57 to 67 lbf/in^2 (4.00 to 4.72 kgf/cm^2)
Oil pressure warning light activation pressure	4.3 to 8.5 lbf/in^2 (0.30 to 0.60 kgf/cm^2)

Oil pump:
Rotor to casing clearance	0.006 to 0.011 in (0.150 to 0.301 mm)
Inner to outer rotor clearance	0.002 to 0.0078 in (0.05 to 0.20 mm)
Rotor endfloat	0.001 to 0.004 in (0.028 to 0.104 mm)
Oil type/specification	Multigrade engine oil, viscosity range SAE 10W/30 to 20W/50, to Ford spec. SSM-2C9001-AA (Duckhams QXR, Hypergrade, or 10W/40 Motor Oil)

Torque wrench settings – ohc engine

	lbf ft	kgf m
Main bearing caps	64 to 74	8.8 to 10.2
Big-end bearing caps	30 to 35	4.1 to 4.8
Crankshaft pulley bolt	40 to 44	5.5 to 6.0
Camshaft and auxiliary shaft sprockets	33 to 36	4.5 to 5.0
Flywheel bolts	47 to 51	6.5 to 7.1
Oil pump to block	12 to 15	1.7 to 2.1
Oil pump cover	7 to 9	0.9 to 1.3
Sump bolts:		
(1)	0.7 to 1.5	0.1 to 0.2
(2)	4 to 6	0.6 to 0.8
(3)	6 to 7	0.8 to 1.0
Sump drain plug	15 to 20	2.1 to 2.8
Oil pressure switch	9 to 11	1.2 to 1.5
Valve adjustment ball-pin	33 to 36	4.5 to 5.0
Cylinder head:		
(1)	30 to 41	4.0 to 5.5
(2)	37 to 52	5.0 to 7.0
(3) After 10 to 20 minutes wait	63 to 70	8.5 to 9.5
(4) After 15 minutes at 1000 rpm	66 to 81	9.0 to 11.0
Rocker cover bolts (see text):		
1 to 6	4 to 5	0.5 to 0.7
7 and 8	1.5 to 2	0.2 to 0.25
9 and 10	4 to 5	0.5 to 0.7
7 and 8	4 to 5	0.5 to 0.7
Timing cover	9 to 12	1.3 to 1.7
Inlet manifold	12 to 15	1.7 to 2.1
Exhaust manifold	15 to 18	2.1 to 2.5
Spark plugs	14 to 20	2.0 to 2.8

Part A : OHV ENGINE

1 General description

The 1598 cc engine is of four-cylinder, ohv, in-line construction.

Two valves per cylinder are mounted vertically in the cast-iron cylinder head and run in integral valve guides. They are operated by rocker arms, pushrods and tappets from the camshaft which is located at the base of the cylinder bores in the right-hand side of the engine. The correct valve stem to rocker arm pad clearance can be obtained by the adjusting screws in the ends of the rocker arms.

A crossflow type cylinder head is used with four inlet ports on the right-hand side and four exhaust on the left.

The cylinder block and the upper half of the crankcase are cast together. The open half of the crankcase is closed by a pressed steel sump.

The pistons are made from anodised aluminium alloy with solid skirts. Two compression rings and one oil control ring are fitted. The gudgeon pin is retained in the small-end of the connecting rod by circlips. The combustion chamber is machined in the piston crown.

The connecting rod bearings are all steel-backed and may be copper/lead, lead/bronze, or aluminium/tin.

At the front of the engine a single chain drives the camshaft via the camshaft and crankshaft chain wheels which are enclosed in a pressed steel cover. The chain is tensioned automatically by a snail cam which bears against a pivoted tensioner arm. This presses against the non-driving side of the chain, so avoiding any lash or rattle.

The camshaft is supported by three renewable bearings located directly in the cylinder block. Endfloat is controlled by a plate bolted to the front bearing journal and the chain wheel flange.

The statically and dynamically balanced cast iron crankshaft is supported by five renewable thin wall shell main bearings which are in turn supported by substantial webs which form part of the crankcase. Crankcase endfloat is controlled by semi-circular thrust washers located on each side of the centre main bearing.

The centrifugal water pump and radiator cooling fan are driven, together with the alternator, from the crankshaft pulley wheel by a flexible belt. The distributor is mounted toward the front of the right-hand side of the cylinder block and is driven at half crankshaft speed from a skew gear on the camshaft.

The oil pump is mounted externally on the right-hand side of the engine under the distributor and is driven by a short shaft from the same skew gear on the camshaft as the distributor and may be of eccentric bi-rotor or sliding vane type.

Bolted to the flange on the end of the crankshaft is the flywheel to which is bolted in turn the clutch. Attached to the rear of the engine is the gearbox bellhousing.

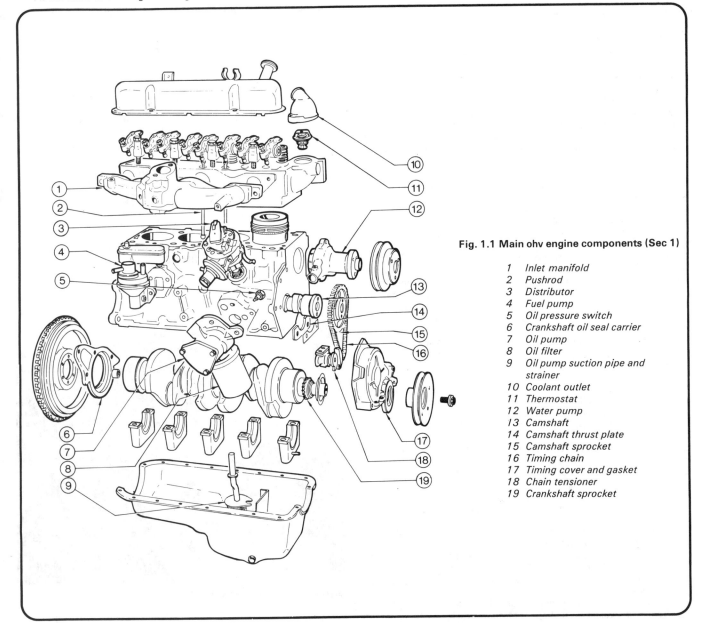

Fig. 1.1 Main ohv engine components (Sec 1)

1   Inlet manifold
2   Pushrod
3   Distributor
4   Fuel pump
5   Oil pressure switch
6   Crankshaft oil seal carrier
7   Oil pump
8   Oil filter
9   Oil pump suction pipe and strainer
10 Coolant outlet
11 Thermostat
12 Water pump
13 Camshaft
14 Camshaft thrust plate
15 Camshaft sprocket
16 Timing chain
17 Timing cover and gasket
18 Chain tensioner
19 Crankshaft sprocket

2 Major operations possible with the engine in the vehicle

1   The following major components can be removed and refitted without taking the engine from the vehicle:

    (a) Cylinder head
    (b) Sump
    (c) Big-end bearings
    (d) Pistons and connecting rods
    (e) Timing chain and gears
    (f) Oil pump
    (g) Engine front mountings
    (h) Engine/gearbox rear mounting

2   The clutch unit can be removed from the flywheel with the engine in position providing the gearbox is removed – See Chapters 6 and 5.

3 Major operations requiring engine removal

The following components can only be removed and refitted with the engine removed from the vehicle:

    (a) Crankshaft rear main bearing oil seal
    (b) Crankshaft and main bearings
    (c) Camshaft and camshaft bushes

4 Methods of engine removal

The engine can be lifted from the vehicle upwards through the bonnet aperture (bonnet removed) if sufficient lifting height is available. Alternatively it can be withdrawn through the front with the radiator and its grille panel removed. This latter method is essential where the engine is being removed together with the gearbox. With the first method the engine must be turned sideways before lifting it out.

5 Engine – removal with transmission

1   Before starting work it is essential to have a good hoist which can be positioned over the engine, and also a trolley jack if an inspection pit is not available.
2   Open the bonnet and disconnect the battery negative terminal.
3   Using a pencil, mark the location of the bonnet hinges then, while an assistant supports the bonnet, unscrew and remove the bonnet retaining bolts and the engine compartment light bracket retaining bolt. Remove the windscreen washer tubing and place the tubing and light to one side, then carefully lift the bonnet away and position it in a safe place.
4   Remove the radiator cap and place a wide 2 gallon (9.0 litre) container beneath the radiator. Disconnect the radiator bottom hose and drain the cooling system.
5   Loosen the radiator top hose clips and remove the top hose.
6   Unscrew and remove the screw retaining each headlamp bezel to the front wings and lift the bezel from the upper flanges.
7   Loosen the bonnet release cable adjuster locknuts, unclip the cable from the front panel and disconnect the inner cable from the release spring; place the cable to one side.
8   Referring to Chapter 12, Section 33, detach and remove the front panel unit complete with radiator which can be left attached to it.
9   Loosen the bottom hose clip and remove the hose from the water pump.
10 Prise the air cleaner support brackets away from the air cleaner, withdraw the air cleaner, and detach the support brackets from the engine.
11 Disconnect the heater hoses from the inlet manifold and water pump. Fold them back and secure them out of the way.
12 Detach the choke cable at the carburettor, and the accelerator cable from its carburettor connection linkage and retaining bracket.
13 Disconnect the fuel line from the petrol pump and plug it to prevent leakage.
14 Disconnect the brake servo vacuum pipe at the inlet manifold.
15 Detach the leads from the oil pressure switch, the temperature gauge sender unit, the alternator, coil and idle cut-off valve on the carburettor. Fold them back and secure them out of the way.
16 Unbolt and detach the exhaust downpipe from the manifold (photo).
17 Disconnect the starter motor leads and remove the starter motor.
18 Disconnect the engine earth lead.
19 From inside the vehicle unscrew and remove the cross-head screws securing the gear lever gaiter plate to the floor, remove the plate, and slide the gaiter up the lever.
20 Working beneath the vehicle, unscrew the gear lever retaining cap and then lift the complete gear lever from the gearbox, into the cab.
21 Loosen the clutch cable adjusting locknuts behind the clutch pedal and screw in the adjuster so that the inner cable is slack.
22 Working beneath the vehicle, pull back the clutch cable rubber gaiter, disconnect the inner cable from the clutch release arm, then withdraw the complete cable through the clutch bellhousing aperture and tie it to one side.
23 Place a container of at least 5 pints (2.8 litres) capacity beneath the gearbox, unscrew and remove the gearbox drain plug and drain the oil. Refit and tighten the drain plug.
24 Refer to Chapter 7 and remove the propeller shaft.
25 Unscrew and remove the bolt, washer and clamp retaining the speedometer cable to the gearbox casing, remove the cable, and tie it to one side.
26 Support the weight of the gearbox with a trolley jack, then

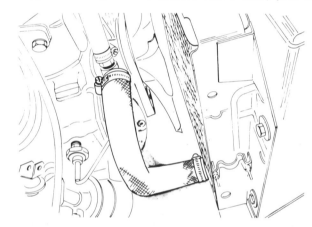

Fig. 1.2 Disconnect the radiator bottom hose at the water pump (Sec 5)

5.16 Disconnecting the exhaust downpipe

5.32 Separating the gearbox from the engine

6.7 Removing the engine (without gearbox)

unscrew and remove the gearbox rear mounting nut, bolt, spacer and washer, noting their location in relation to the gearbox casing.

27 Support the weight of the engine with a suitable hoist, then unscrew and remove the two lower engine mounting nuts. The lifting tackle should be arranged so that it does not damage the wiring loom or brake pipes. It must also be arranged so that when the engine is clear of its mountings it can be tilted as necessary once suspended with the gearbox.

28 An assistant should be at hand to help manoeuvre the engine/transmission clear and also to move the trolley jack in unison with, and supporting, the gearbox.

29 Before lifting and pulling the engine forwards, check that all connections and associate fittings are detached and out of the way.

30 Carefully lift the engine from the front mountings and ease it forwards, at the same time allowing the trolley jack to move forwards as far as possible. If difficulty is experienced in releasing the engine mountings, it may be necessary to unbolt and remove the left-hand side mounting pillar from the engine block.

31 Lift the engine and gearbox assembly from the vehicle and place it on a workbench or large piece of board.

32 Remove the clutch housing bolts and carefully separate the engine and gearbox units. Ensure that the gearbox is not allowed to hang on its input shaft when withdrawing it through the clutch (photo).

6 Engine – removal without transmission

1 Refer to Section 5 and carry out the instructions given in paragraphs 1 to 18 inclusive, omitting paragraph 8 if the front panel is not being removed (engine being lifted through bonnet aperture), but remove the radiator as given in Chapter 2.

2 Unscrew and remove the clutch housing lower cover plate retaining screws and withdraw the cover plate.

3 Support the weight of the gearbox with a trolley jack, then take the weight of the engine with a suitable hoist, ensuring that the engine remains level.

4 Unscrew and remove the remaining clutch housing retaining bolts and the front engine mounting nuts and bolts.

5 Lift the engine clear of the front mountings and separate it from the gearbox by easing it forwards. If the engine mountings will not free, unbolt the left-hand side mounting pillar from the engine block. Do not allow the weight of the engine to hang on the gearbox input shaft.

6 If the front panel has been removed, the engine can be withdrawn through the front end of the vehicle.

7 Where the engine is to be lifted upwards through the bonnet aperture, pull the engine forwards to free it from the gearbox input shaft and then turn the engine sideways (at right-angles to the longitudinal line of the vehicle) (photo). Carefully raise the engine and when the sump is clear of the front panel, move the hoist forwards or

push the vehicle back out of the way (whilst supporting the gearbox – tie it to the bulkhead if necessary), and lower the engine.

7 Engine dismantling – general

1 It is best to mount the engine on a dismantling stand but if one is not available, then stand the engine on a strong bench so as to be at a comfortable working height. Keep the engine upright at least until the sump is removed to avoid sludge running onto the engine components.

2 During the dismantling process the greatest care should be taken to keep the exposed parts free from dirt. As an aid to achieving this, it is a sound scheme to clean thoroughly the outside of the engine, removing all traces of oil and congealed dirt.

3 Use paraffin or a good grease solvent. The latter compound will make the job much easier, as, after the solvent has been applied and allowed to stand for a time, a vigorous jet of water will wash off the solvent and all the grease and filth. If the dirt is thick and deeply embedded, work the solvent into it with a stiff paintbrush.

4 Finally wipe the exterior of the engine with a rag and only then, when it is quite clean, should the dismantling process begin. As the engine is stripped, clean each part in a bath of paraffin or petrol.

5 Never immerse parts with oilways in paraffin, eg the crankshaft, but to clean, wipe down carefully with a petrol dampened rag. Oilways can be cleaned out with wire. If an air line is present all parts can be blown dry and the oilways blown through as an added precaution.

6 Re-use of old engine gaskets is a false economy and can give rise to oil and water leaks, if nothing worse. To avoid the possibility of trouble after the engine has been reassembled **always** use new gaskets throughout.

7 Do not throw away the old gaskets, as it sometimes happens that an immediate replacement cannot be found, and the old gasket is then very useful as a template. Hang up the old gaskets as they are removed on a suitable hook or nail.

8 To strip the engine it is best to work from the top down. The sump provides a firm base on which the engine can be supported with a wooden block in an upright position. When the stage where the sump must be removed is reached, the engine can be turned on its side and all other work carried out with it in this position.

9 Wherever possible, refit nuts, bolts and washers finger tight from wherever they were removed. This helps avoid later loss and muddle. If they cannot be refitted then lay them out in such a fashion that it is clear where they came from.

8 Engine ancillary components – removal

1 Before basic engine dismantling begins the engine should be stripped of all its ancillary components. These items should also be

removed if a factory exchange reconditioned unit is being purchased. The items comprise:

> Alternator and brackets
> Water pump and thermostat housing
> Distributor and spark plugs
> Inlet and exhaust manifold and carburettor
> Fuel pump and fuel pipes
> Oil filter and dipstick
> Oil filler cap
> Clutch assembly (Chapter 5)
> Engine mountings
> Oil pressure sender unit
> Oil separator unit and crankcase ventilation valve

2   Without exception all these items can be removed with the engine in situ, if it is merely an individual item which requires attention. (It is necessary to remove the gearbox if the clutch is to be renewed with the engine in position).

3   Remove each of the listed items as described in the relevant Chapter of this manual.

9   Cylinder head – removal

The operations described in this Section can equally well be carried out with the engine in or out of the vehicle, but with the former, the cooling system must be drained, the battery disconnected and all attachments to the cylinder head removed as described in the appropriate paragraphs of Section 5. If required, the inlet manifold and carburettor can be removed with the cylinder head detached from the engine.

1   Unscrew and remove the four screw-headed bolts and flat washers which retain the rocker cover to the cylinder head and lift off the rocker cover and gasket (photo).

2   Unscrew and remove the four rocker shaft pedestal bolts evenly and remove the washers.

3   Lift off the rocker shaft assembly complete (photo).

4   Remove the pushrods, keeping them in the relative order in which they were removed. The easiest way to do this is to push them through a sheet of thick paper or thin card in the correct sequence (photo).

5   Unscrew the cylinder head bolts half a turn at a time in the reverse order to that shown in Fig. 1.3. When all the bolts are no longer under tension they may be unscrewed from the cylinder head one at a time (photo).

6   The cylinder head can now be removed by lifting upward. If the head is jammed, try to rock it to break the seal. Under no circumstances try to prise it apart from the block with a screwdriver or cold chisel as damage may be done to the faces of the head or block. If the head will not readily free, turn the engine by the flywheel (or starter motor), as the compression in the cylinders will often break the cylinder head joint. If this fails to work, strike the head sharply with a plastic-headed hammer, or with a wooden hammer, or with a metal hammer with an interposed piece of wood to cushion the blows. Under no circumstances hit the head directly with a metal hammer as this

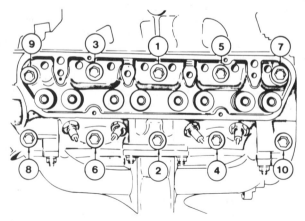

Fig. 1.3 Cylinder head tightening/loosening sequence (Sec 9)

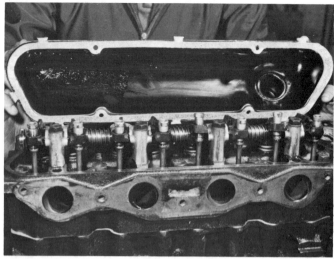

9.1 Remove rocker cover to expose rocker assembly and valves. Note the dovetails in the rocker cover and gasket to assist in gasket location

9.3 Lift the rocker shaft assembly from the cylinder head

9.4 Remove the pushrods and keep in order of location – they must be refitted in their original positions

may cause the iron casting to fracture. Several sharp taps with the hammer at the same time pulling upward should free the head (photo).

7   Do not place the cylinder face downward unless the spark plugs have been removed as they protrude and can easily be damaged.

9.5 Remove the cylinder head bolts only when they are all loosened off

9.6 Lift the cylinder head from the cylinder block

10 Valves – removal

1   The valves can be removed from the cylinder head by compressing each spring in turn with a valve spring compressor until the two halves of the collets can be removed. Release the compressor and remove the spring and spring retainer (photos).

2   If, when the valve spring compressor is screwed down, the valve spring retaining cap refuses to free to expose the split collet, do not continue to screw down on the compressor as there is a likelihood of damaging it.

3   Gently tap the top of the tool directly over the cap with a light hammer. This will free the cap. To avoid the compressor jumping off the valve spring retaining cap when it is tapped, hold the compressor firmly in position with one hand.

4   Slide the rubber oil control seal off the top of each inlet valve stem and then drop out each valve through the combustion chamber (photo).

5   It is essential that the valves are kept in their correct sequence unless they are so badly worn that they are to be renewed. If they are going to be kept and used again, place them in a sheet of card having eight holes numbered 1 to 8, corresponding with the relative positions the valves were in when originally installed. Also keep the valve springs, washers and collets in their original sequence.

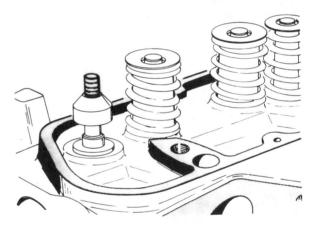

Fig. 1.4 Valve seal and stem shown with spring and collet assembly removed (Sec 10)

10.1a Valve spring partially compressed for removal of collets (arrowed)

10.1b Remove valve spring retaining cap

10.1c Valve spring ready for removal

10.4 Valve stem seal: remove by sliding up valve stem

11 Rocker assembly – dismantling

1   Pull out the split pin from each end of the rocker shaft and remove the flat washer, crimped spring washer and the remaining flat washer.

2   The rocker arms, rocker pedestals, and distance springs can now be slid off the end of the shaft.

12 Timing cover, sprockets and chain – removal

1   The timing cover, sprocket, and chain can be removed with the engine in the vehicle provided the front panel and radiator and water pump are first removed (see Section 5 and Chapter 2).

2   Unscrew and remove the crankshaft pulley centre bolt; this is best achieved by fitting a ring spanner and giving it a sharp blow with a club hammer. If the engine is in the vehicle, engage top gear and apply the handbrake to stop the engine from turning (photo).

3   The crankshaft pulley may pull off quite easily. If not, place two large screwdrivers behind the wheel at 180° to each other, and carefully lever off the wheel. It is preferable to use a proper pulley extractor if this is available (Fig. 1.5) but large screwdrivers or tyre levers are quite suitable, providing care is taken not to damage the pulley flange (photo).

4   Unscrew the bolts which hold the timing cover in place, noting that four sump bolts must also be removed before the cover can be taken off (photo).

5   Check the chain for wear by measuring how much it can be

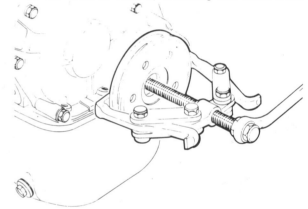

Fig. 1.5 Removing the crankshaft pulley wheel using an extractor (Sec 12)

12.2 Crankshaft pulley centre bolt (arrowed)

12.3 Remove the crankshaft pulley

12.4 Remove the timing cover. Note that sump is already removed

12.6 Oil thrower (arrowed) on crankshaft

12.8 Ease the crankshaft and camshaft sprockets from their respective stubs

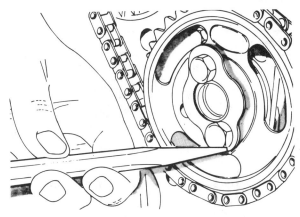

Fig. 1.6 Bend back camshaft sprocket bolt locktabs (Sec 12)

depressed. More than $\frac{1}{2}$ in (12.5 mm) means a new chain must be fitted on reassembly.

6   With the timing cover off, remove the oil thrower. Note that the concave side faces outward (photo).

7   With a drift or screwdriver tap back the tabs on the lockwasher under the two camshaft sprocket retaining bolts and unscrew the bolts (Fig. 1.6).

8   To remove the camshaft and crankshaft sprockets complete with chain, ease each sprocket forward a little at a time, levering behind each sprocket in turn with two large screwdrivers at 180° to each other. If the sprockets are locked solid then it will be necessary to use a proper pulley extractor, and if one is available this should be used in preference to screwdrivers. Remove the sprockets and chain (photo). Take care not to lose the Woodruff key from the crankshaft.

13 Camshaft – removal

1   The camshaft can only be removed from the engine when the engine is removed from the vehicle. This is due to the fact that in order to remove and refit the tappets, the engine must be inverted.

2   With the engine inverted and sump, rocker gear, pushrods, timing cover, oil pump, sprockets and timing chain removed, take off the chain tensioner and arm.

3   Knock back the lockwasher tabs from the two bolts which hold the U-shaped camshaft retainer in place behind the camshaft flange, remove the bolts and slide out the retainer.

4   Rotate the camshaft so that the tappets are fully home and then withdraw the camshaft from the cylinder block. Take great care that

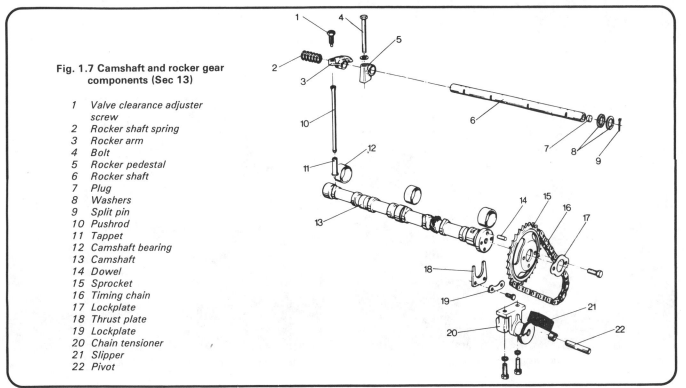

Fig. 1.7 Camshaft and rocker gear components (Sec 13)

1   Valve clearance adjuster screw
2   Rocker shaft spring
3   Rocker arm
4   Bolt
5   Rocker pedestal
6   Rocker shaft
7   Plug
8   Washers
9   Split pin
10 Pushrod
11 Tappet
12 Camshaft bearing
13 Camshaft
14 Dowel
15 Sprocket
16 Timing chain
17 Lockplate
18 Thrust plate
19 Lockplate
20 Chain tensioner
21 Slipper
22 Pivot

the cam lobe peaks do not damage the camshaft bearings as the shaft is pulled forward.

14 Sump – removal

1   The sump can be detached with the engine either in the vehicle or removed, but the starter motor must first be withdrawn (see Chapter 10).
2   Make sure that all oil is drained from the sump, then unscrew and remove the sump retaining bolts (photo); the sump can now be detached from the engine block.
3   If difficulty is experienced in removing the sump due to its being stuck to the gasket, a sharp blow with the palm of the hand on the side of the sump should free it. Failing this, cut the joint with a sharp knife.
4   Thoroughly clean and scrape the mating surfaces of the sump flange and cylinder block and prise out the cork packing strips from the front and rear main bearings caps.

15 Pistons, connecting rods and big-end bearings – removal

1   The pistons, connecting rods and big-end bearings can be removed with the engine either in the vehicle or on a workbench. Note

that in either case, if a pronounced wear ridge exists at the top of the cylinder bores, this should be removed before attempting to extract the pistons. If this is not done, the piston rings may jam against the ridge and cause damage.
2   With the cylinder head and sump removed, unscrew and remove the big-end retaining bolts from number 1 cylinder; the crankshaft will need to be rotated until number 1 piston is at the bottom of its stroke (photo).
3   Remove the big-end cap, noting that the cap and connecting rod are numbered on their right-hand side faces, then extract the big-end shells by pressing them at a point opposite the location tags (photo).
4   Using the wooden handle of a hammer, gently tap the piston up through the cylinder block and remove it from the top, then temporarily refit the shells and cap to the connecting rod.
5   Repeat the procedure given in paragraphs 2 to 4 inclusive on the remaining three cylinders.
6   As an extra precaution, mark each piston crown with the cylinder number from which it was removed to ensure that it is fitted to its original bore on reassembly.

16 Gudgeon pins – removal

1   To remove the gudgeon pin to free the piston from the connecting

14.2 Remove the sump bolts

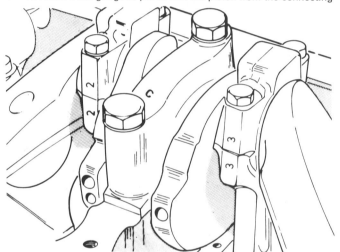

Fig. 1.8 Big-end bearing caps showing numerical identification marks (Sec 15)

15.2 Big-end bearing cap retaining bolts (arrowed)

15.3 Detach big-end cap from rod and crankshaft journal

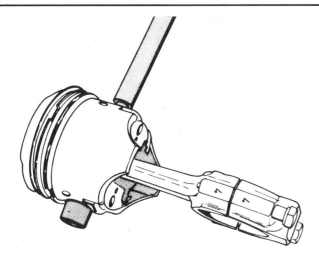

Fig. 1.9 Remove the gudgeon pin (Sec 16)

rod, remove one of the circlips at either end of the pin with a pair of circlip pliers (photo).

2 Press out the pin from the rod and piston.

3 If the pin shows reluctance to move, then on no account force it out, as this could damage the piston. Immerse the piston in a pan of boiling water for three minutes. On removal the expansion of the aluminium should allow the gudgeon pin to slide out easily.

4 Ensure that each gudgeon pin is kept with the piston from which it was removed for exact refitting.

17 Piston rings – removal

1 To remove the piston rings, slide them carefully over the top of the piston, taking care not to scratch the aluminium alloy. Never slide them off the bottom of the piston skirt. It is very easy to break the iron piston rings if they are pulled off roughly so this operation should be done with extreme caution. It is useful to employ three strips of thin metal or feeler gauges to act as guides to assist the rings to pass over the empty grooves and to prevent them from dropping in.

2 Lift one end of the piston ring to be removed out of its groove and insert the end of the feeler gauge under it.

3 Turn the feeler gauge slowly round the piston and as the ring comes out of its groove apply slight upward pressure so that it rests on the land above. It can then be eased off the piston.

18 Flywheel and backplate – removal

1 Remove the clutch (Chapter 5).

2 No locktabs are fitted under the six bolts which hold the flywheel to the flywheel flange on the rear of the crankshaft.

3 Unscrew the bolts and remove them (photo).

4 Lift the flywheel away from the crankshaft flange. Be careful, it is heavy. **Note:** *Some difficulty may be experienced in removing the bolts through the rotation of the crankshaft every time pressure is put on the spanner. To lock the crankshaft in position while the bolts are removed, wedge a block of wood between the crankshaft and the side of the block inside the crankcase.*

5 Unbolt and remove the backplate.

19 Main bearings and crankshaft – removal

1 Detach the engine rear oil seal and carrier, then unscrew each of the ten bolts securing the five main bearing caps and remove them (photo).

2 Remove each main bearing cap in turn, noting that they are

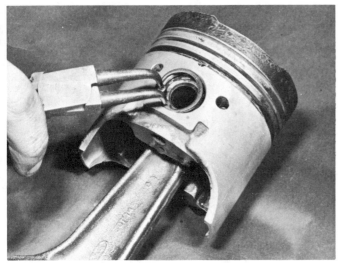

16.1 Remove the gudgeon pin circlip

18.3 Flywheel bolt location

19.1 Remove the main bearing caps

Fig. 1.10 Crankshaft and piston components (Sec 19)

1 Top compression ring
2 Second compression ring
3 Lower oil control ring
4 Piston
5 Gudgeon pin
6 Circlip
7 Connecting rod
8 Small-end bush
9 Big-end shell bearings
10 Big-end bearing cap
11 Big-end bolt
12 Main bearing shell
13 Thrust washer

14 Crankshaft rear oil seal retainer
15 Gasket
16 Oil seal
17 Crankshaft
18 Woodruff key
19 Sprocket
20 Oil thrower
21 Timing cover oil seal
22 Crankshaft pulley
23 Main bearing shell
24 Main bearing cap

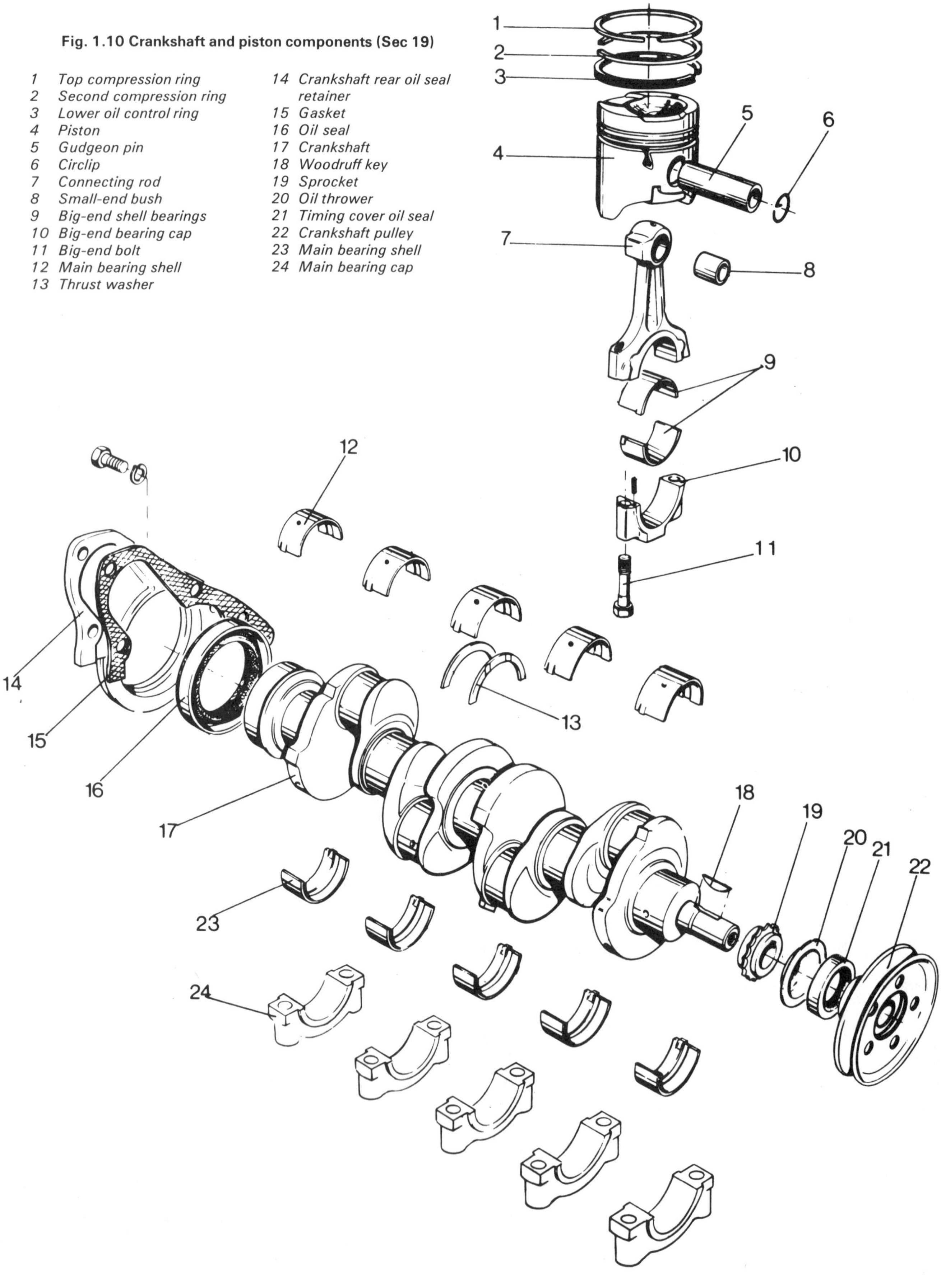

19.2 Main bearing caps removed showing markings, ie 'F', 'R2', 'C', 'R4' and 'R'

19.3 Removing the main bearing thrust washers from their locations each side of the central main bearing

20.1 Remove the two bolts retaining the timing chain tensioner to the underside of the block

marked so that there can be no confusion when refitting regarding sequence or orientation (photo).
3   Remove the thrust washers fitted on each side of the centre main bearing (photo).
4   Lift the crankshaft from the crankcase and then withdraw the shell bearing halves from the crankcase.

20 Timing chain tensioner – removal

1   Unscrew and remove the two bolts and washers retaining the timing chain tensioner and withdraw the tensioner (photo).
2   Pull the timing chain tensioner arm off its hinge pin on the front of the block (photo).

21 Lubrication system – description

1   A forced-feed system of lubrication is fitted, with oil circulated round the engine by a pump drawing oil from the sump below the block (Fig. 1.11).

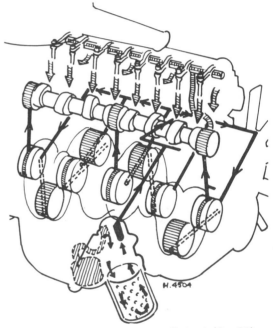

Fig. 1.11 Lubrication system oil circuit (Sec 21)

20.2 Timing chain tensioner arm on tensioner hinge pin

2   The full-flow filter and oil pump assembly is mounted externally on the right-hand side of the cylinder block. The pump is driven by means of a short shaft and skew gear off the camshaft.

3   Oil reaches the pump via a tube pressed into the cylinder block sump face. Initial filtration is provided by a spring-loaded gauze on the end of the tube. Drillings in the block carry the oil under pressure to the main and big-end bearings. Oil at a reduced pressure is fed to the valve and rocker gear and the timing chain and sprockets.

4   One of two types of oil pump may be fitted. The eccentric bi-rotor type can be identified by four recesses cast in the cover whereas the vane type cover is flat. The pumps are directly interchangeable.

22 Oil filter – removal and renewal

1   A full-flow type oil filter is located adjacent to the oil pump on the right-hand side of the engine block.

2   This is a cartridge filter which screws directly into the underside of the pump assembly.

3   Before unscrewing the filter from the pump remember to position a drain tray to catch any oil spillage (photo).

4   Smear the sealing ring of the new filter with clean oil, then screw the filter on to the pump until hand tight. If the engine is in the vehicle and not being overhauled, run the engine and check for leaks.

5   If the filter is difficult to unscrew, use a strap wrench or chain wrench. **Do not** use any such tool to tighten the new filter – tightening by hand should be sufficient.

23 Oil pump – servicing

1   If the pump is worn it is best to purchase an exchange reconditioned unit, as a good oil pump is at the very heart of long engine life.

22.3 Unscrewing the oil filter

Generally speaking, an exchange or overhauled pump should be fitted at a major engine overhaul. If it is wished to overhaul the oil pump, detach the pump and filter unit from the cylinder block and remove the cartridge.

2   Unscrew and remove the four bolts and lockwashers which secure the oil pump cover and remove the cover. Lift out the O-ring seal from the groove in the pump body.

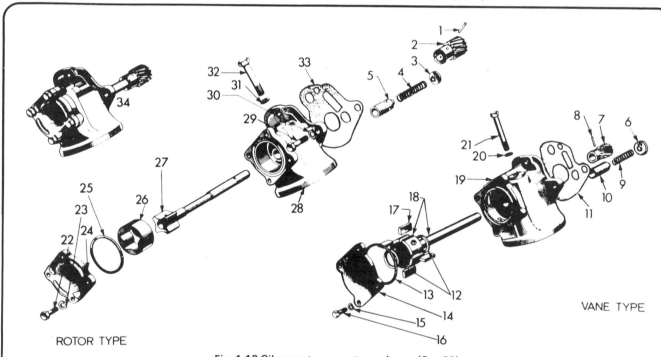

ROTOR TYPE

VANE TYPE

Fig. 1.12 Oil pump types – rotor and vane (Sec 23)

1 Locking pin	9 Relief valve spring	17 Rotor blade (vane)	26 Rotor
2 Oil pump drivegear	10 Relief valve plunger	18 Rotor and shaft assembly	27 Rotor shaft
3 Oil pressure relief valve retainer	11 Gasket	19 Pump assembly	28 Pump body
4 Relief valve spring	12 Spacers	20 Spring washer	29 Bolt
5 Relief valve plunger	13 Oil pump cover sealing ring	21 Bolt	30 Spring washer
6 Oil pressure relief valve retainer	14 Cover	22 Bolt	31 Spring washer
7 Oil pump drivegear	15 Spring washer	23 Spring washer	32 Securing bolt
8 Locking pin	16 Bolt	24 Cover	33 Gasket
		25 Sealing ring	34 Complete pump assembly

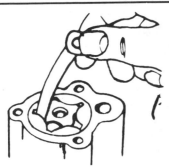

Fig. 1.13 Measure pump inner to outer rotor clearance (Sec 23)

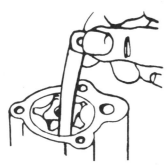

Fig. 1.14 Measure pump body to rotor clearance (Sec 27)

Fig. 1.15 Measure pump rotor endfloat (Sec 27)

Eccentric bi-rotor type pumps

3   Check the clearance between the inner and outer rotors with a feeler gauge (Fig. 1.13). This should not exceed that specified.
4   Check the clearance between the outer rotor and the pump body (Fig. 1.14). This should not exceed that specified.

Rotary vane type pump

5   Check the clearances as indicated (Fig. 1.16).

All pumps

6   Check the endfloat of both types of pump by placing a straight-edge across the open face of the pump casing and measuring the gap between its lower edge and the face of the rotor. This should not exceed the clearance given in the Specifications.
7   Replacement rotors are only supplied as a matched pair so that if the clearance is excessive, a new rotor assembly must be fitted. When it is necessary to renew the rotors, drive out the pin securing the skew gear and pull the gear from the shaft. Remove the inner rotor and driveshaft and withdraw the outer rotor. Install the outer rotor with the chamfered end towards the pump body.
8   Fit the inner rotor and driveshaft assembly, position the skew gear and install the pin. Tap over each end of the pin to prevent it loosening in service. Position a new O-ring in the groove in the pump body, fit the endplate in position and secure with the four bolts and lockwashers.
9   Refit the oil pump assembly together with a new gasket and secure in place with three bolts and lockwashers.

24 Crankcase ventilation system – description and servicing

1   A semi-closed positive crankcase ventilation system is fitted. A breather valve in the oil filler cap allows air to enter as required. Crankcase fumes travel out through an oil separator and emission control valve, and then via a connecting tube back into the inlet manifold. In this way the majority of crankcase fumes are burnt during the combustion process in the cylinders.
2   Clean the valve and rocker box cover breather cap every 18 000 miles (30 000 km). To remove the valve, disconnect the hose and then pull it from its grommet in the oil separator box.

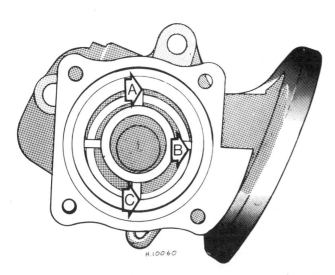

Fig. 1.16 The rotary vane type oil pump clearances (Sec 23)

A = 0.010 in (0.25 mm)   *C = 0.005 in (0.13 mm)*
B = 0.005 in (0.13 mm)

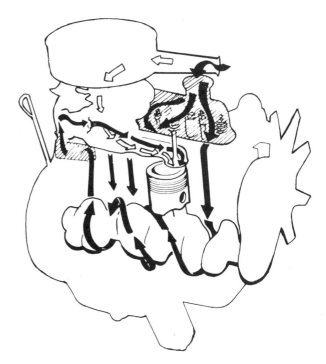

Fig. 1.17 Engine ventilation system circuit (Sec 24)

3   Dismantle the valve by removing the circlip and extracting the seal, valve and spring from the valve body (Fig. 1.19).
4   Wash and clean all components in petrol to remove sludge or deposits, and renew the rubber components if they have deteriorated.
5   Reassembly and refitting are reversals of the removal and dismantling procedures.

25   Engine front mountings – removal and refitting

1   With time, the bonded rubber insulators, one on each of the front mountings, will perish, causing undue vibration and noise from the engine. Severe juddering when reversing or when moving off from rest is also likely and is a further sign of worn mounting rubbers.
2   The front engine mounting rubbers can be changed with the engine in the vehicle.
3   Apply the handbrake firmly, jack up the front of the vehicle and support it adequately on stands.
4   Take the weight of the engine using a trolley jack with a block of wood beneath the front end of the sump.
5   Unscrew and remove the lower mounting nuts and unbolt the mounting pillars from the cylinder blocks, noting from which side of the engine they are removed.
6   Unscrew and remove the rubber mounting pads from the pillars and tighten the new pads into position.
7   Refitting of the engine front mountings is a reversal of the removal procedure.

26   Engine components – examination for wear

1   When the engine has been stripped down and all parts properly cleaned, decisions have to be made as to what needs renewal. The following Sections tell the examiner what to look for. In any borderline case it is always best to decide in favour of a new part. Even if a part may still be serviceable its life will have been reduced by wear and the degree of trouble needed to renew it in the future must be taken into consideration. However these things are relative and it depends on whether a quick 'survival' job is being done or whether the vehicle as a whole is being regarded as having many thousands of miles of useful and economical life remaining.

27   Crankshaft – examination and renovation

1   Examine the crankpin and main journal surfaces for signs of scoring or scratches. Check the ovality of the crankpins at different positions with a micrometer. If more than 0.001 inch (0.0254 mm) out of round, the crankpins will have to be reground. They will also have to be reground if there are any scores or scratches present. Check the main bearing journals in the same fashion.
2   If it is necessary to regrind the crankshaft and fit new bearings, your local Ford garage or engineering works will be able to decide how much metal to grind off and the size of new bearing shells.
3   When new, the main bearing journals will be either standard size or possibly 0.01 in (0.25 mm) undersize. Where a new crankshaft has been machined undersize, the web next to the main journal is marked with a green painted stripe and the bearing shell marked similarly on its edge. The same applies to the big-end journals (crankpins) and shells.

28   Big-end and main bearings – examination and renovation

1   Big-end bearing failure is accompanied by a knocking from the crankcase, and a slight drop in oil pressure. Main bearing failure is accompanied by vibration which can be quite severe as the engine speed rises. Inspect the big-end bearings, main bearings and thrust washers for signs of general wear, scoring, pitting and scratches. The bearings should be matt grey in colour. With lead-indium bearings, should a trace of copper colour be noticed, the bearings are badly worn as the lead bearing material has worn away to expose the copper underlay. Renew the bearings if they are in this condition or if there is any sign of scoring or pitting. Bearing shells are cheap and should be renewed as a matter of course during overhaul.

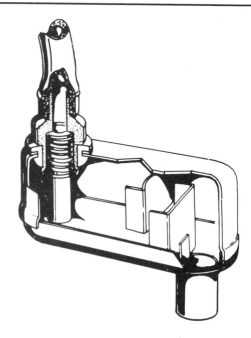

Fig. 1.18 Oil separator and emission control valve (Sec 24)

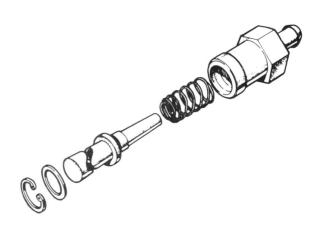

Fig. 1.19 Crankcase emission control valve components (Sec 24)

2   The undersizes available are designed to correspond with the regrind sizes, -0.010 inch (0.2540 mm) bearings are correct for a crankshaft reground -0.010 inch (0.2540 mm) undersize. The bearings are in fact slightly more than the stated undersize, as running clearances have been allowed for during their manufacture.

29   Cylinder bores – examination and renovation

1   A new cylinder is perfectly round and the walls parallel through its length. The action of the piston tends to wear the walls at right-angles to the gudgeon pin due to side thrust. This wear takes place principally on that section of the cylinder swept by the piston rings.
2   It is possible to get an indication of bore wear by removing the cylinder head with the engine still in the vehicle. With the piston down in the bore, first signs of wear can be seen and felt just below the top of the bore where the top piston ring reaches and there will be a noticeable lip. If there is no lip it is fairly reasonable to expect that bore wear is not severe and any lack of compression or excessive oil consumption is due to worn or broken piston rings or pistons (see Section 30).

3   If it is possible to obtain a bore measuring micrometer, measure the bore in the thrust plane below the lip and again at the bottom of the cylinder in the same plane. If the difference is more than 0.006 in (0.15 mm) then a rebore is necessary. Similarly, a difference of 0.006 in (0.15 mm) or more across the bore diameter is a sign of ovality calling for rebore.

4   Any bore which is significantly scratched or scored will need reboring. This symptom usually indicates that the piston or rings are damaged also. In the event of only one cylinder being in need of reboring it will still be necessary for all four to be bored and fitted with new oversize pistons and rings. Your Ford agent or local motor engineering specialist will be able to rebore and obtain the necessary matched pistons. If the crankshaft is undergoing regrinding also, it is a good idea to let the same firm renovate and reassemble the crankshaft and pistons to the block. A reputable firm normally gives a guarantee for such work. In cases where engines have been rebored already to their maximum, new cylinder liners are available which may be fitted. In such cases the same reboring processes have to be followed and the services of a specialist engineering firm are required.

5   Where some bore wear has taken place, but insufficient to justify reboring, proprietary oil control rings may be fitted to the existing pistons in an attempt to reduce oil consumption.

30 Pistons and piston rings – examination and renovation

1   If the old pistons are to be refitted, carefully remove the piston rings and then thoroughly clean them. Take particular care to clean out the piston ring grooves. At the same time do not scratch the aluminium in any way. If new rings are to be fitted to the old pistons, or new piston assemblies are to be fitted to the original (non-rebored) bores, then the top ring should be stepped so as to clear the ridge in the bore left above the previous top ring. If a normal but oversize new ring is fitted, it will hit the ridge and break because the new ring will not have worn in the same way as the old. This will have worn in unison with the ridge.

2   Before fitting the rings on the pistons, each should be inserted approximately 2 in (50 mm) down the cylinder bore and the gap measured with a feeler gauge. This should be as specified. It is essential that the gap is also measured at the bottom of the worn bore, as even if the gap is correct at the top, the ring could easily seize at the bottom. If the ring gap is too small rub down the ends of the ring with a very fine file until the gap, when fitted, is correct. To keep the rings square in the bore for measurement, line each up in turn by inserting an old piston in the bore upside down, and use the piston to push the ring down about 2 in (50 mm). Remove the piston and measure the piston ring gap.

3   When fitting new pistons and rings to a rebored engine, the piston ring gap can be measured at the top of the bore as the bore will not now taper. It is not necessary to measure the side clearance in the piston ring grooves with the rings fitted as the groove dimensions are accurately machined during manufacture. When fitting new oil control rings to old pistons, it may be necessary to have the grooves widened by machining to accept the new wider rings. In this instance the manufacturer's fitting instructions will indicate the procedure.

31 Connecting rods – examination and renovation

1   Examine the mating faces of the big-end caps to see if they have ever been filed in a mistaken attempt to take up wear. If so, the offending rods must be renewed.

2   Insert the gudgeon pin into the little end of the connecting rod. It should go in fairly easily, but if any slackness is present, then take the rod to your local Ford dealer and exchange it for a rod of identical weight.

3   If possible, have the connecting rods checked for alignment by your Ford dealer, and straightened if necessary using the specialised equipment required for this purpose.

32 Camshaft and camshaft bearings – examination and renovation

1   Carefully examine the camshaft bearings for wear. If the bearings

are obviously worn or pitted, then they must be renewed. This is an operation for your local Ford dealer or the local engineering works as it demands the use of specialised equipment. The bearings are removed with a special drift after which new bearings are pressed in, care being taken to ensure the oil holes in the bearing line up with those in the block.

2   The camshaft itself should show no signs of wear. If scoring on the cams is noticed, the only permanently satisfactory cure is to fit a new camshaft.

3   Examine the skew gear for wear, chipped teeth or other damage.

4   Carefully examine the camshaft thrust plates. Excessive wear will be visually self-evident and will require the fitting of a new plate, in which case check that the endfloat is as specified.

33 Timing sprockets and chain – examination and renovation

1   Examine the teeth on both the crankshaft sprocket and the camshaft sprocket for wear. Each tooth forms an inverted V with the sprocket periphery, and if worn, the side of each tooth under tension will be slightly concave in shape when compared with the other side of the tooth. If any sign of wear is present the sprockets must be renewed.

2   Examine the links of the chain for side slackness and renew the chain if any slackness is noticeable when compared with a new chain. It is a sensible precaution to renew the chain if the engine is stripped down for a major overhaul, and has done more than 30 000 miles (48 000 km). The rollers on a very badly worn chain may be slightly grooved.

34 Rockers and rocker shaft – examination and renovation

1   Thoroughly clean the rocker shaft and then check it for distortion by rolling it on a piece of plate glass. If it is out of true, renew it. The surface of the shaft should be free from wear ridges, and score marks.

2   Check the rocker arms for wear of the rocker bushes, for wear at the rocker arm face which bears on the valve stem, and for wear of the adjusting ball-ended screws. Wear in the rocker arm bush can be checked by gripping the rocker arm tip and holding the rocker arm in place on the shaft, noting if there is any lateral rocker arm shake. If shake is present, and the arm is very loose, a new bush or rocker arm must be fitted.

3   Check the top of the rocker arm where it bears on the valve head for cracking or serious wear on the case hardening. If none is present re-use the rocker arm. Check the lower half of the ball on the end of the rocker arm adjusting screw. Check the pushrods for straightness by rolling them on a piece of plate glass. Renew any that are bent.

4   Check that the oil holes in the rocker shaft are not obstructed. Blockage in these holes will lead to rapid wear of the shaft and bushes.

35 Tappets (cam followers) – examination and renovation

Examine the bearing surfaces of the tappets which lie on the camshaft. Any indentation in the surface or any cracks indicate serious wear and the tappets should be renewed. Thoroughly clean them out, removing all traces of sludge. It is most likely that the sides of the tappets will prove worn, but if they are a very loose fit in their bores and can readily be rocked, they should be exchanged for new units. It is very unusual to find any wear in the tappets, and any wear is likely to occur only at very high mileages, or due to failure or neglect of the lubrication system.

36 Cylinder head – decarbonising

1   This can be carried out with the engine either in or out of the vehicle. With the cylinder head off, carefully remove, with a wire brush mounted in an electric drill and blunt scraper, all traces of carbon deposits from the combustion spaces and the ports. The valve heads, stems and valve guides should also be freed from any carbon deposits. Wash the combustion spaces and ports with petrol and scrape the cylinder head surface free of any foreign matter with the side of a steel rule, or similar article.

2   Clean the pistons and the top of the cylinder bores. If the pistons are still in the block then it is essential that great care is taken to ensure that no carbon gets into the cylinder bores as this could scratch the cylinder walls or cause damage to the piston and rings. To ensure that this does not happen, first turn the crankshaft so that two of the pistons are at the top of their bores. Stuff rag into the other two bores or seal them off with paper and masking tape. The waterways and pushrod tunnels should also be covered with small pieces of masking tape to prevent particles of carbon entering the cooling system or oilways and damaging the water pump.

3   There are two schools of thought as to how much carbon should be removed from the piston crown. One school recommends that a ring of carbon should be left around the edge of the piston and on the cylinder bore wall as an aid to low oil consumption. Although this is probably true for early engines with worn bores, on modern engines it is preferable to removal all traces of carbon deposits.

4   If all traces of carbon are to be removed, press a little grease into the gap between the cylinder walls and the two pistons which are to be worked on. With a blunt scraper carefully scrape all the carbon from the piston crown, taking great care not to scratch the aluminium. Also scrape away the carbon from the surrounding lip of the cylinder wall. When all carbon has been removed, scrape away the grease which will now be contaminated with carbon particles, taking care not to press any into the bores. To assist prevention of carbon build-up the piston crown can be polished with a metal polish. Remove the rags or masking tape from the other two cylinders and turn the crankshaft so that the two pistons which were at the bottom are now at the top. Place rag or masking tape in the cylinders which have been decarbonised and proceed as already described.

5   Thoroughly clean out the cylinder head bolt holes in the top face of the block. If these are filled with carbon, oil or water, it is possible for the block to crack when the bolts are screwed in due to the hydraulic pressure created by the trapped fluid.

37 Valves and valve seats – examination and renovation

1   Examine the cylinder head valve seats and the heads of the valves for pitting and burning. The valve heads are specially coated to minimise wear and preferably no attempt should be made to grind them in with valve grinding paste, otherwise the coating will be removed. If the valve seats require attention, the cylinder head should be taken to a garage having valve seat cutting equipment.

2   In extreme cases of valve seat pitting, new inserts will need to be fitted and this is also a job for a suitably equipped garage or engineering works.

3   Where the valves are worn or pitted, it will be necessary to obtain new ones, but if they are still serviceable, all traces of carbon should be removed from them using a scraper, also being careful not to damage the valve head seating.

4   Should the special coating be worn away from the valve heads, and pitting is present, it is recommended that new valves are obtained, although a further lease of life can be given by grinding the valves in as follows. Smear a trace of coarse carborundum paste on the seat face and apply a suction grinder tool to the valve head. With a semi-rotary motion, grind the valve head to its seat, lifting the valve occasionally to redistribute the grinding paste (Fig. 1.20). When a dull matt even surface finish is produced on both the valve seat and valve, wipe off the paste and repeat the process with fine carborundum paste, lifting and turning the valve to redistribute the paste as before. A light spring placed under the valve head will greatly ease this operation. When a smooth, unbroken ring of light grey matt finish is produced, on both valve and valve seat faces, the grinding operation is complete. All traces of grinding compound should be removed with a paraffin-soaked lint-free cloth, making sure that none is left in the cylinder head ports. Blow through with compressed air if possible.

5   Another form of valve wear can occur on the stem where it runs in the guide in the cylinder head. This can be detected by trying to rock the valve from side to side (Fig. 1.21). If there is any movement at all it is an indication that the valve stem or guide is worn. Check the stem first with a micrometer at points along and around its length. If it is not within the specified size, new valves will probably solve the problem. If the guides are worn, however, they will need reboring for oversize valves – refer to Section 38.

38 Valve guides – examination and renovation

1   Examine the valve guides internally for scoring and other signs of wear. If a new valve is a very loose fit in a guide and there is a trace of lateral rocking then the guide must be reamed out (from the valve seat end) to the next oversize and oversize valves of corresponding stem diameter fitted. Valves are available in oversizes as listed in the Specifications.

2   Reaming is best entrusted to your Ford dealer or local automotive machine shop, who will also recut the valve seats as required to ensure they are concentric with the valve stems.

39 Starter ring gear – examination and renewal

1   If the flywheel ring gear teeth are worn, the ring gear can be renewed without the need to renew the flywheel.

2   To remove the starter ring gear from the flywheel, drill two $\frac{1}{4}$ in

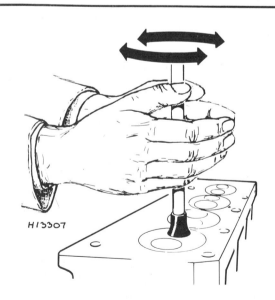

Fig. 1.20 Grind in valves using suction tool (Sec 37)

Fig. 1.21 Check valve stem/guide play by moving it in directions indicated (Sec 37)

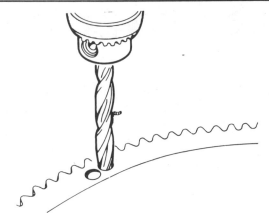

Fig. 1.22 Drilling the ring gear to remove it (Sec 39)

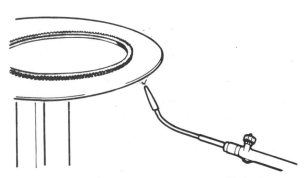

Fig. 1.23 Method of heating ring gear to expand it for fitment to the flywheel (Sec 39)

(6.35 mm) holes next to each other through the ring gear. Take care not to drill the flywheel. Then use a cold chisel to split the ring gear to release it. Take precautions to avoid damage or injury from possible flying fragments.

3   Clean and polish with emery cloth four evenly spaced areas on the outside face of the new starter ring gear.

4   Support the ring gear on a steel plate (2 to 3 mm thick) and heat the plate as shown (Fig. 1.23) with a welding torch to give a uniform temperature of 500° to 540°F (260° to 280°C), at which point the polished ring portions should turn blue. **Do not** exceed this temperature. The ring can now be carefully fitted onto the flywheel with the chamfered portion of the teeth facing the gearbox side of the flywheel. (See also paragraph 6).

5   The ring should be tapped gently down onto its register and left to cool naturally when the contraction of the metal on cooling will ensure that it is a secure and permanent fit. Great care must be taken not to overheat the ring, indicated by it turning light metallic blue, as if this happens the temper of the ring will be lost.

6   It does not matter which way round the ring for pre-engaged

starters is fitted as it has no chamfers on its teeth. This also makes for quick identification between the two ring types.

40   Engine reassembly – general

1   To ensure maximum life with minimum trouble from a rebuilt engine, not only must everything be correctly assembled, but everything must be spotlessly clean, all the oilways must be clear, locking washers and spring washers must always be fitted where indicated and all bearing and other working surfaces must be thoroughly lubricated during assembly.

2   Before assembly begins renew any bolts or studs, the threads of which are in any way damaged, and whenever possible use new spring washers.

3   Apart from your normal tools, a supply of clean rag, an oil can filled with engine oil, a new supply of assorted spring washers, a set of new gaskets, and a torque wrench, should be collected together.

41   Crankshaft – refitting

1   Thoroughly clean the block and ensure that all traces of old gaskets are removed.

2   Position the upper halves of the shell bearings in their correct positions so that the tabs of the shells engage in the machined keyways in the sides of the crankcase locations (photo).

3   Oil the main bearing shells after they have been fitted in position (photo).

4   Fit the thrust washers, one each side of the centre main bearing in the block, with the oil grooves outwards. Stick the thrust washers in place with grease if necessary.

5   Lower the crankshaft into position (photo).

6   Locate the lower half shells into their caps, again making sure that the tabs are engaged. Oil the shells and refit the caps, making sure that

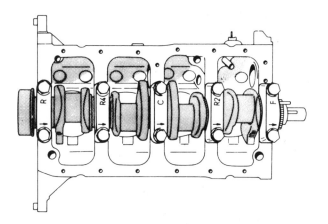

Fig. 1.24 Main bearing cap markings (Sec 41)

41.2 Upper half of main bearing shell in position in cylinder block, with tab engaged in keyway (arrowed)

41.3 Lubricate the main bearing shells

41.5 Lower the crankshaft carefully into position

41.7 Tighten the main bearing cap bolts to the correct torque

41.8 Fit the oil seal housing gasket to the rear of the cylinder block ...

41.9 ... then fit the housing

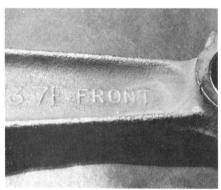

42.1 Connecting rod 'FRONT' marking

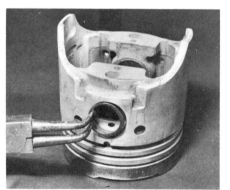

42.2a Refit the gudgeon pin circlip prior to inserting the gudgeon pin and connecting rod

42.2b Locate connecting rod and insert gudgeon pin

they are correctly located. (The front cap is marked 'F', the second 'R2', the centre 'C', the fourth 'R4' and the rear cap 'R').

7   Insert the bearing cap bolts and tighten them to the specified torque (photo). Check the crankshaft endfloat, which should be as specified. Turn the crankshaft and check that it is free to rotate. Some stiffness is to be expected with new bearing shells, but there should be no binding or tight spots.

8   Fit a new rear main oil seal bearing retainer gasket to the rear of the cylinder block (photo).

9   Fit the rear main oil bearing retainer housing (photo). Note that the oil seal is also circular and is simply prised out when removed, a new one being pressed in.

10   Lightly tighten the four retaining bolts with spring washers under their heads, noting that two bolts are dowelled to ensure correct alignment and should be tightened first.

11   Tighten the bolts to the specified torque wrench setting, and check that the housing is centralised.

12   Refit the backplate and bolt it in position.

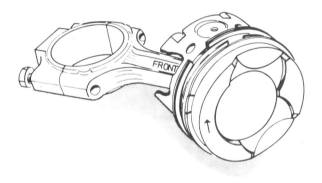

Fig. 1.25 Piston and connecting rod location marks (Sec 42)

42 Pistons and connecting rods – reassembly

1   If the same pistons are being re-used, then they must be mated to the same connecting rod with the same gudgeon pin. If new pistons are being fitted it does not matter which connecting rod they are used with. Note that the word 'FRONT' is stamped on one side of each of the rods. On reassembly the side marked 'FRONT' must be towards the front of the engine (photo).

2   Fit a gudgeon pin in position at one end of the gudgeon pin hole in the piston and fit the piston to the connecting rod by sliding in the gudgeon pin. The arrow on the crown of each piston must be on the same side as the word 'FRONT' on the connecting rod (photos).

3   Fit the second circlip in position. Repeat this procedure for the remaining three pistons and connecting rods.

4   If necessary, heat the pistons in hot water to expand the aluminium and aid insertion of the gudgeon pins. Dry the pistons thoroughly afterwards.

43 Piston rings – fitting

1   Check that the piston ring grooves and oilways are thoroughly clean and unblocked. Piston rings must always be fitted over the head of the piston and never from the bottom.

2   The easiest method to use when fitting rings is to wrap a 0.020 in (0.5 mm) feeler gauge round the top of the piston and place the rings one at a time, starting with the bottom oil control ring, over the feeler gauge.

3   The feeler gauge, complete with ring, can then be slid down the piston over the other piston ring grooves until the correct groove is reached. The piston ring is then gently slid off the feeler gauge into the groove.

4   An alternative method is to fit the rings by holding them slightly open with the thumbs and both of the index fingers. This method requires a steady hand and great care as it is easy to open the ring too much and break it.

5   When assembling the rings note that the compression rings are marked 'top' and that the upper ring is chromium plated. The ring gaps should be spaced as described in the Specifications (photos).

44 Pistons and connecting rods – refitting

1   Fit the connecting rod bearings in position and check that the oil hole in the upper half of each bearing aligns with the oil squirt hole in the connecting rod (photo).

2   With a wad of clean rag wipe the cylinder bores clean, and then oil them generously. The pistons, complete with connecting rods, are fitted to their bores from above. As each piston is inserted into its bore, ensure that it is the correct piston/connecting rod assembly for that particular bore and that the connecting rod is the right way round, and that the front of the piston is towards the front of the bore, ie towards the front of the engine.

3   The piston will only slide into the bore as far as the oil control ring. It is then necessary to compress the piston rings in a clamp (photos).

4   Gently tap the piston into the cylinder bore with a wooden or plastic hammer (photo).

5   Note the directional arrow on the piston crown.

6   Fit the shell bearings to the big-end caps so that the tongue on the back of each bearing lies in the machined recess.

43.5a Piston compression rings showing the 'TOP' markings

43.5b Piston rings in place on piston

44.1 Locate connecting rod upper shell in connecting rod. Note alignment of shell and connecting rod oil holes

44.3a Compress piston rings using a clamp ...

44.3b ... prior to inserting piston in cylinder bore

44.4 Tap piston down its bore with shaft end of hammer

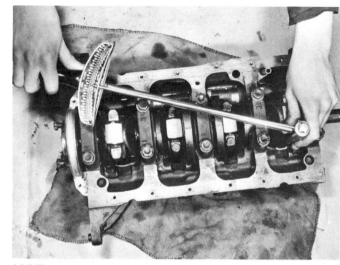

44.7 Tighten connecting rod bearing caps to the correct torque

7   Generously oil the crankshaft connecting rod journals and then refit each cap on the same connecting rod from which it was removed. Fit the locking plates under the heads of the big-end bolts, tap the caps right home on the dowels and then tighten the bolts to the specified torque. Knock up the tabs of the locking plates. To facilitate re-assembly the rod and cap are marked (ie 1 - 2 - 3 -4); these numbers should be on the camshaft side of the engine (photo).
8   When all the connecting rods have been fitted, rotate the crankshaft to check that everything is free, and that there are no high spots causing binding.

45 Cam followers (tappets) and camshaft – refitting

1   The semi-rebuilt engine will now look as in the photograph and is ready for the cam followers and camshaft to be fitted (photo).
2   Fit the eight cam followers into the same holes in the block from which each was removed. The cam followers can only be fitted with the block upside down (photos).
3   Fit the Woodruff key in its slot on the front of the crankshaft and then press the timing sprocket into place so the timing mark faces forward. Oil the camshaft bearings and insert the camshaft into the block (which should still be upside-down)(photo).
4   Make sure the camshaft turns freely and then fit the thrust plate behind the camshaft flange. Tighten the thrust plate bolts to the specified torque. Measure the endfloat with a feeler gauge – it should be as specified. If this is not so, then renew the plate (photo).
5   Turn up the tab under the head of each bolt to lock it in place (photo).

46 Timing chain, sprockets, tensioner and cover – refitting

1   Refit the camshaft sprocket and loosely retain with its two retaining bolts. Use a **new** tab washer.
2   When refitting the timing chain round the sprockets and to the engine, the two timing lines (arrowed) must be adjacent to each other on an imaginary line passing through each sprocket centre (photo).
3   With the timing marks correctly aligned turn the camshaft until the protruding dowel locates in the hole in the camshaft sprocket.
4   Tighten the two retaining bolts and bend up the tabs on the lockwasher (photo).
5   Fit the oil slinger to the nose of the crankshaft, concave side facing outwards. The cut-out locates over the Woodruff key.
6   Slide the timing chain tensioner arm over its hinge pin on the front of the block.
7   Turn the tensioner back from its free position so that it will apply pressure to the tensioner arm and refit the tensioner on the block sump flange.

45.1 Semi-rebuilt engine ready to receive camshaft and tappets

45.2a Insert the cam followers into their bores

45.2b Cam followers located in their respective bores

45.3 Carefully insert the camshaft

45.4 Fit the camshaft thrust plate ...

45.5 ... and bolt in position with tab washers turned up to lock bolt. Note timing gear location peg (arrowed)

46.2 Align the camshaft and crankshaft timing sprocket marks (arrowed)

46.4 Bend lockwasher tabs over bolt heads to secure

46.8 Timing chain tensioner in position

46.9 Renew the front cover oil seal

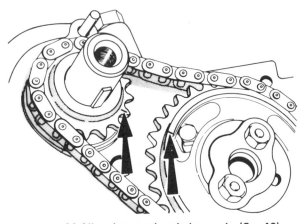

Fig. 1.26 Align the sprocket timing marks (Sec 46)

46.10 Timing cover gasket in position on block prior to fitting the cover

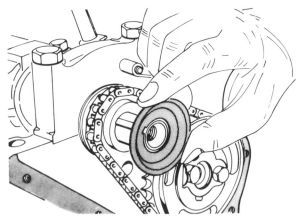

Fig. 1.27 Locate the oil slinger (Sec 46)

8   Bolt the tensioner to the block using spring washers under the heads of the two bolts (photo).
9   Remove the front oil seal from the timing chain cover and carefully press a new seal into position (photo). Lightly lubricate the face of the seal which will bear against the crankshaft.
10 Using jointing compound, fit a new timing cover gasket in place (photo).
11 Fit the timing chain cover, refitting and tightening the two dowel bolts first. These fit in the holes nearest the sump flange and serve to align the timing cover correctly. Ensure that spring washers are used and then tighten the bolts evenly.

47 Sump – refitting

1   Refit the crankcase emission device to its recess adjacent to the top of the petrol pump, tapping it gently into place. Refit the oil pump pick-up pipe using a new tab washer and position the gauze head so that it clears the crankshaft throw and the oil return pipe (where fitted). Tighten the nut and bend back the tab of the lockwasher (photo).
2   Clean the flange of the sump and fit new gaskets in place. Fit a new sealing strip to the flange at the rear of the crankcase and at the front (photos).
3   Locate the flywheel onto the crankshaft flange and tighten the securing bolts to the specified torque (photo).
4   Locate the sump in position on the crankcase and tighten the securing bolts evenly in diagonal sequence, in the stages shown in the Specifications.

48 Oil pump and crankshaft pulley – refitting

1   Stand the engine upright and then coat the oil pump flanges with jointing compound. Fill the pump with engine oil.
2   Fit a new gasket in place on the oil pump.
3   Position the oil pump against the block, ensuring that the skew gear teeth on the driveshaft mate with those on the camshaft (photo).

47.1 Oil pick-up pipe and bracket location on block underside

47.2a Sump gasket in place on block sump flange

47.2b Fit sealing strips to rear oil seal carrier ...

47.2c ... and to front in timing cover groove

47.3 Tighten the flywheel retaining bolts

48.3 Oil pump in position

4   Refit the three securing bolts and spring washers and tighten them down evenly.

5   Moving to the front of the engine, align the slot in the crankshaft pulley with the key on the crankshaft and gently tap the pulley home.

6   Secure the pulley by fitting the large flat washer, the spring washer and then the bolt which should be tightened securely (photo). Jam the flywheel ring gear to prevent the crankshaft rotating whilst the bolt is being tightened.

49 Cylinder head – assembly and refitting

1   Thoroughly clean the faces of the block and cylinder head. Then fit a new cylinder head gasket. In order to position the gasket correctly, it is a good idea temporarily to screw in two lengths of studding (one in each extreme diagonal hole) to act as locating dowels. These should be removed once two of the cylinder head bolts have been screwed into position.

2   With the cylinder head on its side lubricate the valve stems and refit the valves to their correct guides. The valves should previously have been ground in (see Section 37) or renewed.

3   Fit the valve stem oil seals, open ends down.

4   Next slide the valve spring into place. Use new ones if the old set has covered 20 000 miles (32 000 km) or more.

5   Slide the valve spring retainer over the valve stem.

6   Compress the valve spring with a compressor.

7   Refit the split collets. A trace of grease will help to hold them to the valve stem recess until the spring compressor is slackened off and the collets are wedged in place by the spring.

8   Carefully lower the cylinder head onto the block.

9   Refit the cylinder head bolts and screw them down finger tight. Note that two of the bolts are of a different length.

10   With a torque wrench tighten the bolts in the order shown in Fig. 1.3. Do this in the various stages shown in the Specifications.

11   Fit the pushrods into the same holes in the block from which they were removed. Make sure the pushrods seat properly in the cam followers.

12   Reassemble the rocker gear onto the rocker shaft and fit the shaft to the cylinder head (photo). Ensure that the oil holes are clear and that the cut-outs for the securing bolts lie facing the holes in the brackets. When fitted, the rocker arm lubrication port in the shaft must point forwards and downwards. This is marked by a notch cut into the end face of the shaft. Where a new shaft is being fitted, ensure that it has end covers fitted.

13   Tighten the four rocker bracket washers and bolts to the specified torque wrench setting (photo).

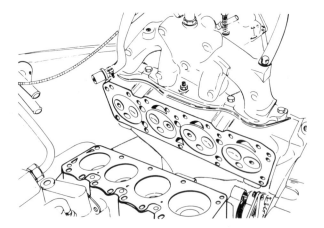

Fig. 1.28 Refit the cylinder head (Sec 49)

50 Valve clearances – adjustment

1   The valve adjustments should be made with the engine cold. The importance of correct rocker arm/valve stem clearances cannot be overstressed as they vitally affect the performance of the engine. If the

48.6 Tighten the crankshaft pulley bolt

49.12 Engage the rocker arm adjustment screws prior to tightening the rocker shaft pedestal bolts

49.13 Tighten the rocker shaft pedestal bolts

clearances are set too open, the efficiency is reduced as the valves open late and close earlier than was intended. If, on the other hand, the clearances are set too close, there is a danger that the stems will expand upon heating and not allow the valves to close properly, which will cause burning of the valve head and seat and possible warping. If the engine is in the vehicle, access to the rockers is by removing the four holding-down screws from the rocker cover, and then lifting the rocker cover and gasket away.

2   Turn the crankshaft, observing the rocker arms, until the valve of one cylinder can be seen to be 'rocking' – ie the exhaust valve is closing and the inlet valve opening. Adjust the valves on the **other** cylinder specified in the table below:

Valves 'rocking' on cylinder	Adjust valves of cylinder
No 1	No 4
No 2	No 3
No 4	No 1
No 3	No 2

Counting from the front of the engine, exhaust valves are Nos 1, 4, 5 and 8; inlet valves are Nos 2, 3, 6 and 7. The correct valve clearances are given in the Specifications.

3   The correct clearance is obtained by inserting a feeler gauge of the correct thickness between the valve stem and the rocker arm. The self-locking adjuster head should be turned until the feeler gauge is a sliding fit (photo).

4   Do not refit the rocker cover before refitting the distributor and setting the ignition timing (if applicable). The details of this are given in Chapter 4.

51 Engine ancillary components – refitting

1   Reconnect the ancillary components to the engine in the reverse order to that in which they were removed.

2   It should be noted that in all cases it is best to reassemble the engine as far as possible before refitting it. This means that the inlet and exhaust manifolds, carburettor, alternator, starter, thermostat, oil filter, distributor and engine mounting brackets, should all be in position.

3   Connect the HT leads as shown in Fig. 1.29.

52 Engine refitting – general

1   Although the engine can be refitted by one person and a suitable hoist, it is easier if two are present so that the upper and lower parts of the assembly can be observed whilst the unit is being guided into position.

2   At this stage, one or two tips may come in useful. Ensure all the loose leads, cables, etc are tucked out of the way. If not, it is easy to trap one and so cause much additional work after the engine is refitted. Smear a little grease on the tip of the gearbox input shaft before fitting the gearbox (if applicable).

3   Always fit a new fanbelt, new cooling hoses and hose clips, as this will help eliminate the possibility of failure while on the road.

53 Engine – refitting with transmission

1   Suspend the engine and gearbox from the hoist at an angle of approximately 30° to the horizontal and place a trolley jack beneath the vehicle engine compartment.

2   Carefully position the assembly into the engine compartment and lower the gearbox onto the trolley jack. Move the engine rearwards until the front engine mountings are in alignment with their brackets and, at the same time, lower the assembly and move the trolley jack rearwards.

3   Jack up the gearbox and enter the rear mounting bolt from the left-hand side of the vehicle together with the spacer and washer, then tighten the nut.

4   Lower the engine front mountings onto their brackets and refit and tighten the retaining nuts and washers.

5   Remove the lifting hoist from the engine and the trolley jack from beneath the gearbox.

6   Insert the speedometer cable into the gearbox location, refit the

50.3 Using feeler gauge and ring spanner to adjust the valve clearances

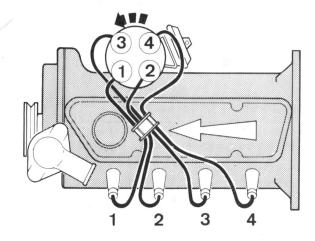

Fig. 1.29 Spark plug HT lead positions (Sec 57)

cable retaining clamp, and tighten the single bolt and spring washer.

7   Refer to Chapter 7 and refit the propeller shaft, making sure that the alignment marks are adjacent.

8   Reconnect the clutch cable to the clutch operating arm by inserting the inner cable through the clutch housing aperture, rubber gaiter, and operating lever large hole, then move the inner cable to the small hole. Position the outer cable firmly in the clutch housing.

9   Refer to Chapter 5 and adjust the clutch cable as necessary.

10   Working inside the cab lower the gear lever through the floor and enter it into the gearbox selector housing with the tapered end facing forwards.

11   From beneath the vehicle position the gasket onto the selector housing and then tighten the nylon retaining cap to secure the lever.

12   Inside the cab, slide the rubber gaiter down the gear lever and secure the retaining plate to the floor.

13   Working from the front of the vehicle, reconnect the fuel pipe to the fuel pump. Refit the fuel pipes to the carburettor.

14   Lift the exhaust downpipe to the manifold joint, insert the sealing ring, and loosely assemble the clamp. Make sure that the exhaust pipe is positioned correctly, with the manifold and clamp faces parallel to each other and the sealing ring central, then tighten the clamp nuts evenly.

15   Refer to Chapter 3, refit the accelerator and choke cables, then adjust them.

16   Connect the electrical leads to the starter motor, water temperature sender and oil pressure sender units, the coil and the carburettor idle cut-off valve.

17 Refit the brake servo vacuum pipe to the inlet manifold.
18 Refit the heater hoses to their bulkhead and engine connections and tighten the hose clips.
19 Refit the air cleaner brackets and air cleaner, refer to Chapter 3 if necessary.
20 Push the radiator bottom hose onto the water pump with the remaining end facing forwards and tighten the clip to secure it.
21 With the aid of an assistant, position the front panel assembly to the front of the vehicle and tighten the retaining bolts. Make sure that the front bumper is correctly aligned. Refit the bumper corner sections – refer to Chapter 12 for further details.
22 Push the radiator bottom hose onto the radiator outlet and the top hose onto the thermostat housing and radiator inlet, then tighten the clips.
23 Fit the bonnet release cable to the front panel in its original position, tighten the locknuts, and clip the outer cable to the front panel. Connect the inner cable to the release spring.
24 Refit the two front headlamp bezels and secure them with the retaining screws.
25 Refill the radiator and cooling system; refer to Chapter 2 if necessary.
26 Refill the gearbox with the correct amount and grade of oil; refer to Chapter 6 if necessary.
27 Refill the engine with the correct quantity and grade of oil.
28 With the help of an assistant, locate the bonnet onto the hinges and loosely screw in the retaining bolts and washers. Move the bonnet so that the previously made marks are in alignment, then tighten the retaining bolts and prop the bonnet in the open position.
29 Refit the windscreen washer tubing and the engine compartment light to the bonnet.
30 Reconnect the battery negative terminal.

54 Engine – refitting without transmission

1 Suspend the engine at the required height. If the front panel is in position, the engine must be arranged at right-angles to the longitudinal line of the vehicle and the sump must be clear of the top edge of the front grille panel.
2 Check that the gearbox is suitably supported in the horizontal position and also ensure that the clutch plate is centralised, otherwise you will encounter difficulties when trying to engage the gearbox input shaft when mating the engine to the gearbox. Refer to Chapter 5 if necessary.
3 Carefully lower the engine into the engine compartment and gradually ease it rearwards until it is aligned with the gearbox. It will help if the gearbox is engaged in top gear to avoid the input shaft rotating in subsequent operations. When level with the gearbox, the transversely suspended engine can be turned so that it is in line.
4 Enter the clutch over the gearbox input shaft as far as it will go. If difficulty is experienced in engaging the splines, rotate the crankshaft with a ring spanner on the crankshaft pulley bolt.
5 Avoid allowing the weight of the engine to rest on the gearbox input shaft otherwise damage could result.
6 Push the engine fully home to the gearbox clutch bellhousing, align the bolt holes, insert the retaining bolts and tighten them to the specified torque.
7 Remove the trolley jack and lower the front engine mountings onto their brackets, tightening the retaining nuts and washers.
8 Remove the lifting hoist from the engine.
9 Refit the clutch housing lower dust cover plate and tighten the retaining screws.
10 Refer to Chapter 10 and refit the starter motor.
11 Refer to Section 53 and carry out the instructions given in paragraph 13 onwards, as applicable.

55 Engine – initial start-up after major overhaul

1 There is no reason why the reassembled engine should not fire at the first operation of the starter switch.
2 If it fails to do so, make two or three more attempts as it may be that the carburettor bowl is empty and requires filling by a few strokes of the camshaft-operated fuel pump.

3 If the engine still does not fire, check the following points:

(a) There is fuel in the tank
(b) Ignition and battery leads are correctly and securely connected. (Check particularly the spark plug HT lead sequence)
(c) The choke is correctly connected
(d) The distributor has been correctly installed and not fitted 180° out
(e) Work systematically through the fault diagnosis chart at the end of this Chapter

4 Run the engine until normal operating temperature is reached and check the torque setting of all nuts and bolts. Retighten the cylinder head bolts as given in the Specifications.
5 With the engine cold check and adjust the valve clearances again.
6 Adjust the slow-running and carburettor mixture control screws (Chapter 3).
7 Check for all oil or water leaks and when the engine has cooled, check the levels in the radiator and sump and top up as necessary.
8 If new bearings, piston rings etc have been fitted, the engine should be run-in for the first few hundred miles at reduced revolutions. It is good practice to renew the engine oil and filter after this initial mileage, to get rid of the metallic particles which will have been produced when the new components bed-in.

56 Fault diagnosis – ohv engine

Refer to Section 120.

PART B: OHC ENGINE

57 General description

The engines covered in this part of Chapter 1 are of four cylinder overhead camshaft design and are available in two capacities, 1593 cc and 1993 cc. An exploded view identifying the main components is shown in Fig. 1.30.
The cylinder head is of the crossflow design with the inlet manifold one side and the exhaust manifold on the other. As flat top pistons are used the combustion chambers are contained in the cylinder head.
The combined crankcase and cylinder block is made of cast iron and houses the pistons and crankshaft. Attached to the underside of the crankcase is a pressed steel sump which acts as a reservoir for the engine oil. Full information on the lubricating system will be found in Section 82.
The cast iron cylinder head is mounted on top of the cylinder block and acts as a support for the overhead camshaft. The slightly angled valves operate directly in the cylinder head and are controlled by the camshaft via cam followers. The camshaft is operated by a toothed reinforced composite rubber belt from the crankshaft. To eliminate backlash and prevent slackness of the belt, a spring-loaded tensioner in the form of a jockey wheel is in contact with the back of the belt. It serves two further functions, to keep the belt away from the water pump and also to increase the contact area of the camshaft and crankshaft sprocket.
The drivebelt also drives the auxiliary shaft sprocket and it is from this shaft that the oil pump, distributor and fuel pump operate.
The inlet manifold is mounted on the left-hand side of the cylinder head and to this the carburettor is fitted. A water jacket is incorporated in the inlet manifold so that the petrol/air charge may be preheated before entering the combustion chambers.
The exhaust manifold is mounted on the right-hand side of the cylinder head and connects to a single downpipe and silencer system.
Aluminium alloy pistons are connected to the crankshaft by forged steel connecting rods and gudgeon pins. The gudgeon pin is a press fit in the small end of the connecting rod but a floating fit in the piston boss. Two compression rings and one scraper ring, all located above the gudgeon pin, are fitted.
The forged crankshaft runs in five main bearings and endfloat is accommodated by thrust washers either side of the centre main bearing.
Before commencing any overhaul work on the engine refer to Section 64, where information is given about special tools that are required to remove the cylinder head, drivebelt tensioner and oil pump.

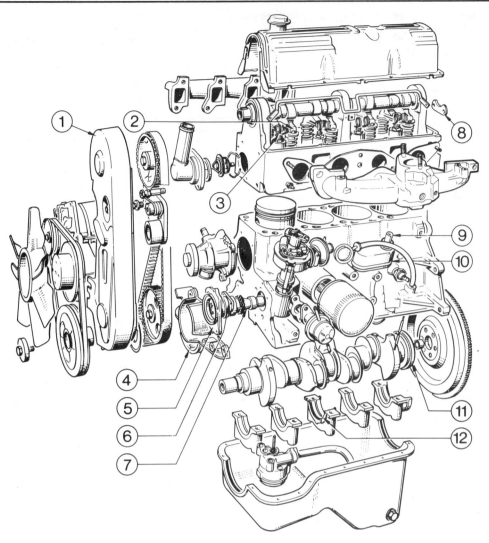

Fig. 1.30 Exploded view of the ohc engine (Sec 57)

1 Belt guard	5 Front cover – auxiliary	7 Auxiliary shaft	10 Oil separator
2 Cam follower	shaft	8 Camshaft thrust plate	11 Oil seal (crankshaft)
3 Spring	6 Auxiliary shaft thrust plate	9 Vent valve	12 Thrust washer
4 Timing cover (crankshaft)			

58 Major operations possible – engine in vehicle

The following major operations may be undertaken with the engine in the vehicle:

(a) Removal and refitting of the camshaft
(b) Removal and refitting of the cylinder head
(c) Removal and refitting of the timing belt
(d) Removal and refitting of the auxiliary shaft
(e) Removal and refitting of the engine front mountings
(f) Removal and refitting of the sump
(g) Removal and refitting of the oil pump
(h) Removal and refitting of the big-end bearings
(i) Removal and refitting of the pistons and connecting rods

59 Major operations requiring engine removal

The following operations can only be carried out with the engine removed from the vehicle:

(a) Removal and renewal of the main bearings
(b) Removal and refitting of the crankshaft
(c) Removal and refitting of the flywheel
(d) Removal and renewal of the crankshaft rear oil seal

60 Methods of engine removal

1 The engine may be lifted out either on its own or in unit with the gearbox. On models fitted with automatic transmission it is recommended that the engine be lifted out on its own, unless a substantial crane or overhead hoist is available, because of the weight factor.

2 The engine or engine and gearbox (as applicable) of all ohc engined variants must be removed through the front end of the vehicle, and therefore it is essential that the radiator and front panel are removed. The radiator and panel can be removed together as described in Chapter 12.

61 Engine – removal with transmission

1 The engine complete with transmission removal procedure is essentially the same as that given for the ohv engine as described in Section 5. However, the following points should also be noted concerning automatic transmission models:

(a) Drain the transmission fluid (Chapter 5)
(b) Disconnect the speedometer cable and transmission controls (Chapter 6, Section 28, paragraphs 7 to 11 and 13)
(c) Disconnect the transmission fluid cooler and plug the lines

2   Information on separating the engine from the automatic transmission will be found in Section 64.

3   Where appropriate, ignore references to the manual choke and substitute those applicable to the automatic choke.

62 Engine – removal without manual transmission

The removal procedure is essentially the same as that for the ohv engine described in Section 6. As the ohc engine can only be withdrawn through the front of the vehicle, the front panel and radiator must be removed, and references to removal of the engine through the bonnet aperture must therefore be ignored. Refer to Chapter 12 for information on the removal of the front end panel and radiator. Make due allowance for the differences between manual and automatic choke versions (where applicable).

63 Engine – removal without automatic transmission

The engine removal procedure for models fitted with automatic transmission is essentially the same as that for the ohv engine detailed in Section 6, but with the following differences:

(a)   *Refer to Chapter 6 and disconnect the downshift cable at the throttle link and bracket*

(b)   *With the bellhousing front cover removed, unscrew the four driveplate to torque converter retaining bolts; it will be necessary to turn the crankshaft in order to gain access to each of the bolts*

(c)   *Make sure when separating the engine from the transmission that the torque converter is held firmly inside the bellhousing, using a piece of wood*

(d)   *The engine can only be removed through the front of the vehicle, necessitating the removal of the front panel and radiator and transmission fluid cooler*

64 Engine dismantling – general

1   Refer to Section 7. In addition you will also require three special tools with which to remove the cylinder head bolts, oil pump bolts and valve springs (photo).

2   When separating the engine from the automatic transmission, remove the bellhousing front cover and then unscrew the four torque converter retaining bolts through the housing aperture. It will be necessary to turn the crankshaft in order to gain access to each of

these bolts. As the engine and transmission are parted, ensure that the torque converter is held firmly inside the bellhousing. The torque converter must be kept in position whilst the transmission is removed and during refitting.

65 Engine ancillary components – removal

Refer to Section 8.

66 Cylinder head – removal (engine in vehicle)

1   Open the bonnet and using a soft pencil mark the outline of both the hinges at the bottom to act as a datum for refitting.

2   With the help of a second person to take the weight of the bonnet, undo and remove the hinge to bonnet securing bolts with plain and spring washers. There are two bolts to each hinge.

3   Lift away the bonnet and put in a safe place where it will not be scratched.

4   Refer to Chapter 10, and remove the battery.

5   Place a container having a capacity of 8 pints (4.55 litres) under the engine and sump and remove the oil drain plug. Allow the oil to drain out and then refit the plug.

6   Refer to Chapter 3, and remove the air cleaner assembly from the top of the carburettor.

7   Mark the HT leads so that they may be refitted in their original positions and detach from the spark plugs (photo).

8   Release the HT leads from the clips on the top of the camshaft cover.

9   Spring back the clips securing the distributor cap to the distributor body. Lift off the distributor cap.

10 Detach the HT lead from the centre of the ignition coil. Remove the distributor cap and HT leads from the engine compartment.

11 Refer to Chapter 2, and drain the cooling system.

12 Refer to Chapter 3, and remove the carburettor.

13 The combined insulation spacer and gasket may now be lifted from the studs. Note that it is marked 'TOP FRONT' and it must be refitted the correct way round.

14 Detach the vacuum hoses from the inlet manifold adaptor.

15 Detach the coolant hose(s) at the central manifold location (photo).

16 It is not necessary to remove the carburettor and inlet manifold, but if it is wished to do so, proceed as follows. Undo and remove the nuts and bolts securing the inlet manifold to the side of the cylinder head. Note that one of the manifold securing bolts also retains the air cleaner support bracket.

17 Lift away the inlet manifold and recover the manifold gasket.

18 Undo and remove the two nuts that secure the exhaust downpipe and clamp plate to the exhaust manifold (photo).

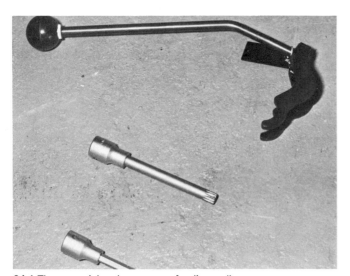

64.1 Three special tools necessary for dismantling

66.7 Disconnect the HT leads from the spark plugs

19 Slide the clamp plate down the exhaust pipe.

20 Detach the thermal transmitter electric cable from the inlet manifold side of the cylinder head.

21 Slacken the radiator top hose clips and completely remove the hose (photo).

22 Undo and remove the bolts, spring and plain washers that secure the top cover to the cylinder head.

23 Lift away the top cover.

24 Undo and remove the two self-locking nuts that secure the heat deflector plate to the top of the exhaust manifold. Lift away the deflector plate.

25 Undo and remove the bolts, spring and plain washers that secure the drivebelt guard (photo).

26 Lift away the guard.

27 Release the tension from the drivebelt by slackening the spring-loaded roller mounting plate securing bolt (photo). If available use special tool No 21-012.

28 Lift the toothed drivebelt from the camshaft sprocket (photo).

29 Using the special tool (21 - 002) or equivalent together with a socket wrench (photo), slacken the cylinder head securing bolts in the sequence shown in Fig. 1.31 until all are free from tension. Remove the ten bolts noting that because of the special shape of the bolt head no washers are used. Unfortunately there is no other tool suitable to

slot into the bolt head so do not attempt to improvise which will only cause damage to the bolt.

30 The cylinder head may now be removed by lifting upwards. If the head is stuck, try to rock it to break the seal. Under no circumstances try to prise it apart from the cylinder block with a screwdriver or cold chisel, as damage may be done to the faces of the cylinder head and block. Neither should any attempt be made to free the head by turning

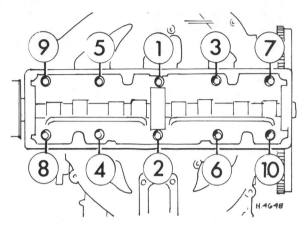

Fig. 1.31 Cylinder head bolt loosening and tightening sequence (Sec 66)

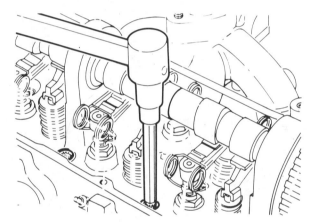

Fig. 1.32 Remove and tighten cylinder head bolts using special tool shown (Ford No 21.002) (Sec 66)

66.15 Detach the hoses from the manifold, noting their respective locations

66.18 Detach the exhaust downpipe from the manifold

66.21 Detach the radiator top hose

66.25 Removing belt guard securing bolts

66.27 Release the belt tensioner mounting plate securing bolt

66.28 Removing the belt from the camshaft sprocket

66.29 Slacken the cylinder head securing bolts using the special tool

the crankshaft on the starter motor, as piston-valve contact may occur. Cautious tapping with a plastic or wooden hammer may be effective.
31 Lift the head away and place it on the bench. Do not allow it to rest on any protruding valves.

67 Cylinder head – removal (engine removed from vehicle)

The procedure for removing the cylinder head with the engine removed is the same as that given in the previous Section, paragraphs 22 to 31 inclusive.

68 Auxiliary shaft – removal

1 Using a metal bar lock the shaft sprocket, and with an open-ended spanner undo and remove the bolt and washer that secure the sprocket to the shaft (photo).
2 Undo and remove the three bolts and spring washers that secure the shaft front cover to the cylinder block (photo).
3 Lift away the front cover (photo).
4 Undo and remove the two crosshead screws that secure the shaft thrust plate to the cylinder block (photo).
5 Lift away the thrust plate (photo).
6 The shaft may now be drawn forwards and then lifted away (photo).

69 Flywheel (manual gearbox) and backplate – removal

1 Refer to Section 18 (photos).
2 Unbolt and remove the engine backplate (photo).

70 Driveplate (automatic transmission) – removal

The driveplate removal is similar to that of the flywheel, therefore refer to Section 18.

71 Sump – removal

Refer to Section 14 (photos).

72 Oil pump and strainer – removal

On the ohc engine the oil pump is located inside the crankcase and therefore the sump must be removed to gain access to it.
1 Undo and remove the screw and spring washer that secure the oil pump pick-up pipe support bracket to the crankcase.
2 Using the special tool (21 - 012) or equivalent undo the two special bolts that secure the oil pump to the underside of the

68.1 Auxiliary shaft sprocket securing bolt removal

68.2 Remove auxiliary shaft front cover securing bolts

68.3 Remove auxiliary shaft front cover

68.4 Remove auxiliary shaft thrust plate securing screws

68.5 Lift away the thrust plate

68.6 Withdraw the auxiliary shaft

69.1a Removal of flywheel securing bolts

69.1b Lift away the flywheel

69.2 Remove the backplate

71.1a Remove the sump securing bolts

71.1b Lift away the sump

72.2 Remove the oil pump securing bolts using the special tool

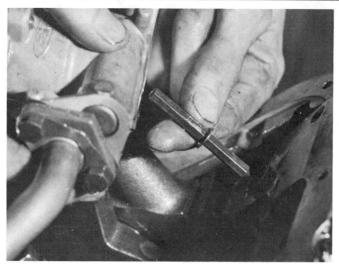

72.3 Remove the oil pump and pick-up pipe

72.4 Oil pump driveshaft removal

crankcase. Unfortunately there is no other tool suitable to slot into the bolt head so do not attempt to improvise which will only cause damage to the screw (photo).

3   Lift away the oil pump and strainer assembly (photo).

4   Carefully lift away the oil pump drive, making a special note of which way round it is fitted (photo).

73 Crankshaft pulley, sprocket and timing cover – removal

1   Lock the crankshaft using a block of soft wood placed between a crankshaft web and the crankcase then using a socket and suitable extension, undo the bolt that secures the crankshaft pulley. Recover the large diameter plain washer.

2   Using a large screwdriver ease the pulley from the crankshaft. Recover the large diameter thrust washer.

3   Again using the screwdriver, ease the sprocket from the crankshaft (photo).

4   Undo and remove the bolts and spring washers that secure the timing cover to the front of the crankcase.

5   Lift away the timing cover and the gasket (photo).

74 Pistons, connecting rods and big-end bearings – removal

1   The removal procedure for the pistons, connecting rods and big-end bearings is the same as that given in Section 15.

2   Note that the pistons have an arrow or notch marked on the crown showing the forward facing side (photo). Inspect the big-end bearing caps and connecting rods to make sure identification marks are visible. This is to ensure that the correct end caps are fitted to the correct connecting rods and the connecting rods placed in their respective bores (Fig. 1.33).

3   Unbolt and remove the big-end caps (photo), then remove the pistons.

75 Crankshaft and main bearings – removal

With the engine removed from the car and separated from the gearbox, and the timing belt, crankshaft pulley and sprocket, flywheel and backplate, oil pump, big-end bearings and pistons all dismantled, proceed to remove the crankshaft and main bearings.

1   Make sure that identification marks are visible on the main bearing end caps, so that they may be refitted in their original positions and also the correct way round (photo).

2   Undo by one turn at a time the bolts which hold the five bearing caps.

3   Lift away each main bearing cap and the bottom half of each

73.3 Ease the sprocket from the crankshaft

73.5 Remove the timing cover and gasket

74.2 Piston identification marks stamped on crown

74.3 Lift away the big-end cap

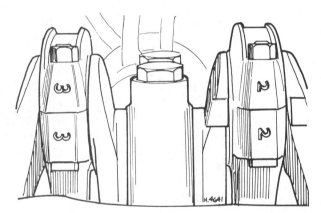

Fig. 1.33 Big-end bearing cap and connecting rod identification marks (Sec 74)

75.1 Main bearing cap identification marks

bearing shell, taking care to keep the bearing shells in the same caps if they are to be re-used (photo).

4   When removing the rear main bearing end cap note that this also retains the crankshaft rear oil seal (photo).

5   When removing the centre main bearing, note the bottom semi-circular halves of the thrust washers, one half lying on either side of the main bearing.

6   As the centre and rear bearing end caps are accurately located by dowels it may be necessary to gently tap the end caps to release them.

7   Slightly rotate the crankshaft to free the upper halves of the bearing shells and thrust washers which can be extracted and placed over the correct bearing cap.

8   Carefully lift away the crankshaft rear oil seal (photo).

9   Remove the crankshaft by lifting it away from the crankcase (photo).

76 Camshaft drivebelt – removal (engine in vehicle)

1   Refer to Chapter 2, Section 2, and drain the cooling system. Slacken the top hose securing clips and remove the top hose. Unbolt and remove the radiator.

2   Turn the engine over so that the TDC marks of the timing cover and crankshaft pulleys are in alignment. The camshaft pulley thrust washer mark must also be aligned with the cylinder head mark. When set in this position, no damage will occur to the pistons and valves with the cylinder head in position. *Be sure not to turn the engine or camshaft during the subsequent operations until the new belt is fitted.*

75.3 Lifting away the No 2 main bearing cap

75.4 Rear main bearing cap removal

75.8 Remove crankshaft rear oil seal

75.9 Cylinder block and crankcase with crankshaft removed

76.7 Lift away the crankshaft pulley

76.9 Timing belt removal

3   Slacken the alternator mounting bolts and push the unit towards the engine. Lift away the drivebelt.
4   Undo and remove the bolts that secure the timing belt guard to the front of the engine. Lift away the guard.
5   Slacken the belt tensioner mounting plate securing bolts and release the tension on the belt. A splined bolt tool (No 21-012) may be required for one of the bolts.
6   Engage a gear (manual gearbox only), and apply the brakes firmly. Undo and remove the bolt and plain washer that secure the crankshaft pulley to the nose of the crankshaft. On vehicles fitted with automatic transmission, the starter must be removed and the ring gear jammed to prevent the crankshaft rotating.
7   Using a screwdriver carefully ease off the pulley (photo).
8   Recover the plain large diameter thrust washer.
9   The drivebelt may now be lifted away (photo).

77 Valves – removal

1   Valve removal requires the use of a special Ford valve spring removal compressor (No 21-005). Should this not be readily available, it is just possible to use a universal valve spring compressor, provided extreme caution is taken.
2   Make a special note of how the cam follower springs are fitted and using a screwdriver remove these from the cam followers (photo).

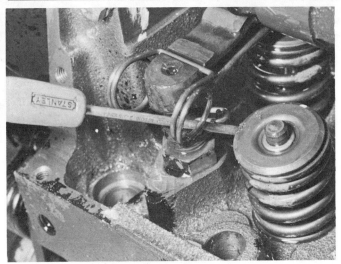

77.2 Cam follower spring removal

77.4 Compressing a valve spring

78.1 Remove camshaft lubrication pipe

78.2 Camshaft lubrication pipe holes

3   Back off fully the cam follower adjustment and remove the cam followers. Keep these in order so that they can be refitted in their original positions.

4   Using the valve spring compressor, compress the valve springs and lift out the collets (photo).

5   Remove the spring cap and spring and using a screwdriver prise the oil retainer caps out of their seats. Remove each valve and keep in order unless they are so badly worn that they are to be renewed. If they are going to be used again, place them in a sheet of card having eight numbered holes corresponding with the relative positions of the valves when fitted. Also keep the valve springs, cups etc, in the correct order.

78 Camshaft – removal

It is not necessary to remove the engine from the car in order to remove the camshaft. However, it will be necessary to remove the cylinder head first (Section 66) as the camshaft has to be withdrawn from the rear.

1   Undo and remove the bolts, and spring washers and bracket that secure the camshaft lubrication pipe. Lift away the pipe (photo).

2   Carefully inspect the fine oil drillings in the pipe to make sure that none are blocked (photo).

3   Using a metal bar, lock the camshaft drive sprocket, then undo and

78.3 Use a metal rod to lock the camshaft sprocket

78.4 Remove the sprocket

78.5 Remove the camshaft thrust plate securing bolts

78.6 Camshaft thrust plate removal

78.8 Tapping the camshaft through the bearings

78.9 Camshaft removal

78.10 Camshaft oil seal removal

79.3 Thermostat housing removal

79.4a Remove the belt tensioner mounting plate securing bolt

remove the sprocket securing bolt and washer (photo).
4   Using a soft-faced hammer or screwdriver, ease the sprocket from the camshaft (photo).
5   Undo and remove the two bolts and spring washers that secure the camshaft thrust plate to the rear bearing support (photo).
6   Lift away the thrust plate, noting which way round it is fitted (photo).
7   Remove the cam follower springs and then the cam followers as detailed in Section 77, paragraphs 2 and 3.
8   The camshaft may now be removed by using a soft-faced hammer and tapping rearwards. Take care not to cut the fingers when the camshaft is being handled as the sides of the lobes can be sharp (photo).
9   Lift the camshaft through the bearing inserts as the lobes can damage the soft metal bearing surfaces (photo).
10 If the oil seal has hardened or become damaged, it may be removed by prising it out with a screwdriver (photo).

79 Thermostat housing and belt tensioner – removal

1   Removal of these parts will usually only be necessary if the cylinder head is to be completely dismantled.
2   Undo and remove the two bolts and spring washers that secure the thermostat housing to the front face of the cylinder head.
3   Lift away the thermostat housing and recover its gasket (photo).
4   Undo and remove the bolt and spring washer that secure the belt tensioner to the cylinder head. It will be necessary to override the tension using a screwdriver as a lever (photos).
5   Using tool number 21-012 (the tool for removal of the oil pump securing bolts) unscrew the tensioner mounting plate and spring securing bolt and lift away the tensioner assembly (photo).

80 Piston rings – removal

Refer to Section 17 – the procedure is the same.

81 Gudgeon pin – removal

Interference fit type gudgeon pins are used and it is important that no damage is caused during removal and refitting. Because of this, should it be necessary to fit new pistons, take the parts along to the local Ford garage who will have the special equipment to do this job.

82 Lubrication and crankcase ventilation systems – description

1   The pressed steel oil sump is attached to the underside of the

79.4b Release the tension with a screwdriver

79.5 Use the special tool to remove the mounting plate and spring securing bolt from the belt tensioner

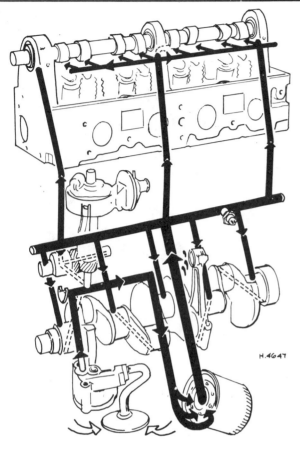

Fig. 1.34 Circulation of lubricant through engine (Sec 82)

crankcase and acts as a reservoir for the engine oil. The oil pump draws oil through a strainer located under the oil surface, passes it along a short passage and into the full flow oil filter. The freshly filtered oil flows from the centre of the filter element and enters the main gallery. Five small drillings connect the main gallery to the five main bearings. The big-end bearings are supplied with oil by the front and rear main bearings via skew oil bores. When the crankshaft is rotating, oil is thrown from the hole in each big-end bearing and splashes the thrust side of the piston and bore.

2   The auxiliary shaft is lubricated directly from the main oil gallery. The distributor shaft is supplied with oil passing along a drilling inside the auxiliary shaft.

3   A further three drillings connect the main oil gallery to the overhead camshaft. The centre camshaft bearing has a semi-circular groove from which oil is passed along a pipe running parallel with the camshaft. The pipe is drilled opposite each cam and cam follower, so providing lubrication to the cams and cam followers. Oil then passes back to the sump, via large drillings in the cylinder head and cylinder block.

4   A semi-enclosed engine ventilation system is used to control crankcase vapour. It is controlled by the amount of air drawn in by the engine when running and the throughput of the regulator valve (Fig. 1.35). The system is known as the PCV system (Positive Crankcase Ventilation) and the advantage of the system is that should the 'blow-by' exceed the capacity of the PCV valve, excess fumes are fed into the engine through the air cleaner. This is caused by the rise in crankcase pressure which creates a reverse flow in the air intake pipe.

5   Periodically, pull the valve and hose from the rubber grommet of the oil separator and inspect the valve for free movement. If it is sticky in action or is choked with sludge, dismantle it and clean the components.

6   Occasionally check the security and condition of the system connecting hoses.

83 Oil pump – dismantling, inspection and reassembly

1   If oil pump wear is suspected it may be possible to obtain a repair kit. Check for wear first as described later in this Section and if confirmed, obtain an overhaul kit or a new pump. The two rotors are a matched pair and form a single replacement unit. Where the rotor assembly is to be re-used the outer rotor, prior to dismantling, must be marked on its front face in order to ensure correct reassembly.

2   Undo and remove the two bolts and spring washers that secure the intake cowl to the oil pump body. Lift away the cowl and its gasket (Fig. 1.36).

3   Note the relative position of the oil pump cover and body and then undo and remove the three bolts and spring washers. Lift away the cover.

4   Carefully remove the rotors from the housing.

5   Using a centre-punch tap a hole in the centre of the pressure relief valve sealing plug (make a note to obtain a new one).

6   Screw in a self-tapping screw and using an open-ended spanner, withdraw the sealing plug as shown in Fig. 1.37.

7   Thoroughly clean all parts in petrol or paraffin and wipe dry using a non-fluffy rag. The necessary clearances may now be checked using a machined straight-edge (a good steel rule) and a set of feeler gauges. The critical clearances are between the lobes of the centre rotor and convex faces of the outer rotor; between the rotor and the pump body; and between both rotors and the end cover plate.

8   Measure the clearances described (Figs. 1.38 and 1.39) and compare them with the limits given in the Specifications.

9   If the only excessive clearance is endfloat it is possible to reduce it by removing the rotors and lapping the face of the body on a flat bed until the necessary clearances are obtained. It must be emphasised, however, that the face of the body must remain perfectly flat and square to the axis of the rotor spindle otherwise the clearances will not be equal and the end cover will not be a pressure tight fit to the body. It is worth trying, of course, if the pump is in need of renewal anyway but unless done properly, it could seriously jeopardise the rest of the overhaul. Any variations in the other two clearances should be overcome with a new unit.

10 With all parts scrupulously clean, first refit the relief valve and spring and lightly lubricate with engine oil.

11 Using a suitable diameter drift drive in a new sealing plug, flat side outwards, until it is flush with the intake cowl bearing face.

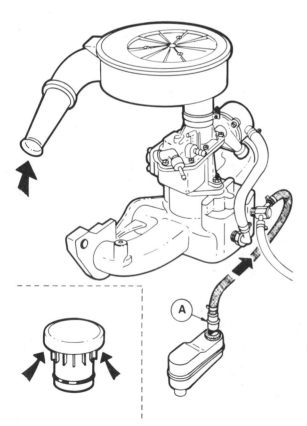

Fig. 1.35 The positive crankcase ventilation system – 'A' is the vent valve (Sec 82)

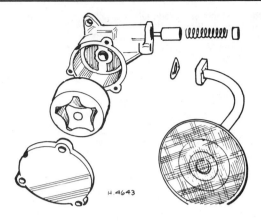

Fig. 1.36 Oil pump components (Sec 83)

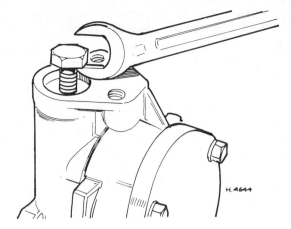

Fig. 1.37 Sealing plug removal method from pump pressure relief valve (Sec 83)

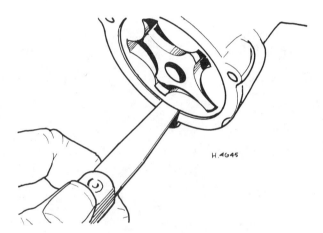

Fig. 1.38 Check the pump body to rotor clearance (Sec 83)

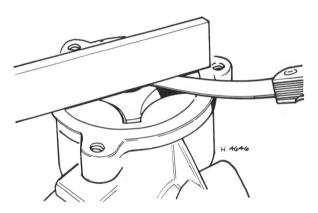

Fig. 1.39 Check the pump rotor endfloat (Sec 83)

12 Well lubricate both rotors with engine oil and insert into the body. Fit the oil pump cover and secure with the three bolts in a diagonal and progressive manner to the specified torque.

13 Fit the intermediate shaft into the rotor driveshaft and make sure that the rotor turns freely.

14 Fit the cowl to the pump body, using a new gasket, and secure with the two bolts.

84 Oil filter – removal and refitting

The oil filter is a complete throwaway cartridge screwed into the left-hand side of the cylinder block. Simply unscrew the old unit, clean the seating on the block and lubricate with engine oil. Screw the new one into position, taking care not to cross the thread. Continue until the sealing ring just touches the block face then tighten between three quarters of a turn and a full turn using the hands only. Always run the engine and check for signs of leaks after installation.

If difficulty is experienced in unscrewing the old filter, use a chain or strap wrench, but **do not** use any such tool on refitting.

85 Engine components – examination for wear

Refer to Section 26 – the same considerations apply.

86 Crankshaft – examination and renovation

Refer to Section 27 – the procedure is the same.

87 Big-end and main bearings – examination and renovation

Refer to Section 28 – the procedure is the same.

88 Cylinder bores – examination and renovation

Refer to Section 29 – the procedure is the same.

89 Pistons and piston rings – examination and renovation

Refer to Section 30 – the procedure is the same.

90 Connecting rods and gudgeon pins – examination and renovation

1 Gudgeon pins are a shrink fit into the connecting rods. Neither of these would normally need replacement unless the pistons were being changed, in which case the new pistons would automatically be supplied with new gudgeon pins.

2 Connecting rods are not subject to wear but in extreme circumstances such as engine seizure they could be distorted. Such conditions may be visually apparent but where doubt exists they should be checked for alignment and if necessary straightened or renewed as applicable.

3 The bearing caps should also be examined for indications of filing down which may have been attempted in the mistaken idea that

bearing slackness could be remedied in this way. If there are such signs then the connecting rods should be replaced.

91 Camshaft and camshaft bearings – examination and renovation

1 The camshaft bearing bushes should be examined for signs of scoring and pitting. If they need renewal they will have to be dealt with professionally as, although it may be relatively easy to remove the old bushes, the correct fitting of new ones requires special tools. If they are not fitted evenly and square from the very start they can be distorted thus causing localised wear in a very short time. See your Ford dealer or local engineering specialist for this work.
2 The camshaft itself may show signs of wear on the bearing journals, or cam lobes. The main decision to take is what degree of wear justifies replacement, which is costly. Any signs of scoring or damage to the bearing journals cannot be removed by regrinding. Renewal of the whole camshaft is the only solution. When overhauling the valve gear, check that oil is being ejected from the nozzles onto the cam followers.
3 The cam lobes themselves may show signs of ridging or pitting on the high points. If ridging is light then it may be possible to smooth it out with fine emery. The cam lobes, however, are surface hardened and once this is penetrated wear will be very rapid thereafter.

92 Cam followers – examination

1 The faces of the cam followers which bear on the camshaft should show no signs of pitting, scoring or other forms or wear. They should not be a loose sloppy fit on the ball-headed bolt.
2 Inspect the face which bears onto the valve stem, and if pitted, the cam follower must be renewed.

93 Timing gears and belt – examination and renovation

1 Any wear which takes place in the timing mechanism will be on the teeth of the drivebelt or due to stretch of the fabric. Whenever the engine is to be stripped for major overhaul a new belt should be fitted.
2 It is very unusual for the timing gears (sprockets) to wear at the teeth. If the securing bolt/nuts have been loose it is possible for the keyway or hub bore to wear. Check these two points, and if damage or wear is evident a new gear must be obtained.

94 Starter ring gear – examination and renewal

Refer to Section 39 – the procedure is the same.

95 Cylinder head – decarbonising

Refer to Section 36 in Part A of this Chapter – the procedure is essentially the same.

96 Valve guides – inspection

Examine the valve guides internally for wear. If the valves are a very loose fit in the guides and there is the slightest suspicion of lateral rocking using a new valve, then the guides will have to be reamed and oversize valves fitted. This is a job best left to the local Ford garage.

97 Engine reassembly – general

All components of the engine must be cleaned of oil, sludge and old gaskets and the working area should also be cleared and clean. In addition to the normal range of good quality socket spanners and general tools which are essential, the following must be available before reassembling begins:

> *Complete set of new gaskets*
> *Supply of clean rags*
> *Clean oil can full of clean engine oil*
> *Torque wrench*
> *All new spare parts as necessary*

98 Crankshaft – installation

Ensure that the crankcase is thoroughly clean and that all oilways are clear. A thin twist drill or a piece of wire is useful for cleaning them out. If possible blow them out with compressed air. Treat the crankshaft in the same fashion, and then inject engine oil into the crankshaft oilways.
1 Wipe the bearing shell locations in the crankcase with a soft, non-fluffy rag.
2 Wipe the crankshaft journals with a soft, non-fluffy rag.
3 If the old main bearing shells are to be renewed (not to do is a false economy unless they are virtually new) fit the five upper halves of the main bearing shells to their location in the crankcase (photo).

98.3 Locate the bearing shells into the crankcase

98.4 Main bearing cap identity mark

4 Identify each main bearing cap and place in order. The number is cast onto the cap and with intermediate caps an arrow is also marked so that the cap is fitted the correct way round (arrow pointing to front of engine) (photo).
5 Wipe the cap bearing shell locations with a soft non-fluffy rag.
6 Fit the bearing half shell onto each main bearing cap (photo).
7 Make sure that the tabs on the shells are engaged in the location slots.
8 Apply a little grease to each side of the centre main bearing so as to retain the thrust washers (photo).
9 Fit the upper halves of the thrust washers into their grooves either side of the main bearing. The slots must face outwards (photo).
10 Lubricate the crankshaft journals and the upper and lower main bearing shells with engine oil (photo).
11 Carefully lower the crankshaft into the crankcase (photo).
12 Lubricate the crankshaft main bearing journals again and then fit

No 1 bearing cap (photo). Fit the two securing bolts but do not tighten yet.
13 Apply a little cement gasket to the crankshaft rear main bearing end cap location (photo).
14 Next fit No 5 cap (photo). Fit the two securing bolts but as before do not tighten yet.
15 Apply a little grease to either side of the centre main bearing cap so as to retain the thrust washers. Fit the thrust washers with the tag located in the groove and the slots facing outwards (photo).
16 Fit the centre main bearing cap and the two securing bolts. Then refit the intermediate main bearing caps. Make sure that the arrows point towards the front of the engine (photo).
17 Lightly tighten all main cap securing bolts and then fully tighten in a progressive manner to the specified torque (photo).
18 Using a screwdriver ease the crankshaft fully forwards and with feeler gauges check the clearance between the crankshaft journal side

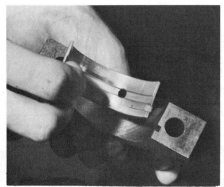
98.6 Fit the shells to the main bearing caps

98.8 Apply grease to either side of the centre main bearing

98.9 Fit the thrust washers to the centre main bearing

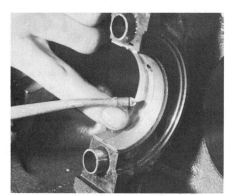
98.10 Lubricate the bearing shells

98.11 Fit the crankshaft to the crankcase

98.12 Refit No 1 main bearing cap – note identity mark

98.13 Apply gasket cement to the rear main bearing cap location

98.14 Refit the rear main bearing cap

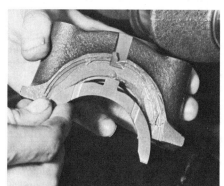
98.15 Fit the thrust washers to the centre main bearing cap – note slots face outwards

98.16 Main bearing caps in position

98.17 Tighten the main bearing cap bolts to the specified torque

98.18 Using a feeler gauge to check crankshaft endfloat

102.2 Insert the oil pump driveshaft

102.3 Tighten the oil pump securing bolts

and the thrust washers. The clearance must be within the specified limit (photo).
19 Test the crankshaft for freedom of rotation. Should it be very stiff to turn or possess high spots, a most careful inspection must be made with a micrometer, preferably by a qualified mechanic, to get to the root of the trouble. It is very seldom that any trouble of this nature will be experienced when fitting the crankshaft. Some stiffness is normal after fitting new bearings.

99 Pistons and connecting rods – reassembly

As a press-type gudgeon pin is used (see Section 81) this operation must be carried out by the local Ford garage.

100 Piston rings – refitting

Refer to Section 43 – the procedure is the same.

101 Pistons and connecting rods – refitting

Refer to Section 44 and prior to fitting each piston, locate the piston ring gaps as specified.

102 Oil pump – refitting

1 Wipe the mating faces of the oil pump and underside of the cylinder block.
2 Insert the hexagonal driveshaft into the end of the oil pump (photo), making sure it is the right way round.
3 Offer up the oil pump and refit the two special bolts. Using the special tool (21-012) and a torque wrench, tighten the bolts to the specified torque (photo).

4 Refit the one bolt and spring washer that secure the oil pump pick-up support bracket to the crankcase.

103 Crankshaft rear oil seal – installation

1 Apply some gasket cement to the slot on either side of the rear main bearing end cap and insert a rectangular shaped seal (photo).
2 Apply some gasket cement to the slot in the rear main bearing end cap and carefully insert the shaped seal (photo).
3 Lightly smear some grease on the crankshaft rear oil seal and carefully ease it over the end of the crankshaft. The spring must be inwards (photo).
4 Using a soft metal drift carefully tap the seal into position (photo).

104 Auxiliary shaft cover – refitting

1 Carefully insert the auxiliary shaft into the front face of the cylinder block (photo).
2 Position the thrust plate into its groove in the auxiliary shaft – countersunk faces of the holes facing outwards – and refit the two screws (photo).
3 Tighten the two crosshead screws using a crosshead screwdriver and an open-ended spanner (photo).
4 Smear some grease on the cylinder block face of a new gasket and carefully fit into position (photo).
5 Apply some gasket cement to the slot in the underside of the crankshaft timing cover. Insert the shaped seal.
6 Offer up the timing cover and secure with the bolts and spring washers (photo).
7 Smear some grease onto the seal located in the auxiliary shaft cover and carefully ease the cover over the end of the auxiliary shaft.
8 Secure the auxiliary shaft cover with the four bolts and spring washers (photo).

103.1 Fit the rectangular seals to the rear of the crankshaft

103.2 Fit the seal into the rear main bearing cap

103.3 Fit the crankshaft rear oil seal

103.4 Tapping the crankshaft seal evenly into position

104.1 Refit the auxiliary shaft

104.2 Locate the thrust plate

104.3 Tighten the thrust plate securing screws

104.4 Locate a new gasket onto the cylinder block front face

104.6a Refit the crankshaft timing cover

104.6b Tighten the crankshaft timing cover securing bolts

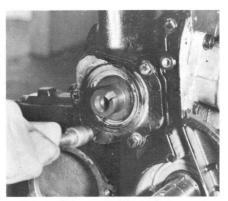

104.8 Tighten the auxiliary shaft cover securing bolts

105 Sump – refitting

1   Wipe the mating faces of the underside of the crankcase and the sump.
2   Smear some grease on the underside of the crankcase.
3   Fit the sump gasket making sure that the bolt holes line up (Fig. 1.40).
4   Offer the sump up to the gasket taking cae not to dislodge the gasket and secure in position with the bolts (photo).
5   Tighten the sump bolts in a progressive manner, to the specified torque (Fig. 1.41). Start at bolt 'A'for the first stage torque, at bolt 'B' for the second stage, then bolt 'A' again for the final stage.

106 Crankshaft sprocket, pulley and auxiliary shaft sprocket – refitting

1   Check that the keyways in the end of the crankshaft are clean and the keys are free from burrs. Fit the keys into the keyways (photo).
2   Slide the sprocket into position on the crankshaft. This sprocket is the small diameter one (photo).
3   Ease the timing belt into mesh with the crankshaft sprocket (photo).
4   Slide the large diameter plain washer onto the crankshaft (photo).
5   Check that the keyway in the end of the auxiliary shaft is clean and that the key is free of burrs. Fit the key to the keyway.
6   Slide the sprocket onto the end of the auxiliary shaft (photo).
7   Slide the pulley onto the end of the crankshaft (photo).
8   Refit the bolt and thick plain washer to the end of the crankshaft (photo).
9   Lock the crankshaft pulley with a metal bar and using a socket wrench fully tighten the bolt (photo).

107 Water pump – refitting

1   Make sure that all traces of the old gasket are removed and then smear some grease on the gasket face of the cylinder block.
2   Fit a new gasket to the cylinder block.
3   Offer up the water pump and secure in position with the four bolts and spring washers (photo).

108 Flywheel and clutch – refitting

1   Remove all traces of the shaped seal from the backplate and apply a little adhesive to the backplate. Fit a new seal to the backplate (photo).
2   Wipe the mating faces of the backplate and cylinder block and carefully fit the backplate to the two dowels (photo).
3   Wipe the mating faces of the flywheel and crankshaft and offer up the flywheel to the crankshaft, aligning the previously made marks unless new parts have been fitted.
4   Fit the six securing bolts and lightly tighten.

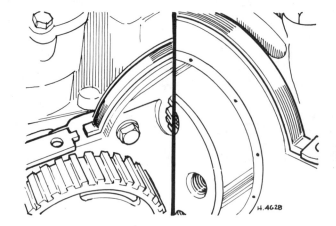

Fig. 1.40 Correct fitment of sump gasket at front and rear main bearing caps (Sec 105)

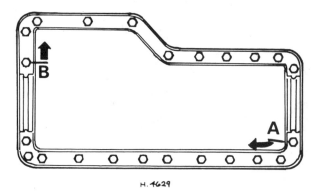

Fig. 1.41 Correct order for tightening sump bolts (Sec 105)

5   Lock the flywheel using a screwdriver engaged in the starter ring gear and tighten the securing bolts in a diagonal and progressive manner to the specified torque (photo).
6   Refit the clutch disc and pressure plate assembly to the flywheel making sure the disc is the right way round (photo).
7   Secure the pressure plate assembly with the six retaining bolts and spring washers.
8   Centralise the clutch disc using an old input shaft or piece of wooden dowel and fully tighten the retaining bolts (photo).

109 Valves – refitting

1   With the valves suitably ground in (see Section 37) and kept in

105.4 New gaskets fitted to greased underside of crankcase, ready for sump

106.1 Refit the Woodruff key to crankshaft

106.2 Slide on the crankshaft sprocket

106.3 Fit a new timing belt to the crankshaft sprocket

106.4 Refit the large diameter plain washer

106.6 Fit the auxiliary shaft sprocket

106.7 Refit the crankshaft pulley

106.8 Locate the pulley bolt and large washer

106.9 Tighten the crankshaft pulley securing bolt

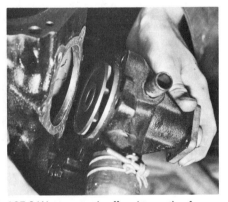

107.3 Water pump is offered to mating face with a new gasket

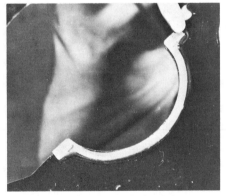

108.1 Fit a new gasket to the backplate

108.2 Locate the backplate

108.5 Tighten the flywheel retaining bolts

108.6 Refit the clutch unit

108.8 Fully tighten the clutch retaining bolts after the disc has been centralised

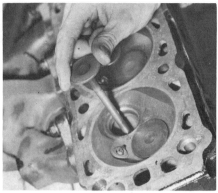

109.1 Insert the valve into its guide

109.2 Slide the seal down the valve stem

109.3 Fit the valve spring and cap

109.4 Locate the collets

110.1 Camshaft oil seal correctly fitted

110.3 Insert the camshaft through the bearings

110.4 Lubricate the camshaft bearings

110.6 Locate the camshaft thrust plate

110.7 Tighten the camshaft thrust plate retaining bolts

110.8 Locate the Woodruff key in the camshaft

110.9 Camshaft sprocket backplate tag

110.10 Camshaft sprocket backplate fitted

their correct order, start with No 1 cylinder and insert the valve into its guide (photo).

2 Lubricate the valve stem with engine oil and slide on a new oil seal. The spring must be uppermost as shown (photo).

3 Fit the valve spring and cap (photo).

4 Using a valve spring compressor, compress the valve spring until the split collets can be slid into position (photo). Note these collets have serrations which engage in slots in the valve stem. Release the valve spring compressor.

5 Repeat this procedure until all eight valves and valve springs are fitted.

110 Camshaft – refitting

1 If the oil seal was removed (Section 78) a new one should be fitted, taking care that it is fitted the correct way round. Gently tap it into position so that it does not tilt (photo).

2 Apply some grease to the lip of the oil seal. Wipe the three bearing surfaces with a clean, non-fluffy rag.

3 Lift the camshaft through the bearings taking care not to damage the bearing surfaces with the sharp edge of the cam lobes. Also take care not to cut the fingers (photo).

4 When the journals are ready to be inserted into the bearings lubricate the bearings with engine oil (photo).

5 Push the camshaft through the bearings until the locating groove in the rear of the camshaft is just rearwards of the bearing carrier.

6 Slide the thrust plate into engagement with the camshaft taking care to fit it the correct way round (photo).

7 Secure the thrust plate with the two bolts and spring washers (photo).

8 Check that the keyway in the end of the camshaft is clean and that the key is free of burrs. Fit the key into the keyway (photo).

9 Locate the tag on the camshaft sprocket backplate. This must locate in the second groove in the camshaft sprocket (photo).

10 Fit the camshaft sprocket backplate, tag facing outwards (photo).

11 Fit the camshaft sprocket to the end of the camshaft and with a soft-faced hammer make sure it is fully home (photo).

12 Refit the sprocket securing bolt and thick plain washer (photo).

111 Cam followers – refitting

1 Undo the ball-headed bolt locknut and screw down the bolt fully. This will faciliate refitting the cam followers (photo).

2 Rotate the camshaft until the cam lobe is away from the top of the cylinder head. Pass the cam follower under the back of the cam until the cup is over the ball-headed bolt (photo).

3 Engage the cup with the ball-headed bolt (photo).

4 Refit the cam follower spring by engaging the ends of the spring with the anchor on the ball-headed bolt (photo).

5 Using the fingers pull the spring up and then over the top of the cam follower (photo).

6 Repeat the above sequence for the remaining seven cam followers.

7 Check that the jet holes in the camshaft lubrication pipe are free and offer the pipe up to the camshaft bearing pedestals (photo).

8 Refit the pipe securing bolts and spring washers.

112 Cylinder head – refitting

1 Wipe the mating faces of the cylinder head and cylinder block. Turn the crankshaft so that No 1 piston is about $\frac{3}{4}$ in (2 cm) below TDC. *Do not turn the crankshaft again until it is necessary to do so when fitting the timing belt.*

2 Carefully place a new gasket on the cylinder block and check to ensure that it is the correct way up, and the right way round (photo).

3 Gently lower the cylinder head, being as accurate as possible first time, so that the gasket is not dislodged (photo).

4 Refit the cylinder head bolts, taking care not to damage the gasket if it has moved (photo).

110.11 Refitting the camshaft sprocket

110.12 Camshaft sprocket retaining bolt and plain washer

111.1 Slackening the ball-headed bolt locknut

111.2 Passing the cam follower under the camshaft

111.3 Cup located over ball-headed bolt

111.4 Cam follower spring engaged with the anchor

111.5a Cam follower spring being lifted over cam follower

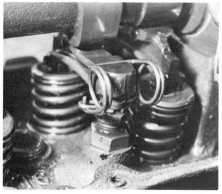
111.5b Cam follower springs correctly fitted

111.7 Refit the lubrication pipe

112.2 Position the cylinder head gasket on top of the cylinder block

112.3 Lower the cylinder head onto the gasket

112.4 Refit the cylinder head bolts

112.5 Special tool engaged in a cylinder head bolt

112.6 Tighten the cylinder head bolts

113.1 Refit the timing belt tensioner

113.3 Use a screwdriver to relieve the tension of the spring

114.1 Line up the camshaft timing marks (arrowed)

114.5 Timing belt fitted

114.6a Fit the belt guard

114.6b Locate the guard between washer and pedestal

5   Using the special tool (21-002) lightly tighten all the bolts (photo).
6   Tighten the cylinder head bolts progressively to the specified torque (photo), in the order shown in Fig. 1.31.

113 Camshaft drivebelt tensioner and thermostat housing – refitting

1   Thread the shaped bolt through the spring and tensioner plate and screw the bolt into the cylinder head (photo).
2   Tighten the bolt securely using the special tool (21-012).
3   Using a screwdriver to overcome the tension of the spring, position the plate so that its securing bolt can be screwed into the cylinder head (photo).
4   Clean the mating faces of the cylinder head and thermostat housing and fit a new gasket.
5   Offer up the thermostat housing and secure in position with the two bolts and spring washers.
6   Tighten the bolts to the specified torque.

114 Camshaft drivebelt – refitting and timing

1   Rotate the camshaft until the pointer is in alignment with the dot mark on the front bearing pedestal (photo). To achieve this always rotate the camshaft in the direction shown in Fig. 1.42.
2   Using a socket wrench on the crankshaft pulley bolt, turn the crankshaft until No 1 piston is at its TDC position. This is indicated by a mark on the crankshaft sprocket (see Fig. 1.42).
3   Engage the drivebelt with the crankshaft sprocket and auxiliary shaft sprocket. Pass the back of the belt over the tensioner jockey wheel and then slide it into mesh with the camshaft sprocket.
4   Slacken the tensioner plate securing bolt and allow the tensioner to settle by turning the crankshaft through two revolutions. Retighten the tensioner plate securing bolt.
5   Line up the timing marks and check that these are correct indicating the belt has been correctly refitted (photo).
6   Refit the belt guard, easing the guard into engagement with the bolt and large plain washer located under the water pump (photos).
7   Refit the guard securing bolts and tighten fully.

115 Valve clearances – checking and adjustment

1   With the engine top cover removed, turn the crankshaft until each cam in turn points vertically upwards. This will ensure that the cam follower will be at the back of the cam (Fig. 1.43).
2   Using feeler gauges as shown (photo) check the clearance which should be as given in the Specifications.

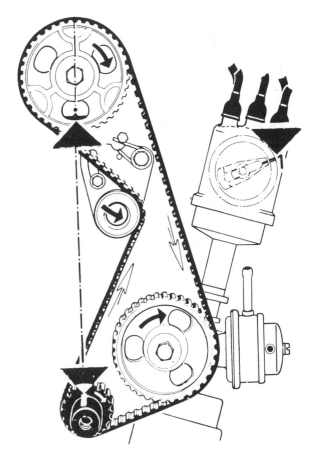

Fig. 1.42 Camshaft, ignition and crankshaft timing set at TDC, firing stroke, No 1 cylinder (Sec 114)

3   If adjustment is necessary, using open-ended spanners, slacken the ball-headed bolt securing locknut (photo).
4   Screw the ball-headed bolt up or down as necessary until the required clearance is obtained (photo). Retighten the locknut.
5   Counting from the front of the engine, exhaust valves are Nos 1, 3, 5 and 7; inlet valves are Nos 2, 4, 6 and 8.

115.2 Checking the valve clearance

115.3 Slackening ball-headed bolt locknut

115.4 Adjust the ball-headed bolt

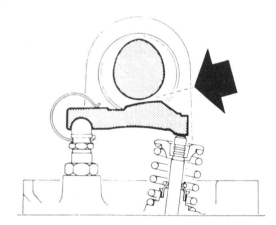

Fig. 1.43 Cam follower to camshaft clearance (Sec 115)

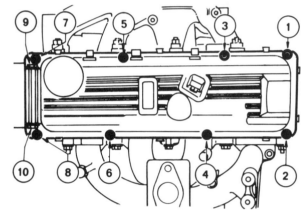

Fig. 1.44 Camshaft cover bolt identification. Tighten in stages given in Specifications (Sec 115)

6   Refit the camshaft cover and tighten the bolts to the specified torque — see Fig. 1.44.

116 Engine/gearbox — reconnecting

If the engine was removed in unit with the gearbox it may be reattached in the following manner.
1   With the engine on the floor and a wood block under the front of the sump, lift up the gearbox and insert the gearbox input shaft in the centre of the clutch and push so that the input shaft splines pass through the internal splines of the clutch disc.
2   If difficulty is experienced in engaging the splines, try turning the gearbox slightly but on no account allow the weight of the gearbox to rest on the input shaft as it is easily bent.
3   With the gearbox correctly positioned on the engine backplate, support its weight using a wooden block.
4   Secure the gearbox to the engine and backplate with the bolts and spring washers.
5   Refit the starter motor to its aperture in the backplate and secure with the two bolts and spring washers.

6   Reconnection of the engine to the automatic transmission is achieved in a similar manner. Reverse the procedure given in Section 63.

117 Engine — installation with gearbox

The engine and gearbox installation procedures are similar to those given for the ohv engine type, details of which are given in Section 53.

118 Engine — installation less gearbox

The installation procedure is basically the same as that for the ohv engine as described in Section 54.

119 Engine — initial start-up after major overhaul or repair

Refer to Section 55, as the details are the same.

120 Fault diagnosis – engine

Symptom	Reason(s)
Engine fails to turn when starter operated	Flat or defective battery Loose battery leads Defective starter solenoid or switch or broken wiring Engine earth strap disconnected Jammed starter motor drive pinion Defective starter motor Inhibitor switch defective (automatic transmission)
Engine turns but will not start	Ignition damp or wet Ignition leads to spark plugs loose Shorted or disconnected low tension leads Dirty, incorrectly set, or pitted contact breaker points Faulty condenser Defective ignition switch Ignition leads connected wrong way round Faulty coil Contact breaker point spring earthed or broken Fuel tank empty Too much choke allowing too rich a mixture to wet plugs Float damaged or leaking or needle not seating Float level incorrect Fuel pump defective
Engine stalls and will not start	Ignition failure (refer to Chapter 4) No petrol in petrol tank Petrol tank breather choked Sudden obstruction in carburettor Water in fuel system
Engine misfires or idles unevenly or stops	Ignition leads loose Battery leads loose on terminals Battery earth spring loose on body attachment point Engine earth lead loose Low tension leads to SW and CB terminals on coil loose Low tension lead from CB terminal side to distributor loose Dirty, or incorrectly gapped plugs Dirty, incorrectly set, or pitted contact breaker points Tracking across inside of distributor cover Ignition too retarded Faulty coil No petrol in petrol tank Vapour lock in fuel line (in hot conditions or at high altitude) Blocked float chamber needle valve Fuel pump filter blocked Choked or blocked carburetor jets Faulty fuel pump Mixture too weak Air leak in carburettor Air leak at inlet manifold Incorrect valve clearances Burnt out exhaust valves Sticking or leaking valves Weak or broken valve springs Worn valve guides or stems Worn pistons and pistons rings
Lack of power	Burnt out exhaust valves Sticking or leaking valves Worn valve guides and stems Weak or broken valve springs Blown cylinder head gasket (accompanied by increase in noise) Worn pistons and piston rings Worn or scored cylinder bores Ignition timing wrongly set Contact breaker points incorrectly gapped Incorrect valve clearances Incorrectly set spark plugs Carburation too rich or too weak Dirty contact breaker points Distributor automatic advance and retard mechanisms not functioning correctly Faulty fuel pump giving top end fuel starvation

Symptom	Reason(s)
Excessive oil consumption	Badly worn, perished or missing valve stem oil seals
	Excessively worn valve stems and valve guides
	Worn piston rings
	Worn pistons and cylinder bores
	Excessive piston ring gap allowing blow-by
	Piston oil return holes choked
	Leaking oil filter gasket
	Leaking timing case gasket (ohv engine)
	Leaking sump gasket
	Loose sump plug
Unusual noises from engine	Worn valve gear (noisy tapping from top cover)
	Worn big-end bearings (regular heavy knocking)
	Worn timing chain or gears (rattling from front of engine) (ohv only)
	Worn main bearings (rumblings and vibrations)
	Worn crankshaft (knocking, rumbling and vibration)
Engine 'pinks'	Wrong grade of fuel used
	Defective automatic transmission vacuum diaphragm

Chapter 2 Cooling system

For modifications, and information applicable to later models, see Supplement at end of manual

Contents

Specifications

General
System type .... Thermosyphon, pump-assisted, belt-driven cooling fan

Thermostat
Type .... Wax
Initial opening temperature .... 180° to 198°F (82° to 92°C)
Fully open temperature .... 210° to 216°F (99 to 102°C)
Location:
    OHV engine .... Cylinder head, top left-hand side
    OHC engine .... Cylinder head, front face, right-hand side

Radiator
Type .... Corrugated fin, downflow
Pressure cap rating .... 13 lbf/in^2 (0.9 kgf/cm^2)

Drivebelt
Deflection .... 0.4 to 0.5 in (10 to 13 mm) under firm thumb pressure at midpoint of longest run

System capacity*
OHV engines .... 10.6 pints (6.0 litres)
OHC engines .... 14.4 pints (8.2 litres)
*Deduct 1.8 pints (1 litre) if no heater fitted

Antifreeze
Type/specification .... Antifreeze to Ford spec SSM-97B-9101-A (Duckhams Universal Antifreeze and Summer Coolant)

Torque wrench settings

	lbf ft	kgf m
Fan blades	5 to 7	0.7 to 1.0
Water pump:		
$\frac{1}{4}$ in bolts	5 to 7	0.7 to 1.0
$\frac{5}{16}$ in bolts	12 to 16	1.7 to 2.1
Thermostat housing	12 to 15	1.7 to 2.0

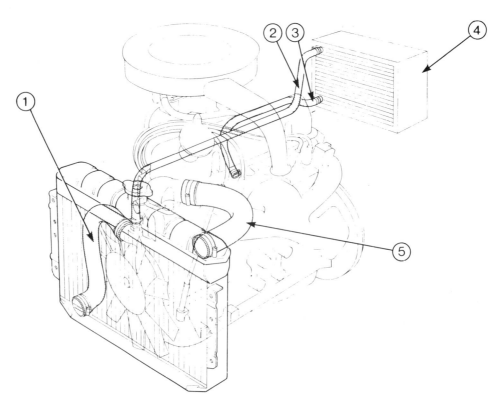

Fig. 2.1 Cooling system layout of the ohv engine (Sec 1)

1	Bottom hose	3	Heater inlet hose	4	Heater matrix	5	Top hose
2	Heater outlet hose						

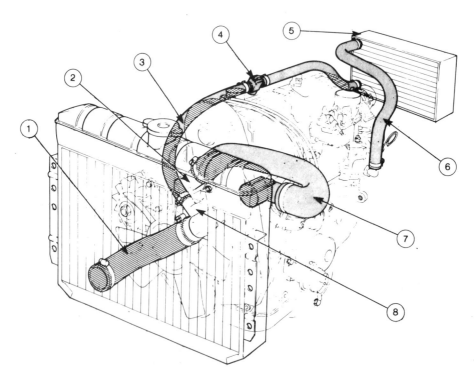

Fig. 2.2 Cooling system layout on the ohc engine (Sec 1)

1	Bottom hose	3	Heater inlet hose	5	Heater matrix	7	Top hose
2	Thermostat housing	4	Heater shut-off valve	6	Heater outlet hose	8	Water pump

1 General description

On both the ohv and ohc engine types, the cooling system operates in the same manner as given below. Certain differences do exist however.

The cooling system is of a water pump assisted thermal syphon type and is pressurised by means of a pressure valve filler cap. The main components of the system include a radiator, impeller type water pump, thermostat, cooling fan, and connecting hoses. The system operates as follows.

Cold water from the bottom of the radiator is drawn towards the water pump where it is then pumped into the water passages of the engine cylinder block and cylinder head. Heat from the moving parts of the engine is absorbed by the water, which is then directed to the top header tank of the radiator. Due to the passage of air through the radiator by the action of the cooling fan and movement of the vehicle, the water cools as it passes down through the radiator matrix and the cycle is then repeated.

To enable the engine to achieve its most efficient operating temperature quickly, a thermostat is fitted to the water outlet from the engine to the radiator top hose. When the coolant is cold the thermostat is closed and the circulation of water is restricted within the engine water passages by means of a bypass route.

When an interior heater is fitted to the vehicle, water from the engine is directed through the heater matrix and returned to the water pump by two hoses. Similarly, two hoses provide coolant for the coolant-operated automatic choke (when fitted).

The system is pressurised in order to allow the engine to achieve its most efficient operating temperature and to reduce the amount of coolant necessary to cool the engine; by pressurisation the boiling point of the coolant is also increased.

2 Cooling system – draining

Where the cooling system is to be drained and left empty for any length of time it is imperative that the coolant is removed from both radiator and cylinder block, otherwise corrosion of the water pump may occur with subsequent early failure of the water pump bearings and impeller.

1 If the engine is cold, remove the filler cap from the radiator by turning the cap anti-clockwise. If the engine is hot, then turn the filler cap very slightly until pressure in the system has had time to be released. Use a rag over the cap to protect your hand from escaping steam. *If with the engine very hot the cap is released suddenly, the drop in pressure can result in the water boiling. With the pressure released the cap can be removed.*

2 If antifreeze is used in the cooling system, drain it into a bowl of suitable capacity and retain for re-use.

3 Detach the radiator bottom hose (photo) and drain the coolant from the radiator. A drain plug is also fitted to the side of the cylinder block and this should be unscrewed to drain the engine.

4 When the water has finished running, probe the drain plug orifices with a short piece of wire to dislodge any particles of rust or sediment which may be causing a blockage.

5 It is important to note that the heater cannot be drained completely and therefore in cold weather an antifreeze solution must be used. Always use an antifreeze with an ethylene glycol base.

3 Cooling system – flushing

1 In time the cooling system will gradually lose its efficiency as the radiator becomes choked with rust, scale deposits from the water, and other sediment. To clean the system out, remove the radiator filler cap and bottom hose and leave a hose running in the filler cap neck for ten to fifteen minutes.

2 In very bad cases the radiator should be reverse flushed. To do this, remove the radiator (Section 6) and invert it, then run water from a hose through it so that the water enters at the bottom hose connection and exits at the top. Flush in the normal direction afterwards.

3 If scaling of the engine waterways is suspected use a proprietary flushing compound in accordance with its maker's instructions.

2.3 Detach the bottom hose to drain the radiator

4 Cooling system – filling

1 Reconnect the radiator bottom hose and insert the cylinder block drain plug.

2 Fill the system slowly to ensure that no air-lock develops. Check that the valve in the heater is open (control at HOT), otherwise an air-lock may form in the heater. The best type of water to use in the cooling system is rain water; use this whenever possible.

3 Do not fill the system higher than within 1 in (25 mm) of the filler neck. Overfilling will merely result in wastage, which is especially to be avoided when antifreeze is in use.

4 On ohc engine models it is suggested that the radiator top hose be loosened off at one end to vent the system and prevent an air-lock. As soon as the coolant reaches the top hose level, retighten the hose connection and continue filling to the specified level.

5 On completion run the engine and check for signs of leaks from the system.

6 Refit the filler cap and turn it firmly clockwise to lock it in position.

5 Antifreeze solution

1 In weather conditions where the ambient temperature is likely to drop below freezing point, it is essential to use an antifreeze solution in the cooling system; if the coolant is permitted to freeze in the engine or radiator, serious damage can result which could be very expensive to repair.

2 The cooling system is initially filled with a solution of 25% antifreeze and it is recommended that this percentage is maintained throughout the year, as the solution supplied by Ford contains a rust and corrosion inhibitor. A suitably equipped Ford garage will have the hydrometer necessary to check the antifreeze strength.

3 After a period of two years the antifreeze solution should be renewed by draining and flushing the cooling system as described in Sections 2 and 3. Check all the hose connections for security and then mix the correct quantity of antifreeze solution in a separate container, which should be clean.

4 Fill the cooling system as described in Section 4.

5 The following table gives a guide to protection, but it is recommended that a 25% minimum concentration is used in order to benefit from the corrosion inhibiting proportion of the antifreeze.

Antifreeze %	Protection provided to
50	-37°C (-34°F)
40	-25°C (-13°F)
30	-16°C (+3°F)
25	-13°C (+9°F)
20	-9°C (+15°F)
15	-7°C (+20°F)
10	-4°C (+25°F)

6 Radiator – removal, inspection, cleaning and refitting

1   Drain the cooling system as described in Section 2.
2   Loosen the clips securing the top and bottom hoses to the radiator and carefully ease the hoses off the connecting tubes.
3   Unscrew and remove the four radiator mounting bolts (Fig. 2.3) and then carefully manoeuvre the radiator from its location.
4   The radiator matrix, header and bottom tanks should be thoroughly examined for signs of damage, deterioration and leakage; very often a rusty sediment will have been deposited where a leak has occurred.
5   The radiator should be flushed through whilst removed as it can be inverted and back flushed. Clean the exterior of dead flies and dirt with a water jet from a garden hose.
6   Radiator repairs are best left to a specialist, as without the relevant equipment it is quite easy to make matters worse, although minor repairs can be tackled with a proprietary compound.
7   Refitting the radiator is a reversal of the removal procedure, but the following additional points should be noted:

   (a) Examine and renew any clips and hoses which have deteriorated
   (b) Refill the cooling system as described in Section 4

7 Thermostat – removal, testing and refitting

1   The function of the thermostat is to enable the engine to reach its most efficient operating temperature in the shortest time, and this is accomplished by restricting the circulation of coolant to the engine during warming up: after reaching the operating temperature the thermostat opens and allows the coolant to circulate through the radiator.
2   A faulty thermostat can cause overheating or slow engine warmup as well as affecting performance of the heater.
3   On ohc engine models the thermostat is located on the front face of the cylinder head (photo) whereas on the ohv engine it is situated on the top face of the cylinder head (Fig. 2.4).
4   To remove the thermostat, partially drain the cooling system, usually 4 pints (2.27 litres) is sufficient, as described in Section 2.
5   Unclip and detach the top hose from the thermostat housing, although if only the thermostat itself is to be checked/renewed the hose can be left attached.
6   Unscrew and remove the thermostat housing retaining bolts and then carefully remove the housing. The gasket will tear but this doesn't matter as it has to be renewed anyway. Extract the thermostat, noting its location in the groove in the aperture in the cylinder head.
7   Clean the old gasket material from the housing and cylinder head mating flanges.
8   To test whether the thermostat is serviceable, suspend it by a

7.3 Thermostat housing location on the ohc engine

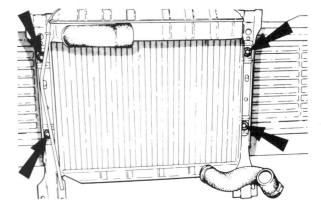

Fig. 2.3 The radiator attachment points (Sec 6)

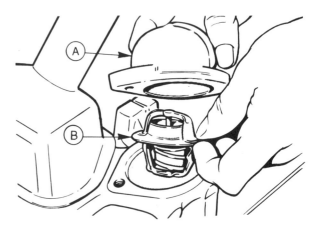

Fig. 2.4 Thermostat location on the ohv engine showing the housing (A) and thermostat (B) (Sec 7)

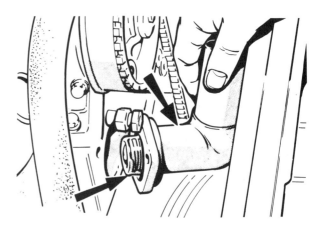

Fig. 2.5 Thermostat location on the ohc engine (Sec 7)

piece of string in a pan of water, which is then heated, but make sure that it does not touch the pan. Use a similarly suspended thermometer to check the operating temperatures of the thermostat with reference to the information given in the Specifications. If the thermostat is faulty it must be renewed.
9   Refitting the thermostat is a reversal of the removal procedure, but it will be necessary to use a new gasket. and the cooling system must be refilled as described in Section 4. To prevent leaks, the mating surfaces of the water outlet and cylinder head must be clean and free of excessive corrosion. Tighten the bolts to the specified torque.

8 Water pump – removal and refitting

1 An impeller type water pump is fitted on the front face of the cylinder block.

2 Drain the cooling system as described in Section 2. Remove the radiator as given in Section 6.

3 Slacken the alternator mounting bolts and push the alternator towards the cylinder block. Lift away the drivebelt.

4 Undo and remove the bolts and washers that secure the fan assembly to the water pump spindle hub. Lift away the fan and pulley.

Fig. 2.6 Remove the belt cover on ohc engine (Sec 8)

5 On ohc engine models, detach the timing belt cover which is secured by three bolts (Fig. 2.6).

6 Disconnect and remove the heater hose and bottom hose from the water pump.

7 Unscrew the water pump retaining bolts and withdraw the pump unit (Fig. 2.7 or 2.8).

8 Whilst it is possible to dismantle the water pump for overhaul, a suitable puller and press are required and it is therefore not a recommended task for the DIY mechanic, even if replacement parts are readily available. It is quicker and more economical to renew the complete pump unit.

9 Refitting the water pump is a reversal of the removal procedure, but note the following points:

> (a) Make certain that the mating surfaces of the pump and cylinder block are perfectly clean, and fit a new gasket
>
> (b) Tighten the pump retaining bolts and fan pulley bolts to the specified torque
>
> (c) Adjust the drivebelt tension as described in Section 9
>
> (d) On completion, run the engine and check for leaks around the pump mating surface and hose connections

9 Drivebelt – adjustment and renewal

1 The belt tension is correct when there is 0.5 in (13 mm) of lateral movement under firm thumb pressure at a point midway between the alternator and fan pulleys (Fig. 2.9 or 2.10).

2 To adjust the belt, loosen the alternator pivot bolt(s) fully but only slightly loosen the alternator adjustment strap bolt. Carefully move the alternator towards or away from the engine until the correct tension

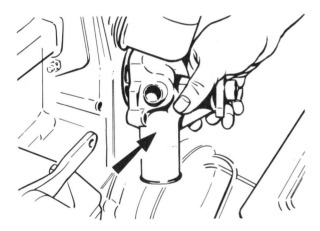

Fig. 2.7 Remove the water pump – ohc engine (Sec 8)

Fig. 2.8 Remove the water pump – ohv engine (Sec 8)

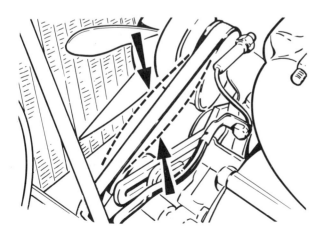

Fig. 2.9 Drivebelt tension check point on the ohv engine (Sec 9)

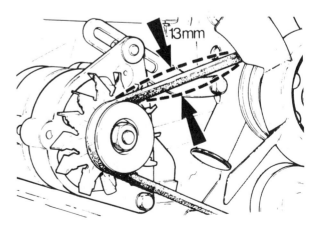

Fig. 2.10 Drivebelt tension check point on the ohc engine (Sec 9)

is obtained, then tighten the adjusting strap bolt and the alternator pivot bolt(s) in that order.

3   If the belt is worn or stretched unduly it should be renewed. However, the most common reason for renewing a belt is that the original has broken, and it is therefore advisable to carry a replacement on the vehicle for such an occurrence.

4   To remove the belt first loosen the alternator mounting and adjustment bolts and swivel the unit towards the engine, thus releasing the tension.

5   Slip the old belt over the crankshaft, alternator, water pump and fan pulleys and lift it over the fan blades. It may be necessary to turn the fan blades by hand in order to assist the belt over the alternator pulley.

6   Place the new belt onto the pulleys and adjust its tension as described in paragraphs 1 and 2.

7   On completion check that the alternator mounting and adjuster bolts are securely tightened. After fitting a new belt, its tension should be rechecked after about 600 miles (1000 km) and if necessary readjusted to take up the initial stretch.

8   If belt renewal is a frequent occurrence, check the pulleys for misalignment and/or damage.

10 Temperature gauge and sender unit – testing, removal and refitting

1   If the temperature gauge is faulty and gives an incorrect reading, either the gauge, sender unit, instrument voltage stabiliser, wiring or connections are responsible.

2   First check that all the wiring and connections are clean and secure. The gauge, sender unit and voltage stabiliser cannot be repaired by the home mechanic, and therefore they must be renewed if faulty. The voltage stabiliser is located on the back of the fuel gauge.

3   The wiring can be checked by connecting a substitute wire between the sender unit and the temperature gauge and observing the result.

4   Before removing the sender unit the cooling system must be partially drained of about 4 pints (2.27 litres) of coolant, then detach the supply lead and unscrew the unit.

5   Refit the sender unit in the reverse order and top up the cooling system.

6   Details of the removal and refitting of the temperature gauge are given in Chapter 10.

11 Fault diagnosis – cooling system

Symptom	Reason(s)
Overheating	Loss of coolant (see below)
	Drivebelt slipping or broken
	Radiator blocked (internally or externally)
	Hose(s) collapsed
	Thermostat faulty
	Water pump defective
	New engine not yet run-in
	Brakes binding
	Engine oil level too low
	Mixture too weak
	Ignition timing incorrect, or automatic advance malfunctioning
	Blockage in exhaust system
Overcooling	Thermostat defective or missing
Coolant loss – external	Overheating (see above)
	Hose(s) leaking or clips loose
	Radiator core leaking
	Heater matrix leaking
	Radiator pressure cap leaking
	Water pump seal defective
Coolant loss – internal	Blown cylinder head gasket (oil in coolant and/or coolant in oil)
	Cylinder head or block cracked

Chapter 3 Fuel and exhaust systems

For modifications, and information applicable to later models, see Supplement at end of manual

Contents

Specifications

General

System type	Centrally mounted fuel tank, mechanical fuel pump, single choke downdraught carburettor
Fuel tank capacity	14.3 gallons (64 litres)
Fuel octane rating	91 RON (UK 2-star)

Carburettor – general

Make	Motorcraft
Model:	
1.6 – ohv	77IF 9510 KNA
1.6 – ohc	78HF 9510 KEA
2.0 – Economy	78HF 9510 KJA
2.0 – manual choke	78HF 9510 KFA
2.0 – manual transmission/auto choke	78HF 9510 KGA
2.0 – auto transmission/auto choke	78HF 9510 KHA

Carburettor specifications

	KNA	KEA	KJA	KFA	KGA	KHA
Throttle barrel diameter (mm)	36	36	32	36	36	36
Venturi diameter (mm)	28	27	23	27	27	27
Main jet	135	137	115	135	135	127
Float level setting (mm)	31	29	29	29	29	29
Accelerator pump stroke (mm)	2.6	2.8	2.0	2.8	2.8	2.8
Manual choke plate pull-down (mm)	4.5	–	3.0	4.5	–	–

Carburettor tuning data

Idle speed – all models	800 ± 25 rpm
Mixture CO at idle:	
1.6 – ohv	1.25 ± 0.2 %
All other models	1.0 ± 0.2 %
Fast idle speed:	
1.6 – ohv	1100 ± 100 rpm
All other manual choke models	1000 ± 100 rpm
All automatic choke models	2000 ± 100 rpm
Automatic choke adjustment:	
De-choke	5.3 mm (0.209 in)
V mark	5.0 mm (0.2 in)
Vacuum pull-down	3.0 mm (0.118 in) KEA, 3.8 mm (0.150 in) others
Bi-metal spring adjustment	Central
Thermostat spring slot	Central

Torque wrench settings

	lbf ft	kgf m
Exhaust manifold to cylinder head	15.5 to 18	2.1 to 2.5
Downpipe to manifold:		
OHV	15.5 to 19	2.1 to 2.6
OHC	25 to 29	3.5 to 4.0
Exhaust brackets	6 to 7	0.8 to 1.0
Exhaust insulator bolts:		
8 mm	6 to 7	0.8 to 1.0
10 mm	10 to 12.5	1.4 to 1.7

1 General description

The fuel system comprises a fuel tank, a mechanically operated fuel pump, a single venturi downdraught carburettor, an air cleaner, and a constant flow fuel line system.

The rectangular fuel tank is located beneath the body floor, and on its upper face a lever type fuel gauge sender unit is fitted. The fuel flow and return hoses and the tank vent pipe are fitted to separate connections on the sender unit, and the sender unit is connected to the fuel gauge on the vehicle dash panel.

The fuel gauge is of the bi-metallic type on which the indicator needle moves slowly, taking approximately thirty seconds initially to give a true reading.

The fuel pump is of the mechanical diaphragm type, attached to the left-hand side of the engine. It incorporates a nylon mesh filter in its top cover.

Fuel entering the carburettor passes into the float chamber and is maintained at a constant level by a float system which closes a needle valve; when the level falls, the needle valve admits more fuel until the correct level is regained.

The air cleaner element is a disposable paper type which must be renewed at the specified mileage intervals. The air intake duct of the cleaner unit swivels to provide a summer or winter climate setting. With the winter setting, the duct is directed towards the exhaust manifold so that hot air enters the cleaner unit. For summer setting the duct is pivoted away from the manifold.

2 Air cleaner – removal, refitting and servicing

1 Every 6000 miles (10 000 km) the air cleaner element should be removed, cleaned and refitted. In dusty operating conditions the air cleaner should be cleaned at more frequent intervals.

2 Every 18 000 miles (30 000 km) the air cleaner element should be discarded and a new element fitted.

3 To remove the element from its container, unscrew the three lid retaining screws, unclip the lid and extract the element.

4 Wipe out the container before inserting the new element. The old element may be re-used if it is well within its recommended renewal mileage and is not congealed with dirt. Tap it lightly to dislodge any minor dirt particles before refitting it into the container (photo).

5 Refit the lid and retaining screws to secure.

6 To remove the complete filter unit on ohv engines, use a screwdriver and prise free the three mounting stays from the cleaner unit.

2.4 The air filter element fitted into its container

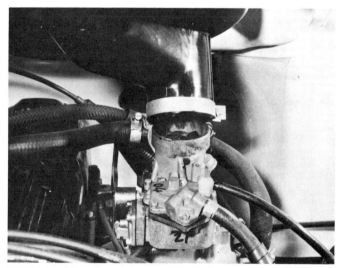

2.7 Detaching the air cleaner on the ohc engine

7   On ohc engine models, the cleaner unit can be removed after unscrewing and removing the single bolt and loosening off the carburettor to cleaner clamp (photo).

8   Refit in the reverse order to removal, then adjust (if necessary) the seasonal setting of the intake nozzle.

3   Fuel pump – routine service

1   At the specified intervals, undo and pull the fuel pipe from the pump inlet tube.

2   Undo and remove the centre screw and O-ring and lift off the cap, filter and seal (photo).

3   Thoroughly clean the cap, filter and pumping chamber, using a paintbrush and clean petrol to remove any sediment.

4   Reassembly is the reverse sequence to dismantling. Do not overtighten the centre screw as it could distort the cap.

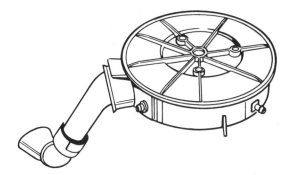

Fig. 3.1 The ohv engine air cleaner unit (Sec 2)

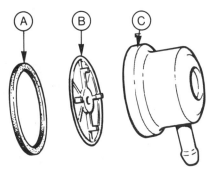

Fig. 3.2 Fuel pump service items

A   Seal washer   C   Cover
B   Filter

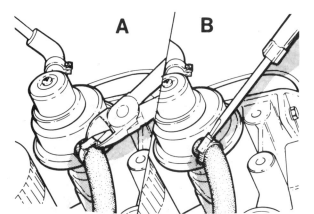

Fig. 3.3 Snip free crimped type hose clamp (A) and refit using a screw type clip (B) (Sec 4)

3.2 Fuel pump location on the ohc engine. Remove screw (arrowed) to detach cap for access to filter

4   Fuel pump – removal and refitting

1   Apart from removing the pump cap and filter for cleaning at the specified intervals, this type of pump cannot be dismantled for repair and therefore should a fault develop, it must be renewed as a unit. If required, your Ford dealer will be able to test the output of your old pump if you are uncertain of its efficiency. Remove the pump as follows.

2   Remove the inlet and outlet pipes at the pump and plug the ends to stop petrol loss or dirt finding its way into the fuel system. Crimped hose clips should be snipped free and new clips fitted on assembly.

3   Undo and remove two bolts and spring washers that secure the pump to the cylinder block.

4   Lift away the fuel pump and gasket and recover the pushrod.

5   Refitting the fuel pump is the reverse sequence to removal, but there are several additional points that should be noted:

(a)   Always fit a new gasket
(b)   Check that the hoses and their connections are in good condition. Check for leaks on completion when the engine is running
(c)   It may be necessary to loosen the fuel supply pipe at the carburettor and crank the engine so that any possible airlocks are expelled. As soon as petrol issues from the open end of the pipe, reconnect it.

5   Fuel tank – removal and refitting

1   Disconnect the battery earth terminal.

2   Pump or syphon out any remaining fuel in the tank into a suitable container.

3   Raise and support the vehicle at the rear with axle stands. Chock the front wheels.

4   Working underneath the vehicle, unscrew the fuel inlet pipe retaining clips and detach the pipe connection (Fig. 3.4).

5   Loosen the tank retaining straps (photo), support the tank underneath and then release the straps. Lower the tank and then detach the gauge sender unit wires and the fuel outlet and vent pipes. Lower and remove the tank.

6   Using two screwdrivers in the slots in the sender unit retaining ring, unscrew the sender unit from the fuel tank. Lift away the sealing ring and the sender unit, noting that the float must hang downwards. Cover the aperture in the tank to keep dirt out.

7   Refit in the reverse order to removal, using a new seal, and check that the four insulator pads are located correctly as indicated in Fig. 3.6.

8   With all of the pipes, wires and straps securely in place, refill the tank and check for any signs of fuel leaks. Switch on the ignition and wait 30 seconds, then check the fuel gauge reading.

5.5 Fuel tank retaining strap

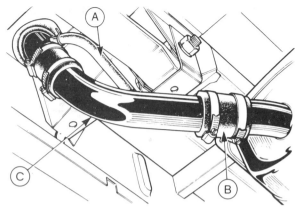

Fig. 3.4 The fuel inlet pipe (C), interconnecting hose (B) and ventilation pipe (A) (Sec 5)

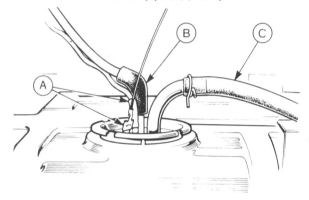

Fig. 3.5 Fuel tank sender unit (Sec 5)

A   Wires   C   Ventilation pipe
B   Fuel feed pipe

6   Fuel tank – cleaning

1   With time it is likely that sediment will collect in the bottom of the fuel tank. Condensation, resulting in rust and other impurities, will usually be found in the fuel tank of any car more than three or four years old.

2   When the tank is removed it should be vigorously flushed out and turned upside down. If facilities are available at the local garage the tank may be steam cleaned and the exterior repainted with a lead-based paint.

3   Never weld or bring a naked light close to an empty fuel tank until it has been steam cleaned out for at least two hours or washed internally with boiling water and detergent and allowed to stand for at least three hours. This work should be left to specialists.

4   Any small holes may be repaired using a proprietary product which gives satisfactory results provided that the instructions are rigidly adhered to.

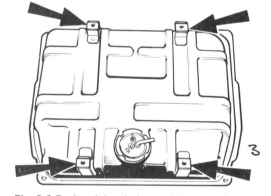

Fig. 3.6 Fuel tank insulation pad locations (Sec 5)

7   Fuel tank filler pipe – removal and refitting

1   Disconnect the battery earth lead.

2   Raise the vehicle at the rear and make secure on axle stands. Chock the front wheels.

3   If the fuel tank is more than a quarter full, the level must be lowered by syphoning or pumping the fuel out. Store in a suitable container.

4   Detach the ventilation tube from the filler pipe.

5   Disconnect the filler pipe extension and remove the pipe to body sealing ring.

6   Remove the filler cap and pull out the sealing ring. Unscrew the three filler pipe neck-to-body retaining screws.

7   From within the vehicle detach the filler pipe cover panel (where applicable) and remove the pipe.

8   Refit in the reverse order to removal and as the tank is topped up, check the filler pipe for any signs of leakage.

8   Accelerator cable – adjustment

1   Get an assistant to sit in the vehicle and hold down the throttle pedal.

2   Referring to Fig. 3.7, screw the adjuster sleeve nut to the point where the throttle linkage of the carburettor is just fully open. Release the throttle pedal and then reapply it to its fullest extent and check that the throttle linkage is fully actuated.

3   On automatic transmission models the kickdown cable adjustment must also be checked to make certain that the kickdown cable is not preventing the throttle being fully opened. This adjustment is given in Chapter 6.

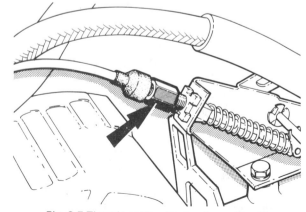

Fig. 3.7 Throttle cable adjuster sleeve (Sec 8)

9 Accelerator cable – removal and refitting

1   Working inside the vehicle, detach the accelerator cable from the pedal shaft.

2   Working from the engine side, detach the outer cable and grommet from the mounting bracket by prising free with a screwdriver as shown (Fig. 3.8). Prise the grommet from the cable.

3   Remove the air cleaner as given in Section 2.

4   Detach the inner cable from the carburettor, then depressing the four clip pegs using a screwdriver, twist and remove the cable from its bracket. Great care must be taken not to damage the cable during removal from the bracket (Fig. 3.9).

5   Fit the cable in the reverse order to removal and adjust the cable as described in the previous Section.

10 Choke cable – adjustment, removal and refitting

1   To adjust the choke cable, slacken the inner cable retaining screw at the carburettor (Fig. 3.10). Pull the inner cable through from the dash panel end so that it protrudes about $\frac{1}{4}$ in (6 mm). Hold the choke plate in the fully open position and remove any slack in the inner cable, then retighten the clamp screw. Push the choke knob fully home so that it butts against the dash panel.

2   If the choke cable is to be removed, disconnect the inner cable at the carburettor end by loosening the retaining screw, and unclip the outer cable retaining clamp.

3   Remove the bulkhead cable grommet by prising it free with a suitable screwdriver.

4   Referring to Fig. 3.11, unscrew and remove the heater control panel screws from the points indicated. Detach the control panel.

5   Remove the outer choke cable-to-dash retaining nut. Before pulling the cable through and free from the dash panel side, tie a length of string to the other end of the cable so that when pulled through it can be used to draw the new cable back through the bulkhead on reassembly.

6   Refit in the reverse order, detach the draw cord and reassemble the cable at the carburettor end and at the dash panel. Adjust the cable as given previously.

11 Carburettor – description and maintenance

1   On all models, a Motorcraft carburettor is fitted, being a single venturi downdraught type with a fixed jet system. The specification of the carburettor fitted depends on the engine size and model of vehicle to which it is fitted, the main differences being either a manually operated or automatic choke, and other detailed differences to suit a manual or automatic transmission.

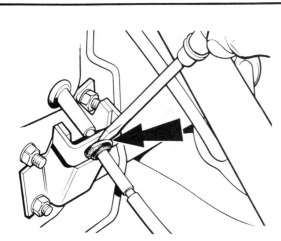

Fig. 3.8 Prise free the outer cable and grommet (Sec 9)

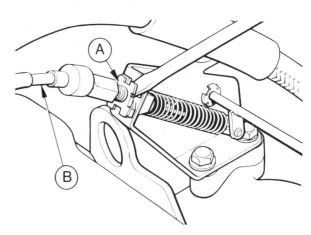

Fig. 3.9 Free cable (B) by detaching clip (A) from bracket (Sec 9)

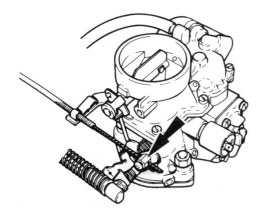

Fig. 3.10 Inner cable retaining clamp (arrowed) (Sec 10)

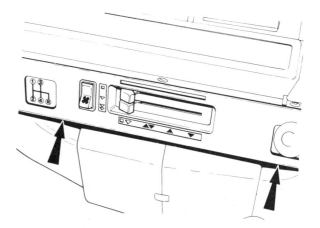

Fig. 3.11 Control panel screw locations (Sec 10)

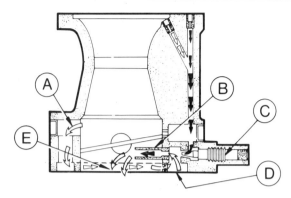

Fig. 3.12 The bypass idle system (Sec 11)

A   Air enters bypass
B   Sonic discharge tube
C   Idle mixture screw
D   Air/fuel mixture chamber
E   Air distributor channel

2   The 2-litre Economy model carburettor has a smaller throttle barrel diameter, venturi diameter and main jet than any of the other models.

3   A sonic by-pass idle system is fitted whereby the main airflow at idle comes from the bypass system, whilst a small proportion of air is procured through the slightly open throttle valve (butterfly). The air passage of the bypass idle system is shown in Fig. 3.12. The air from the bypass mixes with the air/fuel mixture and is then drawn in the normal manner into the engine through the sonic discharge tube. The idle mixture setting screw is set during manufacture and sealed with a tamperproof plug to prevent unauthorised adjustment.

4   An idle mixture shut-off valve is fitted to prevent the engine from running on (dieseling) when the ignition is switched off.

5   The main jet system in the carburettor regulates the fuel/air flow as required and the accelerator pump injects fuel when the throttle is depressed at speeds above idle. At high engine speeds a vacuum-operated power valve enables a richer mixture to be supplied.

6   Maintenance of the carburettor is confined to 6000 mile (10 000 km) intervals when the idling and mixture settings should be checked and the carburettor linkages lubricated with engine oil. When fitted, the automatic choke fast idle setting should be checked and adjusted at the same interval.

7   The modern carburettor is a reliable instrument which is unlikely to give trouble so long as clean fuel is used. Haphazard tinkering is liable to do more harm than good, and is to be avoided.

12 Carburettor – slow running adjustment

1   The carburettor slow running adjustment should be checked every 6000 miles (10 000 km). Although the idle mixture screw is covered by a tamperproof plug to prevent unauthorised adjustment of the screw, (which is preset at the factory), the plug can be prised out and the screw adjusted. This action should not normally be required, however, and may in any case be forbidden by local or national anti-pollution laws. Satisfy yourself on this point before proceeding.

2   Run the engine until it reaches normal operating temperature. Connect a tachometer to the engine in accordance with its maker's instructions and check that the idle speed is as given in the Specifications. Adjust if necessary using the idle speed adjustment screw (Fig. 3.13).

3   If maladjustment of the idle mixture is suspected, and all other tuning adjustments (ignition timing and valve clearances) are known to be correct, proceed as follows.

4   Ideally a CO meter (exhaust gas analyser) should be used in accordance with its maker's instructions. As this is rather expensive for the home mechanic, a proprietary device such as Gunson's Colortune may be used instead. A tachometer will also be needed.

5   With the engine warmed up and idling at the correct speed, run it at 3000 rpm for 30 seconds, then check the mixture with the device employed. If a CO meter is being used, refer to the Specifications for the correct CO level.

6   If mixture adjustment is necessary, remove the air cleaner and prise out the tamperproof plug (refer to paragraph 1). Refit the air

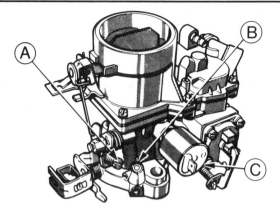

Fig. 3.13 Manual choke carburettor (Sec 12)

A   Idle speed adjustment screw
B   Tamperproof plug over idle mixture screw
C   Idle mixture shut-off valve

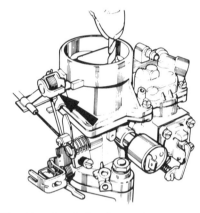

Fig. 3.14 Checking the choke plate pull-down with a drill shank. Adjust tag (arrowed) if necessary (Sec 13)

cleaner loosely – it is not necessary to bolt it in position – and adjust the mixture and idle speed adjustment screws to achieve the correct idle speed and mixture.

7   If adjustment cannot be achieved within 30 seconds, run the engine at 3000 rpm again for 20 to 30 seconds to clear any excess fuel from the inlet manifold before proceeding.

8   On a worn engine which is burning some oil, it may be impossible to achieve a correct mixture reading, even through the engine may run satisfactorily.

9   When adjustment is complete, remove the air cleaner and fit a new tamperproof plug. Refit the air cleaner securely and disconnect the test gear.

10   It is emphasised that the above procedure only serves to adjust the mixture at idle speed. Mixture at higher rpm is controlled by the size of the main jet, venturi and throttle barrel, and is not adjustable.

13 Manual choke carburettor – fast idle adjustment

1   Before checking or adjusting the fast idle, first check that the idle speed and fuel mixture settings are correct as given in the previous Section.

2   Remove the air cleaner unit (Section 2).

3   Referring to Fig. 3.14, rotate the cam to its stop to fully shut the choke. Now open the choke plate through the venturi using a screwdriver and when against its stop, measure the choke plate to carburettor pull-down clearance using a twist drill or rod gauge of the specified diameter. If adjustment is necessary bend the tag to provide the correct clearance as given in the Specifications.

4   Run the engine to its normal operating temperature, then hold the choke valve fully open and actuate the choke control mechanism as far as it will go without interfering with the choke valve position, which should be about one-third of the full choke control travel.

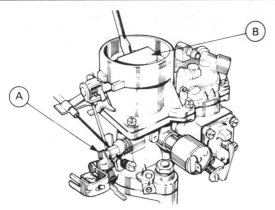

Fig. 3.15 Checking the fast idle with valve (plate) held open (B). 'A' is the adjuster tag (Sec 13)

5 With the choke valve held open, note the fast idle rpm and if necessary stop the engine and adjust as required by bending the tag illustrated in Fig. 3.15.
6 With the choke fast idle reset, you must now recheck the basic idle speed and if necessary readjust as given in the previous Section.
7 Refit the air cleaner on completion.

14 Automatic choke carburettor – fast idle adjustment

1 Run the engine to its normal operating temperature then switch off the ignition. Connect a tachometer to the engine.
2 Remove the air cleaner unit as given in Section 2.
3 Hold the choke plate fully open by hand, then open the throttle partially to enable the fast idle cam to engage in the high cam position (Fig. 3.16). Release the throttle and choke plates. A mirror may be useful for observing the fast idle cam.
4 Push the fast idle cam down to the first stage, which is V-marked as shown (Fig. 3.17). In this position the choke plate must be fully open. If not, either the engine has not reached its normal operating temperature, or the auto choke mechanism is at fault.
5 Restart the engine but do not touch the throttle. Note the engine speed, and if necessary adjust as required by bending the tag (A) on the throttle lever shown in Fig. 3.17.
6 On completion refit the air cleaner.

15 Carburettor – removal and refitting

1 Open the bonnet and disconnect the battery negative terminal.
2 Remove the air cleaner assembly by following the instructions given in Section 2.
3 Disconnect the fuel pipes from the carburettor; if a crimped type clip is fitted it should be replaced with a screw type clip.
4 Carefully detach the distributor vacuum pipe from the carburettor.
5 Disconnect the throttle linkage and (if applicable) the choke cable from the carburettor.
6 On automatic choke carburettor versions check that the cooling system is cold and that there is no pressure present; to do this, temporarily remove the radiator cap then refit it firmly. Disconnect the automatic choke hoses at the carburettor and tie them to one side facing upwards to prevent the loss of coolant (photo).
7 Unscrew and remove the two carburettor flange nuts and spring washers and carefully lift the carburettor from the inlet manifold together with the gasket.
8 Refitting the carburettor is a reversal of the removal procedure but the following points should be noted:

   (a) Always use a new gasket and ensure that the mating surfaces of the carburettor and inlet manifold are clean
   (b) Refer to Section 10 for information concerning refitting and adjustment of the choke cable (manual choke variants)
   (c) Adjust the carburettor idle and mixture settings as necessary on completion, details of which are given in Sections 12, 13 or 14 (as applicable)

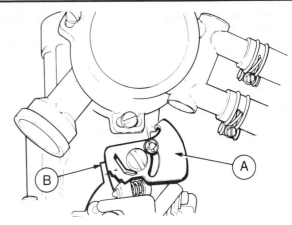

Fig. 3.16 Set auto choke mechanism in 'high cam' position (Sec 14)

A   Fast idle cam
B   High cam position

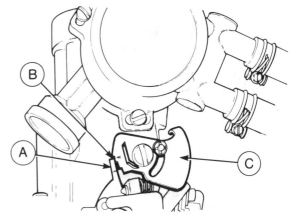

Fig. 3.17 Auto choke fast idle position (Sec 14)

A   Adjustment lever
B   V mark aligned with top edge of throttle lever at fast idle
C   Fast idle cam

15.6 Carburettor (ohc engine) shown with air cleaner removed. Detach fuel and auto choke coolant pipes

16 Carburettor – dismantling and reassembly (general)

1 With time the component parts of the carburettor will wear and petrol consumption will increase. The diameter of the drillings and jets may alter due to erosion, and air and fuel leaks may develop around

the spindles and other moving parts. Because of the high degree of precision involved, it is best to purchase an exchange rebuilt carburettor. This is one of the few instances where it is better to take the latter course rather than rebuild the component itself.

2   It may be necessary to partially dismantle the carburettor to clear a blocked jet or renew a gasket. Providing care is taken there is no reason why the carburettor may not be completely reconditioned at home, but ensure a full repair kit can be obtained before you strip the carburettor down. **Never** poke out jets with wire, blow them out with compressed air or with air from a car tyre pump.

17 Carburettor – dismantling and reassembly

1   Before starting to dismantle the carburettor, clean its outer surfaces with a soft brush and petrol.
2   Where fitted, remove the automatic choke unit (see Section 20).
3   Detach the upper body section by unscrewing and removing the seven retaining screws. Lift the upper body from the main body with care, trying not to split the gasket, as this can be used as a pattern to make another if one is not readily available on reassembly.
4   Disengage the choke actuating rod.

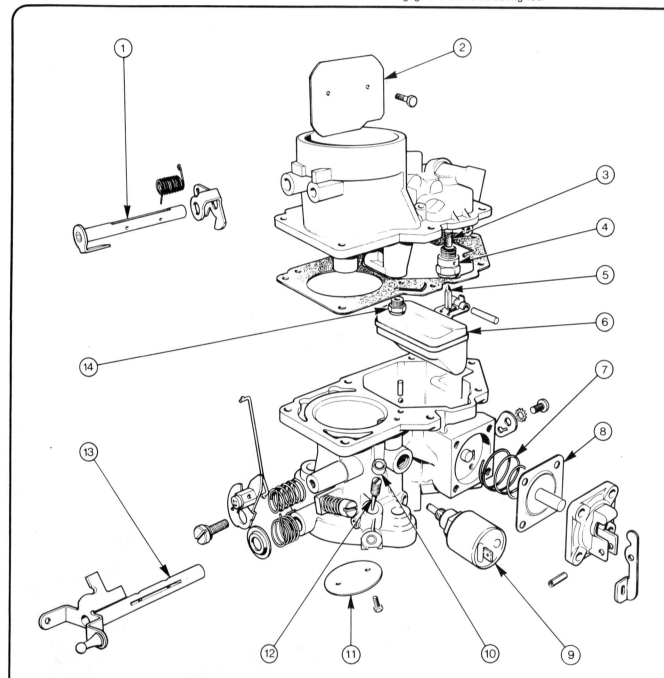

Fig. 3.18 The Motorcraft carburettor fitted with the manual choke
(Sec 17)

1 Choke spindle	6 Float	9 Idle mixture shut-off valve	11 Throttle plate (valve)
2 Choke plate (valve)	7 Pump return spring		12 Mixture screw
3 Fuel inlet filter	8 Accelerator pump diaphragm	10 Tamperproof seal (mixture screw)	13 Throttle spindle
4 Needle valve housing			14 Main jet
5 Needle valve			

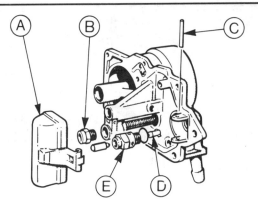

Fig. 3.19 Carburettor upper body and float components (Sec 17)

A   Float   D   Filter
B   Main jet   E   Valve housing
C   Float pivot pin

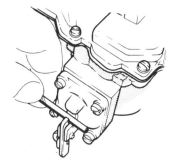

Fig. 3.20 Check the lever clearance on the accelerator pump (Sec 17)

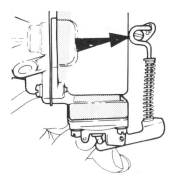

Fig. 3.21 Adjust control link at U section (arrowed) (Sec 17)

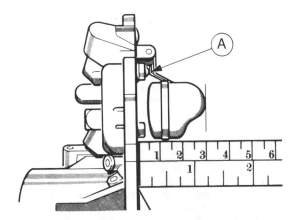

Fig. 3.22 Float level – adjust at tag (A) if necessary (Sec 18)

5   From the main body extract the accelerator ball valve and weight – invert the carburettor to allow them to fall out into your cupped hand.

6   Carefully extract the float pivot pin by lightly tapping it free. Withdraw the float, needle valve and upper gasket (Fig. 3.19).

7   Unscrew and remove the needle valve housing and filter.

8   Unscrew and remove the main jet.

9   Remove the retaining screws and carefully withdraw the accelerator pump unit complete with spring.

10   Unscrew and remove the idle shut-off valve.

11   To remove the idle mixture screw, use a suitable screwdriver and break the tamperproof seal. Extract the seal and remove the mixture adjuster screw.

12   Wash the respective components in clean petrol and blow dry (compressed air from a tyre pump is ideal).

13   Inspect the jets for signs of damage or possibly blockage.

14   Check the accelerator pump and diaphragm for any signs of splits, perishing or possible leakage faults.

15   Check the float for signs of leakage and the needle valve, mixture screw and throttle spindle for signs of wear or damage. Renew any damaged, worn or suspect components as necessary. The needle valve should be renewed as a matter of course.

16   Obtain a new set of gaskets, and if possible a new accelerator pump diaphragm, for reassembly.

17   Reassembling the carburettor is basically a reversal of the removal procedure, but the following points should be noted:

(a)   When refitting the accelerator pump, ensure that the return spring tapers outwards

(b)   Insert a new seal washer and filter into the float valve housing prior to fitting the housing to the carburettor. Check and adjust the float level as given in Section 18

(c)   Don't forget to fit a new seal washer to the idle mixture shut-off valve

(d)   On manual choke models, the cranked end of the choke linkage must be fitted at the lower end when in position. As the upper body is fitted, hold the choke mechanism in the fully shut position to ensure that the choke cam does not over-centre as the body is located

(e)   On manual choke models, check and adjust the choke pull-down setting as given in Section 13. On automatic choke models, refer to Section 19

(f)   Check and if necessary adjust the accelerator pump stroke by winding back the idle speed adjuster screw so that it is clear of the linkage, then with the throttle shut, push the accelerator pump diaphragm to its stop and check the clearance between the lever and diaphragm using a drill shank as shown (Fig. 3.20). The pump stroke should be as given in the Specifications. If adjustment is required, open or close the control link U section accordingly (Fig. 3.21)

18 Float level – checking and adjustment

1   Refer to the previous Section and remove the carburettor upper body as given in paragraphs 1 to 3, having first removed the air cleaner unit (Section 2). There is no need to remove the carburettor from the engine.

2   Hold the upper body vertically and with the needle valve fully shut, check the clearance between the base of the float and the inner flange face of the upper body – see Fig. 3.22.

3   Check the clearance measured against that specified for your carburettor model and if necessary adjust the float setting by bending the tag (A) in the required direction.

4   Refit the upper body and check the idle speed and choke settings before refitting the air cleaner.

19 Automatic choke – adjustment

1   Before attempting to adjust the automatic choke it is recommended that the carburettor is removed from the engine as described in Section 15.

2   Unscrew and remove the three cover retaining screws and withdraw the cover and spring assembly together with the sealing joint.

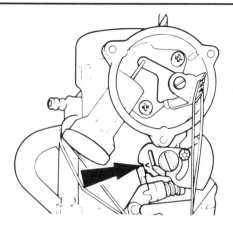

Fig. 3.23 Align V mark (arrowed) with throttle lever (Sec 19)

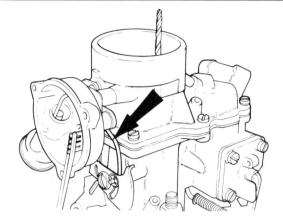

Fig. 3.24 Bend control rod to adjust V mark setting (Sec 19)

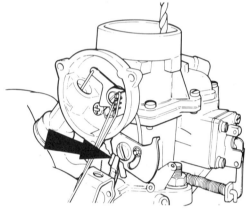

Fig. 3.25 De-choke adjustment tag (arrowed) on the fast idle cam
(Sec 19)

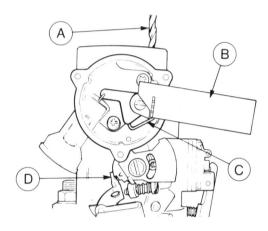

Fig. 3.26 Checking the vacuum plate pull-down (Sec 19)

A	Drill shank (gauge rod)	C	Pull-down lever
B	Preload tool (23 011)	D	Throttle at high cam position

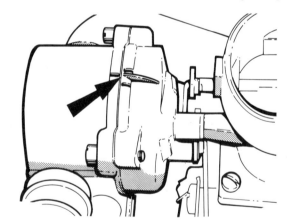

Fig. 3.27 Align the auto choke housing and cover marks (arrowed)
(Sec 19)

Adjusting the V mark

3   Fasten an elastic band around the choke plate lever and set the band so that it holds the choke plate closed. Operate the throttle lever to open the throttle and allow the choke plate to close fully, then release the throttle.

4   Insert a drill shank of the specified diameter between the choke plate and the air horn on the accelerator pump side. Allow the fast idle cam to drop into its operating position by partially opening the throttle, then check that the V mark on the cam aligns with the throttle lever (Fig 3.23).

5   If necessary bend the choke control rod to achieve the correct alignment (Fig. 3.24).

De-choke adjustment

6   With the choke plate still held in the fully closed position, turn the throttle lever so that the throttle is wide open. The choke plate should de-choke (ie open) just before full throttle.

7   If the choke plate action is not correct, check the adjustment by inserting a twist drill of the specified diameter between the choke plate and the air horn on the accelerator pump side of the carburettor. If necessary bend the de-choke lever on the fast idle cam (Fig. 3.25).

Vacuum choke plate pull-down adjustment

8   To check the vacuum choke plate pull down adjustment you will require the use of the Ford auto choke pre-load tool No 23 011. If this is available, proceed as follows. The engine must be at normal operating temperature.

9   Position the throttle in the high cam position as shown in Fig. 3.26. Start the engine, but do not touch the throttle pedal. Locate the special preload tool as shown on the choke lever.

10 With the preload tool floating, measure the choke plate to air horn clearance on the accelerator pump side using a twist drill of the specified size.

11 If necessary adjust the clearance by bending the choke plate pull-down lever accordingly.

Reassembly

12 Having completed the three checks and made any necessary adjustments, the choke housing can be reassembled. Engage the choke spring into the central slot on the operating linkage, and then locate the housing with gasket and insert the three retaining screws, but do not fully tighten them until the alignment mark on the housing is opposite the central mark on the auto choke body (Fig. 3.27).

13 Refit the air cleaner to complete.

20 Automatic choke mechanism – dismantling, inspection and reassembly

1 Refer to Section 2 and remove the air cleaner. Clamp and detach the automatic choke hoses, then tie them to one side facing upwards to prevent loss of coolant.
2 Remove the choke body outer housing, which is retained by three screws. Note the housing gasket.
3 Unscrew and remove the two screws from within the choke housing (Fig. 3.28).
4 Unscrew the choke linkage-to-spindle screw (Fig. 3.29) and remove the choke body from the rear face of the carburettor.
5 Remove the screw retaining the choke operating spindle and extract the vacuum piston linkage (Fig. 3.30).
6 Clean the respective components and carefully inspect for signs of damage or excessive wear. Renew any defective components.
7 Before reassembly, ensure that all parts are perfectly clean and dry – do not lubricate any components.

8 Reassemble in the reverse order to dismantling. Ensure that the plastic sleeve is fitted to the spindle and also that the seal rubber is located between the carburettor and main choke body. Reset the V mark alignment, check the de-choke setting and the vacuum pull-down as given in the previous Section, and refit the air cleaner to complete.

21 Exhaust system – general

1 The exhaust system layout fitted depends on the engine and body types.
2 The front pipe section is attached to the manifold at its forward end and to the front silencer connection at its rear end.
3 Two silencers are fitted. On the ohc engine models a silencer is fitted to both front and rear section pipes, whilst on the ohv engine models the two silencers are both incorporated into the front pipe section.
4 The pipe connections are secured by U-bolt clamps and the

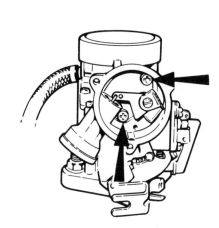

Fig. 3.28 Choke housing retaining screws (arrowed) (Sec 20)

Fig. 3.29 Detach choke linkage (Sec 20)

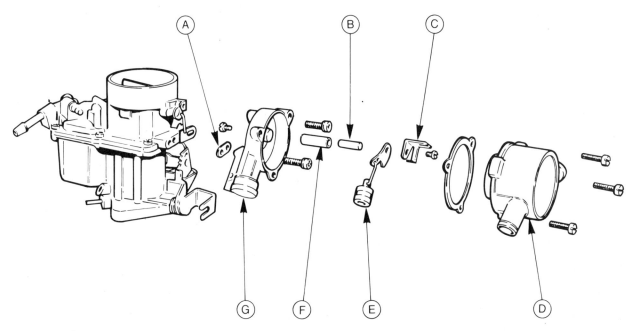

Fig. 3.30 The auto choke components (Sec 20)

A Seal rubber	C Actuating link	E Vacuum piston unit	G Housing
B Choke spindle	D Outer housing and bi-metal spring	F Sleeve	

systems are suspended from the underframe by means of welded brackets (interconnected by means of rubber insulators) or support straps (Figs. 3.31 and 3.32).

5   A regular inspection of the exhaust system must be made to check for insecurity, damage and corrosion to the point where the system leaks.

6   The system can either be removed and renewed as a complete unit, or a single section can be renewed,. As the clamps and fittings are invariably well rusted, penetrating oil should be applied to assist in unscrewing damp nuts and also to separate pipe sections where necessary.

7   The insulators and flexible straps will almost certainly be perished,

distorted and in need of replacement and they should also therefore be renewed.

8   When refitting the system, loosely attach all the fittings until the system is located satisfactorily before tightening them up. Check for leaks on completion.

9   Whilst repairs to an exhaust system can be made with exhaust bandage and various silencer repair kits that are readily available, they cannot be expected to last for any prolonged period.

10 If the vehicle is to be kept for longer than a couple of years, consideration should be given to fitting a stainless steel system. Various proprietary stainless steel exhaust systems are available, most of them carrying guarantees of five years or more.

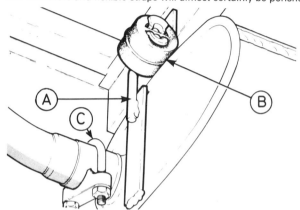

Fig. 3.31 Front silencer and mounting (Sec 21)

A   Mounting hanger   C   Pipe clamp
B   Insulator

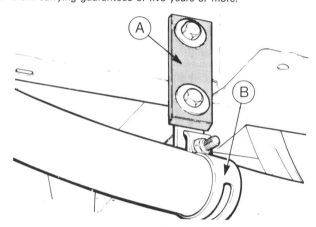

Fig. 3.32 The rear tailpipe support strap (A) and bracket clamp (B)
(Sec 21)

22   Fault diagnosis – fuel and exhaust systems

Unsatisfactory engine performance and excessive fuel consumption are not necessarily the fault of the fuel system or carburettor. In fact they more commonly occur as a result of ignition and timing faults. Before acting on the following it is necessary to check the ignition system first. Even though a fault may lie in the fuel system it will be difficult to trace unless the ignition is correct. The faults below, therefore, assume that this has been attended to first (where appropriate).

Symptom	Reason(s)
Fuel consumption excessive	Air cleaner choked and dirty giving rich mixture
	Fuel leaking from carburettor, fuel pump or fuel lines
	Float chamber flooding
	Generally worn carburettor
	Distributor condenser faulty
	Balance weights or vacuum advance mechanism in distributor faulty
	Carburettor choke mechanism defective
	Carburettor incorrectly adjusted, mixture too rich
	Idling speed too high
	Contact breaker gap incorrect
	Valve clearances incorrect
	Incorrectly set spark plugs
	Tyres under-inflated
	Wrong spark plugs fitted
	Brakes dragging
Insufficient fuel delivery or weak mixture	Petrol tank air vent restricted
	Partially clogged filters in pump and carburettor
	Dirt lodged in float chamber needle housing
	Incorrectly seating valves in fuel pump
	Fuel pump diaphragm leaking or damaged
	Gasket in fuel pump damaged
	Fuel pump valves sticking due to petrol gumming
	Too little fuel in fuel tank (prevalent when climbing steep hills)
	Union joints on pipe connections loose
	Split in fuel pipe on suction side of fuel pump
	Inlet manifold to block or inlet manifold to carburettor gasket leaking
Engine will not idle	Cut-off solenoid defective or disconnected
	Idle system blocked
	Air leaks at carburettor or manifold

Chapter 4 Ignition system

For modifications, and information applicable to later models, see Supplement at end of manual

Contents

Specifications

General

System type .... 12 volt, contact breaker and coil, with ballast resistor
Firing order:
    OHV engine 1-2-4-3
    OHC engines 1-3-4-2
Location of No 1 cylinder .... Crankshaft pulley end

Spark plugs

Type:
    OHV engine .... Motorcraft AGR 22 or equivalent
    OHC engine (1.6) .... Motorcraft BF 22 or equivalent
    OHC engine (2.0) .... Motorcraft BF 32 or equivalent
Electrode gap (all types) .... 0.025 in (0.6 mm)

Coil

Make .... Lucas, Bosch, Femsa or Polmot
Primary resistance .... 0.95 to 1.35 ohms
Secondary resistance .... 5000 to 9000 ohms
Ballast resistor .... 1.5 ohms
Output (open-circuit condition, on vehicle) .... 23 kV minimum

Distributor

Make .... Motorcraft
Drive:
    OHV engine .... From camshaft
    OHC engines .... From auxiliary shaft
Direction of rotation:
    OHV engine .... Anti-clockwise
    OHC engines .... Clockwise
Automatic advance mechanisms .... Centrifugal and vacuum
Contact breaker points gap .... 0.025 in (0.6 mm)
Dwell angle .... 48° to 52° (53% to 58%)
Shaft endfloat .... 0.025 to 0.033 in (0.6 to 0.8 mm)

Ignition timing

Initial advance .... 6° BTDC static or at 800 rpm (vacuum advance disconnected)

Torque wrench settings

	lbf ft	kgf m
Spark plugs:		
OHV engine	22 to 29	3.0 to 3.9
OHC engines	15 to 20	2.0 to 2.8

1 General description

The main function of the ignition system is to provide an electrical spark in the engine combustion chamber in order to ignite the fuel-air mixture, which has been drawn into the cylinder by the induction stroke of the piston. There are three major components involved: the coil, the distributor and the spark plug. All three play an important role in converting the electrical power available at the battery into a spark at the spark plug at precisely the right time in the engine cycle.

Since the fuel-air mixture is under compression at the point of ignition, the voltage required to bring about the electrical discharge across the plug electrodes may be as high as 12 000 volts, and in order to produce this, the system is divided into two circuits, namely the low tension circuit (LT), and the high tension circuit (HT).

The low tension circuit or primary circuit consists of the battery lead (+) to the ignition switch, the lead from the ignition switch to the coil primary windings, and the lead from the coil to the contact breaker points and condenser in the distributor.

The high tension circuit or secondary circuit consists of the coil secondary windings, the heavy lead from the centre of the coil to the distributor cap, the rotor arm, spark plug leads and spark plugs.

The system functions in the following manner. Low tension voltage (12V) is supplied by the battery to the primary coil winding and an electromagnetic field is produced around the secondary winding when the contact points close. This initial process is a controlled action, and the magnetic field gradually builds up, but when the contact breaker points separate, the collapse of the negative field across the secondary coil winding induces a much higher voltage in the secondary winding. This high tension voltage is fed from the coil to the distributor cap and via the carbon brush to the rotor arm.

The distributor cap houses four segments which are connected by high tension leads to the four spark plugs. As the rotor arm turns, it releases the high tension current to the four segments as required with the result that the spark jumps across the spark plug electrodes.

The ignition is advanced and retarded automatically to ensure that the spark occurs at just the right instant for the particular load at the prevailing engine speed. A mechanical governor mechanism, consisting of two weights embodied in the distributor, controls the amount of advance required in relation to the engine speed. A vacuum unit also mounted on the distributor controls the amount of advance required in relation to the load and is operated by vacuum in the carburettor.

The ignition system uses a 6 volt coil and a ballast resistor; during starting a 12 volt supply is fed to the coil which has the effect of boosting the voltage at the spark plug. However, once the starting current is released, the voltage to the coil is reduced to 6 volts by means of the ballast resistor (photo). The accompanying ignition circuit diagrams show how the circuits are affected when the ignition/starter switch is operated.

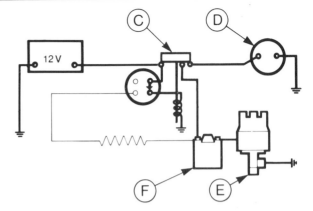

Fig. 4.1 Ignition circuit with switch in the 'start' position (Sec 1)

C   Starter solenoid   E   Distributor
D   Starter motor   F   Ignition coil

Fig. 4.2 Ignition circuit with switch in the 'On' position showing ballast resistor (G) (Sec 1)

2 Contact breaker points – adjustment

1   To adjust the contact breaker points accurately, the use of a dwell meter is required (following the manufacturer's instructions) but, as many owners will not possess one, the following paragraphs also describe adjusting the points with a feeler gauge.

2   First prise the distributor cap retaining clips away and lift the cap from the distributor, clean the cap thoroughly with a dry cloth and check that the segments are not excessively burnt. If they are, the cap must be renewed (photo).

1.0 The ignition coil and ballast resistor unit

2.2 Check each segment within the distributor cap

Measuring plug gap. A feeler gauge of the correct size (see ignition system specifications) should have a slight 'drag' when slid between the electrodes. Adjust gap if necessary

Adjusting plug gap. The plug gap is adjusted by bending the earth electrode inwards, or outwards, as necessary until the correct clearance is obtained. Note the use of the correct tool

Normal. Grey-brown deposits, lightly coated core nose. Gap increasing by around 0.001 in (0.025 mm) per 1000 miles (1600 km). Plugs ideally suited to engine, and engine in good condition

Carbon fouling. Dry, black, sooty deposits. Will cause weak spark and eventually misfire. Fault: over-rich fuel mixture. Check: carburettor mixture settings, float level and jet sizes; choke operation and cleanliness of air filter. Plugs can be re-used after cleaning

Oil fouling. Wet, oily deposits. Will cause weak spark and eventually misfire. Fault: worn bores/piston rings or valve guides; sometimes occurs (temporarily) during running-in period. Plugs can be re-used after thorough cleaning

Overheating. Electrodes have glazed appearance, core nose very white — few deposits. Fault: plug overheating. Check: plug value, ignition timing, fuel octane rating (too low) and fuel mixture (too weak). Discard plugs and cure fault immediately

Electrode damage. Electrodes burned away; core nose has burned, glazed appearance. Fault: pre-ignition. Check: as for 'Overheating' but may be more severe. Discard plugs and remedy fault before piston or valve damage occurs

Split core nose (may appear initially as a crack). Damage is self-evident, but cracks will only show after cleaning. Fault: pre-ignition or wrong gap-setting technique. Check: ignition timing, cooling system, fuel octane rating (too low) and fuel mixture (too weak). Discard plugs, rectify fault immediately

3 Check that the carbon brush is unbroken and stands proud of the plastic surface.

4 Carefully lift the rotor arm off the cam and then use a screwdriver to prise the contact points open. Examine the surfaces of both contacts; if they are rough, pitted or dirty it will be necessary to remove them for resurfacing or renewal as described in Section 3.

5 Assuming that the points are satisfactory, turn the engine using a spanner on the crankshaft pulley nut, until the moving contact heel is positioned on the highest point of one of the cam lobes.

6 Using a feeler gauge of the correct size (see Specifications) check the contact breaker gap; the blade of the feeler gauge should be a sliding fit between the contact points.

7 If adjustment is required, slightly loosen the one or two fixed contact retaining screw(s) and move the fixed contact as required; a notch is provided to facilitate adjustment by the use of a suitable screwdriver (photo).

8 After adjustment, tighten the retaining screw(s) and recheck the gap, then turn the engine until the heel of the moving contact is on the peak of the next cam lobe and check the gap again. Any variation indicates that the distributor spindle is bent or worn, and if excessive it must be renewed.

9 Refit the rotor arm and distributor cap and make sure that the clips are secure.

10 If a dwell meter is available, this is a quicker and more accurate method of checking the contact breaker points. Dwell angle is the number of degrees through which the distributor shaft turns between the instants of closure and opening of the contact breaker points. The angle is directly proportional to the points gap. Increasing the points gap decreases the dwell angle, and vice versa.

11 According to the type of dwell meter in use, the angle may be measured whilst the engine is being cranked on the starter motor, or with the engine running. Follow the meter manufacturer's instructions on this subject.

12 If the dwell angle is correct, no further action is required. If the dwell angle is too small, reduce the points gap; if the angle is too large, increase the gap. If the dwell angle fluctuates, this may be due to wear or damage in the distributor.

13 Whenever the contact breaker gap is altered, the ignition timing should be checked and if necessary adjusted, as described in Section 10.

3 Contact breaker points – removal, servicing and refitting

1 If the contact breaker points are excessively burnt or pitted, they must be removed for refacing or renewal.

2 To remove the points unclip the distributor cap and lift it away, then pull the rotor arm off the cam.

3 Loosen the terminal screw and extract the two fork tabs of the low tension leads. On some models you will also have to disconnect the radio suppressor lead, which has a bullet connector.

4 Unscrew and remove the contact breaker unit retaining screws, serrated washers, and flat washers, and withdraw the assembly from the distributor.

5 Dress the face of each contact squarely on an oilstone or a piece of fine emery cloth until all traces of 'pips' or 'craters' have been removed. After much dressing of the contact points, the tungsten tips will be reduced to the base metal and it will then be necessary to fit new points.

6 Refitting the contact breaker points is a reversal of the removal procedure but the following additional information should be noted:

   (a) Clean the points with methylated spirit before assembling
   (b) Lightly lubricate the peaks of the cam lobes with petroleum jelly
   (c) Adjust the contact points gap (and dwell angle, if possible) as described in Section 2

4 Condenser – removal, testing and refitting

1 The condenser acts as a 'buffer' in the low tension circuit of the ignition system by absorbing the surges of current which are produced by the contact breaker points opening and closing. This greatly reduces the arcing at the points, and its action also assists in the rapid collapse of the magnetic field set up by the primary winding within the coil.

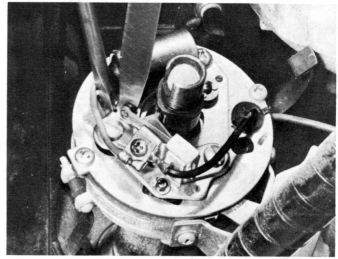

2.7 Using a feeler gauge and screwdriver to adjust the contact breaker points clearance

Failure of the condenser will reduce the spark plug voltage in the high tension circuit, and if difficulty in starting the engine is experienced accompanied by 'missing' under load, the fault may well be in the condenser.

2 To remove the condenser, first unclip the distributor cap and remove it, then lift the rotor arm off the cam.

3 Loosen the terminal screw and slide out the condenser lead fork tab. Unscrew and remove the cross-headed condenser retaining screw and lift the condenser away from the distributor.

4 Without the use of specialist equipment the only sure way of diagnosing a faulty condenser is to renew it and note if there is any improvement. However, a simple test is to separate the points by hand with the ignition switched on; if this action is accompanied by a **strong** blue flash across the points, condenser failure is indicated (a **weak** flash is normal).

5 Refitting the condenser is a reversal of the removal procedure, but make sure that the retaining screw is tightened securely and that the lead end tab is not touching the baseplate.

5 Distributor – lubrication

1 Every 6000 miles (10 000 km) the distributor should be lubricated. Smear a little petroleum jelly or high melting-point grease on the lobes of the distributor cam to provide lubrication for the contact point heel.

2 Remove the rotor arm and apply two drops of engine oil into the cam recess; a felt pad is provided to accept the oil.

3 Apply a few drops of oil through the baseplate aperture to lubricate the governor weights.

4 Great care should be taken not to use too much lubricant, otherwise surplus oil may contaminate the contact points and cause ignition failure.

6 Distributor – removal and refitting

1 To remove the distributor from the engine, mark the four spark plug leads so that they may be refitted to the correct plugs and pull off the spark plugs lead connectors – **do not** pull the leads.

2 Detach the high tension and the low tension CB lead from the coil by pulling their connectors – not the leads. Remove the distributor cap.

3 Pull off the rubber union holding the vacuum pipe to the distributor vacuum advance housing.

4 If it is not wished to disturb the timing, turn the crankshaft until the timing marks (Fig. 4.12) are in line and the rotor arm is pointing to No 1 spark plug segment in the distributor cap. This will facilitate refitting the distributor providing the crankshaft is not moved whilst the distributor is away from the engine. Mark the position of the rotor in relation to the distributor body (Fig. 4.3).

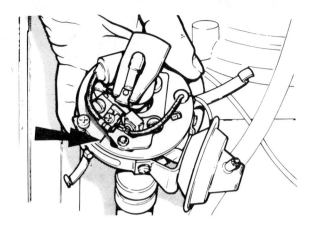

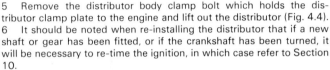

Fig. 4.3 Mark the relative positions of the rotor arm and body
(Sec 6)

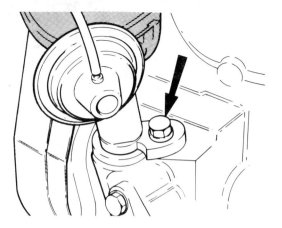

Fig. 4.4 The distributor retaining bolt (Sec 6)

5   Remove the distributor body clamp bolt which holds the distributor clamp plate to the engine and lift out the distributor (Fig. 4.4).
6   It should be noted when re-installing the distributor that if a new shaft or gear has been fitted, or if the crankshaft has been turned, it will be necessary to re-time the ignition, in which case refer to Section 10.
7   Insert the distributor into its location with the vacuum advance assembly to the rear.
8   Notice that the rotor arm rotates as the gears mesh. The rotor arm must settle in exactly the same direction that it was in before the distributor was removed. To do this, lift out the assembly far enough to rotate the shaft one tooth at a time, lowering it home to check the direction of the rotor arm. When it points in the desired direction with the assembly fully home fit the distributor clamp plate, bolt and plain washer.
9   With the distributor assembly fitted, reconnect the low tension lead from the side of the distributor to the CB terminal on the coil. Reconnect the HT lead to the coil and refit the rubber union of the vacuum pipe which runs from the induction manifold to the vacuum advance unit.

7   Distributor – dismantling

1   With the distributor removed from the engine, clear a work area on the bench so that as the respective components are removed they can be laid out in order of appearance for cleaning and inspection. Refer to Fig. 4.5 or 4.6 as applicable.
2   Pull the rotor arm from the cam.
3   Remove the contact breaker points as given in Section 3.
4   Remove the condenser and lead, which are secured by a single screw.
5   Unclip the vacuum pivot post circlip and unscrew the two baseplate retaining screws. Withdraw the baseplate (Fig. 4.7).
6   Detach the vacuum unit, which is retained to the outer body by two screws.
7   Prise free the plastic bump stop as shown (Fig. 4.8). Before extracting the cam and plate assembly, a note must be made of the relative position of the cam plate and bump stop. Also note that the two advance springs are of different sizes, so note their positions also (Fig. 4.9).
8   Extract the felt pad from the recess in the top of the cam pivot, compress the circlip using suitable circlip pliers and remove it.
9   Disconnect the advance springs and then remove the cam spindle from the distributor body.
10   Should it be necessary to remove the drivegear, using a suitable diameter parallel pin punch tap out the gear lockpin. If the original gear is to be re-used, mark its position relative to the shaft for reference during assembly.
11   The gear may now be drawn off the shaft with a universal puller. If there are no means of holding the puller legs these must be bound together with wire to stop them springing apart during removal.
12   Finally withdraw the shaft from the distributor body.

8   Distributor – inspection and repair

1   Check the contact breaker points for wear, as described in Section 3. Check the distributor cap for signs of tracking, indicated by a thin black line between the segments. Renew the cap if any signs of tracking are found.
2   If the metal portion of the rotor arm is badly burned or loose, renew the arm. If only slightly burned, clean the end with a fine file. Check that the contact spring has adequate pressure and that the bearing surface is clean and in good condition.
3   Check that the carbon brush in the distributor cap is unbroken and stands proud of its holder.
4   Examine the centrifugal weights and pivots for wear and the advance springs for slackness. They can best be checked by comparing with new parts. If they are slack they must be renewed.
5   Check the points assembly for fit on the breaker plate, and the cam follower for wear.
6   Examine the fit of the spindle in the distributor body. If there is excessive side movement it will be necessary either to fit a new bush or obtain a new body (assuming that the spindle itself is not worn).
7   The baseplate can be dismantled for inspection by removing the circlip retaining the upper plate spindle post. Withdraw the upper plate spring and washers, noting their relative positions. Renew any worn or damaged components.
8   Reassemble the baseplate in the reverse order to dismantling, referring to Fig. 4.10.

9   Distributor – reassembly

1   Locate the thrust washer onto the mainshaft and then smear a liberal amount of grease (lithium-based) onto the upper shaft.
2   Refit the cam and plate unit, ensuring that the cam plate is correctly positioned relative to the bump stop (as noted on removal). Where a new cam plate is being fitted, the markings on it should be the same and so must its position relative to the bump stop. Secure the cam plate with the circlip, positioning the clip tangs at 90° to the slot in the rotor arm.
3   Engage the governor springs to their respective posts, then refit the bump stop (Fig. 4.11).
4   The vacuum advance unit can now be refitted to the body and the two retaining screws (their threads smeared with a small amount of sealant such as Loctite 601) screwed into position.
5   Fit the low tension lead rubber grommet into its cut-out in the body, locate the baseplate and secure with screws.
6   Refit the vacuum unit and use a new circlip to secure the vacuum pivot post to the baseplate.
7   Locate and secure the condenser with its single screw. Reconnect the LT and condenser leads.
8   Refer to Section 2 and adjust the contact breaker points gap prior to refitting the distributor.

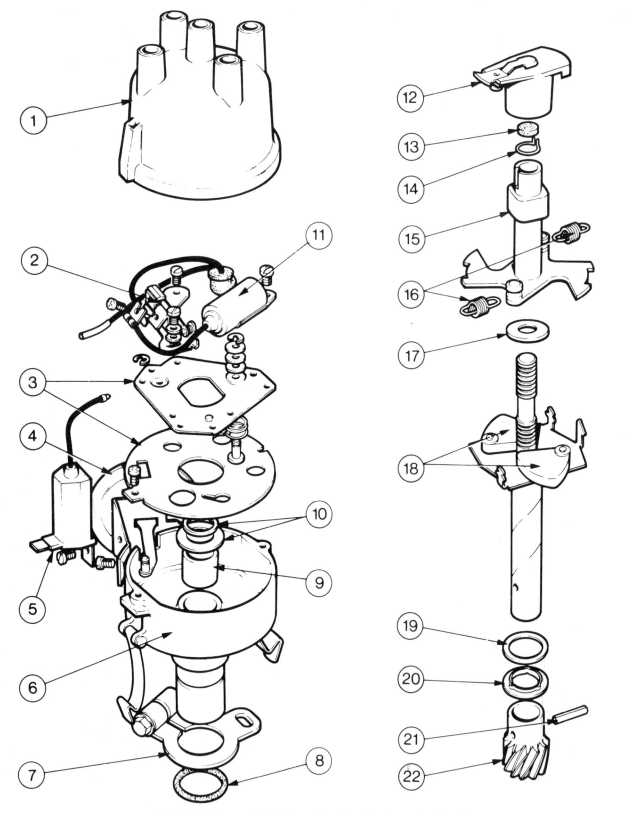

Fig. 4.5 The Motorcraft distributor fitted to the ohv engine (Sec 7)

1	Cap	7	Distributor clamp	13	Felt pad	18 Advance weight assembly
2	Points assembly	8	Seal	14	Circlip	19 Spacer
3	Baseplate	9	Bush	15	Cam	20 Washer
4	Vacuum unit	10	Thrust washers	16	Advance springs	21 Pin
5	Radio suppressor	11	Condenser	17	Washer	22 Gear
6	Body	12	Rotor arm			

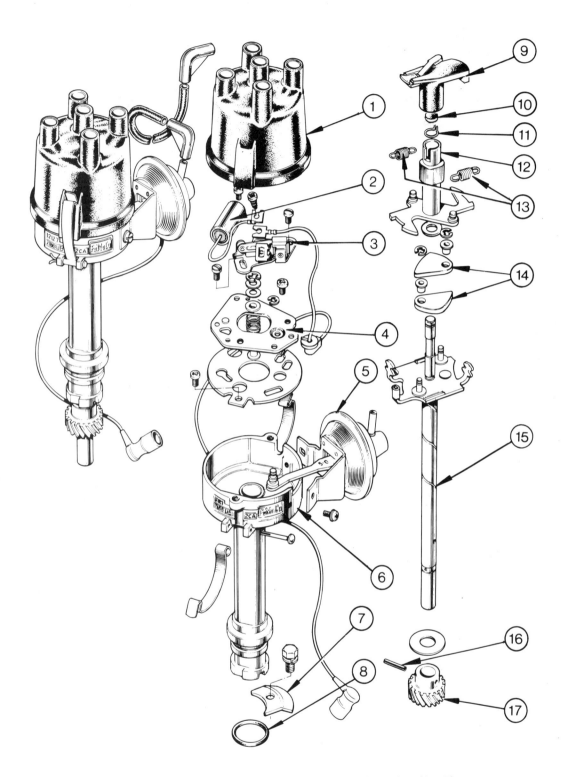

Fig. 4.6 The Motorcraft distributor fitted to ohc engines (Sec 7)

1	Cap	6	Body	10	Felt pad	14	Advance weights
2	Condenser	7	Distributor clamp	11	Circlip	15	Shaft
3	Contact breaker	8	Seal	12	Cam	16	Pin
4	Baseplate	9	Rotor arm	13	Advance springs	17	Gear
5	Vacuum unit						

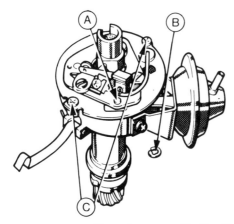

Fig. 4.7 The contacts and baseplate assembly (Sec 7)

A   Vacuum unit hinge post   C   Baseplate retaining screws
B   Circlip

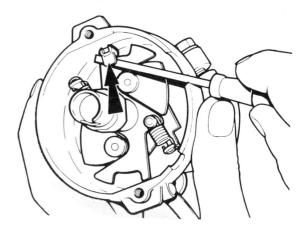

Fig. 4.8 Prise free the plastic bump stop (arrowed) (Sec 7)

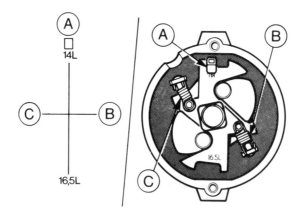

Fig. 4.9 Typical cam plate and advance spring position, showing
the bump stop position (A), the thin advance spring (B) and the
thick advance spring (C) locations (Sec 7)

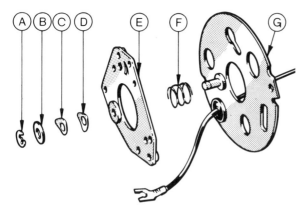

Fig. 4.10 Baseplate components

A   Circlip   E   Upper plate
B   Washer   F   Spring
C   Curved washer   G   Baseplate
D   Curved washer

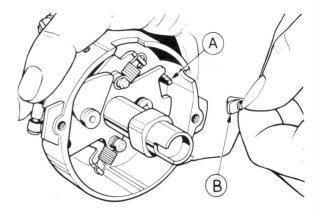

Fig. 4.11 Refit the bump stop (B) onto the governor weight (A)
(Sec 9)

10 Ignition timing – checking and adjustment

1   After overhauling the distributor or fitting new contact points, the ignition timing should be checked and adjusted to ensure that the spark at the spark plugs is occurring at the exact moment in relation to the rotation of the engine. The basic ignition timing can be checked and if necessary adjusted using the static method, or using a stroboscopic timing light, if available, for more accurate adjustment.

2   *To adjust the ignition timing using a static timing light,* first rotate the engine with a spanner on the crankshaft pulley nut until the No 1 piston moves up on its compression stroke; this can be ascertained by removing No 1 spark plug and placing the thumb over the exposed hole, when pressure will be felt as the piston moves upwards.

3   Refer to the Specifications to determine the correct amount of ignition advance required for static timing, then continue to rotate the engine until the notch on the rear of the crankshaft pulley is aligned with the relevant mark on the timing cover (Fig. 4.12). If the pulley is rotated past the timing marks, do not turn it back, otherwise the slack in the distributor gear and timing chain or belt will effectively retard the timing; the pulley should be rotated two complete turns and the marks aligned again.

4   Unclip the distributor cap and place it to one side.

5   Connect a 12 volt bulb between the distributor low tension terminal or the coil CB terminal and a suitable earth point on the engine or the battery negative terminal.

6   Loosen the distributor retaining bolt and switch on the ignition, then turn the distributor body so that the moving contact heel is released from the cam and the points are closed. The distributor should be turned in the same direction as the normal rotation of the rotor arm viewed from the top (clockwise for ohc engine models, anti-clockwise for ohv engine models).

7   Now turn the distributor slowly in the opposite direction until the points just open; at this exact point the timing light will come on and the distributor retaining bolt should then be tightened.

8   If the retaining bolt elongated hole does not provide enough adjustment, the clamp bolt will need to be loosened.

9   With the distributor locked in position, the rotor arm should be facing the direction of the No 1 segment of the distributor cap, but if this is not the case, the skew gear is probably engaged incorrectly with the camshaft/auxiliary shaft and it will therefore be necessary to withdraw the distributor and refit it correctly as detailed in Section 6.

10 Check that the ignition timing is correct by rotating the engine two complete turns and noting when the timing light comes on; this should occur when the timing marks are aligned.

11 *To adjust the ignition timing using a stroboscopic timing light,* carry out the instructions given in paragraphs 2 to 4 inclusive then loosen the distributor retaining bolt and position the distributor so that the contact points are about to open, with the rotor arm pointing towards the No 1 segment of the distributor cap. (This is only necessary if timing has been lost completely – if the engine will run, commence at paragraph 12).

12 Refit the distributor cap and connect the timing light to the engine in accordance with the manufacturer's instructions, then disconnect the vacuum unit pipe.

13 Clean the timing marks on the crankshaft pulley and timing cover and, if necessary, mark them with chalk or white paint to make them more visible. Start the engine and shine the timing light towards the timing marks (Fig. 4.12).

14 With the engine idling, the correct mark on the pulley should appear aligned with the pointer on the timing cover. If adjustment is necessary turn the distributor anti-clockwise to advance and clockwise to retard on ohc engines, vice versa for ohv engines. Tighten the distributor retaining bolt when the adjustment is correct.

15 To check the operation of the distributor advance weights, increase the engine speed to a fast idle and check that the timing marks advance accordingly. Similarly check the operation of the vacuum advance by holding the fast idle speed and reconnecting the vacuum pipe, when the timing marks should advance again. Any irregularity indicates a fault and the distributor should be dismantled and the particular component checked as described in Section 8.

11 Spark plugs and HT leads – general

1   The correct functioning of the spark plugs is vital for the correct running and efficiency of the engine.

2   At intervals of 6000 miles (10 000 km) the plugs should be removed, examined, cleaned, and if worn excessively, renewed. The condition of the spark plugs will also tell much about the overall condition of the engine.

3   If the insulator nose of the spark plug is clean and white, with no deposits, this is indicative of a weak mixture, or too hot a plug. (A hot plug transfers heat away from the electrode slowly – a cold plug transfers it away quickly).

4   If the tip and insulator nose are covered with hard black looking deposits, then this is indicative that the mixture is too rich. Should the plug be black and oily, then it is likely that the engine is fairly worn, as well as the mixture being too rich.

5   If the insulator nose is covered with light tan to greyish brown deposits, then the mixture is correct and it is likely that the engine is in good condition.

6   If there are any traces of long brown tapering stains on the outside of the white portion of the plug, then the plug will have to be renewed, as this shows that there is a faulty joint between the plug body and the insulator, and compression is being lost.

7   Plugs should ideally be cleaned by a sand blasting machine, which will free them from carbon more thoroughly than cleaning by hand.

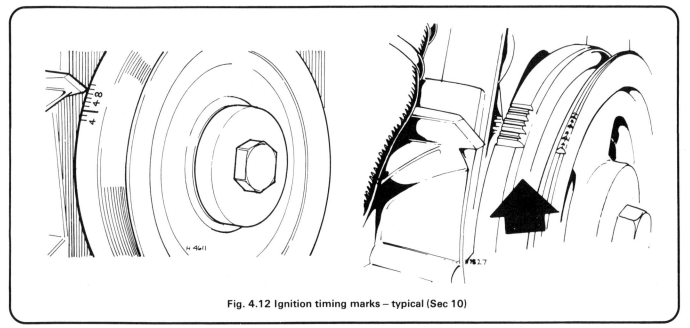

Fig. 4.12 Ignition timing marks – typical (Sec 10)

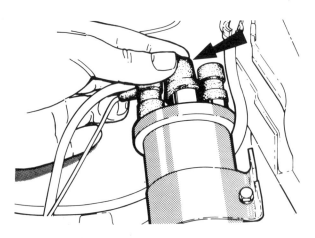

Fig. 4.13 When detaching HT leads, pull on connector – not the lead (Sec 11)

Some machines will also test the condition of the plugs under compression. Any plug that fails to spark at the recommended pressure should be renewed.

8   The spark plug gap is of considerable importance, as, if it is too large or too small, the size of the spark and its efficiency will be seriously impaired. The spark plug gap should be set to the figure given in the Specifications.

9   To set it, measure the gap with a feeler gauge, and then bend open, or close, the **outer** plug electrode until the correct gap is achieved. The centre electrode should **never** be bent as this may crack the insulation and cause plug failure if nothing worse.

10 When refitting the plugs, remember to fit the leads from the distributor in the correct firing order in accordance with the rotation of the rotor arm. The cylinders on all engine types are numbered front to rear, but the firing order and distributor rotation for the ohc and ohv engines differ – refer to the Specifications.

11 The HT leads fitted when new are of the carbon impregnated rayon or glass fibre core type for radio interference suppression. It is most important when removing this type of HT lead from the spark plugs, that they are gripped by their terminals – do not pull the lead! Provided the leads are not bent in a tight loop and compressed, there is no reason why this type of lead should fail. A legend has arisen which blames this type of lead for all ignition faults and many owners replace them with the older copper-cored type and install separate suppressors. In the majority of cases, it would be more profitable to establish the real cause of the trouble before going to the expense of new leads.

12 The plug leads require no routine attention other than being kept clean and wiped over regularly. At intervals of 6000 miles (10 000 km), however, pull the leads off the plugs and distributor one at a time and make sure no water has found its way onto the connections. Remove any corrosion from the brass ends, wipe the collars on top of the distributor cap and refit the leads.

13 Every 10 000 to 12 000 miles (16 000 to 20 000 km) it is recommended that the spark plugs are renewed to maintain optimum engine performance.

12 Fault diagnosis – ignition system

By far the majority of breakdown and running troubles are caused by faults in the ignition system either in the low tension or high tension circuit. There are two main symptoms indicating ignition faults. Either the engine will not start or fire, or the engine is difficult to start and misfires. If it is a regular misfire, ie the engine is only running on two or three cylinders, the fault is almost sure to be in the secondary, or high tension, circuit. If the misfiring is intermittent, the fault could be in either the high or low tension circuits. If the car stops suddenly or will not start at all, it is likely that the fault is in the low tension circuit. Loss of power and overheating, apart from cooling system faults or faulty carburation settings, are normally due to faults in the distributor or incorrect ignition timing.

Engine fails to start

1   If the engine fails to start and the car was running normally when it was last used, first check there is fuel in the petrol tank. If the engine turns normally on the starter motor and the battery is evidently well charged, then the fault may be in either the high or low tension circuits. First check the HT circuit. **Note:** *If the battery is known to be fully charged, the ignition light comes on, and the starter motor fails to turn the engine, check the tightness of the leads on the battery terminal and the security of the earth lead at its connection to the body.* It is quite common for the leads to have worked loose, even if they look and feel secure. If one of the battery terminal posts gets very hot when trying to work the starter motor, this is a sure indication of a faulty connection to that terminal.

2   One of the commonest reasons for bad starting is wet or damp spark plug leads and distributor. Remove the distributor cap. If condensation is visible internally, dry the cap with a rag and wipe over the leads. Refit the cap.

3   If the engine still fails to start, check that current is reaching the plugs, by disconnecting each plug lead in turn at the spark plug end. Turn the engine on the starter motor and hold the end of the lead with an insulated tool about $\frac{3}{16}$ in (5 mm) from the cylinder block.

4   Sparking between the end of the cable and the block should be fairly strong with a regular blue spark. If current is reaching the plugs, then remove them and clean and regap them to the specified gap. The engine should now start.

5   If there is no spark at the plug leads, take off the HT lead from the centre of the distributor cap and hold it to the block as before. Spin the engine on the starter once more. A rapid succession of blue sparks between the end of the lead and the block indicate that the coil is in order and that the distributor cap is cracked, the rotor arm faulty or the carbon brush in the top of the distributor cap is not making good contact with the spring on the rotor arm.

6   If there are no sparks from the end of the lead from the coil, check the connections at the coil end of the lead. If it is in order start checking the low tension circuit. First clean and regap the points.

7   Use a 12 volt voltmeter or a 12 volt bulb and two lengths of wire. With the ignition switch on and the points open test between the low tension wire to the coil (it is marked SW or +) and earth. No reading indicates a break in the supply from the ignition switch. Check the connections at the switch to see if any are loose. Refit them and the engine should run. A reading shows a faulty coil or condenser or broken lead between the coil and the distributor.

8   Take the condenser wire off the points assembly and with the points open, test between the moving point and earth. If there now is a reading, then the fault is in the condenser. Fit a new one and the fault is cleared.

9   With no reading from the moving point to earth, take a reading between earth and the CB or (-) terminal of the coil. A reading here indicates a broken wire which must be renewed between the coil and distributor. No reading confirms that the coil has failed and must be renewed. Remember to connect the condenser wire to the points assembly. For these tests it is sufficient to separate the contact breaker points with a piece of paper.

10 It should be noted that the coil is of 6 volt rating and is fitted with a ballast resistor unit. The details of this are explained in Section 1. If renewing the coil, be certain to obtain the correct replacement type or further difficulty could be encountered when starting the engine.

11 Note also that if the ballast resistor is defective, the engine will fire when the starter motor is operated but will cut out when the ignition key is released from the starting position. Do not simply bypass the resistor in this case, or the coil may overheat. In an emergency a suitable bulb (6V, 24W) may be substituted for the resistor.

Engine misfires

12 If the engine misfires regularly, run it at a fast idling speed. Pull off each of the plug caps in turn and listen to the note of the engine. Hold the plug cap in a dry cloth or with a rubber glove as additional protection against a shock from the HT supply.

13 No difference in engine running will be noticed when the lead from the defective circuit is removed. Removing the lead from one of the good cylinders will accentuate the misfire.

14 Remove the plug lead from the end of the defective plug and hold it about $\frac{3}{16}$ in (5 mm) away from the block. Restart the engine. If the sparking is fairly strong and regular, the fault must lie in the spark plug.

15 The plug may be loose, the insulation may be cracked, or the points may have been burnt away, giving too wide a gap for the spark

to jump. Worse still, one of the points may have broken off. Either renew the plug, or clean it, reset the gap, and then test it.

16 If there is no spark at the end of the plug lead, or if it is weak and intermittent, check the ignition lead from the distributor to the plug. If the insulation is cracked or perished, renew the lead. Check the connections at the distributor cap.

17 If there is still no spark, examine the distributor cap carefully for tracking. This can be recognised by a very thin black line running between two or more electrodes, or between an electrode and some other part of the distributor. These lines are paths which now conduct electricity across the cap, thus letting it run to earth. The only answer is a new distributor cap. As a temporary measure it may be possible to interrupt the track by scraping or filing away its ends.

18 Apart from the ignition timing being incorrect, other causes of misfiring have already been dealt with under the section dealing with the failure of the engine to start. To recap, these are that:

(a) The coil may be faulty giving an intermittent misfire
(b) There may be a damaged wire or loose connection in the low tension circuit
(c) The condenser may be short-circuiting
(d) There may be a mechanical fault in the distributor (broken driving spindle or contact breaker spring)

19 If the ignition timing is too far retarded, it should be noted that the engine will tend to overheat, and there will be a quite noticeable drop in power. If the engine is overheating and the power is down, and the ignition timing is correct, then the carburettor should be checked, as it is likely that this is where the fault lies.

Chapter 5 Clutch

Contents

Specifications

General
Type .... Single dry plate, diaphragm spring
Actuation .... Cable

Clutch disc outer diameter
1.6 ohv engine .... 8.5 in (21.59 cm) Ferodo or 9.0 in (22.8 cm) Porner
1.6 and 2 litre ohc engines .... 8.5 in (21.59 cm) Ferodo or 9.5 in (24.13 cm) Mintex

Clutch pedal stop clearance .... 0.13 to 0.18 in (3.5 to 4.5 mm)

Release bearing type .... Sealed ball

Clutch pedal free play .... 0.49 to 0.78 in (12.5 to 20.0 mm)

Torque wrench setting

	lbf ft	kgf m
Pressure plate to flywheel	11.5 to 14.7	1.6 to 2.0

1 General description

All manual transmission models are fitted with a single dry plate diaphragm clutch which is bolted to the rear face of the flywheel.

The clutch disc or driven plate is splined to the gearbox input shaft and is free to move in either direction between the faces of the flywheel and pressure plate. The double lining on the outer portion of the disc is attached to the inner hub by means of a number of spring dampers which cushion the initial take-up of the drive.

The gearbox input shaft locates in a bearing positioned in the end of the crankshaft which requires little lubrication as, with the gearbox in neutral or the clutch engaged, both shaft and crankshaft rotate at the same speed.

The pressure plate is actuated by a release bearing which slides on a locating sleeve and depresses the diaphragm centre fingers; this causes the annular plate to move away from the driven plate friction linings, and drive from the engine flywheel to the gearbox input shaft ceases.

The release arm is actuated by the clutch pedal and cable. The cable unit incorporates an adjuster with which to set the necessary clutch pedal to stop clearance.

On release of the clutch pedal, the diaphragm spring forces the pressure plate into contact with the linings on the clutch disc, which is then forced into contact with the engine flywheel; drive is then restored through the clutch assembly.

The main components of the clutch are shown in Fig. 5.1.

2 Clutch − adjustment

1 Every 6000 miles (10 000 km) the clutch cable ends should be lubricated, and the clutch play checked and where necessary adjusted. Proceed as follows.

2 Working inside the vehicle, measure the clearance between the clutch pedal and its stop and also check the clutch pedal free play. These two check points are shown in Fig. 5.2 together with the respective specified clearances.

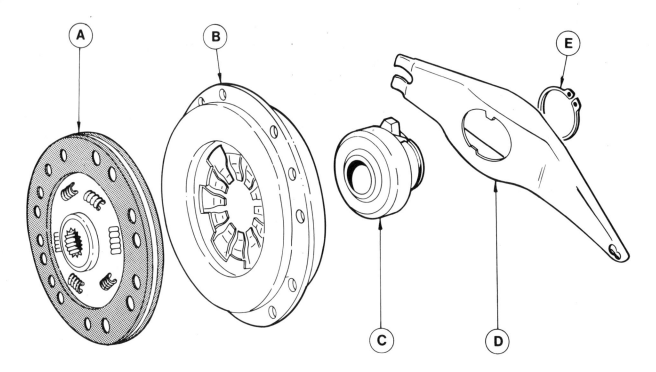

Fig. 5.1 The principal clutch components (Sec 1)

A Clutch disc
B Pressure plate
C Thrust bearing and hub
D Release lever
E Circlip

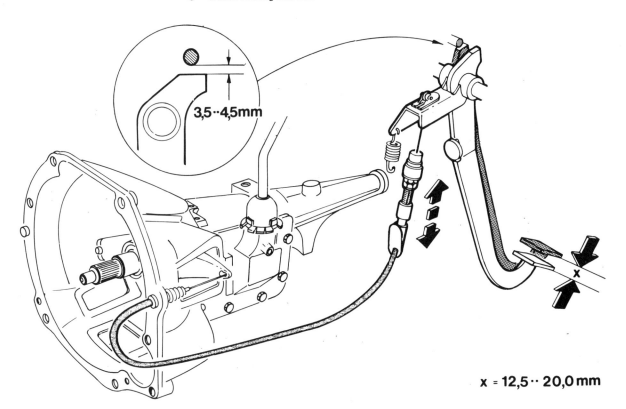

3,5··4,5mm

x = 12,5 ·· 20,0 mm

**Fig. 5.2 The clutch operating cable and pedal adjustment check
points (LH drive shown) (Sec 2)**

3   If adjustment is necessary, loosen the clutch cable locknut and adjustment nut and then turn the adjuster nut just sufficiently to give the necessary pedal free play.

4   Tighten the locknut and check that the clearance is still maintained.

3   Clutch operating cable – removal and refitting

1   Working inside the vehicle, loosen the clutch cable at the pedal by unscrewing the locknut and cable adjustment nut.

2   Extract the cable-to-pedal yoke retaining pin.

3   Raise and securely support the vehicle at the front so that you can work underneath it in safety.

4   Working underneath, pull the rubber gaiter from the clutch housing to expose the cable-to-release lever connection (photo).

5   Slide the cable inwards along the lever and withdraw the location nipple through the larger section of the slotted hole in the lever. Withdraw the gaiter over the cable.

6   Raise and support the bonnet. Press the cable seal from its location in the bulkhead and withdraw the cable.

7   Refitting the clutch cable is a reversal of the removal procedure. It will be necessary to adjust the clutch as described in Section 2.

4   Clutch pedal – removal and refitting

1   Working inside the vehicle, loosen the clutch cable locknut and adjuster nut.

2   Unhook the return spring (see Fig. 5.3) and then prise free the pedal shaft retaining clip from its location groove in the end of the shaft (Fig. 5.4).

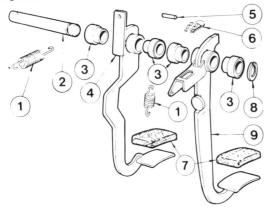

Fig. 5.3 The clutch and brake pedal components (Sec 4)

1	Return springs	6	Yoke
2	Shaft	7	Pedal rubbers
3	Bushes	8	Circlip
4	Brake pedal	9	Clutch pedal
5	Pin		

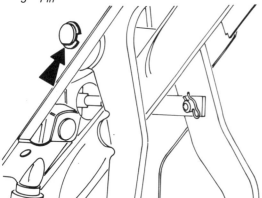

Fig. 5.4 Remove the shaft retaining clip (arrowed) (Sec 4)

3.4 Prise gaiter from housing to gain access to cable end

3   The pedal shaft can now be withdrawn from the brake pedal end sufficiently to allow the clutch pedal to be released.

4   Press the pedal retaining pin from the plastic yoke and withdraw it. Detach the clutch operating cable and remove the pedal complete with bushes.

5   Examine the clutch pedal and bushes for signs of wear and renew as necessary. Also check the pivot shaft for wear and if necessary fully remove it for renewal. To save taking the brake pedal assembly apart, feed a temporary rod through the brake pedal as the pedal shaft is withdrawn from the clutch pedal side. A wooden dowel rod of suitable diameter will do. This can then be withdrawn when the new pedal shaft is fitted.

6   Refitting the clutch pedal is basically a reversal of the removal procedure, but note the following special points:

(a)   Lubricate the pedal shaft and bushes with molybdenum disulphide grease

(b)   Reconnect the return spring and align the pedal with the opening before sliding the shaft back to the stop

(c)   Use a new pedal shaft circlip if the old one was distorted on removal

(d)   On completion readjust the clutch as given in Section 2

5   Clutch – removal

1   Remove the gearbox as described in Chapter 6, or the engine as described in Chapter 1.

2   Scribe an alignment mark on the clutch pressure plate assembly and the flywheel, then loosen each of the six pressure plate retaining

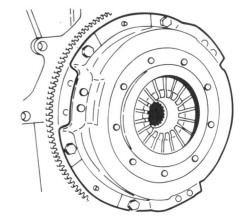

Fig. 5.5 View of pressure plate bolted to flywheel (Sec 5)

bolts a turn at a time in diagonal sequence until the diaphragm spring tension has been released.

3   Check that the pressure plate is not binding on the location dowels, then remove the retaining bolts and carefully lift the pressure plate and driven plate from the flywheel; note which way round the driven plate is so that it can be refitted correctly.

6   Clutch – inspection and renewal

1   The clutch disc (driven plate) should be examined for wear or deterioration of the friction lining and damper springs. If the linings have worn to within 0.04 in (1.0 mm) of the rivets, or if they are contaminated with oil, the disc should be renewed. The source of oil contamination must be rectified.

2   Check the machined faces of the pressure plate and flywheel for grooves and heavy scoring. If damage is evident, either renew the items as an assembly, or have the faces machined within limits by an engineering works. Dismantling of the pressure plate is not advisable for the home mechanic, as special jigs and tools are required.

3   The release bearing, located in the gearbox bellhousing, should be checked for wear by spinning it and observing whether there is any excessive wear or harshness present; bear in mind that it is pre-packed with grease. Renewal of this component is covered in Section 8. If the clutch disc or pressure plate are being renewed, it is always wise to renew the release bearing at the same time.

7   Clutch – refitting

1   It is important to avoid getting oil or grease onto the clutch disc friction linings or the pressure plate and flywheel faces. Install the clutch with clean hands and wipe down the pressure plate and flywheel faces with a clean dry rag before starting. A guide tool will be required in order to centralise the clutch driven plate.

2   Place the clutch disc against the flywheel with the hub facing outwards; the disc should be marked on the flywheel side and, if it is not fitted correctly, it will be quite impossible to operate the clutch.

3   Depending on the dimensions of the guide tool, this can be located into the crankshaft spigot bearing now, or alternatively after the procedure in the next paragraph.

4   Offer the clutch pressure plate up to the flywheel locating dowels ensuring that the previously made marks are in alignment, then tighten the retaining bolts finger tight (photo).

5   Check that the clutch disc is centralised so that the gearbox input shaft splines will enter the disc and locate the crankshaft spigot bearing on reassembly. If a centralisation tool is not available use an old input shaft or, if nothing else is available, a suitable diameter bar, moving it sideways and up and down to achieve the central position of the disc (Fig. 5.6).

6   With the guide tool still in position, tighten the pressure plate retaining bolts in diagonal sequence and in three or four stages, until the specified torque setting is achieved. Check the disc centralisation again, then remove the guide tool (if used).

7   Refit the gearbox as described in Chapter 6, or the engine as described in Chapter 1.

8   Clutch release bearing – removal and refitting

1   Remove the gearbox (Chapter 6) or engine (Chapter 1) so that the release bearing is accessible within the gearbox bellhousing.

2   If the engine has been removed it will be necessary to disconnect the clutch cable from the release lever and prise the rubber gaiter free from the bellhousing.

3   Withdraw the release bearing away from the gearbox as far as it will go; if the clutch bellhousing is being separated from the gearbox, the release arm assembly can be withdrawn at the same time. Using a pair of circlip pliers, disengage the circlip and withdraw the release bearing assembly over the gearbox input shaft; it may be necessary to rotate the circlip until the 'eyes' can be seen. Slide the release arm from the locating pin and withdraw it from the clutch bellhousing, then remove the circlip from the input shaft.

4   It is unnecessary to dismantle the release bearing and hub, as the parts are not serviced separately.

7.4 Locate the clutch disc and pressure plate assembly onto the flywheel. Note dowel pegs in flywheel to ensure correct location of plate

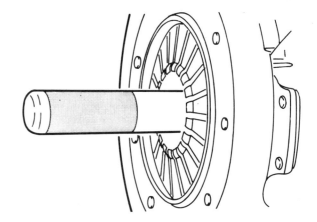

Fig. 5.6 Locate centering tool before fully tightening the pressure plate bolts (Sec 7)

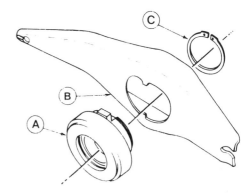

Fig. 5.7 Clutch release bearing (A), release lever (B) and circlip (C) (Sec 8)

5   Refitting the clutch release bearing is a reversal of the removal procedure, but the following additional points should be noted:

(a)   *Using a fine file, carefully remove any burrs from the hub locating sleeve, then smear it sparingly with high melting-point grease*

(b)   *Make sure that the release arm is located correctly in the dowel pin*

9   Fault diagnosis – clutch

There are four main faults to which the clutch and release mechanism are prone. They may occur by themselves or in conjunction with any of the other faults. They are clutch squeal, slip, spin and judder.

Clutch squeal

1   If, on taking up the drive or when changing gear, the clutch squeals, this is a sure indication of a badly worn clutch release bearing.

2   As well as regular wear due to normal use, wear of the clutch release bearing is much accentuated if the clutch is ridden, or held down for long periods in gear, with the engine running. To minimise wear of this component, the car should always be taken out of gear at traffic lights and for similar hold-ups.

3   The clutch release bearing is not an expensive item, but is difficult to get at, and requires the gearbox or engine to be removed for access to it.

Clutch slip

4   Clutch slip is a self-evident condition which occurs when the clutch friction plate is badly worn, oil or grease has got onto the flywheel or pressure plate faces, or the pressure plate itself is faulty. (It will also occur if the operating cable is too tight).

5   The reason for clutch slip is that, due to one of the faults listed above, there is either insufficient pressure from the pressure plate, or insufficient friction from the friction plate, to ensure solid drive.

6   If small amounts of oil get onto the clutch, they will be burnt off under the heat of the clutch engagement, and in the process will gradually darken the linings. Excessive oil on the clutch will burn off leaving a carbon deposit which can cause quite bad slip, or fierceness, spin and judder.

7   If clutch slip is suspected, and confirmation of this condition is required, there are several tests which can be made.

8   With the engine in second or third gear and pulling lightly up a moderate incline, sudden depression of the accelerator pedal may cause the engine to increase its speed without any increase in road speed. Easing off on the accelerator will then give a definite drop in engine speed without the vehicle slowing.

9   In extreme cases of clutch slip the engine will race under normal acceleration conditions.

Clutch spin

10 Clutch spin is a condition which occurs when the release arm travel is excessive, there is an obstruction in the clutch, either on the input shaft splines, or in the operating lever itself, or the oil has partially burnt off the clutch linings and has left a resinous deposit which is causing the clutch disc to stick to the pressure plate or flywheel.

11 The reason for clutch spin is that due to any, or a combination, of the faults just listed, the clutch pressure plate is not completely freeing from the centre plate even with the clutch pedal fully depressed.

12 If clutch spin is suspected, the condition can be confirmed by extreme difficulty in engaging first gear from rest, difficulty in changing gear, and very sudden take-up of the clutch drive at the fully depressed end of the clutch pedal travel as the clutch is released.

13 Check that the clutch is correctly adjusted and if in order, then the fault lies internally in the clutch. It will then be necessary to remove the clutch for examination and to check that the clutch disc moves freely on the gearbox input shaft splines, without binding or excessive slack caused by worn splines.

Clutch judder

14 Clutch judder is a self-evident condition which occurs when the gearbox or engine mountings are loose or too flexible, when there is oil on the faces of the clutch friction plate, or when the clutch pressure plate has been incorrectly adjusted during assembly.

15 The reason for clutch judder is that, due to one of the faults just listed, the clutch pressure plate is not freeing smoothly from the direction disc, and is snatching.

16 Clutch judder normally occurs when the clutch pedal is released in first or reverse gears, and the vehicle shudders as it moves backward or forward.

17 If on inspection, oil on the clutch linings is found to be the fault, the linings will have to be renewed and all traces of oil washed from the clutch components and housing. It will also be necessary to renew the faulty gearbox seal or engine rear oil seal, whichever is at fault. If the gearbox oil level is below normal then the gearbox seal is probably at fault, but if in doubt renew both engine and gearbox seals.

Chapter 6 Manual gearbox, overdrive and automatic transmission

For modifications, and information applicable to later models, see Supplement at end of manual

Contents

Specifications

Manual gearbox
General
Type .... 4 forward speeds, 1 reverse, Synchromesh on all forward gears. Overdrive optional extra

Ford designation:
    Standard .... Type F
    Heavy duty .... Type G
    Identification tag marking:
        Type F .... FOG
        Type G .... FOB

Lubrication
Oil type .... Hypoid gear oil, viscosity SAE 80EP, to Ford spec SQM-2C9008-A (Duckhams Hypoid 80)

Oil capacity:
    Type F (non-overdrive) .... 2.6 pints (1.5 litres)
    Type G (non-overdrive) .... 3.5 pints (2.0 litres)
    All types with overdrive .... 4.4 pints (2.5 litres)

Gear ratios (:1)

	Type F (wide ratio)	Type F (close ratio)	Type G
1st	3.96	3.65	4.41
2nd	2.28	1.97	2.35
3rd	1.41	1.37	1.51
4th	1.00	1.00	1.00
Reverse	4.238	3.66	4.67

Overhaul data

Countershaft gear axial play:
  Type F .... 0.005 to 0.017 in (0.15 to 0.46 mm)
  Type G .... 0.007 to 0.020 in (0.18 to 0.53 mm)
Countershaft diameter:
  Type F (wide ratio) .... 0.6837 to 0.6843 in (17.367 to 17.380 mm)
  Type F (close ratio) .... 0.7600 to 0.7604 in (19.301 to 19.314 mm)
  Type G .... 0.7610 to 0.7615 in (19.329 to 19.342 mm)

Overdrive

Type .... Laycock de Normanville, model J

Gearbox mainshaft

Diameter of oil transfer .... 0.9840 to 0.9650 in (24.485 to 24.511 mm)
Inside diameter of main case at oil transfer .... 0.9660 to 0.9670 in (24.536 to 24.561 mm)
Diameter at sunwheel .... 0.9410 to 0.9430 in (23.901 to 23.951 mm)
Inside diameter of sunwheel bush (where fitted) .... 0.9470 to 0.9490 in (24.052 to 24.103 mm)
Diameter at mainshaft spigot .... 0.5620 to 0.5625 in (14.274 to 14.2875 mm)
Inside diameter at spigot bearing .... 0.5628 to 0.5638 in (14.294 to 14.320 mm)

Operating pistons

Operating piston diameter .... 1.2492 to 1.2497 in (31.3297 to 31.7424 mm)
Operating piston bore diameter .... 1.2500 to 1.2512 in (31.75 to 32.0091 mm)

Pump

Pump plunger diameter .... 0.4996 to 0.500 in (12.6898 to 12.700 mm)
Pump body bore .... 0.5003 to 0.5009 in (12.7076 to 12.7228 mm)

Relief valve

Outside diameter of relief valve piston .... 0.2496 to 0.2498 in (6.3398 to 6.3449 mm)
Inside diameter of relief valve body .... 0.2500 to 0.2505 in (6.35 to 6.3627 mm)
Outside diameter of dashpot piston .... 0.9370 to 0.9373 in (23.799 to 23.8066 mm)
Inside diameter of dashpot sleeve .... 0.9375 to 0.9385 in (23.8125 to 23.8377 mm)

Speedometer pinion

Outside diameter of speedometer pinion .... 0.3105 to 0.3110 in (7.8867 to 7.9004 mm)
Inside diameter of speedometer bearing .... 0.3120 to 0.3135 in (7.924 to 7.9629 mm)

Sliding member travel from direct drive to overdrive
(Measured at bridge pieces) .... 0.0510 to 0.1000 in (1.2954 to 2.54 mm)

Minimum engagement/disengagement speed .... 30 mph (48 kph) (Top gear)

Hydraulic system residual pressure .... 20 lbf/in² (1.41 kgf/cm²)

Automatic transmission
General

Transmission type .... Ford C3
Transmission fluid:
Type:
  Black dipstick (up to Sept. 1980) .... ATF to Ford spec. SQM-2C-9007-AA (Duckhams Q-Matic)
  Red dipstick (from Oct. 1980) .... ATF to Ford spec. SQM-2C-9010-A (Duckhams D-Matic)
Capacity (approx) .... 11.4 pints (6.5 litres) (including converter)

Gear ratios (:1)

1st 2.47
2nd 1.47
3rd 1.00
Reverse 2.11
Converter .... 2.35 (maximum)

Torque wrench settings

	lbf ft	kgf m
Manual gearbox		
Clutch housing-to-gearbox bolts	41 to 48	5.6 to 6.5
Input shaft bearing retainer bolts	11 to 13	1.5 to 1.8
Extension housing to gearbox:		
Type F	33 to 36	4.6 to 5.0
Type G	40 to 44	5.5 to 6.2
Selector housing to gearbox:		
Type F	15 to 18	2.1 to 2.5
Type G	11.5 to 14	1.6 to 2.0
Mainshaft nut (Type G only)	25 to 29	3.5 to 4.1

	lbf ft	kgf m
Overdrive		
Pump non-return valve to main case	16	2.2
Pressure filter base plug	16	2.2
Speedometer drivegear retaining nut	50 to 60	6.9 to 8.3
Coupling flange retaining nut	80 to 130	11.0 to 17.9
Relief valve base plug	16	2.2
Automatic transmission		
Converter housing-to-engine bolts	22 to 27	3.0 to 3.7
Converter drain plug	20 to 29	2.7 to 4.0
Starter inhibitor switch	12 to 14	1.6 to 1.9
Oil pan to transmission housing	12 to 17	1.6 to 2.4
Downshift cable bracket	12 to 17	1.6 to 2.4
Downshift lever nut (outer)	7 to 11	1.0 to 1.5
Downshift lever nut (inner)	30 to 39	4.1 to 5.4
Brake band adjuster screw locknut	34 to 44	4.7 to 6.1
Oil line to connector	7 to 10	0.9 to 1.4
Connector to oil cooler line	12 to 14	1,6 to 2.0
Oil line connector to transmission housing	10 to 14	1.4 to 2.0
Governor to governor hub	7 to 9	0.9 to 1.3
Vacuum diaphragm bracket	1.17 to 2.17	0.17 to 0.3
Servo housing cover	7 to 9	0.9 to 1.3
Torque converter housing to transmission housing	26 to 28	3.6 to 5.3
Transmission extension to transmission housing	26 to 38	3.6 to 5.3

PART A: MANUAL GEARBOX

1 General description – manual gearbox

Two basic types of manual gearbox are fitted, these being designated type F and type G. The type fitted depends on the model and engine.

Both gearbox types are similar in design and have four constant mesh, helically cut forward gears and one straight cut reverse gear. All forward gear selection is by synchromesh operation.

The clutch bellhousing, selector housing and extension housing are separate castings and are bolted to the main gearbox casing.

The input shaft (main drive gear) and mainshaft are in line and rotate on ball-bearings. The mainshaft spigot runs in needle roller bearings, as does the countershaft (layshaft) gear assembly.

The synchronisers are of blocker ring and bar type and operate in conjunction with tapered cones machined onto the gears. When engaging a gear, the synchroniser sleeve pushes the blocker ring against the tapered gear cone by means of the three spring tensioned blocker bars. The drag of the blocker ring causes the gear to rotate at the same speed as the synchroniser unit, and at this point further movement of the sleeve locks the sleeve, blocker ring and gear dog teeth together.

In the F type gearbox the 1st/2nd gear synchronizer hub is a tight press fit onto the mainshaft and cannot be removed during overhaul. The mainshaft endfloat is controlled by selective circlips.

Reverse gear is obtained by moving the reverse idler gear into mesh with the countershaft gear and the spur teeth of the 1st/2nd synchroniser.

In both gearbox types a three-rail selector mechanism is used, whereby the rails are located in the housing and move in accordance with the gear lever selection position. The selector forks are located in position on the rails and these actuate the gear selection.

On the type F gearbox the selector forks of 1st/2nd and 3rd/4th gears differ in that they are slotted into their respective guides fixed to the selector rails.

2 Gearbox – removal and refitting

1   The gearbox can be removed in unit with the engine from the front of the vehicle as described in Chapter 1, or alternatively, separated from the rear of the engine and lowered from the vehicle. The following paragraphs describe the latter method.
2   Open the bonnet and disconnect the battery negative terminal.
3   Place a container of adequate capacity beneath the gearbox, unscrew and remove the drain plug, and allow the oil to drain. Refit the drain plug.
4   Jack up the front of the vehicle (unladen), and support it adequately on stands; allow plenty of room beneath the vehicle for lowering and removing the gearbox. Ensure that the handbrake is fully applied and chock the rear wheels.
5   From inside the vehicle cab, unscrew and remove the gear lever

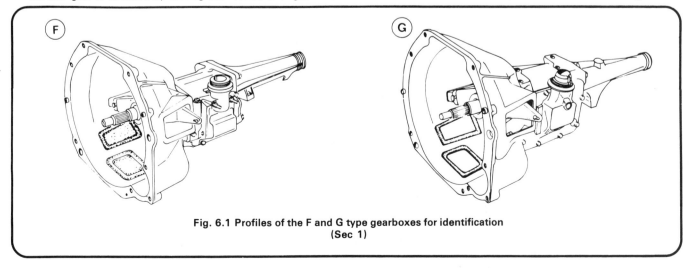

Fig. 6.1 Profiles of the F and G type gearboxes for identification
(Sec 1)

cover plate retaining screws and lift the plate and gaiter from the floor. From beneath the vehicle unscrew and remove the gear lever retaining cap, then carefully lift the gear lever from the gearbox and withdraw it into the cab.

6   Unscrew the clutch cable adjuster locknut and slacken off the cable adjustment at the clutch pedal.

7   Working underneath the vehicle, detach the reversing light leads at the gearbox connection.

8   Remove the propeller shaft as described in Chapter 7.

9   Prise the rubber gaiter from the gearbox bellhousing, and disconnect the clutch cable from the release lever.

10   Detach the gearbox earth strap.

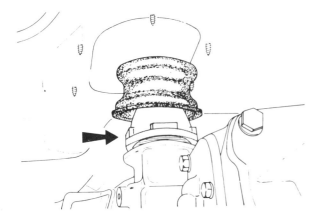

Fig. 6.2 Detach gear lever from underneath (Sec 2)

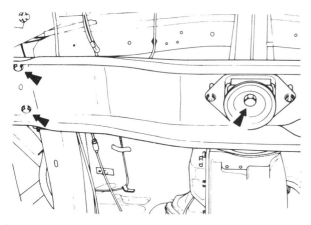

Fig. 6.3 Gearbox crossmember outer retaining bolts and the single gearbox retaining bolt in the middle (Sec 2)

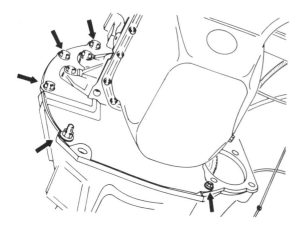

Fig. 6.4 Clutch housing bolt positions (Sec 2)

11   Disconnect and note the respective connections of the starter motor leads.

12   Unbolt and remove the starter motor.

13   Disconnect the speedometer drive cable at the gearbox.

14   Unbolt and remove the clutch housing cover.

15   Jack or block up the rear of the engine for support.

16   Position a jack (preferably a trolley type) under the gearbox to support it centrally.

17   Where an overdrive unit is fitted, disconnect the supply cables from it, noting their locations.

18   Unscrew and remove the respective clutch housing-to-engine retaining bolts.

19   Unscrew and remove the gearbox crossmember retaining bolts from the chassis on each side. A single central bolt retains the crossmember to the gearbox as shown in Fig. 6.3, but this can be removed after the gearbox has been withdrawn.

20   If an assistant is available, get him or her to steady the rear of the gearbox and support it whilst you pull it rearwards away from the engine. When the gearbox input shaft is clear of the clutch, the gearbox can be lowered and removed from underneath the vehicle. *It is most important during the gearbox removal that its complete weight is not allowed to hang on the input shaft, otherwise damage could occur to the shaft and/or clutch.*

21   On removal of the gearbox the crossmember can be detached by unscrewing the central retaining bolt.

22   To refit the gearbox, first ensure that the clutch driven plate is aligned to the crankshaft pilot bearing; refer to Chapter 5 if necessary.

23   Jack up the gearbox and carefully insert the input shaft into the clutch driven plate; if difficulty is experienced in engaging the splines it will help temporarily to select top gear with the gear lever and then to turn the gearbox output shaft until the splines engage. Do not allow the gearbox to hang on the input shaft.

24   Once the gearbox is fully entered, refit the clutch housing bolts and earth strap to prevent unnecessary strain on the input shaft.

25   If not already located, refit the rear crossmember support to the gearbox and then to the chassis on each side, but do not fully tighten the bolts until they are all located. The jacks can then be removed from under the engine and gearbox.

26   Reconnect the following:

     (a)   *Speedometer cable*
     (b)   *Reversing light wire connections*
     (c)   *The clutch cable to release lever (and relocate the rubber gaiter in the housing aperture)*
     (d)   *The overdrive cables (where applicable)*

27   Refit the starter motor and connect up the leads to it.

28   Refit the clutch housing cover and secure with the two retaining bolts.

29   Refit the propeller shaft, aligning the respective markings – refer to Chapter 7.

30   Insert the gear lever into the gearbox from within the cab and tighten the retaining cap down into the joint from beneath the vehicle.

31   Reposition the gaiter and tighten the gear lever cover plate retaining screws to the floor.

32   Remove the support stands and lower the vehicle to the ground.

33   Refer to Chapter 5 and adjust the clutch.

34   Refill the gearbox with the correct grade and quantity of oil (see Specifications).

35   Reconnect the battery leads.

3   Gearbox (type F) – dismantling

1   Place the complete unit on a firm bench or table and ensure that you have the following tools available, in addition to the normal range of spanners etc:

     (a)   *Good quality circlip pliers, 2 pairs – 1 expanding and 1 contracting*
     (b)   *Copper headed mallet, at least 2 lb (0.9 kg)*
     (c)   *Drifts, steel and brass, 0.375 in (9.525 mm) diameter*
     (d)   *Small containers for needle rollers*
     (e)   *Engineer's vice mounted on firm bench*
     (f)   *Selection of metal tubing*

Any attempt to dismantle the gearbox without the foregoing is not

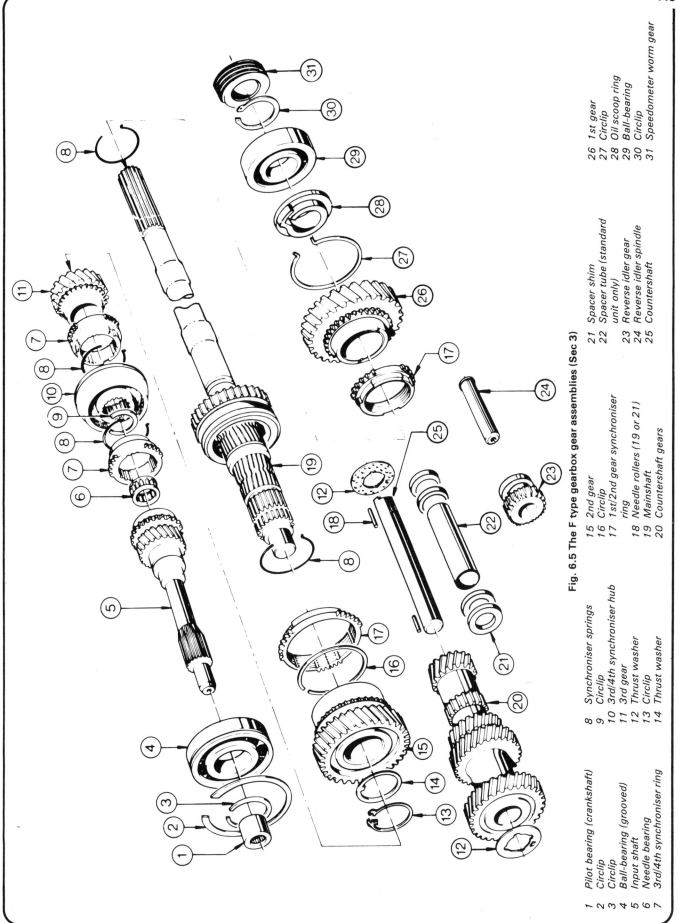

Fig. 6.5 The F type gearbox gear assemblies (Sec 3)

1 Pilot bearing (crankshaft)
2 Circlip
3 Circlip
4 Ball-bearing (grooved)
5 Input shaft
6 Needle bearing
7 3rd/4th synchroniser ring

8 Synchroniser springs
9 Circlip
10 3rd/4th synchroniser hub
11 3rd gear
12 Thrust washer
13 Circlip
14 Thrust washer

15 2nd gear
16 Circlip
17 1st/2nd gear synchroniser ring
18 Needle rollers (19 or 21)
19 Mainshaft
20 Countershaft gears

21 Spacer shim
22 Spacer tube (standard unit only)
23 Reverse idler gear
24 Reverse idler spindle
25 Countershaft

26 1st gear
27 Circlip
28 Oil scoop ring
29 Ball-bearing
30 Circlip
31 Speedometer worm gear

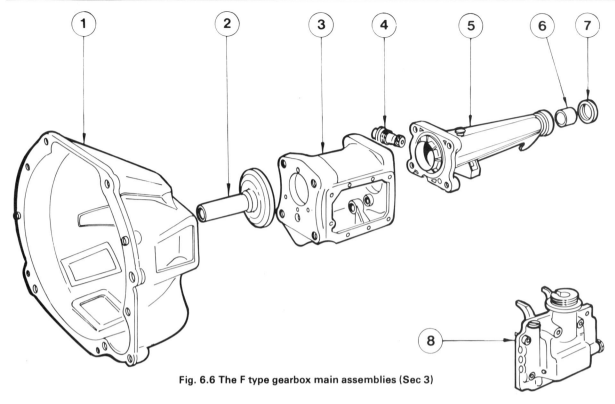

Fig. 6.6 The F type gearbox main assemblies (Sec 3)

1 Clutch housing	3 Gearbox casing	5 Gearbox extension housing	7 Oil seal
2 Guide sleeve	4 Speedometer drive pinion	6 Extension housing bush	8 Selector housing

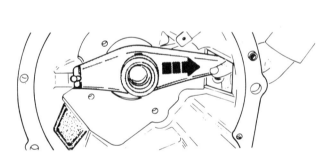

Fig. 6.7 Withdraw the clutch release lever through the side aperture in the clutch housing (Sec 3)

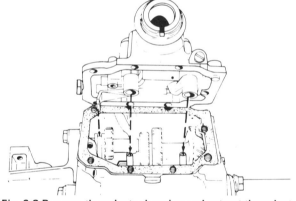

Fig. 6.8 Remove the selector housing and extract the selector forks (Sec 3)

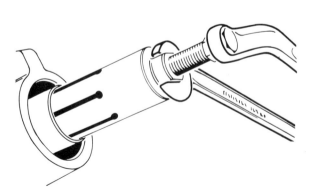

Fig. 6.9 Special tool No 16-025 used for removal of the extension housing bush (Sec 3)

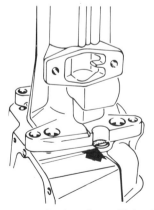

Fig. 6.10 Rotate extension housing sufficiently to enable the countershaft and cutaway to align as shown (Sec 3)

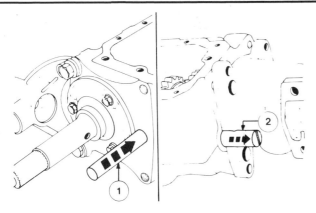

Fig. 6.11 Use a dummy shaft (1) to drive out the countershaft rearwards (2) (Sec 3)

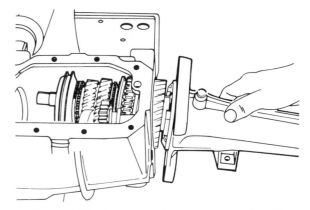

Fig. 6.12 Withdraw the mainshaft assembly (Sec 3)

impossible, but will certainly be very difficult and inconvenient.

2   Read the whole of this Section before starting work.

3   The internal parts of the gearbox are shown in Fig. 6.5 and the housing components in Fig. 6.6.

4   Unscrew and remove the four clutch housing retaining bolts and withdraw the housing from the gearbox front face.

5   Disconnect the clutch release lever and withdraw it through the side aperture of the housing (Fig. 6.7).

6   Unbolt and remove the gear selector housing, which is secured by 7 bolts. If the housing is stuck, tap it lightly with a block of wood to break the seal.

7   Extract the selector forks (1st/2nd and 3rd/4th), noting their location positions (Fig. 6.8).

8   Use a suitable implement and prise out the rear extension oil seal, taking care not to damage the housing. If the extension housing bush is to be removed you will need a suitable extractor, or if available, use the Ford special tool number 16-025 (Fig. 6.9). Should you not possess a suitable tool for removing the bush, get your Ford dealer to remove it for you. *It is important to note that both the extension seal and bush must be removed and renewed only when the extension housing and mainshaft are in their assembled positions.*

9   Unscrew and remove the four bolts retaining the extension housing to the gearbox. Partially pull the extension from the gearcase seat to the point where the extension can be rotated sufficiently to align the cutaway section in the flange with the countershaft, see Fig. 6.10.

10   Use a suitable diameter drift and drive the countershaft rearwards out of the gearbox, (Fig. 6.11). If possible use an old countershaft for this purpose. Cut it to a length of 7 inches (177 mm). The drift must follow the countershaft through as it is driven out so that the needle rollers are retained in position. Drive the drift through just far enough to locate the countershaft, its bearings and thrust washers, allowing them to drop in unison to the bottom of the gearbox.

11   Unbolt and withdraw the main drivegear bearing retainer from the gearbox front face. It is retained by three bolts.

12   Reach down in the gearbox, move the countershaft to one side and extract the input shaft through the front face of the casing.

13   The rear extension housing complete with mainshaft can now be withdrawn rearwards from the gearcase (Fig. 6.12).

14   Lift out the countershaft gears together with the thrust washers, but leave the dummy countershaft (drift) in position in the shaft to prevent the bearings from falling out until ready for inspection.

15   To remove the reverse idler gear, use a suitable length soft drift and drive the gear idler shaft out rearwards, then lift out the gear. Note which way round it is fitted (grooved shoulder section to rear).

16   Unscrew and remove the speedometer drive from the extension housing and then remove the bearing from the drivegear.

17   With the gearbox main assemblies now separated, they can be cleaned for inspection and further dismantling as necessary.

18   If it is apparent at this stage that the gear assemblies and their associated components are badly worn and have possibly suffered damage, it will almost certainly be more economical and practical to purchase a new or good secondhand gearbox instead of trying to repair the existing one.

19   The dismantling procedures for the main component assemblies are given in the following sub-sections.

Input shaft dismantling

20   Support the input shaft in a soft-jawed vice taking care not to damage the splines, then prise open the circlip retaining the bearing in position and remove it (photo). If suitable circlip pliers are not available for this purpose, lever the ends of the circlip apart using two screwdrivers.

21   Using suitable tubing, the input shaft bearing should preferably be pressed from the shaft. An alternative method is to rest the bearing outer track on a soft-jawed vice and to drive the shaft through the bearing using a soft-headed mallet.

22   If the main bearing is to be renewed, remove the circlip from the outer bearing race and transfer it to the new bearing (photo).

Countershaft gears dismantling

23   Withdraw the dummy countershaft from the gear unit and place the gear on the bench, together with its thrust washers and bearings which should be kept adjacent to their respective fitted positions ready for inspection. According to the gearbox type there will be 19 or 21 needle rollers at each end.

Mainshaft dismantling

24   First extract the mainshaft bearing retaining circlip from its groove in the extension housing (Fig. 6.13).

25   Support the extension housing and using a soft-headed mallet, drive the mainshaft from it, taking care not to damage the shaft or housing.

26   From the front end of the mainshaft, extract the small diameter circlip which secures the 3rd/4th gear synchro hub in position (photo). The synchro hub can now be withdrawn as a unit.

3.20 Input shaft bearing circlip removal

3.22 Remove the main bearing outer race circlip from its groove

3.26 Circlip removal from front end of mainshaft

3.29 Remove the mainshaft rear bearing retaining circlip

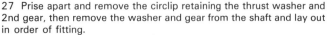

Fig. 6.13 Extract the retaining circlip from the extension housing (Sec 3)

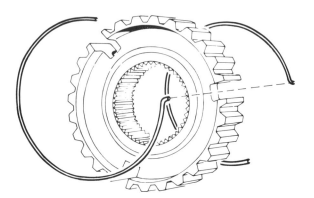

Fig. 6.14 Synchroniser spring location positions (Sec 3)

27 Prise apart and remove the circlip retaining the thrust washer and 2nd gear, then remove the washer and gear from the shaft and lay out in order of fitting.

28 Next on the shaft is the 1st/2nd gear synchro hub assembly. The hub itself is in unit with the mainshaft and cannot therefore be removed. The synchroniser springs and blocker bars can be removed though, but keep them in order of fitting and note how each spring is fitted relative to each other (Fig. 6.14).

29 Working at the rear end of the shaft, remove the circlip retaining the main bearing (photo).

30 Depending on facilities the speedometer drivegear, bearing and 1st gear can be withdrawn from the shaft collectively or individually. If removing collectively, either use a tube drift of suitable diameter and length to support the front face of the 1st gear and drive or press the shaft through from the rear, or use a suitable puller and withdraw the gear, bearing and speedometer drivegear from the rear. To remove individually, either use a puller or fabricate suitable U-shaped plates with which to support each component on its front face and with each plate in turn supported in a vice, drive the shaft through the respective components to remove them from the shaft.

31 To dismantle the 3rd/4th gear synchro hub unit, remove the selector ring, the blocker bars and springs, keeping in order of fitting.

32 For dismantling of the selector housing refer to Section 6.

4 Gearbox (all types) – inspection

1 With the gearbox dismantled the respective components can be cleaned, dried and inspected.

2 Examine all gears for excessively worn, chipped or damaged teeth. Any such gears should be renewed. It will usually be found that if a tooth is damaged in the countershaft geartrain, the mating gear teeth on the mainshaft will also be damaged. In any case it is not good policy to mesh new gears with worn gears as they are usually noisy when in operation.

3 Check the synchro hubs and components for signs of wear or damage. The synchro rings will almost definitely need renewing, the

tell-tale signs of excessive wear being if the oil reservoir grooves are worn smooth or uneven. Also, when fitted to their mating cones – as they would be when in operation – there should be no rock. This would signify ovality, or lack of concentricity. One of the most satisfactory ways of checking is by comparing the fit of a new ring on the hub with the old one. If the grooves of the ring are obviously worn or damaged (causing engagement difficulties) the ring should be renewed.

4 The sliding hubs themselves are also subject to wear and where the fault has been failure of any gear to remain engaged, or actual difficulty in engagement, then the hub is one of the likely suspects.

5 The ends of the splines are machined in such a way as to form a 'keystone' effect on engagement with the corresponding mainshaft gear. Do not confuse this with wear. Check also that the blocker bars (sliding keys) are not sloppy and move freely. If there is any rock or backlash between the inner and outer sections of the hub, the whole assembly must be renewed, particularly if there has been a complaint of jumping out of gear.

6 The thrust washers at the ends of the countershaft gear train should also be renewed as they will almost certainly have worn if the gearbox is of any age (as will the bearings).

7 The caged bearing between the input shaft and the mainshaft will usually be found in good order, but if in any doubt, renew the bearing.

8 All ball-bearings should be checked for chatter. It is advisable to renew these anyway, even though they may not appear to be too badly worn.

9 Circlips, which in the F type gearbox are all important in locating bearings, gears and hubs, should also be checked to ensure that they are not distorted or damaged. In any case a selection of new circlips of varying thickness should be obtained to compensate for variations in new components fitted, or wear in old ones.

10 Check and if necessary dismantle for overhaul the selector housing as described in Section 6 or 9 as applicable.

5 Gearbox (Type F) – reassembly

1 When reassembling the gearbox, rebuild each sub-assembly in

turn, taking care not to damage any parts. Lubricate each part as it is assembled using the specified gearbox oil, or with a multi-purpose grease where indicated.

Mainshaft assembly

2 Commence by assembling the 1st gear synchroniser hub, inserting the blocker bars and retaining them with the synchroniser springs. Arrange the springs each side so that their hooked ends are offset relative to each other as shown in Fig. 6.14.

3 Fit the synchroniser ring and 1st gear to the mainshaft.

4 Slide the oil scoop ring, larger diameter to the rear of the mainshaft, and the bearing onto the mainshaft.

5 Using a piece of suitable diameter tube drift the bearing into position on the mainshaft.

6 If a new mainshaft rear bearing or extension housing are being fitted, the location circlip thickness must be calculated. To do this, fit a circlip into the housing groove and press it outwards so that it butts against the shoulder. Use a depth gauge to measure the distance from the circlip top edge to the bearing stop flange – see Fig. 6.16. Measure the total width of the new bearing and deduct this from the previously noted height measurement to give the necessary thickness of circlip required. Circlips are available in varying thicknesses and it is important to fit one that when in position gives no axial play.

7 Smear the bearing location on the mainshaft with a multi-purpose grease and refit the bearing, pressing it into position. The bearing retaining circlip is then fitted loosely.

8 Relocate the speedometer drivegear, pressing in onto the shaft so that when fitted the distance from the speedometer gear rear face to the front face of the bearing is 3.238 in (82.25 mm) as shown in Fig. 6.17.

9 Check that the 1st/2nd synchro hub is correctly assembled. The sliding gear and hub markings must align, with the selector groove pointing forwards.

10 Slide the 2nd gear into position on the shaft together with its synchroniser ring and thrust washer (photo). Make secure by fitting the circlip, ensuring that it is fully located.

11 Reassemble the 3rd/4th gear synchroniser hub, fitting the blocker bars and springs so that when in position the springs are staggered but with their opposing ends located in alignment in the same blocker bar. The selector ring and hub markings must align when fitted (Fig. 6.18).

12 Slide the 3rd gear together with its synchroniser ring into position on the mainshaft and then locate the 3rd/4th synchro hub assembly. The long side of the hub unit must face the forward end of the shaft. Make secure by fitting the circlip, ensuring that it is fully engaged (photo).

13 The extension housing is now fitted onto the rear of the mainshaft. Warm the housing first by immersing in hot water. Locate the housing and then fit the previously loosely fitted circlip into its extension housing groove.

Countershaft reassembly

14 Insert the dummy countershaft into the countershaft gears and then fill the cavity at each end between the shaft and bore with a multi-purpose grease. Do not forget to fit the spacer tube (if applicable).

15 The spacer shims and bearings can now be refitted. Ensure that the longer needle roller bearings are inserted into the rear end of the shaft. With the needle rollers installed, fit the second spacer shims (photos).

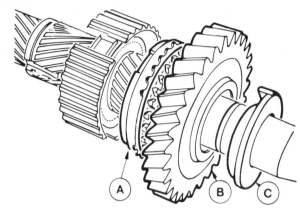

Fig. 6.15 Assemble 1st gear (B) with synchroniser ring (A) and oil scoop ring (C) (Sec 5)

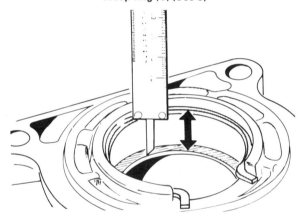

Fig. 6.16 Check depth for circlip requirement (Sec 5)

5.10 Fit 2nd gear synchroniser sleeve and 2nd gear

5.12 Fit 3rd gear, synchroniser sleeve and hub

5.15a Insert spacer shim into countershaft, followed ...

5.15b ... by the needle rollers smeared with grease

5.15c Fit second spacer shim when needle rollers are located

Input shaft

16 Smear the ball-bearing location on the input shaft with a multi-purpose grease, then locate the new bearing and press it into position using a suitable size tube drift of the same diameter as the bearing inner race. The bearing outer race circlip groove must be offset to the front.

17 With the bearing in position on the shaft, locate the small circlip to retain it in position and locate the large circlip into the bearing outer race groove.

Gearbox general assembly

18 If not already fitted, insert the new oil seal into the input shaft bearing retainer, ensuring that the seal lip faces the gearbox casing. The seal lip must be smeared with a multi-purpose grease prior to assembly.

19 Support the reverse idler gear in line with its shaft location holes in the gearbox and then pass the shaft through, driving it in with a soft-headed mallet until it is 0.008 to 0.031 in (0.2 to 0.8 mm) below the gearbox rear face. When fitted the gear must have its grooved hub section offset to the rear.

20 Smear the faces of the countershaft thrust washers with grease. Locate the front one in position as shown in the inside of the gearbox (Fig. 6.19).

21 Carefully lower the countershaft gear into position in the gearbox so that the thrust washer is not disturbed. Stick the rear thrust washer to the rear of the countershaft gear.

22 The mainshaft together with extension housing can now be fitted from the rear. The flange gasket should be located and stuck to the extension flange face by smearing with grease. This ensures that when the housing is turned after fitting the countershaft, the gasket is not

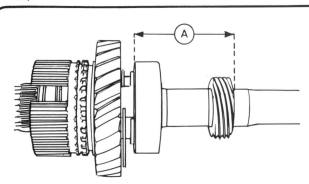

Fig. 6.17 Check bearing to speedometer worm gear clearance (Sec 5)

A = 3.238 in (82.25 mm)

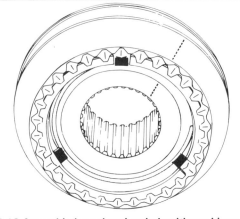

Fig. 6.18 Assembled synchroniser hub with markings aligned (Sec 5)

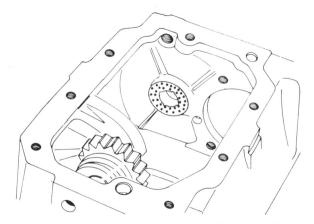

Fig. 6.19 Locate the front thrust washer for the countershaft gear (Sec 5)

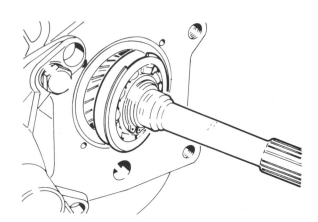

Fig. 6.20 Locate the input shaft (Sec 5)

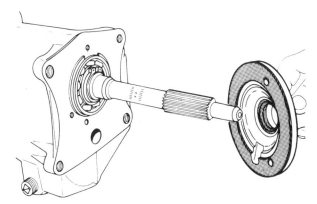

Fig. 6.21 Fit guide sleeve housing with gasket – align groove with oil hole in gearbox front face (Sec 5)

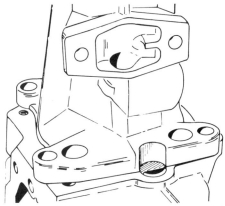

Fig. 6.22 Ensure that the countershaft end section is positioned as shown (Sec 5)

damaged. Initially the extension housing must be located so that the recess for fitment of the countershaft is aligned with the countershaft aperture in the rear gearbox face. This is shown in Fig. 6.22.

23 Lubricate the needle bearing with oil and locate it into the input shaft.

24 Locate the synchroniser ring onto the cone of the input shaft and then carefully fit the shaft into position through its location aperture in the front face of the gearbox (Fig. 6.20). When in position ensure that the circlip in the bearing outer race is butting against the gearbox front face.

25 Locate the guide sleeve housing flange gasket, smearing with grease for security of location during fitting. To avoid damaging the oil seal as the housing is fitted, temporarily tape the splines of the input shaft.

26 Fit the guide sleeve housing into position, ensuring that the oil channel in the gasket and housing is aligned with the oil hole in the gearbox (Fig. 6.21). Smear the housing retaining bolts with a sealing compound, insert and tighten to the specified torque. Remove the protective tape from the input shaft splines.

27 Position the gearbox so that the countershaft gear can be engaged with the corresponding mainshaft and input shaft gears, aligning the countershaft gear with the thrust washers and countershaft location holes in the gearbox front and rear faces. Carefully refit the countershaft from the rear, with the flat section on the rear end of the shaft positioned as shown in Fig. 6.22. Drive the shaft through, keeping it against the dummy shaft in order that the needle bearings are not dislodged.

28 With the countershaft fully located, the rear extension housing can be turned to align its bolt holes with those in the rear gearbox face. Smear the retaining bolts with sealing compound, insert them and tighten to the specified torque.

29 If a new extension housing bush is to be fitted it can now be driven into position using a suitable tube drift, or if available, Ford special tool No 16-015. It is most important that when fitted the oil return groove is located at the bottom of the housing to the rear, with the notch in the bush **not** situated over the oilway.

30 Smear the extension housing oil seal with grease and carefully tap it into position so that it butts against its location shoulder in the housing.

31 Locate the selector housing gasket onto the gearbox, aligning the bolt holes.

32 The 1st/2nd and 3rd/4th gear selector forks are now located into the grooves of their respective hubs. Ensure that each fork is fitted so that the casting number faces forwards.

33 Lower the selector housing into position, engaging the selector fork rods. The reverse gear selector fork must engage with the hub groove of the reverse idler gear (Fig. 6.8). Insert the retaining bolts (smear the threads with sealant) and tighten to the specified torque.

34 Reassemble the clutch release lever and bearing and locate them in the clutch housing.

35 Refit the clutch housing to the front face of the gearbox, smear the retaining bolts with sealant, then fit and tighten them to the specified torque.

36 With the gearbox now reassembled, check that all gears can be selected by temporarily fitting the gear lever and rotating the mainshaft with each gear engaged in turn.

37 On refitting, do not forget to refill the gearbox with the correct grade and quantity of oil. If new components have been fitted, the gearbox should be run-in as if it were new for the first few hundred miles.

6 Selector housing (type F gearbox) – removal, dismantling, reassembly and refitting

1 The gearbox selector housing can be removed with the gearbox in position. First drain the oil from the gearbox, then raise and support the vehicle so that it is safe to work underneath.

2 The selector housing is located on the side face of the gearbox and is secured with bolts. Before unscrewing these bolts, disconnect the gear lever from its location on top of the housing. Detach the reversing light switch wires (where fitted).

3 Remove the selector housing retaining bolts. Prise or tap free the housing from the gearbox and take it to the bench for cleaning and inspection.

4 Having cleaned the housing and its associated components, check for signs of obvious wear or damage to the selector forks, the fork carriers and selector rails. The selector fork carriers should have a precise movement along the rails with a distinctly 'notchy' feel when aligned for gear engagement. If a sloppy movement is apparent, dismantle the housing components as follows. Refer to Fig. 6.23.

5 Unscrew and remove the detent plug and extract the spring and ball (Fig. 6.24).

6 From the housing end remove the blanking discs and plug (or reversing light switch as applicable), then support the housing and drive out the selector fork carrier retaining pins (Fig. 6.25).

7 The respective rails can now be withdrawn and the carriers lifted out of the housing. Remove 1st/2nd rail, then the 3rd/4th rail, and as they are withdrawn collect the interlock ball and spring.

8 Extract the interlock plungers and then withdraw the reverse gear selector rail and fork. Remove the ball and detent spring, then the guide rod.

9 Clean and check the respective components for wear or damage and renew as necessary.

10 Commence reassembly by inserting the selector fork guide rod as shown in Fig. 6.26.

11 Locate the reverse gear selector rail and fork, having first inserted the spring and ball. Compress the ball and spring to enable the selector rail to be fitted.

12 Fit the 3rd/4th speed gear selector rail and fork carrier in a similar manner to the reverse rail and fork. Additionally, fit an interlock pin through the hole in the 3rd/4th selector rail. The reverse to 3rd/4th interlock plunger must also be located.

13 Insert the 1st/2nd selector rail and fork carrier. Locate the interlock plunger between 3rd/4th and 1st/2nd gear selector rails before pressing home the rail.

14 Drive the rail pins into position to locate the respective rails and selector fork carriers.

15 Smear the blanking discs with a sealant and carefully fit them into the end of the housing. Screw the blanking plug (or reversing light switch) into position.

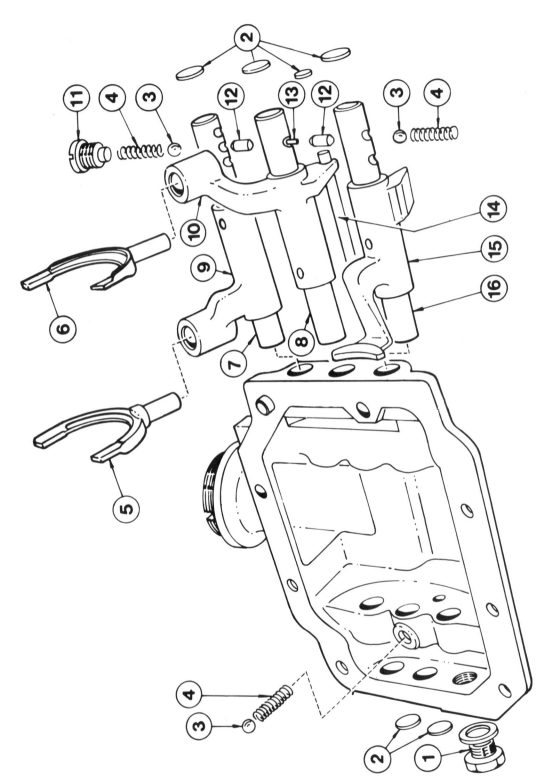

Fig. 6.23 Selector housing components – F type gearbox (Sec 6)

1 Plug with seal or reversing lamp switch
2 Blanking discs
3 Interlock balls
4 Springs
5 1st/2nd gear selector fork
6 3rd/4th gear selector fork
7 1st/2nd gear selector rail
8 3rd/4th gear selector rail
9 1st/2nd gear fork carrier
10 3rd/4th gear fork carrier
11 Selector detent plug
12 Interlock plungers
13 Interlock pin
14 Fork guide rod
15 Reverse gear selector fork
16 Reverse gear selector rail

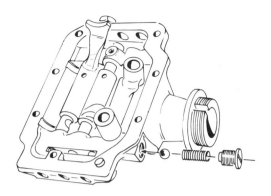

Fig. 6.24 Extract the spring and ball (Sec 6)

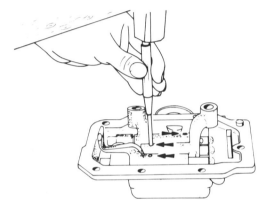

Fig. 6.25 Drive out the selector fork retaining pins (Sec 6)

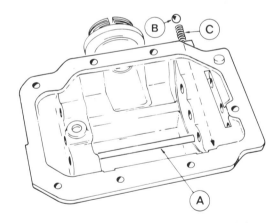

Fig. 6.26 Fit the selector guide fork rod (A). Spring (C) and ball (B) must be fitted before reverse selector rail (Sec 6)

16 Insert the 1st/2nd gear selector rail spring and ball and screw the detent plug in to secure. Smear the plug thread with sealant prior to fitting.

17 Align the selector rails in the neutral position before refitting to the gearbox.

18 Use a new gasket between the gearbox and selector housing joint faces and check that all traces of the old gasket are removed from the flange faces.

19 Refit the housing, taking care to align and locate the selectors with their respective forks. The forks must be fitted with their casting marks facing forwards.

20 Smear the housing retaining bolt threads with sealant, then insert the bolts and tighten evenly to the specified torque.

21 Reconnect the gear lever to the selector housing.

22 Refill the gearbox with the specified quantity and grade of oil, then test drive the vehicle to check gear selection.

7 Gearbox (type G) – dismantling

1 Position the gearbox unit on a clean workbench or firm table and check that before starting to dismantle you have the following tools at your disposal, in addition to the normal range of spanners etc:

- (a) *Good quality circlip pliers, 2 pairs – 1 expanding and 1 contracting*
- (b) *Soft-headed mallet*
- (c) *Drifts (steel and brass) 0.375 in (9.525 mm) diameter*
- (d) *Suitable containers for small components, particularly the needle rollers*
- (e) *Engineer's vice on a firm workbench*
- (f) *Selection of metal tubing (for driving out bearings and seals)*
- (g) *A bearing puller*

2 Read through the whole of this Section before starting work.

3 The gearbox components and their layout are shown in Fig. 6.27 and 6.28.

4 Unscrew and remove the clutch housing bolts and withdraw the housing from the front face of the gearbox.

5 Disconnect the clutch release bearing lever and withdraw it through the side aperture of the clutch housing.

6 Unbolt and remove the gear selector housing which is secured by eight bolts. Detach the gasket.

7 Before removing the rear extension housing, consideration must be given as to whether to renew the oil seal and housing bush, since *they must only be removed and refitted with the housing in position.*

8 The oil seal should always be renewed and this can be prised from the housing, taking care not to damage the housing.

9 The extension housing bush is best removed using Ford special tool number 16-011. This is similar to the tool shown in Fig. 6.9 (the bush removal method is also the same as that for the F type gearbox). Remove the four extension housing retaining bolts and remove the housing. Fit the new bush and seal when the extension housing is relocated on assembly.

10 Use a drift of suitable diameter and length and remove the countershaft rearwards from the gearbox. The drift or dummy shaft should be the same length as the countergear, so that on removal it can remain in the countershaft gear cluster to retain the needle roller bearings in position at each end (photo).

11 Allow the countershaft gear cluster to drop down in the gearbox so that it is disengaged from the input and mainshaft gears.

12 The rear extension and mainshaft can now be withdrawn from the rear of the gearbox.

7.10 Countershaft removal using a drift

124

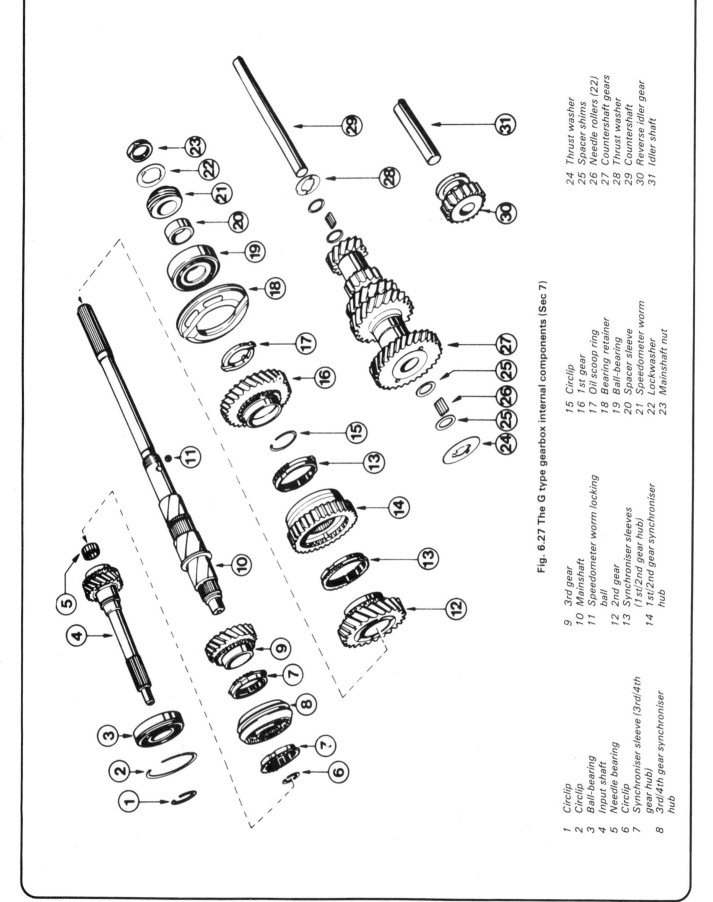

Fig. 6.27 The G type gearbox internal components (Sec 7)

1 Circlip
2 Circlip
3 Ball-bearing
4 Input shaft
5 Needle bearing
6 Circlip
7 Synchroniser sleeve (3rd/4th gear hub)
8 3rd/4th gear synchroniser hub

9 3rd gear
10 Mainshaft
11 Speedometer worm locking ball
12 2nd gear
13 Synchroniser sleeves (1st/2nd gear hub)
14 1st/2nd gear synchroniser hub

15 Circlip
16 1st gear
17 Oil scoop ring
18 Bearing retainer
19 Ball-bearing
20 Spacer sleeve
21 Speedometer worm
22 Lockwasher
23 Mainshaft nut

24 Thrust washer
25 Spacer shims
26 Needle rollers (22)
27 Countershaft gears
28 Thrust washer
29 Countershaft
30 Reverse idler gear
31 Idler shaft

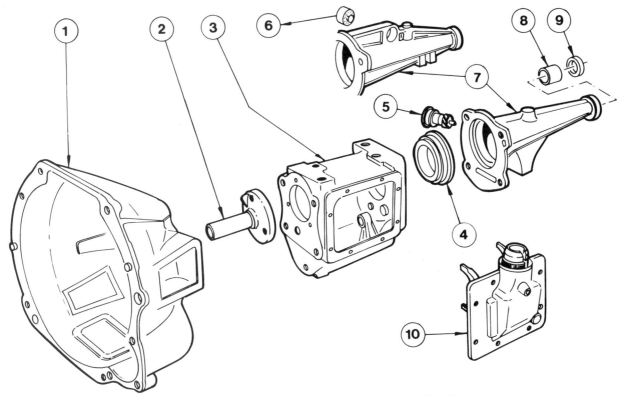

Fig. 6.28 The G type gearbox housing components (Sec 7)

1 Clutch housing
2 Main drive gear bearing
   retainer
3 Gearbox casing

4 Bearing retainer
5 Speedometer drive pinion
6 Rubber bush – extension
   housing

7 Extension housing
8 Extension housing
   bush

9 Oil seal
10 Selector housing

13 Unscrew the three retaining bolts and withdraw the input shaft bearing retainer housing. This housing contains the front oil seal so if it is intended to re-use the seal (unwise), tape the splines of the input shaft to prevent damaging the seal during removal and refitting of the housing. Pull or drive out the input shaft to remove it from the gearbox (photo).

14 To remove the reverse idler gear and shaft, draw it from the gearbox by screwing an M8 x 60 mm bolt into the end of the shaft. The bolt must be fitted with a nut and a suitable socket to act as a spacer

– see Fig. 6.29. Hold the bolt still and tighten the nut to draw out the shaft. Remove the gear, noting its direction of fitting.

15 With the main assemblies removed from the gearbox they can be cleaned and dried for inspection and further dismantling as necessary.

16 Should it be apparent at this stage that the gear assemblies and their associated components are badly worn and possibly damaged, it will almost certainly be more economical and practical to purchase a new or good secondhand gearbox instead of trying to repair the existing one.

7.13 Prise bearing outer track from main casing with a screwdriver

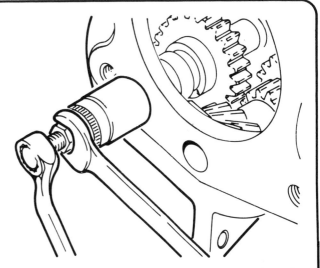

Fig. 6.29 Reverse gear idler shaft removal method (Sec 7)

17 The dismantling procedures for the main assemblies are given in the following sub-sections.

Input shaft dismantling

18 Refer to Section 3, paragraphs 20 and 21. The dismantling instructions are identical.

Countershaft gear dismantling

19 Withdraw the dummy countershaft from the gear cluster and lay the gear on the bench together with the thrust washers, spacer shims and needle roller bearings. There are 22 needle roller bearings at each end. Keep them separate and safe if they are likely to be refitted.

Mainshaft diamantling

20 Start at the front end of the shaft. Prise open the circlip retaining the 3rd/4th synchroniser hub and remove the clip.
21 To remove the 3rd/4th synchroniser hub and 3rd gear you will need a suitable puller which must be located as shown in Fig. 6.30. Draw the hub and 3rd gear from the shaft.
22 Support the mainshaft in a soft-jawed vice and remove the mainshaft nut at the rear, having released its lockwasher tab. The nut will be fairly tight so ensure that you have the shaft securely supported.
23 Depending on facilities, the speedometer drivegear can be withdrawn from the shaft using a suitable puller, or by fabricating a U-shaped plate which will slot in front of the gear. Whilst the plate is supported in a vice, and the mainshaft assembly supported by hand, use a soft-headed mallet and drive the shaft forwards through the gear to release it from its shaft location. On removing the speedometer drivegear, retain its interlock ball.
24 Withdraw the spacer sleeve.
25 The bearing and bearing retainer can now be pressed or driven off rearwards using a suitable tube drift, but take care not to damage the retainer or 1st gear. Remove the ball-bearing from the retainer when it is withdrawn.
26 Withdraw the oil scoop and 1st gear rearwards.
27 Prise open and remove the circlip retaining the 1st/2nd gear synchroniser hub in position. The synchroniser hub can then be removed from the shaft together with 2nd gear (Fig. 6.31).
28 To dismantle the synchroniser hubs first note the alignment markings on the hub and ring, then remove the rings and blocker bars, keeping them in their relative positions.
29 With the gearbox fully dismantled, the respective components can be cleaned and inspected as detailed in Section 4.
30 To dismantle the selector housing refer to Section 9.

---

8 Gearbox (type G) – reassembly

---

1 When reassembling the gearbox, rebuild each sub-assembly in turn, taking care not to damage any parts. Lubricate each part as it is assembled with the specified gearbox oil, or with a multi-purpose grease where indicated.

Mainshaft assembly

2 Commence by reassembling the synchroniser hubs. Locate the blocker bars and retain with the springs, which must be fitted so that their gaps are offset to each other but with the opposing hooked ends aligned as shown in Fig. 6.14. The check marks on the ring and hub must be in alignment when fitted.
3 Slide 2nd gear into position on the shaft together with its synchroniser ring.
4 Locate the 1st/2nd gear synchroniser hub unit and make secure by fitting the retaining circlip (ensuring that it is fully located). The peripheral groove of the sliding gear must face rearwards when fitted.
5 Slide 1st gear into position together with its synchroniser hub, followed by the oil scoop ring. The scoop ring is fitted with its oil groove facing the gear as shown in Fig. 6.33.
6 Smear the mainshaft bearing location in its retainer with multi-purpose grease. Similarly lubricate the ball-bearing, then locate the bearing into its retainer. The bearing and retainer are then pressed or drifted into position using a suitable piece of tubing.
7 Check that the bearing and spacer are fully located and then slide the spacer into position on the shaft.

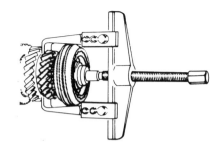

Fig. 6.30 Use a puller to withdraw the 3rd/4th gear synchro hub and 3rd gear (Sec 7)

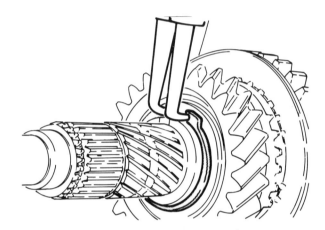

Fig. 6.31 Remove the circlip retaining 1st/2nd gear synchro hub (Sec 7)

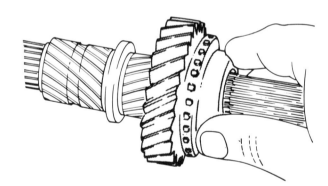

Fig. 6.32 Locate 2nd gear as shown (Sec 8)

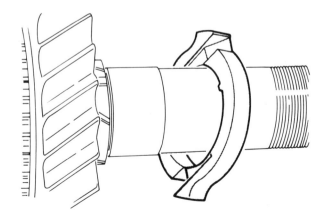

Fig. 6.33 Fit the oil scoop ring facing as shown (Sec 8)

8   Grease and locate the interlock ball and then slide the speed-ometer gear into position on the shaft and over the interlock ball.
9   Slide the lockwasher into position, engaging its tab into the recess in the speedometer drivegear. Fit the mainshaft nut and tighten it to the specified torque whilst supporting the mainshaft in a soft-jawed vice. Bend over the lockwasher tabs to secure the nut. (If a suitable torque wrench adaptor is not available, the correct torque for the mainshaft nut may have to be estimated).
10 Working at the front end of the shaft, fit the 3rd gear together with its synchroniser ring.
11 The 3rd/4th synchroniser hub is fitted next by pressing into position on the shaft using a length of tube of the correct diameter, ie to press on the hub inner shoulder. The synchroniser hub is fitted with the selector fork groove offset to the rear (Fig. 6.34).

Input shaft assembly
12 If the bearing has been removed for renewal, locate and press the new bearing into position on the front of the shaft. Smear the shaft with grease to assist fitment of the bearing.
13 With the bearing in position, fit the retaining circlip, ensuring that it is secure in its groove.
14 The larger circlip can also be fitted at this stage into the groove in the periphery of the outer bearing race.

Countershaft assembly
15 Insert the dummy countershaft into the countergear and then fill the cavity at each end with multi-purpose grease (between the dummy shaft and bore).
16 Locate the inner spacer shim, the 22 needle roller bearings and the outer spacer shim, then repeat at the other end of the gear (photo).

Gearbox general assembly
17 If not already fitted, insert a new oil seal into the input shaft bearing retainer housing so that when fitted the seal lip faces the gearbox side of the housing. Smear the seal lip with grease.
18 Before refitting any of the gear assemblies to the gearbox, check that it is thoroughly clean.
19 Hold the reverse idler gear in position in the gearbox with its selector groove in the hub section facing rearwards. Insert the idler gear shaft (lubricated with grease), and drive it into position from the rear. When fitted the shaft must be located so that its rear flat end aligns with the countershaft bore – see Fig. 6.35.
20 Smear the faces of the countershaft thrust washers with grease and locate them into their recesses in the gearbox. The large washer fits at the front end of the case and the tabs of both washers must point towards the casing when fitted (Fig. 6.36).
21 The countershaft gear and dummy shaft can now be carefully lowered into the gearbox. Take care not to dislodge the thrust washers.

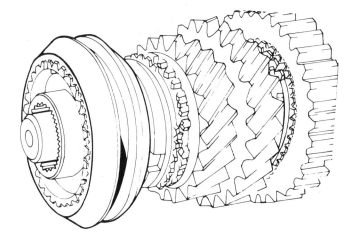

Fig. 6.34 Fit the 3rd/4th synchroniser hub (Sec 8)

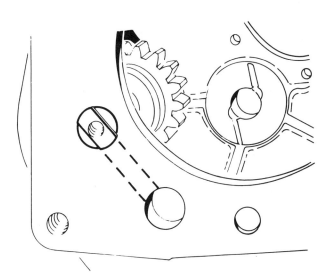

Fig. 6.35 Reverse idler shaft to be positioned as shown (Sec 8)

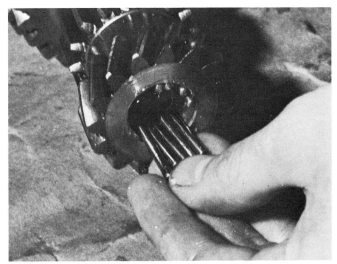

8.16 Insert the spacer shim, needle rollers and outer spacer shim to the countershaft gear at each end

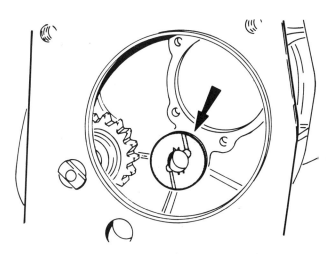

Fig. 6.36 Locate the countershaft thrust washers in the gearbox (Sec 8)

22 Locate the input shaft into the front face of the gearbox so that the bearing outer circlip butts against the gearbox (photo).

23 The input shaft bearing retainer housing can now be fitted, but first locate its flange gasket. Smear the gasket with grease to enable it to stick in position on the flange. It is most important to ensure that when fitted the gasket and bearing housing are correctly located, with the oil hole in the front of the gearbox aligned with the grooved section of the gasket and retainer housing (Fig. 6.37). Temporarily tape the input shaft splines to avoid damaging the retainer oil seal.

24 The retainer housing bolts must be smeared with a sealing compound prior to fitting. Tighten them to the specified torque.

25 Lubricate the needle roller bearing and fit it onto its location on the front end of the mainshaft (or into the input shaft). Slide the synchro ring onto the cone on the input shaft.

26 Smear the extension housing gasket with grease and locate it in position on the rear gearbox face.

27 The mainshaft can now be carefully fitted into the gearbox and the front bearing guided into the input shaft.

28 Turn the gearbox onto its side and align the countergear with the shaft location holes in the gearbox end faces, with the respective gears engaged with those of the input and mainshaft assemblies.

29 Check that the end thrust washers are in position and then push the countershaft through from the rear to locate the countergear. As the shaft is pushed through, keep it against the dummy shaft to ensure that the needle rollers are retained in position.

30 When in position the countershaft must be located with the shaft flat end section pointing along the recess for the reverse idler shaft in the extension housing.

31 Align the bearing retainer hole with the guide pin in the extension housing, locate the housing (Fig. 6.38) and make secure with the four retaining bolts. The retaining bolts must be coated with a suitable sealing compound before fitting.

8.22 Drift input shaft into position in front of gearbox

32 With the extension housing fitted, a new bush can be driven into position using a suitable piece of tubing. When in position ensure that the bush oil return groove is at the bottom of the extension housing to the rear and that the notch in the bush is **not** situated over the oilway.

33 Tap a new oil seal carefully into position in the end of the extension housing, lubricating its seal lip before fitting.

34 Refit the gear selector housing. Smear the housing gasket with grease and with the gears and selector forks in neutral, lower the

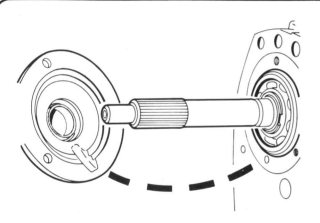

Fig. 6.37 Align the oil return ports as indicated (Sec 8)

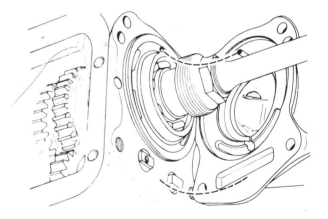

Fig. 6.38 Align the bearing retainer hole with the guide pin (top) (Sec 8)

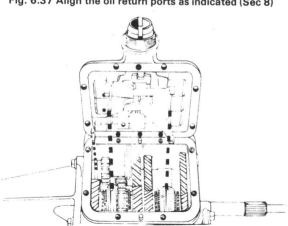

Fig. 6.39 Locate the selector forks and housing (Sec 8)

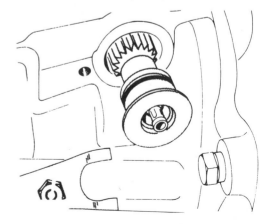

Fig. 6.40 Insert the speedometer drivegear fitted with a new O-ring seal (Sec 8)

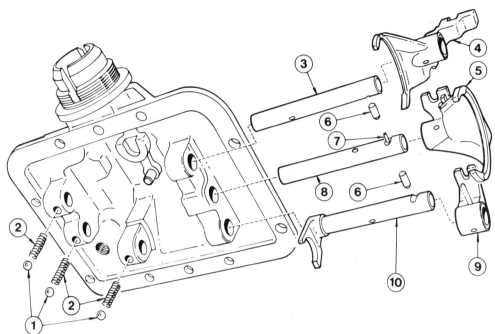

Fig. 6.41 The G type gearbox selector housing components (Sec 9)

1	Interlock balls	4	1st/2nd gear selector fork	7	Interlock pin	9	Reverse gear selector dog
2	Springs	5	3rd/4th gear selector fork	8	3rd/4th gear selector rail	10	Reverse gear selector rail with fork
3	1st/2nd gear selector rail	6	Interlock plunger				

housing onto the gearbox. The selector forks must fit into the synchroniser hub grooves as shown in Fig. 6.39. Tighten the bolts to the specified torque.

35 Refit the speedometer drive gear unit, with a new O-ring seal (Fig. 6.40).

36 Reassemble the clutch release lever and bearing and locate in the clutch housing.

37 Refit the clutch housing to the front face of the gearbox, smear the threads of the retaining bolts with sealant, then insert and tighten them to the specified torque.

38 With the gearbox now reassembled, check that all gears can be selected by temporarily fitting the gear lever and turning the mainshaft with each gear engaged in turn.

39 On refitting the gearbox, do not forget to refill it with the correct grade and quantity of oil. If new components have been fitted, the gearbox should be run-in gently for the first few hundred miles.

9 Selector housing (type G gearbox) – removal, dismantling, reassembly and refitting

1 To remove the housing and initially inspect it, refer to Section 6, paragraphs 1 to 4 inclusive. If the assembly is to be dismantled, refer to Fig. 6.41 and proceed as follows.

2 Extract the 1st/2nd gear selector fork to rail lockpin, then withdraw the rail and detach the selector fork, catching the ball and spring as they are removed.

3 Repeat the above operation for the 3rd/4th gear selector fork and rail.

4 Remove the reverse gear selector rail and fork in a similar manner to that given in paragraph 2.

5 Extract the interlock plungers by turning the housing onto its side.

6 Reassembly is a reversal of the removal procedure, but care must be taken to fit the selector forks correctly. Use new retaining pins for their location on the rails. Don't forget to insert the interlock fitting the respective rails and forks.

7 Refer to Section 6, paragraphs 17 to 22 inclusive, for details of housing fitment, but take note that the selector forks differ and instead of aligning the forks with the selectors, the selector forks must align with the grooves in the synchroniser hubs.

10 Speedometer driven gear – removal and refitting

1 Drive the vehicle onto a pair of ramps, or jack up and support at the front end with a pair of axle stands.

2 On models fitted with the type F gearbox, the cable is detached from its gearbox location by unscrewing the knurled knob. The driven gear unit is then unscrewed from the gearbox for removal.

3 On the type G gearbox, the cable is disconnected from the gearbox by removing the retaining bolt of the cable bracket and then pulling the cable clear. Withdraw the pinion bearing and pinion from the gearbox (Fig. 6.42).

4 Allow for a certain amount of oil spillage from both gearbox types when the speedometer driven gear unit is withdrawn.

5 If the gear itself is badly worn or damaged, it must be renewed. With the G type assembly, also renew the O-ring seal on the bearing.

6 Refit in the reverse order, having lubricated the gear and cleaned the area around the location aperture and the cable.

7 Check the gearbox oil level and top up to complete.

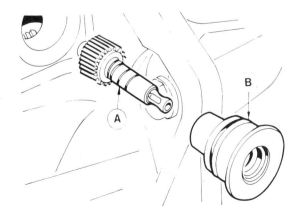

Fig. 6.42 The G type gearbox speedometer gear (A) and bearing (B) (Sec 20)

11 Fault diagnosis – manual gearbox

Symptom	Reason(s)
Weak or ineffective synchromesh	Blocker rings or bars worn or damaged
	Blocker bar springs weak
Jumps out of gear	Selector fork shaft detent springs weak or broken
	Selector forks or synchroniser and reverse gear location grooves worn
	Synchroniser, blocker ring and gear dog teeth worn
	Selector fork loose on shaft
Excessive noise	Incorrect grade oil in gearbox or level too low
	Worn ball-bearings or countershaft needle rollers
	Countershaft gear thrust washers worn
	Gear teeth excessively worn or damaged
Excessive difficuty in engaging gears	Clutch pedal free play out of adjustment
	Faulty clutch disengagemnet
	Worn gearchange lever or selector fork gates

Note: *It is sometimes difficult to decide whether it is worthwhile removing and dismantling the gearbox for a fault which may be nothing more than a minor irritant. Gearboxes which howl, or where the synchromesh can be 'beaten' by a quick gearchange, may continue to perform for a long time in this state. A worn gearbox usually needs a complete rebuild to eliminate noise because the various gears, if re-aligned on new bearings, will continue to howl when different wearing surfaces are presented to each other. The decision to overhaul, therefore, must be considered with regard to time and money available, relative to the degree of noise or malfunction that the driver has to suffer.*

PART B: OVERDRIVE

12 Overdrive – general description

An overdrive unit is fitted as a factory optional extra to those vehicles with a manual gearbox only. It is attached to the rear of the gearbox and takes the form of an hydraulically operated epicyclic-gear. Overdrive operates on third and top gears to provide fast cruising at lower engine revolutions. The overdrive is engaged or disengaged by a driver-controlled switch which controls an electric solenoid mounted on the overdrive unit. A further switch called an inhibitor switch is included in the electrical circuit to prevent accidental engagement of overdrive in reverse, first or second gears.

The overdrive unit is designed to be engaged or disengaged when engine power is being transmitted through the power line and also without the use of the clutch pedal at any throttle opening or road speed. It is important that the overdrive is not disengaged at high road speeds as this will cause excessively high engine speeds.

It will be seen from Fig. 6.43 that the overdrive gears are epicyclic and comprise a central sun wheel which is in mesh with three planet wheels. These three gears are also in mesh with an internally toothed annulus. The planet carrier is splined to the input shaft which is, in fact, the mainshaft of the manual gearbox. The annulus is an integral part of the output shaft.

When the overdrive is disengaged the engine torque is transmitted from the input shaft (A in Fig. 6.43) to the inner member of a uni-directional clutch (N) and then onto the outer member of the clutch (C) via rollers (B) which are driven up inclined faces, and wedge or lock the inner and outer members. The outer member of the clutch (C) forms part of the combined annulus (H) and the output shaft (D). Thus, as the gear train is not operative the drive is direct through the overdrive unit.

Mounted on the externally splined extension shaft (F) of the sun gear is the cone clutch (E) and this is pressed onto the annulus by a number of springs which press against the overdrive unit casing. The spring pressure is transmitted to the clutch member by a thrust ring and ball-bearing, so causing the inner friction lining of the cone clutch to be in contact with the outer cone of the annulus (H) and rotate with the annulus whilst the springs and thrust ring remain stationary.

As the sun wheel is splined to the clutch member, the whole geartrain is locked together so permitting overrun and engine torque in reverse gear to be transmitted through the overdrive unit. Also an additional load is imparted to the clutch during overrun and reverse conditions by the sun wheel, which, due to the special helix angle of the gear teeth, thrusts rearwards and has for its reaction member the cone clutch.

When the overdrive unit is engaged, the cone clutch takes up a new position, whereby it is no longer in contact with the annulus, but has now moved rearwards so that its outer friction lining is in contact with the brake ring which is part of the overdrive unit casing. The sun wheel to which the clutch is attached is now held still. The planet carrier rotates with the input shaft (A) and the three planet wheels are caused to rotate about their own axis and drive the annulus at a greater speed than the input shaft. This is made possible because the uni-directional clutch outer member can overrun the inner member. Hydraulic pressure generated by a pump in the overdrive unit acts on two pistons when a little valve is opened and moves the cone clutch rearwards. The little valve is controlled by the solenoid which is operated by the driver using an electric switch. This hydraulic pressure is sufficient to overcome the spring pressure that holds the clutch member onto the annulus and causes the clutch to engage with the brake ring and hold the sunwheel at rest. As the overdrive unit is attached to the rear of the gearbox, it is able to share the oil in the gearbox. The cam-operated plunger pump draws the oil from the overdrive oil sump and via drillings, passes it to the two operating piston chambers, the ball type operating valve and the pressure relief valve. Oil is also passed to the various other parts of the overdrive unit for lubrication purposes. (Figs. 6.44 and 6.45).

When the driver moves the overdrive switch to the 'engaged' position current passes to the solenoid and causes the operating valve to open. Pressure built up in the hydraulic system causes the two pistons to move against the action of the springs which hold the sliding member onto the annulus. Therefore, the sliding member is moved into contact with the brake ring.

Oil continues to be pumped into the hydraulic operating system, so compressing the modulator springs that are inside the pistons, resulting in a cushioning effect by the progressive application of the load between the sliding member and the brake ring. As the sunwheel is now in a locked condition and the planet gears are free to revolve, the overdrive condition is in evidence. Any further delivery of oil will open the pressure relief valve which will allow oil to pass to the various components for lubrication pruposes and then return to the overdrive oil sump.

When the driver moves the overdrive switch to the 'disengaged' position, current will cease to flow to the solenoid and the operating valve will close. The spring load on the sliding member will force oil to pass from the piston chambers whilst, at the same time, oil will continue to be pumped into the circuit. The sliding member is, therefore, disengaged from the brake ring and this time engaged with the annulus at a controlled rate.

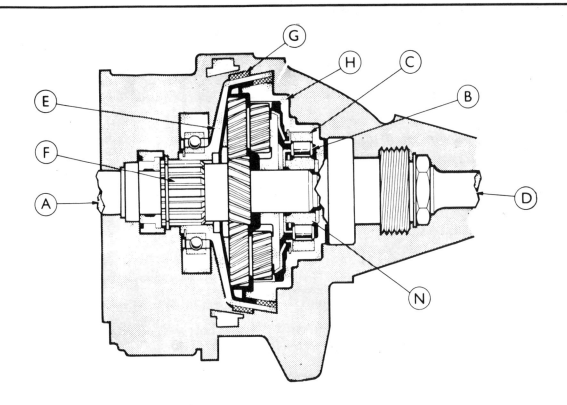

Fig. 6.43 Sectional view of overdrive unit (Sec 12)

A   Input shaft
B   Rollers

C   Outer member –
     unidirectional clutch
D   Output shaft

E   Cone clutch
F   Extension shaft
G   Friction band

H   Annulus
N   Unidirectional clutch
     inner member

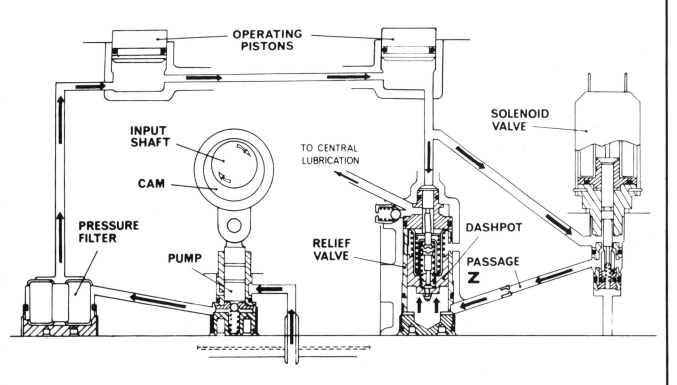

Fig. 6.44 Hydraulic circuit – overdrive condition (Sec 12)

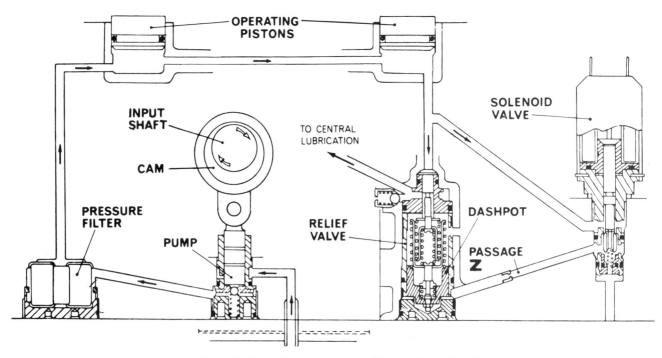

Fig. 6.45 Hydraulic circuit – direct drive condition (Sec 12)

13 Overdrive – removal and refitting

1   It should not be necessary to remove the overdrive unit from the vehicle to attend to the following: Solenoid and operating valve, relief and low pressure valve, pump and non-return valve.

2   If the unit as a whole requires overhaul it must be removed from the vehicle together with the gearbox as described in Section 2 and unbolted from the gearbox. It should however, be pointed out that several special tools are required to dismantle and reassemble the overdrive unit, so before work commences make sure that these are available. Illustrations of tools are shown in Figs. 6.47, 6.48 and 6.49. They are usually to be found at the local Ford agents.

3   Before beginning the sequence to remove the gearbox and overdrive unit it is preferable to drive the vehicle and engage overdrive and then disengage with the clutch depressed. This will release the spline loading between the planet carrier and uni-directional clutch which can make removal difficult.

4   Refitting is a reversal of the removal procedure.

14 Overdrive – dismantling, overhaul and reassembly

1   Refer to Fig. 6.46 which shows all the components of the overdrive unit.

2   Using a screwdriver or small chisel, bend back the tab washers that lock the four nuts that secure the operating piston bridge pieces and unscrew the four nuts. Lift away the four nuts and tab washers followed by the two bridge pieces.

3   Unscrew and remove the six nuts that secure the main casing to the rear casing in a progressive manner, as these two parts will be under the influence of the clutch return spring pressure. Note the position of the copper washers which fit on the two studs at the top of the casing.

4   The main casing complete with brake ring can now be separated from the rear casing.

5   Lift out the sliding member assembly complete with the sun wheel followed by the planet carrier assembly. This should be done with care as it is easy accidentally to damage the oil catcher which is located under the planet carrier assembly.

6   To dismantle the main casing and brake ring, first tap the brake ring from its spigot in the main casing using a suitable drift.

7   Using a pair of pliers carefully remove the two operating pistons.

8   Unscrew and remove the six bolts and spring washers securing the sump to the main casing. Lift away the sump, gasket and suction filter.

9   To remove the relief valve and dashpot assembly a special tool is now necessary. It has a part number of L354A. Remove the relief valve and then withdraw the dashpot piston complete with its component springs and cap, followed by the residual pressure spring. It should be noted that this spring is the only loose spring in the general assembly.

10 The relief valve piston assembly can now be withdrawn by pulling down carefully using a pair of pliers.

11 A further special tool is required to remove the relief valve. Using tool number 401A inserted into the now exposed relief valve bore, withdraw the relief valve together with the dashpot sleeve. Take great care not to damage these parts during removal.

12 Using tool number L354A undo and remove the pump plug, taking care not to lose the non-return valve spring and ball-bearing.

13 The pump valve seat can now be withdrawn. The pump body will be held in position by its O-ring, so to remove this hook a piece of wire into the inlet port and draw the assembly downwards. To remove the pressure filter use tool number L354A and unscrew the pressure filter base plug. The filter element will be released with the plug. Note the aluminium washer which locates on the shoulder in the filter bore.

14 Using an 1 inch (25 mm) AF open-ended spanner unscrew the solenoid control valve. Do not use a wrench on the cylindrical body as it will be irreparably damaged.

15 With a screwdriver carefully remove the circlip from the sun wheel extension and lift out the sun wheel.

16 Again using a screwdriver remove the circlip from its groove on the cone clutch hub and tap the clutch from the thrust ring bearing with a soft-faced hammer.

17 If necessary the bearing may be removed from its housing using a vice and suitable packing. It will be necessary to remove the larger circlip which retains it before removal commences.

18 Using a screwdriver, remove the circlip which retains the uni-directional clutch. Lift away the oil thrower.

19 Place tool number 178A over the now exposed uni-directional clutch and lift the inner member complete with rollers into the special tool. Lift away the bronze thrust washer.

20 Withdraw the speedometer driven gear and bearing.

21 To remove the annulus first drive a centre punch into the welch plug located at the top of the rear casing and lever it out.

22 Using a pair of circlip pliers expand the circlip which secures the annulus bearing.

23 Place the rear casing vertically over supports and with a light blow

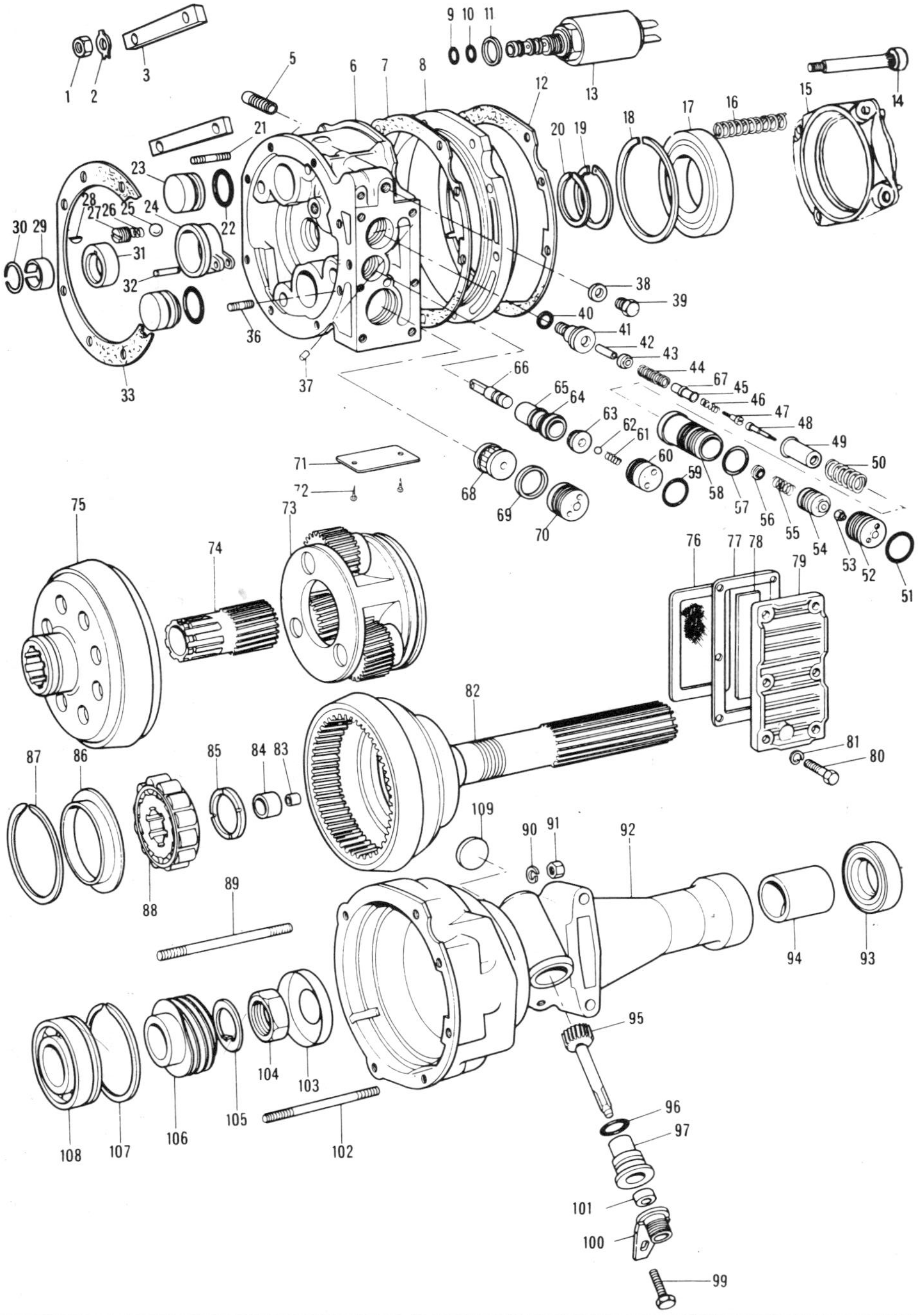

Fig. 6.46 Overdrive unit components (Sec 14)

1 Nut
2 Tab washer
3 Bridge piece
4 Breather
5 Main case
6 Gasket
7 Gasket
8 Brake ring
9 O-ring
10 O-ring
11 Washer
12 Gasket
13 Solenoid
14 Thrust pin
15 Thrust ring
16 Clutch return spring
17 Thrust ball race
18 Retaining circlip
19 Circlip for sliding member
20 Circlip for sunwheel
21 Stud
22 O-ring
23 Operating piston
24 Pump strap
25 Steel ball
26 Lubrication relief valve spring
27 Lubrication relief valve plug
28 Woodruff key
29 Spring ring for mainshaft
30 Circlip
31 Cam
32 Pump pin
33 Gasket
36 Stud
37 Restrictor plug
38 Washer
39 Pressure tapping plug
40 O-ring
41 Relief valve body
42 Relief valve spindle
43 Relief valve spring plate
44 Relief valve spring
45 Relief valve spring cup
46 Residual spring
47 Relief valve spindle
48 Dashpot spindle
49 Dashpot spring cup
50 Dashpot spring
51 O-ring
52 Dashpot plug
53 Dashpot piston locknut
54 Dashpot piston
55 Double dashpot spring
56 Spring retainer
57 O-ring
58 Dashpot sleeve
59 O-ring
60 Pump plug
61 Non-return valve spring
62 Steel ball
63 Non-return valve seat
64 O-ring
65 Pump body
66 Pump plunger
67 Packing washer
68 Pressure filter
69 Pressure filter washer
70 Pressure filter plug
71 Name plate
72 Securing screws
73 Planet carrier assembly
74 Sun wheel
75 Clutch sliding member
76 Sump filter
77 Sump gasket
78 Sump magnet
79 Sump
80 Sump setscrew
81 Shakeproof washer
82 Annulus
83 Restrictor plug
84 Mainshaft support bush
85 Thrust washer
86 Oil thrower
87 Circlip
88 Unidirectional clutch
89 Stud
90 Shakeproof washer
91 Nut
92 Rear case
93 Oil seal
94 Bearing bush
95 Speedo driven gear
96 O-ring
97 Speedo gear bearing
99 Setscrew
100 Retainer
101 Oil seal
102 Stud
103 Weir
104 Locking nut
105 Tab washer
106 Speedo driving gear
107 Annulus ball race circlip
108 Annulus front ball race
109 Welch plug

from a soft-faced hammer on the end of the annulus, drive the annulus complete with bearing downwards from the rear casing.

24 Unscrew and remove the nut that secures the speedometer driving gear and with the aid of a universal puller withdraw the ball-race.

25 The overdrive unit is now fully dismantled and may be inspected for wear.

26 Inspect the teeth and cone surface of the annulus for wear. Check that the uni-directional clutch rollers are not chipped and that the inner and outer members are free from damage.

27 Examine the spring and cage for distortion. Check the lubrication port at the rear of the annulus is clear.

28 Inspect the rear casing bush and oil seal for wear or damage.

29 Examine the clutch linings on the sliding member for signs of excessive wear or overheating. Should there be signs of these conditions the whole sliding member assembly must be removed. It is not possible to fit new linings as these are precision machined after bonding.

30 Make sure that the ball-race rotates smoothly as this can be a source of noise when in direct gear.

31 Inspect the clutch return springs for any signs of distortion, damage or loss of springiness.

32 Check the sun wheel teeth for signs of wear or damage.

33 Inspect the main casing for cracks or damage. Examine the operating cylinder bores for scores or wear. Check the operating pistons for wear and renew the sealing rings if there is any sign of damage.

34 Check the pump plunger assembly. Ensure that the strap is a good fit on the mainshaft cam and that there is no excess play between the plunger and strap.

35 Should the pump plunger assembly be worn or damaged, this must be renewed as a complete assembly.

36 WIth the non-return valve assembly clean, inspect the ball and valve seat and also the O-rings for signs of damage.

37 Check the relief valve and dashpot assembly for wear. The pistons must move freely in their respective housings. Ensure that the rings are in good order.

38 Do not dismantle the dashpot and relief valve piston assemblies, otherwise the pre-determined spring pressures will be disturbed.

39 Finally examine the O-rings on the solenoid valve for damage; if evident they should be renewed together with the sealing washers.

40 Clean the sump filter in petrol and if any particles are stuck in the gauze, rub with an old toothbrush. Wipe the magnetic plug free of any metallic particles.

41 Reassembly of the unit can commence after any damaged or worn parts have been exchanged and new gaskets and seals obtained. Do not use jointing compound during assembly.

42 Fit a new annulus ball-race and then position the speedometer driving gear so that the plain portion is facing the ball-race. Secure with the nut and a new locking washer. Tighten the nut to the specified torque.

43 Place the ball-race circlip in the rear casing and expand using a pair of circlip pliers.

44 Press the annulus through the circlip and into the casing until the bearing is fully home and the circlip is located in its groove. This must be done carefully so that the rear bush and oil seal are not damaged.

45 Fit a new welch plug and secure by striking lightly in the centre with a suitable size flat faced punch.

46 Next position the spring and inner member of the uni-directional clutch into the cage, locating the spring so that the cage is spring loaded in an anti-clockwise direction when viewed from the front.

47 Place this assembly onto tool 178A with the open side of the cage uppermost and feed the clutch in a clockwise direction until all the rollers are in place. Refit the bronze thrust washer in the recess in the annulus.

48 Transfer the uni-directional clutch assembly from the special assembly tool into its outer member in the annulus.

49 Refit the oil thrower and secure with the circlip. Check that the clutch rotates in an anti-clockwise direction only.

50 To assemble the clutch sliding member assembly, fit the ball-race into its housing and secure with the large circlip.

51 Place this assembly onto the hub of the cone clutch and fit the circlip into its groove.

52 Insert the sun wheel into the hub and refit the circlip onto the sun wheel extension.

53 Lightly smear the operating pistons with oil and refit to the main casing.

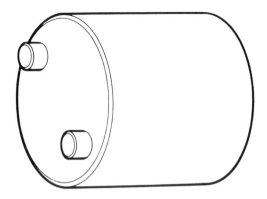

Fig. 6.47 Special tool L354A – dowelled plug spanner (Sec 14)

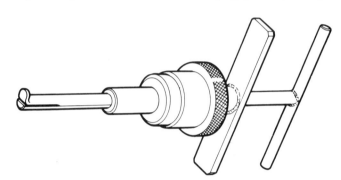

Fig. 6.48 Special tool 401A – relief valve body and dashpot sleeve remover (Sec 14)

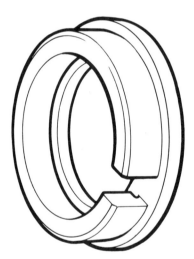

Fig. 6.49 Special tool 178A – assembly ring for unidirectional clutch (Sec 14)

54 Place a new gasket into the main casing and fit the brake ring, ensuring it is fully home on its spigot location.

55 Before refitting the relief valve and dashpot assembly ensure that all component parts are clean and lightly oiled. Insert the relief body in the bore, and using the relief valve outer sleeve push it fully home. Note the end with the O-ring is nearest to the outside of the casing.

56 Next place the relief valve spring and piston assembly into the dashpot cup, taking care that the ends of the residual pressure spring are correctly located.

57 Place these parts in the relief valve outer sleeve whilst at the same time engaging the relief valve piston in its housing.

58 Finally fit the base plug and tighten flush with the housing to the specified torque.

59 Place the pump non-return valve spring in the non-return valve plug and then place the ball on the spring.
60 The non-return valve seat can now be located on the ball and the complete assembly screwed into the main casing using tool L354A. Tighten to the specified torque.
61 Refit the pressure filter and new aluminium washer. Tighten the plug to the specified torque wrench setting.
62 Refit the overdrive sump, suction filter and gasket, and secure with the six bolts and spring washers.
63 Refit the solenoid control valve and tighten firmly using an open-ended spanner.
64 Mount the rear casing assembly vertically in a bench vice and insert the planet carrier assembly. The gears may be meshed in any position.
65 Place the sliding member assembly complete with clutch non return springs onto the cone of the annulus, at the same time engaging the sun wheel with the planet gears. Fit the brake ring into its spigot in the tail casing using a new joint washer on both sides.
66 Position the main casing assembly onto the thrust housing pins, at the same time entering the studs in the brake ring.
67 Fit the two operating piston bridge pieces and secure with the four nuts and new tab washers.
68 Fit the six nuts which secure the rear and main casing assemblies, ensuring that the two copper washers are correctly located on the two top studs. It will be observed that as the nuts are tightened the clutch return spring pressure will be felt.
69 The unit is now ready for refitting to the gearbox.

15 Solenoid control valve (overdrive) – removal, testing and refitting

1 The solenoid and operating valve are a self-contained factory sealed unit.
2 Disconnect the two terminals at the rear of the solenoid noting which way round the cables are fitted.
3 Using a 1 inch (25 mm) AF open-ended spanner unscrew the

assembly. Do not use a wrench around the cylindrical body of the solenoid valve otherwise it will be severely damaged.
4 To test the solenoid connect it in series with a 12 volt battery and ammeter. The solenoid should require approximately 2 amps.
5 Check that the plunger in the valve moves forwards when the solenoid is energised and is returned to its direct drive position by spring pressure when de-energised.
6 It should be noted that this type of solenoid does not operate with a 'click' as observed in other types of overdrive.
7 Inspect the O-rings on the solenoid valve for damage and if necessary renew them together with a sealing washer.
8 If it is necessary to clean the operating valve, immerse this part of the solenoid valve only in paraffin until the valve is clean.
9 If the solenoid proves to be faulty it should be renewed as a complete unit.
10 Refitting is the reverse sequence to removal.

16 Relief valve and dashpot assembly (overdrive) – removal and refitting

1 For this a special tool is necessary to remove the relief valve plug. If the vehicle has been recently used, take care to avoid burns from hot oil which will be released.
2 Unscrew and remove the six bolts and spring washers securing the overdrive sump oil gauze filter. Lift away the sump gasket and gauze filter.
3 Lift out the dashpot piston complete with its component springs and cup, followed by the residual pressure spring.
4 The relief valve piston assembly may now be withdrawn by carefully pullling down with a pair of pliers. The components are shown in Fig. 6.52.
5 Another special tool is required, part number 401A (Fig. 6.48) which should be inserted into the now exposed relief valve bore. Withdraw the relief valve together with the dashpot sleeve taking extreme care not to damage the valve bore.
6 Do not attempt to dismantle the dashpot and relief valve piston

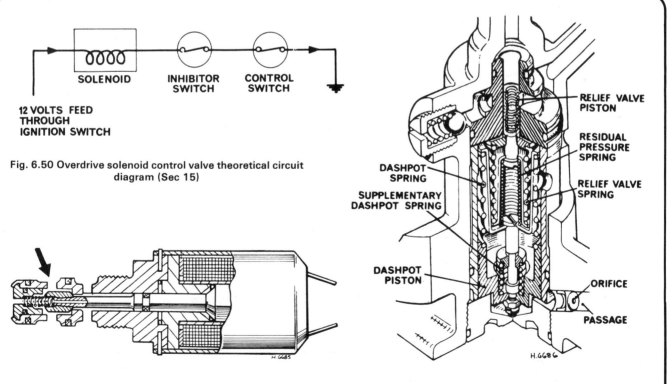

Fig. 6.50 Overdrive solenoid control valve theoretical circuit diagram (Sec 15)

Fig. 6.51 Overdrive solenoid control valve (arrow shows valve assembly) (Sec 15)

Fig. 6.52 Overdrive relief valve and dashpot assembly (Sec 16)

assemblies, otherwise the pre-determined pressures will be disturbed.
7 Inspect the pistons and ensure that they move freely in their respective housings. Make sure the O-rings are not damaged.
8 Before assembly make sure all components are clean and lightly oiled.
9 Insert the relief valve body in the bore and using the relief valve outer sleeve push fully home.
10 It should be noted that the end with the O-ring is nearest the outside of the main casing.
11 Next position the relief valve spring and piston into the dashpot cup, taking care that both ends of the residual pressure spring are correctly located. Carefully position these components in the relief valve outer sleeve, at the same time engaging the relief valve piston in its housing. Fit the base plug and tighten flush with the main housing to the specified torque.
12 Refit the filter, gasket and sump and secure with the six bolts and spring washers.

17 Pump non-return valve (overdrive) – removal and refitting

1 For removal a special tool L354A (Fig. 6.47) is necessary to remove the pump plug. If the vehicle has been recently used take care to avoid burns from hot oil which will be released.
2 Unscrew and remove the six bolts and spring washers securing the overdrive sump and gauze filter. Lift away the sump, gasket and gauze filter.
3 Using tool L354A remove the pump plug taking care not to lose the non-return valve spring and ball. The pump valve seat can now be lifted away (Fig. 6.53).
4 The pump body will be held in position by its O-ring. Should it be necessary to remove this, rotate the propeller shaft until the pump plunger is at the top of its stroke.
5 Next carefully withdraw the pump body by hooking a piece of wire into the now exposed inlet port.
6 Carefully clean and then inspect the non-return valve ball and valve seat and make sure that the O-rings are not damaged. Fit new O-rings if necessary.
7 To refit the non-return valve assembly, first place the spring in the non-return valve plug, then position the ball on the spring.

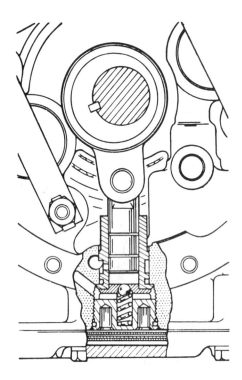

Fig. 6.53 Overdrive pump assembly (Sec 17)

8 The non-return valve seat can now be located on the ball and the complete assembly screwed into the main case using tool L354A. Tighten to the specified torque.
9 Refit the suction filter, sump gasket and sump and secure with the six bolts and spring washers.

18 Pressure filter (overdrive) – removal and refitting

1 For removal a special tool L354A (Fig. 6.47) is necessary to remove the pump plug. If the vehicle has been recently used take care to avoid burns from hot oil which will be released.
2 Unscrew and remove the six bolts and spring washers securing the overdrive sump and gauze filter. Lift away the sump, gasket and gauze filter.
3 Using tool L354A remove the pressure filter base plug.
4 The filter element will come away with the plug. Note the aluminium washer which locates on the shoulder in the filter bore.
5 Remove any dirt and thoroughly wash the element in petrol or paraffin.
6 Refitting is the reverse sequence to removal. Always fit a new aluminium washer. Tighten the plug to the specified torque.

19 Fault diagnosis – overdrive

This is a cumulative diagnosis sequence. There are four faults mentioned. Each fault has a list of checks and remedies listed in order of their likelihood which should be strictly followed. After each check is undertaken, if the fault does not disappear, go on to the next check.

Overdrive does not engage

1 Check oil level. Top up if necessary.
2 Check electrical circuit to solenoid. Rectify break or renew switch if necessary.
3 Remove the solenoid valve to check operation. Renew if inoperative.
4 Check hydraulic pressure with pressure gauge (see Specifications). If incorrect clean blocked filters. If clean check the pump non-return valve seat for clogging and pitting. Renew if dirty or damaged. If satisfactory check relief valve for sticking piston. Renew assembly if piston will not free.
5 Remove overdrive for specialist inspection.

Overdrive does not disengage

Note: *If in this condition* **do not reverse the vehicle.** It will damage the overdrive beyond repair.
6 Check electrical system for closed circuit and repair if necessary.
7 Remove solenoid control valve and check for seized plunger. If seized renew total valve.
8 Check residual pressure with a pressure gauge (see Specifications). If incorrect check relief valve for sticking piston. If clean check control orifice for blocking, otherwise renew parts.
9 Check cone for sticking. If sticking, free by tapping brake ring with soft-faced hammer. (This may occur with a new unit before it is run-in).
10 Remove overdrive for specialist inspection.

Overdrive slips in engagement

Carry out the first four checks under 'does not engage'. If these prove satisfactory, carry out the following.
11 Remove overdrive and check for worn and/or glazed clutch linings or a mechanical obstruction of the cone clutch.
12 Remove overdrive for further specialist inspection.

Overdrive disengagement slow, and/or freewheel on over-run

13 Check the relief valve for sticking piston. If sticking, free off defective parts or renew total relief valve assembly.
14 Check solenoid for sticking or blocked control valve. Clean and free off valve or renew solenoid assembly.
15 Check restrictor orifice for partial blockage. Clean orifice.
16 Remove overdrive for further specialist inspection.

PART C: AUTOMATIC TRANSMISSION

20 Automatic transmission – general description

A three-speed automatic transmission is available as an optional fitting on the 2-litre model. The selector lever is centrally located and incorporates a button in the side of the T-handle. The button must be pressed before the selector can be moved from 'N' and between those positions indicated by arrows in Fig. 6.54.

Forward movement is obtained by selecting 'D' (fully automatic) or '1' (low gear) followed by '2' (2nd gear). It should be noted that both 1st and 2nd gears must only be selected and used within their maximum speed capabilities, which are 55 mph (90 kph) for 2nd gear and 22 mph (35 kph) for 1st gear. This applies for both upward and downward changes.

With the selector lever in 'P' (Park), an internal pawl locks the transmission. Reverse gear is engaged by selecting 'R'.

The system includes a three-element hydrokinetic torque converter which transmits the power from the engine to the transmission unit; the torque converter is capable of variable torque multiplication.

The hydraulically-operated epicyclic gearbox responds to both road speed and throttle pedal demand by means of an internal governor and valve control, and the correct gear for the current conditions is therefore automatically selected.

Should it be necessary to tow the vehicle, the selector lever must be moved to the 'N' (neutral) position but the vehicle must not be towed at speeds in excess of 30 mph or for distances in excess of 15 miles. The propeller shaft should be disconnected if these limits are to be exceeded.

The transmission fluid is cooled by means of a fin-type oil cooler mounted to the right of the radiator.

An inhibitor switch is fitted to the transmission to prevent inadvertent starting of the engine whilst the selector lever is in any position other than 'N' or 'P'.

Due to the complexity of the automatic transmission unit, if performance is not up to standrard, or overhaul is necessary, it is

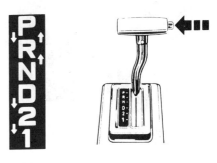

Fig. 6.54 T-handle selector button must be pressed to move selector to respective positions indicated (Sec 20)

imperative that this be left to a main agent who will have the special equipment and knowledge for fault diagnosis and rectification. The contents of the following Sections are therefore confined to supplying general information and any service information and instructions that can be used by the owner.

A cutaway view of the automatic transmission is shown in Fig. 6.55.

The automatic transmission should not be operated with a broken or disconnected downshift cable, otherwise considerable damage may occur due to overheating. As a temporary measure, the downshift inner cable should be pulled out as far as possible and secured in this position. The kickdown facility will thus be engaged but it will be safe to drive the vehicle to the nearest garage.

It is most important that the handbrake be fully applied and 'P' selected whenever the vehicle is being worked on, particularly when making under-bonnet adjustments. This is necessary since if left in gear with the engine running, an increase above the normal speed will provoke vehicle 'creep'.

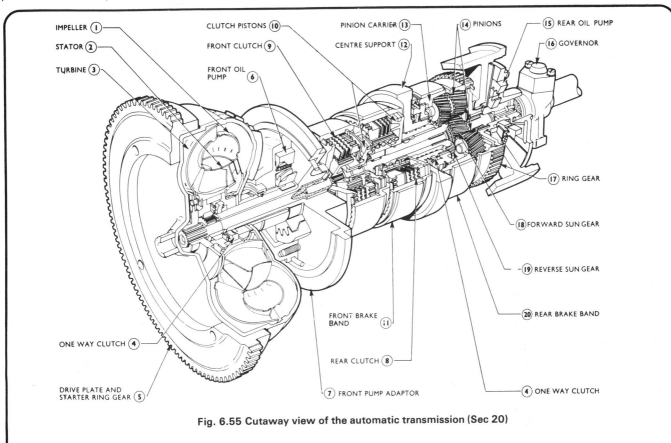

Fig. 6.55 Cutaway view of the automatic transmission (Sec 20)

Fig. 6.56 Automatic transmission dipstick for checking the fluid level (Sec 21)

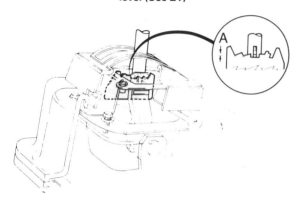

Fig. 6.57 Selector pawl stub to notch clearance (A) (Sec 22)

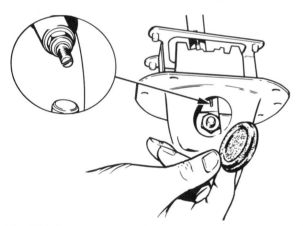

Fig. 6.58 Remove grommet for access to cable adjuster and locknut (Sec 22)

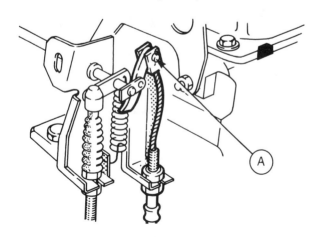

Fig. 6.59 Carburettor downshift cable connection (A) (Sec 23)

21 Automatic transmission – maintenance

1   Every 6000 miles (10 000 km) the automatic transmission fluid level should be checked and topped up as necessary with the correct specified fluid. To do this, run the engine until it reaches its normal operating temperature, then select 'P' and let the engine idle for a further two minutes. Withdraw the transmission dipstick with the engine still running and wipe it clean with a lint-free cloth, then fully reinsert it and withdraw it again to check the level of the fluid. Top up the transmission as necessary by adding fluid through the dipstick tube. Persistent fluid loss should be investigated.
2   To prevent overheating, it is recommended that the exterior of the transmission and oil cooler be cleaned at 6000 mile (10 000 km) intervals.
3   If the vehicle is operating in severe conditions, it is recommended that the transmission front band is adjusted regularly. Refer to Chapter 13.

22   Selector cable (automatic transmission) – adjustment

1   Remove the selector indicator housing and engage the selector lever in 'D' position.
2   Prise the grommet from the side face of the selector housing and insert a feeler gauge between the selector pawl stub and notch (see Fig. 6.57). This clearance (A) must be 0.004 to 0.008 in (0.1 to 0.2 mm) with the lever set in the 'D' position.
3   Where adjustment is necessary, loosen the cable locknut and adjust the cable accordingly by means of the screw head (Fig. 6.58). Tighten the locknut on completion.
4   Refit the grommet and selector housing indicator unit.
5   Removal and refitting of the cable is covered in Section 25.

23 Downshift cable (automatic transmission) – removal, refitting and adjustment

1   Open and support the bonnet.
2   Referring to Fig. 6.59, disconnect the downshift cable from the carburettor linkage. The clevis pin is secured by a split pin which when withdrawn enables the pin to be extracted and the cable detached from the linkage.
3   Refer to Fig. 6.60, and disconnect the cable from the slotted bracket by unscrewing the upper nut, screwing the lower nut back fully and then pulling the cable down to unhook it from its support bracket.
4   Fully engage the handbrake and then raise and support the front of the vehicle with axle stands.
5   The cable can now be detached from its transmission location bracket by loosening the locknuts and releasing the cable from its slot in the bracket.

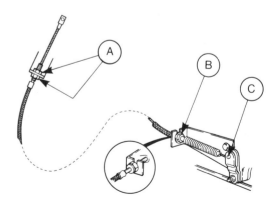

Fig. 6.60 Downshift cable connections (Sec 23)

A   Adjuster nuts (upper end)   C   Downshift lever connection
B   Retaining nuts (lower end)

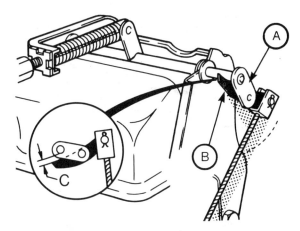

Fig. 6.61 Operating shaft lever (A) and cable connection lever (B). Clearance (C) to be as specified (Sec 23)

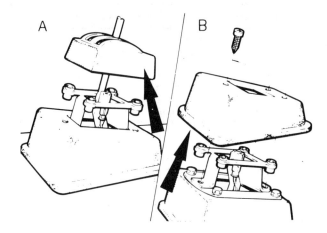

Fig. 6.62 Remove selector indicator housing (A) and sound insulator (B) (Sec 24)

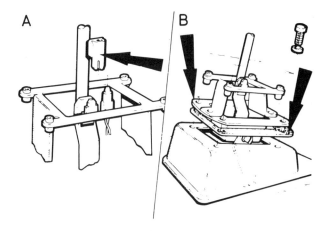

Fig. 6.63 Detach the lamp shroud (A) and selector lever bracket (B) (Sec 4)

Fig. 6.64 Selector lever cable top linkage (Sec 25)

6   Unhook the cable from the downshift lever and withdraw the cable.
7   Refit in the reverse order to removal. Adjust the cable on completion before fully tightening the upper adjustment/retaining nuts.
8   To check the cable adjustment, press the cable connection lever away from the operating shaft lever using a screwdriver and then check the clearance between the two using feeler gauges (Fig. 6.61). The correct clearance is 0.008 to 0.04 in (0.2 to 1.0 mm). If necessary lengthen or shorten the cable accordingly by loosening or tightening the adjuster nut of the cable upper thread.

24 Selector mechanism – removal and refitting

1   Lift clear the indicator housing from the selector lever bracket and then unscrew and remove the three screws securing the sound insulator to the selector lever bracket (Fig. 6.62). Remove the sound insulator.
2   Slide the lever indicator lamp shroud upwards and remove the bulb assembly (Fig. 6.63).
3   Unscrew and remove the four selector lever bracket retaining bolts with washers. Remove the bracket and gasket.
4   Tie a suitable length of cord or wire to the upper selector rod to prevent it from dropping downwards when disconnected. Lift the selector mechanism and remove the retaining clip at the shift rod end.
5   Unhook and withdraw the selector lever unit.
6   Refit in the reverse order to removal. Adjust the selector rods as given in Section 26 if necessary. Tighten the selector bracket retaining bolts to the specified torque.

25 Selector – dismantling and reassembly

1   With the selector mechanism removed from the vehicle (as given in the previous Section), first prise out the rubber grommet and then remove the nut retaining the lever arm. Press the lever arm from the housing.
2   Unscrew the operating cable locknut and then remove the selector pawl and spring from the selector lever bottom end.
3   From the selector lever handle remove the socket-headed cap screw and then remove the handle.
4   Detach the cable nipple from the roller unit at the lever top end and remove the pushbutton.
5   Use a suitable punch to drive out the operating cable guide bush-to-top linkage retaining pin (Fig. 6.64). Remove the cable guide bush and top linkage from the lever arm bottom end.
6   Inspect all parts for wear and renew as necessary.
7   Reassemble in the reverse order to removal, but note the following special points:

(a)   When refitting the pushbutton into the handle, the long keyway must be fitted first
(b)   Hold the pushbutton against its spring, fit the handle to the lever and retain in position with the cap screw
(c)   Smear some medium grease onto the selector pawl before refitting, with spring and guide bush, into the lever lower end
(d)   Apply a general purpose grease into the selector lever housing slots before fitting the lever arm
(e)   Adjust the selector cable as necessary as given in Section 22 on completion

26 Selector rods – removal, refitting and adjustment

1   Both the upper and lower shift rods are secured by means of clips at each end and these can be prised free to release the rods (Fig. 6.65).

2   Renew the rod(s) and bushes if worn or damaged.

3   To refit and adjust the selector control rods, first locate the transmission control lever (attached to the forward end of the lower shift rod) in the 'D' position. To ensure that the lever is in the 'D' position, move it forwards to the '1' position, then move it back by two notches when it will be in 'D' (Fig. 6.66). Keep the lever in this position when adjusting the two rods.

4   Fit the fixed end of the upper rod to the forward pin on the relay lever and secure with its clip. The adjustable end of the upper rod should be allowed to rest against the transmission.

5   Fit the lower rod to the rear pin on the relay lever and retain with clips. Check at this point that the selector lever and the transmission control lever are still engaged in 'D'.

6   Fit the upper rod to the location pin of the selector lever arm, if necessary adjusting the end of the rod so that it is in exact alignment with the location pin. Loosen the locknut, rotate the end of the rod accordingly and retighten the locknut. When fitted onto the location pin, refit the retaining clip.

7   Check that full engagement of all gear selector positions is possible.

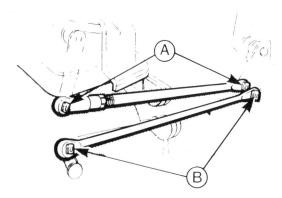

Fig. 6.65 Selector rods upper (A) and lower (B) retaining clips (Sec 26)

27 Inhibitor switch (automatic transmission) – removal, refitting and adjustment

1   Locate the inhibitor switch on the left-hand side of the transmission and, after noting their respective positions, disconnect the two electrical wires.

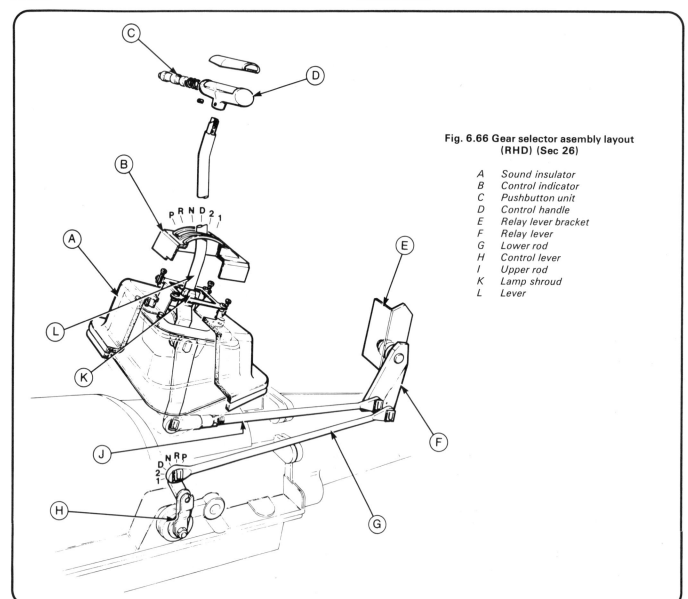

Fig. 6.66 Gear selector asembly layout (RHD) (Sec 26)

A   Sound insulator
B   Control indicator
C   Pushbutton unit
D   Control handle
E   Relay lever bracket
F   Relay lever
G   Lower rod
H   Control lever
I   Upper rod
K   Lamp shroud
L   Lever

2   Loosen the locknut and unscrew the switch from the transmission casing.

3   To refit the inhibitor switch, screw it into the transmission casing and carry out the following adjustment.

4   Connect a 12 volt test lamp and leads across the two switch terminals in series with a 12 volt battery then move the selector lever inside the cab to position 'P'.

5   Screw in the inhibitor switch until the test lamp just lights then screw it in a further quarter of a turn and tighten the locknut.

6   Remove the test lamp and leads and connect the two electrical wires to their respective terminals.

7   Engage each of the five positions separately with the selector lever and check that the engine will only start in positions 'P' and 'N'.

8   Some models may be equipped with a combined inhibitor/reversing lamp switch, screwed vertically into the left-hand side of the transmission. Removal and refitting of this type of switch is as given above, except that there is no locknut and the switch must be screwed home when refitting. Correct adjustment is achieved automatically when the switch is installed.

28 Automatic transmission – removal and refitting

1   Remember that automatic transmission internal faults can only be diagnosed successfully whilst the transmission is still fitted to the vehicle, and therefore the advice of a suitably equipped garage should be sought before removing the unit, unless renewal is the only object.

2   Open the bonnet and disconnect the battery negative terminal.

3   Jack up the front and rear of the vehicle and support it adequately on stands, or alternatively position it over an inspection pit; ensure that the vehicle is unladen.

4   Place a container of at least 1½ gallons (7 litres) beneath the transmission, unscrew and remove the drain plug, and drain the fluid from the transmission. Refit and tighten the drain plug.

5   Refer to Chapter 7 and remove the propeller shaft from the vehicle.

6   Disconnect the exhaust front downpipe from the exhaust manifold and silencer, and withdraw it from beneath the vehicle.

7   Disconnect the speedometer cable from the rear of the transmission.

8   Remove the selector rods from the transmission (Section 26).

9   Withdraw the fluid level dipstick, then unscrew the retaining bolt and remove the dipstick tube assembly from the transmission.

10 Locate the inhibitor switch on the left-hand side of the transmission, note the wiring connections and disconnect the wires.

11 Detach the downshift cable at the downshift lever and bracket and tie it back out of the way.

12 Refer to Chapter 10 and remove the starter motor.

13 Detach the vacuum pipe from its diaphragm and tie it back out of the way.

14 Unscrew and remove the transmission lower cover plate and remove the plate and cable bracket.

15 Working through the front of the bellhousing, unscrew and remove the four driveplate-to-torque converter retaining bolts; it will be necessary to rotate the engine with a spanner on the crankshaft pulley nut to gain access to each of these bolts.

16 Wipe the area around the oil cooler connections to the right-hand side of the transmission, then unscrew and remove the unions, plug the pipe ends and tie the pipes out of the way. (Fig. 6.67).

17 Take the weight of the transmission with a trolley jack positioned beneath the transmission sump; to prevent damage to the sump interpose a block of wood between the jack and sump, but make sure that there is no chance of the transmission slipping in subsequent operations,

18 Unscrew and remove the extension housing support bolt and bushes, then lower the transmission approximately two or three inches.

19 Using a further jack and block of wood, support the rear end of the engine beneath the sump.

20 Unscrew and remove the remaining bellhousing retaining bolts and carefully withdraw the transmission rearwards to separate the torque converter spigot from the crankshaft adaptor. It would be wise to enlist the help of an assistant during this operation in order to steady the transmission on the trolley jack and hold the torque converter in the transmission.

21 Lower the transmission and withdraw it from beneath the vehicle.

22 If necessary the torque converter may be carefully withdrawn from the bellhousing complete with the starter ring gear but, as there will be considerable spillage of fluid, it will be necessary to place the transmission on a suitable container.

23 If necessary the bellhousing and extension housing may also be detached from the transmission by unscrewing and removing the retaining bolts and spring washers (remove the drive flange as applicable).

24 Refitting the automatic transmission is a reversal of the removal procedure, but the following points should be noted:

(a) When refitting the converter, align the oil drain plug with the driveplate opening. When the converter is fully fitted and engaged with the oil pump drivegear, ensure that the distance between the converter flange end face and the converter housing flange is as shown in Fig. 6.68

(b) When the converter case and engine flanges are flush, check that the converter rotates freely, then insert the flange bolts and tighten to the specified torque

(c) Adjust the selector rods and inhibitor switch as described in Sections 26 and 27, then refill the transmission with the correct grade of fluid as given in Section 21

(d) Adjust the downshift cable as described in Section 23 and lower the vehicle to the ground

(e) On completion run the engine and operate the transmission to ensure that it is satisfactory. Check the oil cooler pipes and connections for any signs of leakage

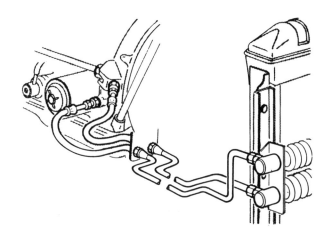

Fig. 6.67 Oil cooler pipe connections to automatic transmission (Sec 28)

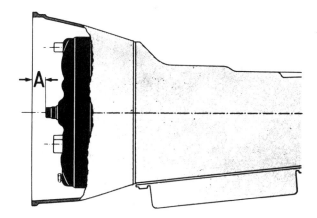

Fig. 6.68 Check the torque converter engagement (Sec 28)

A = 0.4 in (10 mm) minimum

29 Fault diagnosis – automatic transmission

Faults in these units are nearly always the result of low fuel level or incorrect adjustment of the selector linkage or downshift cable. Internal faults should be diagnosed by your main Ford dealer who has the necessary equipment to carry out the work.

Symptom	Reason(s)
Engine will not start with selector in any position	Disconnected or defective inhibitor switch
Engine starts in all selector positions	Defective or short-circuited inhibitor switch
Gearchange speeds incorrect	Selector linkage adjustment incorrect Kickdown cable broken or maladjusted
Parking pawl inoperative	Incorrect linkage adjustment Internal linkage
Selector lever action stiff	Defective lever, selector linkage or inhibitor switch
Fluid loss	Defective vacuum diaphragm

Chapter 7 Propeller shaft

For modifications, and information applicable to later models, see Supplement at end of manual

Contents

Specifications

Type .... Two-section open shaft, with three universal joints and a central flexible coupling mounting

Centre bearing type .... Flexible rubber-mounted ball-bearing

Torque wrench settings

	lbf ft	kgf m
Propeller shaft flange bolts	44 to 49	6.0 to 6.5
Centre bearing to support member	14 to 18	2.0 to 2.5

1 General description

Drive is transmitted from the gearbox to the rear axle by means of a two-section propeller shaft.

The propeller shaft assembly is fitted with three universal joints, one at the front end of the forward shaft and one at each end of the rear shaft. The centre bearing is supported by a flexible rubber mounting which is clamped to the vehicle underframe, and the rear shaft has a sliding spline connection to the front shaft to allow for rear axle movement.

The universal joints are of sealed construction and require no maintenance. When they become worn, renewal of the shaft may be the only solution. If a proprietary UJ repair kit is purchased, make sure that you have the necessary tools and equipment to use it.

2 Propeller shaft assembly – removal and refitting

1 Jack up the rear of the vehicle and support it adequately with stands, then chock the front wheels. Alternatively the vehicle can be placed over an inspection pit or on a ramp.

2 Apply the handbrake firmly to ensure that the propeller shaft remains stationary whilst the retaining bolts are loosened.

3 The propeller shaft is finely balanced and it is imperative that it is refitted in its original position; therefore check that the alignment marks exist on the front and rear sections of the shaft as well as on the rear axle drive flange.

4 Unscrew and remove the four self-locking nuts and bolts securing the propeller shaft rear section to the rear axle drive flange (photo).

5 Unscrew and remove the two bolts retaining the centre bearing to the floor pan whilst supporting the weight of the shaft (photo).

6 Carefully withdraw the complete shaft assembly rearwards and disengage it from the gearbox rear extension (photo), then lower and remove it complete.

7 A small amount of oil spillage may occur from the rear extension of the gearbox, so plug the end or catch the oil in a suitable container.

8 Refit the shaft by first engaging its forward end into the gearbox rear extension (remove plug if inserted).

9 Lift and support the two shaft sections and reconnect the rear

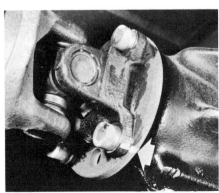

2.4 Propeller shaft coupling to rear axle flange – note alignment marks (arrowed)

2.5 Detach the centre bearing

2.6 The front universal joint and gearbox extension

section to the axle drive flange, aligning the marks before fitting the bolts. Where a new shaft assembly is being fitted, shaft alignment is not necessary.

10 Raise and support the centre bearing so that the two retaining bolts can be fitted. Tighten all bolts to the specified torque settings.

11 Check the transmission oil level and top up should it be necessary.

3 Universal joints and shaft splines – examination for wear

1 Wear in the needle roller bearings is characterised by vibration in the transmission, 'clonks' on taking up the drive, and in extreme cases of lack of lubrication, metallic squeaking, and ultimately grating and shrieking sounds as the bearings break up.

2 It is easy to check if the needle roller bearings are worn with the propeller shaft in position, by trying to turn the shaft with one hand, the other hand holding the rear axle flange when the rear universal is being checked, and the front half coupling when the front universal is being checked. Any movement between the propeller shaft and the front and rear half couplings is indicative of considerable wear. Similarly check the centre universal joint by attempting to turn the yokes either side of the joint in opposite directions.

3 A further check can be made by attempting to lift the shaft near the joint and observing any movement in the joint.

4 Examine the propeller shaft splines for wear by lifting the coupling and observing if there is any play in them; if worn it will be necessary to purchase an exchange propeller shaft.

5 Refer to Section 1 if overhaul of the universal joints is contemplated.

4 Centre bearing – renewal

1 Before separating the shaft sections make alignment markings (if not already made) to ensure correct positioning when reassembling, otherwise the balance may be upset.

2 Bend the retaining bolt locktab straight and then unscrew the bolt. Withdraw the U-shaped retainer sideways.

3 Remove the housing and rubber insulator from the ball-bearing, then pull the insulator from the housing.

4 Using a two-legged puller, carefully withdraw the bearing and caps (Fig. 7.1).

5 Wash the bearing in paraffin and then check it for wear by spinning it and observing any roughness. Hold the inner track stationary and attempt to rock the outer track laterally to show up any excess bearing wear; the bearing must be renewed if faulty.

6 Reassembling the centre bearing is a reversal of the dismantling procedure, but the following points should be noted.

7 The flexible rubber mounting and its clamp should be thoroughly clean prior to refitting. Use a suitable length of tubing to drive the centre bearing into position.

8 With the bearing and caps in position on the shaft, fit the rubber insulator in the housing and bend out the metal tabs to enable its insertion. Bend the tabs back over the rubber with pliers.

9 Fit the housing and insulator over the bearing with the mark facing in the vehicle's direction of travel (Fig. 7.2).

10 Fit the bolt and lockplate into the front section of the shaft to enable the U-retainer to be slid into position (with its peg towards the splines – see Fig. 7.3). Align the shaft markings when assembling.

11 Tighten the bolt and secure with the lockplate.

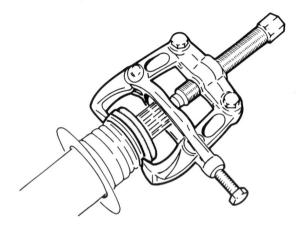

Fig. 7.1 Bearing and cap removal method (Sec 4)

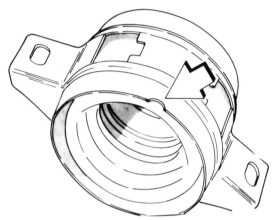

Fig. 7.2 Mark (arrowed) must face direction of travel (Sec 4)

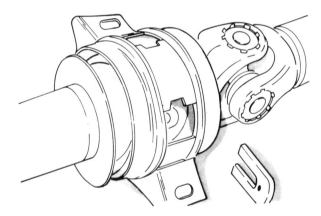

Fig. 7.3 Fit U retainer with peg to splines (Sec 4)

Chapter 8 Rear axle

For modifications, and information applicable to later models, see Supplement at end of manual

Contents

Specifications

Axle type	Fully floating or three-quarter floating, hypoid

Ratios

1.6 ohv – F axle	4.63 : 1, 5.14 : 1
1.6 ohv – H axle	4.56 : 1, 5.14 : 1
1.6 (LC) ohc – F axle	4.63 : 1, 5.14 : 1
1.6 (LC) ohc – H axle	4.56 : 1, 5.14 : 1
2.0 ohc – G axle	4.63 : 1, 5.14 : 1, 5.83 : 1
2.0 ohc – H axle	4.11 : 1, 4.44 : 1, 4.56 : 1, 5.14 : 1
2.0 ohc – H axle (automatic)	4.44 : 1 HD

Lubrication

Oil type/specification	Hypoid gear oil, viscosity SAE 90EP, to Ford spec. SRM-2C-9102-A (Duckhams Hypoid 90S)
Oil capacity:	
80 to 120 models	4.75 Imp pints (2.7 litres)
130 to 190 models	3.25 Imp pints (1.9 litres)

Torque wrench settings

	lbf ft	kgf m
Bearing cap to axle case:		
F axle	44 to 52	6.0 to 7.0
G axle	74 to 87	10 to 12
H axle	72 to 81	9.9 to 11
Differential housing to axle case (H)	39 to 44	5.3 to 6.0
Crownwheel to differential:		
F axle	58 to 63	8.0 to 8.6
G axle	74 to 87	10 to 12
H axle	50 to 55	6.9 to 7.5
Propeller shaft to pinion flange	44 to 49	5.3 to 6.7
Differential housing/bearing cap lockbolts:		
G axle	12 to 15	1.7 to 2.0
H axle	13 to 15	1.8 to 2.0
Wheel hub nut:		
F and H axles	148 to 184	20.4 to 25.3
G axle (locknut)	52	7.1
Drive pinion nut:		
G axle	74 to 87	10 to 12
F and H axles	See text (Section 7)	
Rear axle case to cover (F and G)	15 to 18	2.0 to 2.5

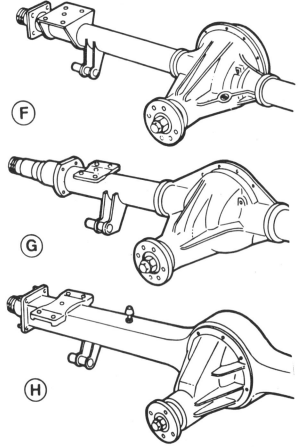

Fig. 8.1 The identifying features of the three axle types (Sec 1)

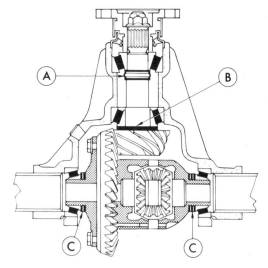

Fig. 8.2 Sectional view of the F type axle unit (Sec 1)

A   Collapsible sleeve   C   Housing shims
B   Pinion shim

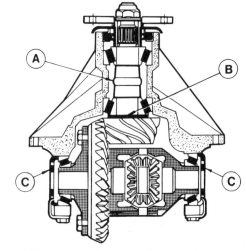

Fig. 8.3 Sectional view of the H type axle unit (Sec 1)

A   Collapsible sleeve   C   Ring nuts
B   Pinion shim

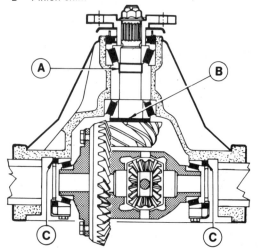

Fig. 8.4 Sectional view of the G type axle unit (Sec 1)

A   Spacer sleeve   C   Ring nuts
B   Pinion shim

1   General description

Three axle types are fitted, being known as the type F, type G and type H. The type F axle is only fitted to 1.6-litre variants. The type G axle is only fitted to 2-litre variants. The type H axle is fitted to both 1.6 and 2-litre variants. Axle ratios differ according to model and type.

On the F and G type axles, the differential unit is a fully floating hypoid (Salisbury) type and is mounted direct into the axle casing, access being through the rear inspection cover.

The H type (Timken) differential is of the three-quarter floating type and is bolted to its own carrier, which is attached to the front face of the axle case.

For external identification of the three axle types, refer to Fig. 8.1.

On the H and F type axles, the pinion bearing spacer is of the collapsible sleeve type (Figs. 8.2 and 8.3). Special care must be taken when renewing the pinion seal not to overtighten the flange retaining nut, or the sleeve could become distorted and the pinion to crownwheel setting be disturbed.

The G type axle has a fixed pinion spacer sleeve (Fig. 8.4).

The pinion to crownwheel mesh is adjusted by means of suitable shims fitted between the pinion inner bearing and the pinion gear. This applies on all axle types.

The axleshafts (halfshafts) are splined on their inner ends and locate in the differential side gears. On the F type axle, the preload to the inner taper roller bearings is made by shims of suitable thickness fitted between the axle case and differential. On the G type axle, the preload is by ring nuts on the axle case. The H. type axleshaft bearing preload is set by means of ring nuts in the differential housing itself.

The outer wheel hubs of the H and F type axles are the same, having ball-bearings as shown in Fig. 8.5. The outer hub of the G type axle is fitted with two taper roller bearings, the free play of which is set by an adjuster nut which is secured by a lockwasher and locknut. This hub assembly is shown in Fig. 8.6.

On all three axle types, the outer hub bearings are lubricated by rear axle oil.

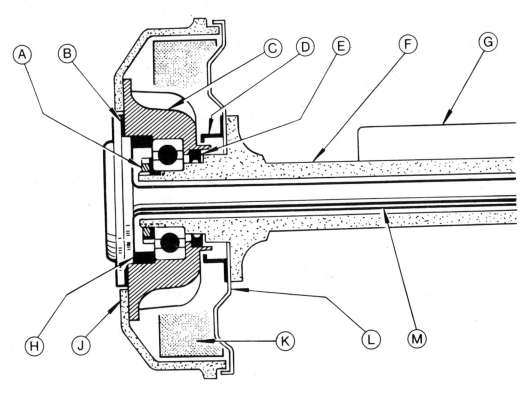

Fig. 8.5 Axle hub on the F and H type axles (Sec 1)

A	Nut	D	Guard	G	Spring bearer	K	Brake shoe
B	Gasket location	E	Oil seal	H	Spacer ring	L	Brake carrier plate
C	Hub	F	Axle tube	J	Brake drum	M	Halfshaft

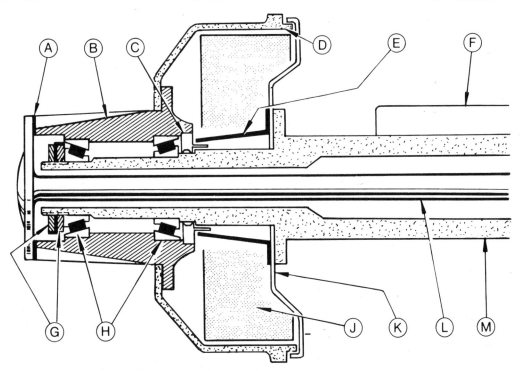

Fig. 8.6 The G type axle hub (Sec 1)

A	Gasket location	D	Brake drum	G	Locknuts	K	Brake carrier plate
B	Hub	E	Guard	H	Taper roller bearing	L	Halfshaft
C	Seal	F	Spring bearer	J	Brake shoe	M	Axle tube

2   Rear axle – removal and refitting

1   Ensure that the vehicle is unloaded, then chock the front wheels, jack up the rear of the vehicle and support it adequately beneath the underframe side members in front of the rear springs.
2   Support the weight of the rear axle with a trolley jack positioned beneath the differential housing and stands on each end of the axle.
3   Apply the handbrake firmly, unscrew the rear wheel nuts, and remove the rear wheels. (Remember that 6-stud wheels have left-hand thread wheel nuts on the left-hand side).
4   Mark the pinion and propeller shaft drive flanges so that they can be refitted to their original position, then unscrew and remove the four self-locking nuts and bolts and detach the propeller shaft, supporting it on a stand.
5   Wipe the area around the brake fluid reservoir filler cap, unscrew the cap, and tighten it down onto a piece of polythene sheeting; this will reduce the loss of hydraulic fluid in subsequent operations.
6   Carefully unscrew and detach the flexible brake hose at its forward union and plug the end with a pencil or similar object to prevent the ingress of dirt or foreign matter.
7   Detach the coil spring from the load conscious brake valve by extracting the split pin and withdrawing the clevis pin (at the top of the spring). This is shown in Fig. 8.7. Note that if the spring is detached at the bottom end, the load conscious valve will have to be readjusted. Do not therefore detach the spring at its bottom end unless absolutely necessary. Refer to Chapter 9 for details.
8   Disconnect the exhaust system rear supports.
9   Unscrew and remove the locknut securing the handbrake cable retainer to the handbrake rod after removing the return spring and releasing the handbrake.
10 Unbolt the handbrake cable brackets from the underframe and

then loosen the retaining nuts and detach the cable from the brackets.
11 Unbolt and disconnect the shock absorbers from their upper mountings on each side.
12 Unscrew the shackle bolt nuts and extract the four shackle bolts from the rear springs at their forward and rear locations.
13 Check that all associated axle components are disconnected, then lower and withdraw the axle unit complete with springs and shock absorbers (Fig. 8.8).
14 The springs and shock absorbers can be detached as necessary with the axle free from the vehicle.
15 Refitting the rear axle is a reversal of the removal procedure, but the following points should be noted:

(a)   The pinion and propeller shaft flanges must be aligned to the previously made marks
(b)   Tighten all nuts and bolts to the specified torques. The rear spring mountings must only be finally tightened with the suspension under load (vehicle free standing)
(c)   Bleed the braking system as described in Chapter 9
(d)   Check and top up the axle oil level

3   Axleshaft (halfshaft) – removal and refitting

1   Chock the front wheels and jack up the rear of the vehicle, supporting it firmly and adequately on stands placed at each end of the rear axle.
2   On H axle models only, remove the hub cap and with the handbrake fully applied, unscrew and remove the wheel nuts and withdraw the wheel. Refer to Chapter 9 and remove the brake drum.
3   On all models, unscrew and remove the 6 nuts or 5 bolts and remove the axleshaft. Release the axleshaft by carefully tapping the flange, then withdraw the shaft from the axle, being careful not to damage the splines which engage with the differential unit. Be prepared for some oil spillage.
4   Recover the gasket and seal from the flange.
5   Refitting the axleshaft is a reversal of the removal procedure, but the following additional points should be noted:

(a)   Clean the mating faces of the axleshaft flange and hub flange and fit a new gasket
(b)   Check and top up the rear axle oil level

4   Rear hub (F and H type axles) – removal, overhaul and refitting

1   Refer to the previous Section and remove the axleshaft on the side concerned.
2   Lever up the hub nut locking washer tab and straighten it, then unscrew and remove the hub nut and lockwasher; a special tool is manufactured for this purpose but the careful use of a soft drift will suffice.

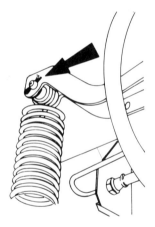

Fig. 8.7 Disconnect the load conscious brake valve spring at the top (Sec 2)

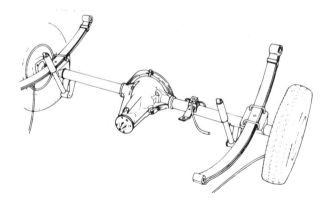

Fig. 8.8 Remove axle assembly complete with springs and shock absorbers (Sec 2)

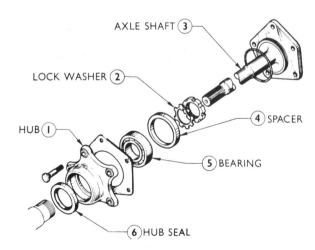

Fig. 8.9 Exploded view of the rear hub fitted to the F and H type axles (Sec 4)

3   Withdraw the hub assembly from the rear axle either by attaching a slide hammer to the hub flange, or alternatively by using spacers and attaching the axleshaft (outer face first) to the flange with the wheel nuts; tightening the wheel nuts will release the hub assembly.

4   Drive out the hub bearing and spacer with a soft metal drift, then use a screwdriver to extract the grease retainer from the hub.

5   Wash and clean all the components in paraffin then carefully examine each item for damage and deterioration. Check the bearing wear by spinning the outer track whilst holding the inner track stationary and observing any roughness. Similarly with the bearing stationary, attempt to move the outer track laterally; excessive movement is an indication of wear. Any component which is unserviceable must be renewed.

6   Refitting the rear hub is a reversal of the removal procedure, but the following additional points should be noted:

(a) Fit a new grease retainer and hub nut lockwasher
(b) Use suitable diameter tubing to drive the grease retainer, bearing and spacer into position squarely
(c) Pack the hub bearing with a lithium-based grease prior to assembling
(d) The hub nut should be tightened to the minimum torque wrench setting given in the Specifications, but if a locking tab does not align with the nut slot, tighten the nut further until alignment occurs.

5   Rear hub (G type axle) – removal, overhaul and refitting

1   Refer to Section 3 and remove the axleshaft on the side concerned.
2   Remove the roadwheel(s) if not already removed.
3   Refer to Chapter 9 and remove the brake drum.
4   Using a screwdriver or chisel, bend up the hub lockwasher tab and

unscrew and remove the locknut, lockwasher and adjusting nut. A special tool is manufactured for this purpose, and should be borrowed from a local garage if possible, as the nuts are not easily accessible with a spanner.

5   Drive out the outer bearing, then the inner bearing cups and oil seal using a soft metal drift, but keep each bearing inner and outer tracks together.

6   Wash and clean all the components in paraffin then carefully examine each item for wear and deterioration. Check the bearing tapered rollers and inner and outer tracks for pitting and scoring, and if necessary obtain new bearings.

7   Refitting the rear hub is a reversal of the removal procedure, but the following points should be noted:

(a) Use suitable diameter tubing to drive the bearing cups squarely into the hub
(b) Grease the bearings with a lithium-based grease prior to assembly, and fit a new oil seal to the inner bearing
(c) The bearings should be adjusted by first tightening the adjusting nut to 50 to 60 lbf ft (7 to 9 kgf m), then loosening the nut by $\frac{1}{16}$ to $\frac{1}{3}$ of a turn. Fit the lockwasher and tighten the locknut to a torque of 50 to 65 lbf ft (7 to 9 kgf m), then bend the locktab onto the locknut to retain it. The special tool or a large box spanner and torque wrench will be required for this operation

6   Drive pinion oil seal (G type axle) – renewal

1   The G type axle has a fixed length spacer sleeve fitted at the rear of the pinion taper roller bearing and this is shown in Fig. 8.4. The G type axle is fitted to the 2-litre models.
2   Raise the vehicle at the rear and support with axle stands.
3   With a scriber or file mark a line across the propeller shaft and

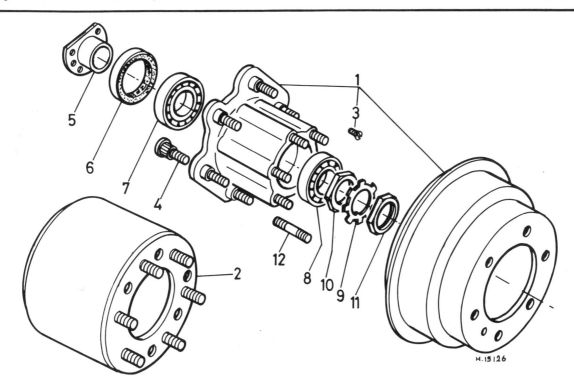

H.15126

Fig. 8.10 The G type rear hub components (Sec 5)

1　Brake drum and hub	4　Wheel stud	7　Bearing (inner)	10　Adjuster nut
2　Intermediate hub	5　Oil baffle	8　Bearing (outer)	11　Locknut
3　Screw (drum retainer)	6　Oil seal	9　Lockwasher	12　Stud

pinion driving flanges so that they may be refitted together in their original positions.

4   Undo and remove the four bolts and spring washers securing the propeller shaft and pinion driving flanges and carefully lower the propeller shaft.

5   Carefully clean the front of the final drive housing as there will probably be a considerable amount of oil and dirt if the seal has been leaking for a while.

6   Using a mole wrench or large bar bolted to the flange, grip the drive pinion flange and with a socket undo and remove the pinion flange retaining self locking nut. This nut must be discarded and a new one obtained ready for reassembly.

7   Place a container under the front of the final drive housing to catch any oil that may issue once the oil seal has been removed.

8   Using a universal puller and suitable thrust pad pull off the drive pinion flange from the drive pinion.

9   Using a screwdriver or small chisel, carefully remove the old oil seal. It will probably be necessary to partially dismantle it. Note which way round it is fitted with the lip facing inwards.

10 Before fitting a new seal apply some grease to the inner face between the two lips of the seal.

11 Apply a little jointing compound to the outer face of the seal.

12 Using a tubular drive of suitable diameter carefully drive the oil seal into the final drive housing. Make quite sure that it is fitted squarely into the housing.

13 Refit the drive pinion flange and once again hold securely with a mole wrench or large bar. Fit a new self-locking nut and tighten to the specified torque wrench setting.

14 Reconnect the propeller shaft, aligning the previously made marks on the flanges, and refit the bolts with new spring washers. Tighten to the specified torque wrench setting.

15 Finally check the rear axle oil level and top up if necessary.

---

7   Drive pinion oil seal (F and H type axles) – renewal

The F and H type axles are fitted with a collapsible spacer and this is shown in Figs. 8.2 and 8.3. Renewal of the drive pinion oil seal should only be attempted by the more experienced DIY mechanic. A special torque wrench or a spring balance will be needed, and a new pinion nut must be fitted on reassembly. No difficulty should be encountered unless the pinion nut is overtightened (paragraph 12), in which case removal of the taper roller bearing to renew the collapsible spacer may present problems.

1   Jack up the rear of the vehicle and support it securely under the bodyframe.

2   Disconnect the propeller shaft from the rear axle drive pinion after marking them for correct alignment.

3   Remove the rear roadwheels and brake drums.

4   Using a spring balance and length of cord wound round the drive pinion flange, determine the torque required to turn the drive pinion and record it.

5   Alternatively, a socket wrench fitted to the pinion nut and a suitable torque wrench may be used.

6   Mark the coupling in relation to the pinion splines for exact replacement.

7   Hold the pinion coupling flange by placing two 2-inch long bolts through two opposite holes and bolting them up tight. Undo the self-locking nut whilst holding a large screwdriver or tyre lever between the two bolts as a lever. Remove the flange, using a puller if necessary.

8   Carefully prise free the old oil seal using a blunt screwdriver or similar implement, then clean out the housing.

9   Fit the new oil seal first having greased the mating surfaces of the seal and the axle housing. The lips of the oil seal must face inwards. Using a piece of brass or copper tubing of suitable diameter, carefully drive the new oil seal into the axle housing recess until the face of the seal is flush with the housing. Make sure that the end of the pinion is not knocked during this operation.

10 Refit the coupling to its original position on the pinion splines.

11 Fit a new pinion nut and holding the coupling still with the screwdriver or tyre lever, tighten the nut until the pinion endfloat only just disappears. **Do not** overtighten.

12 Rotate the pinion to settle the bearing and then check the preload using the cord and spring balance method previously described. By slight adjustment of the nut and rotation of the pinion obtain a spring balance preload figure 2 to 3 lbf in (2 to 4 kgf cm) greater than that

which applied before dismantling (paragraph 4). The additional torque is to compensate for the friction of the new seal.

---

8   Differential carrier (H type axle) – removal and refitting

On the H type axle the differential unit is mounted to the pinion carrier, and this is mounted on studs to the front face of the axle casing. The differential unit and carrier can therefore be removed complete with the axle casing still in position in the vehicle, but the axleshafts must first be removed. Proceed as follows.

1   Refer to Section 3 and remove both axleshafts.

2   Place a large container of at least 5 pints capacity beneath the differential carrier to catch the oil which will drain out.

3   Mark the pinion and propeller shaft flanges so that they can be refitted in their original position, then unscrew and remove the four self-locking nuts and bolts, detach the shaft, and support it with a stand.

4   Unscrew and remove the eight self-locking nuts which retain the differential carrier to the axle casing, then lift the carrier slightly to allow the oil to drain into the container.

5   Using a trolley jack or with the aid of an assistant, withdraw the differential carrier off the studs and remove it from beneath the vehicle (Fig. 8.11).

6   Peel the gasket from the axle casing studs; a new gasket will need to be fitted on reassembly.

7   Further dismantling of the differential unit is not recommended. If it is worn or damaged, its overhaul should be entrusted to your Ford dealer who will have the necessary tools required for this task. Alternatively, purchase an exchange unit.

8   Refitting the differential carrier is a reversal of the removal procedure but the following points should be noted:

   (a)   Check the mating faces of the differential carrier and axle housing for burrs and file them flat; always use a new gasket

   (b)   Make sure that the differential carrier is fitted with the pinion to the bottom, and tighten the retaining nuts in diagonal sequence in three or four stages

   (c)   The pinion and propeller shaft flanges must be aligned to the previously made marks

   (d)   Tighten all nuts and bolts to the specified torque wrench settings

   (e)   Fill the rear axle with the correct grade of oil until the level is up to the lower edge of the filler plug hole, then refit and tighten the plug

   (f)   If a new differential carrier unit has been installed, it should be run-in for 500 miles (800 km) to ensure that the new bearings bed in correctly. Change the oil after this mileage

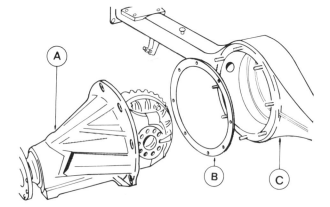

Fig. 8.11 H type axle differential unit and carrier (A), flange gasket (B) and axle case (C) (Sec 8)

---

9   Differential unit (G and F type axles) – repair and overhaul

1   The design and layout of the G and F type axles is such that any attempt to remove the differential unit or pinion assembly from the axle housing will upset their preset meshing.

2   Since special tools and skills are required to set up the

crownwheel and pinion mesh, the removal, overhaul and assembly of these differential types is not recommended and should be entrusted to your Ford dealer.

3   In any case the latest trend is for rear axle components not to be supplied individually, but the complete factory-built unit only to be supplied as a replacement.

10 Fault diagnosis – rear axle

Symptom	Reason(s)
Oil leakage	Faulty pinion oil seal Faulty axleshaft oil seals/gasket Defective cover gasket
Noise	Lack of oil Worn bearings General wear
'Clonk' on taking up drive and excessive backlash	Incorrectly tightened pinion nut Worn components Worn axleshaft splines Elongated roadwheel bolt holes Worn propeller shaft universal joints

Chapter 9 Braking system

Contents

Specifications

System type .... Disc front brakes, drum rear brakes, hydraulic operation, servo-assisted. Handbrake to rear wheels only with mechanical operation

Hydraulic system
Fluid type/specification .... Hydraulic fluid to Ford spec. SAM-6-9103 A (amber) (Duckhams Universal Brake and Clutch Fluid)

Front disc brakes
Disc diameter:
    Single solid or inner ventilated .... 10.62 in (270 mm)
    Outer ventilated .... 6.14 in (156 mm)
Disc thickness:
    Solid .... 0.55 in (14.15 mm)
    Ventilated .... 0.94 in (23.90 mm)
Disc thickness minimum (solid) .... 0.551 in (14.0 mm)
Maximum disc run-out (including hub) .... 0.005 in (0.13 mm)
Piston bore diameters .... 2.25 in (57.15 mm) and 1.63 in (41.40 mm)
Minimum pad thickness (friction material) .... 0.06 in (1.5 mm)
Total pad areas (both wheels) .... 24 in² (154.83cm²) and 30 in² (193.54 cm²)

Rear drum brakes
Drum diameter .... 9.00 in (228.6 mm) or 10.00 in (254.0 mm)
Shoe width .... 1.75 in (44.4 mm), 2.25 in (57.1 mm) or 2.75 in (69.8 mm)
Minimum lining thickness .... 0.06 in (1.5 mm)
Wheel cylinder diameter .... 0.8 in (20.3 mm), 0.87 in (22.2 mm) or 0.93 in (23.8 mm)

Torque wrench settings

	lbf ft	kgf m
Caliper to front suspension unit	66 to 81	9.0 to 11.0
Disc to hub	37 to 44	5.1 to 6.1
Carrier plate to axle	22 to 25	3.0 to 3.5
Hydraulic unions	8 to 11	1.2 to 1.5
Bleed valves	8 maximum	1.0 maximum

1 General description

Disc brakes are fitted to the front wheels and drum brakes to the rear. All are operated under servo assistance from the brake pedal, this being connected to the master cylinder and servo assembly, mounted on the bulkhead.

A dual line brake system is fitted and may be of vertical or horizontal split design, see Fig. 9.1 and 9.2. The object of the dual line brake system is to enable the brakes to remain operative in the event of a failure in the front or rear hydraulic circuit, although the brake efficiency will of course be reduced. Servo assistance in this condition is still available.

The front disc brakes operate in a conventional manner. The brake disc is secured to the hub flange and the caliper is mounted on the steering knuckle and wheel stub, so that the disc is able to rotate in between the two halves of the caliper. Inside each half of the caliper is a hydraulic cylinder, this being interconnected by a drilling which allows hydraulic fluid pressure to be transmitted to both halves. A piston operates in each cylinder, and is in contact with the outer face of the brake pad. By depressing the brake pedal, hydraulic fluid pressure is transmitted to the caliper by a system of metal and flexible hoses, whereupon the pistons are moved outwards so pushing the pads onto the face of the disc and slowing down the rotational speed of the disc.

On models with a horizontally split braking system, a four-piston caliper is fitted to each front wheel. In this system, the secondary chamber of the master cylinder transmits fluid pressure to the rear brakes and the two lower pistons in each front brake. The primary chamber fluid is fed to the upper pistons.

On models fitted with the vertically split braking system, two sizes of master cylinder have been fitted. On the master cylinder with the 0.937 in (23.8 mm) inside diameter, the primary chamber supplies fluid to the front brakes and the secondary cylinder supplies the rear brake circuit. On models fitted with a 0.875 in (22.2 mm) inside diameter master cylinder, the primary chamber feeds the rear circuit whilst the secondary chamber feeds the front circuit.

The rear drum brakes have one cylinder operating two shoes. When the brake pedal is depressed, hydraulic fluid pressure, increased by the servo unit, is transmitted to the rear brake wheel cylinders by a system of metal and flexible pipes. The pressure moves the pistons outwards so pushing the shoe linings into contact with the inside circumference of the brake drum and slowing down the rotational speed of the drum.

The linings are bonded into position on the shoes. The leading shoe lining is about double the thickness of the trailing shoe lining. This ensures an even working life for both front and rear linings since the leading shoe suffers from extra wear in service.

The drum brake linings can be easily inspected for wear through two apertures in each backplate after removal of the seal plugs. This dispenses with the need to remove the wheels and drums.

The handbrake operates on the rear wheels only, and the centrally mounted lever is connected to the rear brake assemblies by rod and cable. Adjustment of the handbrake is possible but is not normally

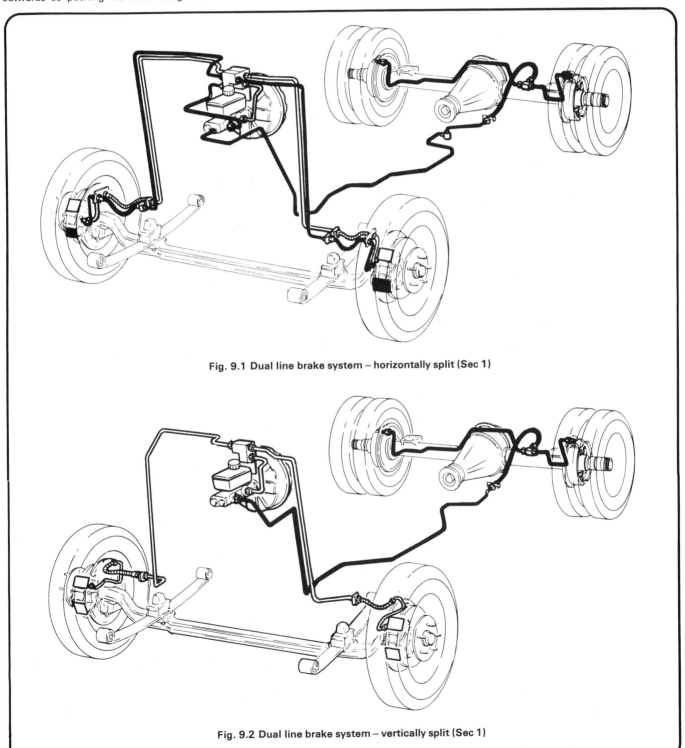

Fig. 9.1 Dual line brake system – horizontally split (Sec 1)

Fig. 9.2 Dual line brake system – vertically split (Sec 1)

necessary as the rear brakes are fitted with automatic adjusters.

A metering valve is fitted in the hydraulic circuit and this restricts the initial pressure supply to the front brakes until the rear brakes are under equal pressure. In this manner the front and rear brake balance is maintained.

The servo unit, which reduces the amount of pedal pressure required to actuate the brakes, is of a vacuum type and is located between the master cylinder and the brake pedal. In the event of the servo unit failing for any reason the brakes will remain operational but greater braking effort will be required by the driver.

Some models are fitted with a load conscious brake valve (also known as a load apportioning valve). This device senses the loading on the rear axle and adjusts the hydraulic pressure to the rear brakes accordingly to prevent the rear wheels from locking up under light loading.

2 Braking system – maintenance

1   At the specified intervals, or more frequently if necessary, check the brake fluid level in the reservoir. Always use the recommended brake fluid for topping up, as use of non-standard fluid may result in perishing or swelling of the system seals with consequent brake failure. Any sudden fall in the reservoir fluid level should be investigated immediately.

2   Also at the specified intervals, the brake linings and pads should be checked for wear. Check the brake pipe and hoses for leaking of fluid caused by corrosion, chafing or faulty unions. The handbrake linkage should be checked, lubricated and adjusted as necessary at the same interval. Refer to Fig. 9.3 for the lubrication points.

3   Every 36 000 miles (60 000 km) or two years, whichever comes sooner, it is advisable to change the fluid in the braking system and at the same time renew all hydraulic seals and flexible hoses. This is because hydraulic fluid absorbs moisture from the air, leading to internal corrosion and reducing the boiling point of the fluid.

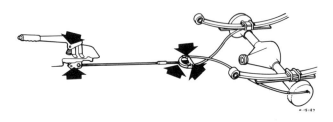

Fig. 9.3 Lubrication points (arrowed) of the handbrake cable (Sec 2)

3 Bleeding the hydraulic system

1   If any of the hydraulic components in the braking system have been removed or disconnected, or if the fluid level in the master cylinder has been allowed to fall appreciably, it is inevitable that air will have been introduced into the system. The removal of air from the hydraulic system is essential if the brakes are to function correctly, and the process of removing it is known as bleeding.

2   There are a number of one-man, do-it-yourself, brake bleeding kits currently available from motor accessory shops. It is recommended that one of these kits should be used wherever possible as they greatly simplify the bleeding operation and also reduce the risk of expelled air and fluid being drawn back into the system.

3   If one of these kits is not available then it will be necessary to gather together a clean jar and a suitable length of clear plastic tubing which is a tight fit over the bleed screw, and also to engage the help of an assistant.

4   Before commencing the bleeding operation, check that all rigid pipes and flexible hoses are in good condition and that all hydraulic unions are tight. Take great care not to allow hydraulic fluid to come

into contact with the vehicle paintwork, otherwise the finish will be seriously damaged. Wash off any spilled fluid immediately with cold water.

5   If hydraulic fluid has been lost from the master cylinder, due to a leak in the system, ensure that the cause is traced and rectified before proceeding further or a serious malfunction of the braking system may occur.

6   To bleed the system, clean the area around the bleed screw at the wheel cylinder to be bled. If the hydraulic system has only been partially disconnected and suitable precautions were taken to prevent further loss of fluid, it should only be necessary to bleed that part of the system. However, if the entire system is to be bled, start at the wheel furthest away from the master cylinder.

7   Remove the master cylinder filler cap and top up the reservoir. Periodically check the fluid level during the bleeding operation and top up as necessary, using only new brake fluid of the specified type.

8   If a one-man brake bleeding kit is being used, connect the outlet tube to the bleed screw and then open the screw half a turn. If possible position the unit so that it can be viewed from the car, then depress the brake pedal to the floor and slowly release it. The one-way valve in the kit will prevent air from returning to the system at the end of each stroke. Repeat this operation until clean hydraulic fluid, free from air bubbles, can be seen coming through the tube. Now tighten the bleed screw and remove the outlet tube.

9   If a one-man brake bleeding kit is not available, connect one end of the plastic tubing to the bleed screw and immerse the other end in the jar containing sufficient clean hydraulic fluid to keep the end of the tube submerged. Open the bleed screw half a turn and have your assistant depress the brake pedal to the floor and then slowly release it. Tighten the bleed screw at the end of each downstroke to prevent expelled air and fluid from being drawn back into the system. Repeat this operation until clean hydraulic fluid, free from air bubbles, can be seen coming through the tube. Now tighten the bleed screw and remove the plastic tube.

10 If the entire system is being bled the procedures described above should now be repeated at each wheel, finishing at the wheel nearest to the master cylinder. Do not forget to recheck the fluid level in the master cylinder at regular intervals and top up as necessary. Figs. 9.4, 9.5 and 9.6 show the bleed nipple locations.

11 Front calipers of four-piston construction are fitted with three bleed nipples and these must be bled simultaneously by using three lengths of tubing; it may also be necessary to depress the button(s) located on the metering valve to assist the bleeding operations (photo).

12 When completed, recheck the fluid level in the master cylinder, top up if necessary and refit the cap. Check the 'feel' of the brake pedal which should be firm and free from any 'sponginess' which would indicate air still present in the system.

3.11 Metering valve (vertically split system) is located on top of servo unit

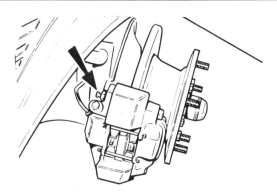

Fig. 9.4 Single bleed nipple (arrowed) on two-piston caliper
(Sec 3)

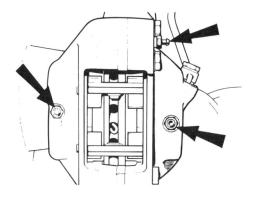

Fig. 9.5 Three bleed nipples (arrowed) on four-piston caliper
(Sec 3)

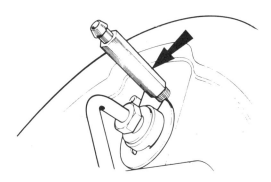

Fig. 9.6 Rear brake bleed nipple (arrowed) (Sec 3)

13   Discard any expelled hydraulic fluid as it is likely to be contaminated with moisture, air and dirt which makes it unsuitable for
further use.

4   Flexible hose – inspection, removal and refitting

1   Inspect the condition of the flexible hydraulic hoses leading to
each of the front disc brake calipers and also the one at the front of the
rear axle. If they are swollen, damaged or chafed, they must be
renewed.
2   Wipe the top of the brake master cylinder reservoir and unscrew
the cap. Place a piece of polythene sheet over the top of the reservoir
and refit the cap. This is to stop hydraulic fluid syphoning out during
subsequent operations.

Front hoses
3   Jack up and support the front of the vehicle. If access is difficult,
remove the roadwheel on the side concerned.
4   Disconnect the flexible hose at the caliper.
5   From inside the engine compartment, disconnect the hose at the
bulkhead union (photo).
6   When refitting, make sure the key on the hose end fitting locates
in the slot in the bulkhead mounting hole. Note that the hoses are
handed, ie left and right-hand hoses are not interchangeable. If there
is a white stripe on the hose, it should face forwards.
7   When the bulkhead union is secured, attach the hose at the caliper
end. Make sure that the hose is positioned so that it cannot chafe
against steering or suspension components.

Rear hose
8   Disconnect the rear hose at its forward mounting bracket first,
then at the axle 3-way union. If the 3-way union is integral with the
end of the hose, disconnect the rigid pipes from the union and unbolt
the union (photos).
9   Refit in the reverse order to removal.

All hoses
10   Bleed the brake hydraulic system on completion (Section 3) and
check for satisfactory brake operation. If only one hose has been
renewed, it should only be necessary to bleed that part of the system.

5   Handbrake – adjustment

1   Normally the automatic adjustment of the rear brakes will also
remove any excess handbrake lever movement, but where the handbrake cable has stretched it will be necessary to carry out the following
adjustment.
2   Jack up the rear of the vehicle, chock the front wheels and support
it adequately with suitable stands.
3   Fully release the handbrake lever and then working underneath the
vehicle, loosen off the cable adjuster locknuts. (One locknut has a left-
hand thread). Turn the adjuster until all tension is removed from the

4.5 Front flexible hose

4.8a Rear flexible hose to three-way connector
location

4.8b Rear flexible hose to front location
bracket on chassis

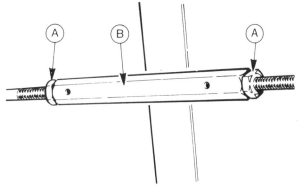

Fig. 9.7 Handbrake cable adjuster (B) with locknuts (A) (Sec 5)

5.3 Handbrake cable yoke. End of adjuster assembly is visible at top of photo

operating rods and cable, and then clean and lubricate the adjuster threads thoroughly (photo). Operate the footbrake pedal several times to ensure that the rear brakes are adjusted, then pull the handbrake lever up 6 notches.

4   Retighten the adjuster until it is hand tight but no more and then tighten the locknuts against the adjuster; the threads each side of the adjuster should be of equal length and the threads should be visible through the adjuster holes.

5   Under normal operation, the handbrake should be effective when applied 7 to 8 notches. Release the handbrake fully and check that the rear wheels are free to turn, then lower the vehicle to the ground.

6   Front disc pads – inspection, removal and refitting

1   Apply the handbrake firmly and remove the hub cap (when fitted). Loosen the wheel nuts and jack up the front of the vehicle, supporting it adequately on suitable stands. Remove the front wheels.

2   On inspection, if the disc pad lining thickness is found to be less than the minimum given in the Specifications, the pads must be renewed. The pads should be renewed in sets of four, and a single or single pair of pads should never be renewed alone.

3   To remove the disc pads, first open the bonnet and remove the brake fluid reservoir filler cap, and disconnect the battery negative terminal.

4   On ventilated disc brakes fitted with a four-piston caliper, use a length of dowel rod of suitable diameter to drive the two pad retaining pins out of the caliper, at the same time depressing the anti-rattle clips (Fig. 9.8).

5   On solid disc brakes fitted with a two-piston caliper, straighten the split pin ears and extract them with a pair of pliers, at the same time depressing the anti-rattle clips.

6   On both types of caliper, note the fitted position of the anti-rattle clips before removing them.

7   The disc pads can now be removed from the caliper; if they prove difficult to move by hand, a pair of long-nosed pliers can be used (Fig. 9.9).

8   The next operation will raise the level of the brake fluid in the fluid reservoir and it is advisable to remove a quantity of fluid with a pipette, or alternatively to place some rag around the reservoir to absorb any fluid which overflows.

9   Using a flat iron bar or length of wood, carefully push the pistons fully back into their caliper bores. Be careful not to damage or distort the brake disc.

10   Clean the recesses in the caliper and the exposed faces of each piston of all traces of dirt and rust.

11   Refitting the disc pads is a reversal of the removal procedure, but it will be necessary to depress the footbrake pedal several times to reposition the caliper pistons and provide the disc pads with the correct adjustment. Check the brake fluid level in the reservoir and top up as necessary with fresh fluid before refitting the filler cap and wiping away any excess fluid (photo).

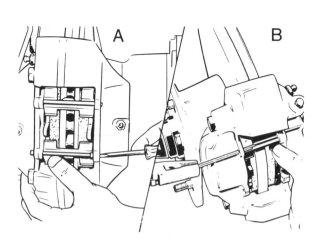

Fig. 9.8 Remove the disc pad retaining pins (Sec 6)

A   Four-piston caliper   B   Two-piston caliper

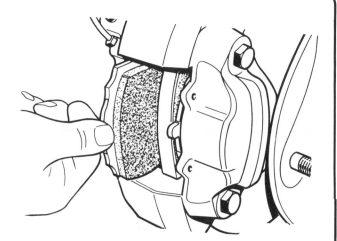

Fig. 9.9 Extracting the disc pads from the caliper (Sec 6)

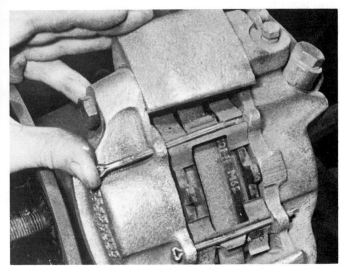

6.11 Refitting disc pad retaining pins

7 Front brake caliper – removal and refitting

1   Remove the front brake disc pads as described in Section 6.
2   Wipe the area around the brake fluid reservoir filler cap, remove the cap and then tighten it down firmly onto a piece of polythene sheeting; this will prevent an excessive amount of fluid being lost from the hydraulic system and will thus assist the final bleeding operation.
3   Preferably using a split ring spanner, unscrew and remove the union nut(s) securing the hydraulic brake pipe(s) to the caliper, and plug the end(s) with a pencil or similar item to prevent the ingress of dirt or foreign matter.
4   Using a screwdriver, bend up the caliper retaining bolt locktabs then unbolt the caliper from the stub axle mounting and withdraw the

caliper; make sure where a horizontally split dual line braking system is fitted that the two hydraulic brake pipes are identified with their original locations on the caliper (Fig. 9.10).
5   Refitting the front brake caliper is a reversal of the removal procedure but the following additional points should be noted:

    (a) *Wipe the disc contact faces clean of any spilt brake fluid or foreign matter*
    (b) *Tighten all nuts and bolts to the correct torque wrench settings*
    (c) *Bleed the brake hydraulic system as described in Section 3 and remember to remove the polythene sheeting from the fluid reservoir filler cap*

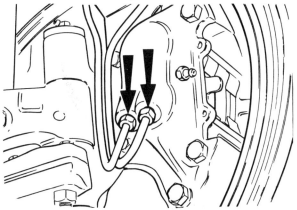

Fig. 9.10 Hydraulic pipe locations (arrowed) at the caliper – horizontally split system (Sec 7)

8 Front brake caliper – dismantling, overhaul and reassembly

1   Remove the front brake caliper as described in Section 7. Note that under no circumstances should the two halves of the caliper be separated as they are specially bolted together during manufacture (Fig. 9.11).

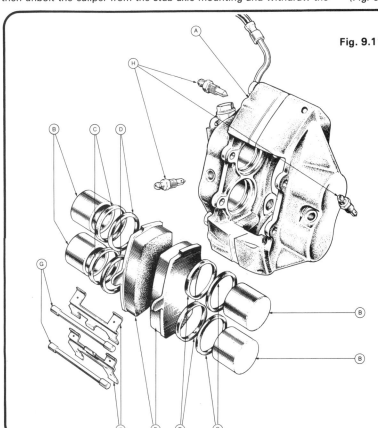

Fig. 9.11 Exploded view of the four-piston type front brake caliper (Sec 8)

    A *Caliper*
    B *Pistons*
    C *Seals*
    D *Retainer*
    E *Brake pads*
    F *Anti-rattle clips*
    G *Retaining pins*
    H *Bleed nipples*

2   Place a block of wood of suitable width into the caliper between the faces of the pistons and then carefully apply air pressure from a tyre pump to the inlet port(s) to partially remove the pistons from their bores.

3   Prise the sealing bellows skirts from the caliper when these are fitted and then remove the pistons; prise the bellows from the pistons (when fitted) and note the location of each piston.

4   Note the fitted position of the piston seals, then carefully prise them out of their locating grooves.

5   Wash all components in clean hydraulic fluid or methylated spirit, and then examine the surfaces of the pistons and caliper bores for scoring, scratching, or bright wear areas. If these exist renew the caliper unit complete, but, if the piston and caliper are in good condition, discard the oil seals and obtain a repair kit.

6   Dip the internal components in clean hydraulic fluid and then assemble the new seals to the pistons using the fingers only to manipulate them into position; make sure the seals are fitted the correct way round.

7   Assemble the sealing bellows (if fitted) to the pistons, lubricate the caliper bores with hydraulic fluid and then carefully insert each piston into its original bore, finally manipulating the sealing bellows (if fitted) onto the caliper grooves.

8   Remember that hydraulic fluid is an effective paint stripper, and therefore do not spill any on the vehicle bodywork.

Fig. 9.12 Refitting the front brake caliper pistons (Sec 8)

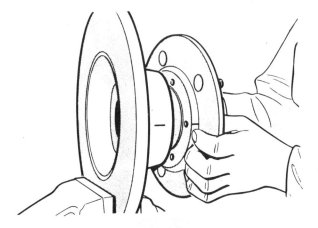

Fig. 9.13 Front hub and disc alignment marks (Sec 9)

9   Front brake disc – examination, removal and refitting

1   Remove the disc pads as described in Section 6.

2   Examine the surface of the disc for deep scoring or grooving. Light scoring is normal but anything more severe should be removed by taking the disc to be surface ground, provided the thickness of the disc is not reduced below the specified minimum; otherwise a new disc will have to be fitted.

3   The disc should be checked for run-out, but before doing this, the front wheel bearings must be adjusted as described in Chapter 11. The run-out is best checked with a dial gauge, although using feeler blades between the face of the disc and a fixed point will give a satisfactory result. The check should be made on both sides of the disc at a radius of 5.1 in (130 mm), the disc being slowly moved by hand.

4   If the disc run-out exceeds that given in the Specifications and it is confirmed that the disc is faulty, it must be renewed.

5   To remove the disc first remove the hub assembly as described in Chapter 11 and check that the hub and disc alignment marks are clearly visible as shown in Fig. 9.13.

6   Using a screwdriver, bend back the locktabs and unbolt the disc from the hub assembly in diagonal sequence.

7   Refitting the front brake disc is a reversal of the removal procedure but the following additional points should be noted:

   (a)   *Clean the mating surfaces of the disc and hub assembly before reassembling them and ensure that the alignment marks are adjacent to each other*

   (b)   *Tighten the retaining bolts to the correct torque wrench settings*

   (c)   *Always use new locktabs*

   (d)   *Adjust the wheel bearings as described in Chapter 11*

10   Rear brake shoes – inspection, removal and refitting

1   Two rubber inspection plugs are fitted to each rear backplate and these can be prised free to allow inspection of the brake linings through the apertures. This eliminates the need to remove the brake drums unless the linings are to be renewed (photo).

2   After prising out the rubber plugs, clean the edge of the shoe to ascertain how much wear has taken place and compare it with the minimum lining thickness given in the Specifications. Repeat the procedure for each shoe of both rear wheels. If it is found that any show is below the minimum limit, it will be necessary to renew all the rear brake shoes.

3   Remove the hub cap (when fitted), loosen the wheel nuts, chock the front wheels and then fully release the handbrake.

4   Jack up the rear of the vehicle and support it adequately on suitable stands, then remove the wheels. Note that on 6-stud wheels,

10.1 Inspection plugs (arrowed) in the rear brake backplate

the wheel nuts are right-hand threaded on the right-hand side of the vehicle and left-hand threaded on the left-hand side.

5   The following instructions refer to axle types G, or F and H. Refer to Chapter 8 for the identification and description of the axle types.

6   On the G type axle, unscrew and remove the axleshaft nuts in diagonal sequence and withdraw the axleshaft together with its gasket. Using a chisel or screwdriver, bend up the tabs of the

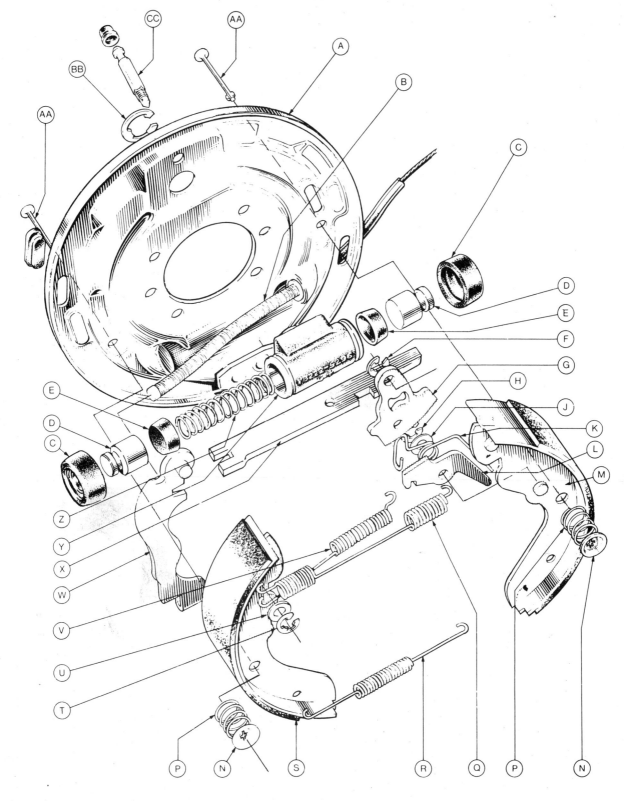

Fig. 9.14 Rear brake components (Sec 10)

A	Backplate	J	Washer	R	Lower return spring	X	Spacer strut
B	Handbrake cable	K	Spring	S	Brake shoe	Y	Wheel cylinder
D	Dust cover	L	Ratchet	T	Spring clip	Z	Spring
E	Seal	M	Brake shoe	U	Washer	AA	Pin
F	Spring clip	N	Washer	V	Handbrake spring	BB	Circlip
G	Ratchet	P	Spring	W	Handbrake lever	CC	Bleed valve
H	Spring clip	Q	Upper return spring				

lockwasher and then unscrew and remove the bearing locknut; a special tool is required to loosen the bearing locknut and adjusting nut and should be obtained from the local tool hire agent or local garage if possible. Remove the lockwasher, adjusting nut, and the outer bearing cone and rollers assembly, then carefully lift the hub and drum off the rear axle extension. Wipe the assembly clean of any surplus bearing grease which may have dropped onto the brake drum inner surface.

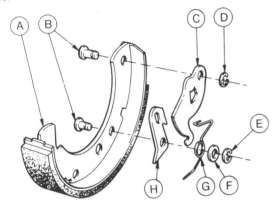

Fig. 9.15 Exploded view of the self-adjusting mechanism components (Sec 10)

A	Leading brake shoe	E	Spring clip
B	Pivot pins	F	Washer
C	Large ratchet	G	Spring
D	Spring clip	H	Small ratchet

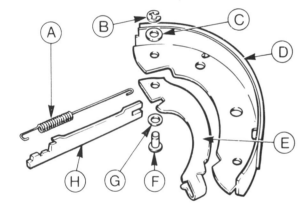

Fig. 9.16 Rear brake shoe and handbrake components (Sec 10)

A	Spring	E	Lever
B	Spring clip	F	Pivot pin
C	Washer	G	Washer
D	Trailing shoe	H	Spacer strut

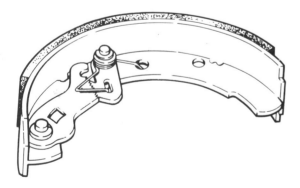

Fig. 9.17 Assembly position of self-adjusting ratchet (Sec 10)

7   On the F and H type axle (fitted to all LCX models except the 125 variant), remove the brake drum retaining screw and withdraw the drum from the hub. If necessary use a soft-headed mallet and tap evenly round the drum outer circumference to ease it free. The rear brake components are now accessible (photo).

8   With the brake drum removed, clean it and examine the contact surfaces for signs of excessive scoring and wear. The drum must be renewed or alternatively machined if extensive wear has taken place.

9   Check the brake shoe lining thickness and, if it is below the minimum limit given in the Specifications, or if the lining rivets are flush with the lining surface, it will be necessary to renew all four rear brake shoes. Renewal is also necessary if the linings are contaminated with oil or hydraulic fluid. In this case the source of contamination must also be rectified.

10   To remove the brake shoes, first remove the holding-down spring from the leading shoe by depressing the top washer, turning it through 90° and withdrawing the washers, spring, and pin from the backplate.

11   Note the position of each brake shoe return spring, and mark the outer surface of the shoe webs to indicate their front and rear locations.

12   Unhook the lower return spring from both shoes using a pair of pliers.

13   Pull the lower end of the leading shoe away from the abutment and unhook it from the upper return spring; detach the return spring from the trailing shoe.

14   Remove the holding-down spring from the trailing shoe using the procedure described in paragraph 10.

15   Pull the upper end of the trailing shoe away from the wheel cylinder, pull the handbrake cable spring back, and disconnect the handbrake cable from the handbrake lever. The trailing shoe can now be removed from the backplate.

16   The self-adjusting mechanism must now be removed from the leading shoe by prising the two clips from the pivot pins. Note the correct position of the ratchet spring (Fig. 9.15).

17   Finally remove the handbrake lever and spacer strut from the trailing shoe by pulling the lever and twisting the strut, and then unhooking the retaining spring. Prise the pivot pin clip out of its groove and remove the handbrake lever and washers from the trailing shoe.

18   With the brake shoes removed, locate an elastic band around the wheel cylinder to prevent the pistons from coming out. Take care not to depress the footbrake pedal whilst the brake shoes and drums are removed.

19   Thoroughly clean all traces of lining dust from the shoes and backplate but do not inhale the dust as it is hazardous to health.

20   Check that the wheel cylinder pistons are free to move in their bores. Check the wheel cylinder dust covers for damage and the wheel cylinders and brake pipe unions for hydraulic fluid leaks.

21   Check the handbrake lever, adjuster, and self-adjusting mechanism for wear, and renew any items as necessary.

10.7 Rear brake assembly with drum removed

22 Refitting of the rear brake shoes is a reversal of the removal procedure, but the following additional points should be noted:

(a) *When refitting the brake shoes note that the leading shoe is the one with the thicker lining*

(b) *Ensure that the spacer strut is fitted at right-angles to the handbrake lever. The adjuster ratchets should be positioned as shown in Fig. 9.17 prior to fitting the leading shoe*

(c) *When reassembling the G type axle, readjust the rear hub bearings as given in Chapter 8, Section 5*

(d) *Depress the footbrake several times to bring the brake shoes into the correct position*

(e) *Adjust the handbrake as described in Section 5*

23 Finally remove the stands, lower the vehicle to the ground, and road test the vehicle to check the operation of the brakes. If new linings have been fitted, the efficiency of the brakes may be slightly reduced until the linings have bedded-in.

11 Rear brake wheel cylinder – removal and refitting

1 If the wheel cylinder is seized or the internal seals leaking it will be necessary to overhaul or renew the unit; the removal and refitting procedure is as follows (photo).

2 Remove the rear brake shoes by referring to Section 10, then thoroughly clean the area around the wheel cylinder to prevent the ingress of foreign matter into the hydraulic system.

3 Wipe clean and then remove the brake fluid reservoir cap, and screw it down tightly onto a piece of polythene sheeting to prevent all the brake fluid from draining out of the hydraulic pipes.

4 Unscrew and remove the bleed nipple from the rear of the wheel cylinder and then, using a split ring spanner if possible, unscrew the union nut securing the metal brake pipe to the wheel cylinder. Plug the end with a pencil or cover it with masking tape to prevent dirt contaminating the brake fluid.

5 Using a screwdriver, prise the retaining clip from the rear of the wheel cylinder and then remove the wheel cylinder and gasket from the brake backplate.

6 Clean the wheel cylinder location on the backplate on both sides.

7 Refitting the rear wheel cylinder is a reversal of the removal procedure but the following additional points should be noted:

(a) *Fit a new gasket and retaining clip to the wheel cylinder each time it is removed*

(b) *A special tool is required to fit the retaining clip to the wheel cylinder and this is shown in Fig. 9.18; if the tool is not readily available, a suitable length of tubing, a threaded stud, a nut, and washer can be made into a tool quite easily by the home mechanic*

(c) *It is important to ensure that the location peg on the wheel cylinder locates with the hole in the backplate*

(d) *Tighten all nuts and bolts to the torque wrench settings given in the Specifications*

(e) *Bleed the braking system as described in Section 3 and then depress the brake pedal several times to centralise and adjust the brake shoes by actuation of the automatic adjuster. Don't forget to remove the polythene sheet from the brake fluid reservoir*

(f) *Adjust the handbrake as described in Section 5.*

12 Rear brake wheel cylinder – dismantling and reassembly

1 Remove the wheel cylinder as described in the previous Section, then brush and clean away all external dirt.

2 Prise each rubber boot from its groove in the cylinder body.

3 Extract each piston together with its seal from the cylinder bore; if difficulty is experienced apply air pressure from a tyre pump to the fluid inlet, and wrap the assembly in a clean cloth to catch the parts in as they emerge. The bleed nipple must be fitted or the injected air will escape through its hole.

4 The cylinder components and their order of fitting are shown in Fig. 9.14.

5 Inspect the inside of the cylinder for score marks caused by impurities in the hydraulic fluid. If any are found, the cylinder and pistons will require renewal. If the wheel cylinder requires renewal

11.1 Rear brake wheel cylinder

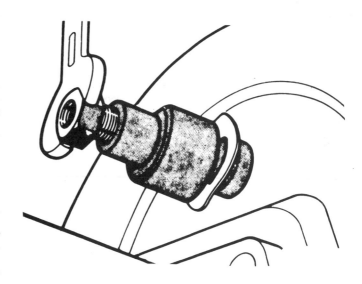

Fig. 9.18 Tool for refitting the rear wheel cylinder retaining clip (Sec 11)

always ensure that the replacement is exactly similar to the one removed.

6 If the cylinder is sound, thoroughly clean it out with fresh hydraulic fluid.

7 The old rubber seals will probably be swollen and visibly worn. Smear the new rubber seals with hydraulic fluid and refit to the pistons, making sure they are the correct way round.

8 Wet the cylinder bore with clean hydraulic fluid and then insert the return spring, followed by the seal and piston at each end. Ensure that the seal is correctly located and not distorted or damaged during fitting into the cylinder bore.

9 Relocate the rubber boots on each end of the cylinder and check that they are fully engaged in the cylinder grooves to complete.

13 Master cylinder – removal and refitting

1 Raise and support the bonnet.

2 Wipe the area around the hydraulic fluid reservoir filler cap, unscrew the cap, and tighten it down firmly onto a piece of polythene sheeting; this will help retain the fluid in the reservoir while the master cylinder is being removed.

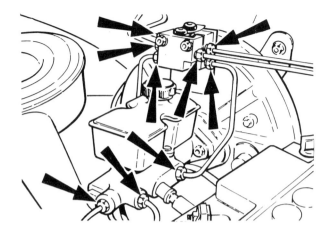

Fig. 9.19 Master cylinder and pressure metering valve hydraulic fluid line connections (horizontally split system) (Sec 13)

3   Referring to Fig. 9.19, disconnect the fluid lines at their connections to the master cylinder and brake pressure metering valve as applicable. Note the pipe locations. Plug the pipe ends to prevent spillage and the ingress of dirt. Disconnect the brake warning light switch wire.

4   Undo and remove the two nuts and spring washers that secure the master cylinder to the rear of the servo unit. Lift away the master cylinder taking care that no hydraulic fluid is allowed to drip onto the paintwork. Wipe any fluid spillage from paintwork or fittings in the engine compartment as the fluid will damage paintwork.

5   Refit in the reverse sequence to removal. Refer to Section 14 if fitting a new unit. When reattaching the fluid line unions, they should be loosely assembled until all are located. The master cylinder should also be loosely attached to assist if necessary in allowing the pipe

connections to be engaged easily and without the danger of cross-threading. With all pipes connected, tighten the fittings and the master cylinder retaining nuts.

6   Top up the hydraulic reservoir fluid level and bleed the system as described in Section 3.

14 Master cylinder – dismantling, overhaul and reassembly

If a replacement master cylinder is to be fitted, it will be necessary to lubricate the seals before fitting to the vehicle as they have a protective coating when originally assembled. Remove the blanking plugs from the hydraulic pipe union seatings. Inject clean hydraulic fluid into the master cylinder and operate the primary piston several times so that the fluid spreads over all the internal working surfaces.

If the master cylinder is to be dismantled after removal, proceed as follows.

1   First remove the reservoir filler cap and invert the cylinder to allow the fluid to drain from the cylinder. Detach the reservoir from the cylinder by unscrewing the two retaining screws. On some models the reservoir is removed by simply pulling upwards from the cylinder and removing the rubber seals. Do not re-use fluid emptied from the cylinder.

2   Mount the cylinder in a soft-jawed vice, then use a length of dowel rod to depress the primary piston and, with it held down, locate and remove the stop pin from the front reservoir inlet (Fig. 9.21).

3   Extract the circlip frm the mouth of the cylinder and then remove the internal components, placing them on a clean surface in the exact order of removal; tap the cylinder on a wooden block to remove the secondary piston assembly.

4   Remove the primary piston spring by unscrewing and removing the retaining screw and sleeve.

5   Prise the seals from the pistons as necessary and then wash all components in clean hydraulic fluid and methylated spirit. Examine the pistons and cylinder bore surfaces for scoring, scratches, or bright wear areas and if any are observed, renew the master cylinder as a complete unit. If the surfaces are in good condition, discard the old seals and obtain a repair kit.

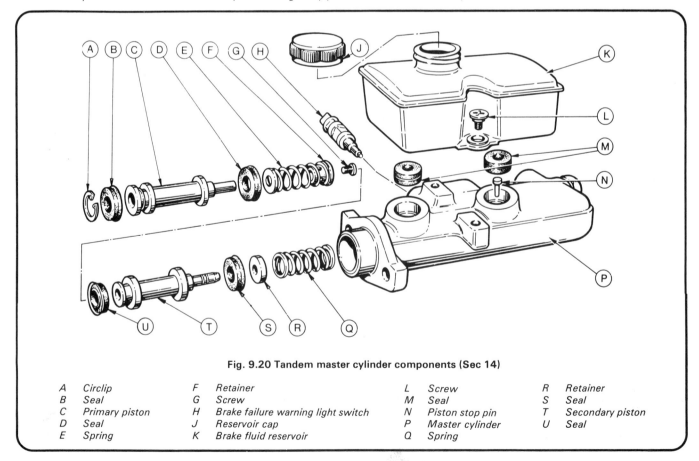

Fig. 9.20 Tandem master cylinder components (Sec 14)

A	Circlip	F	Retainer	L	Screw	R	Retainer
B	Seal	G	Screw	M	Seal	S	Seal
C	Primary piston	H	Brake failure warning light switch	N	Piston stop pin	T	Secondary piston
D	Seal	J	Reservoir cap	P	Master cylinder	U	Seal
E	Spring	K	Brake fluid reservoir	Q	Spring		

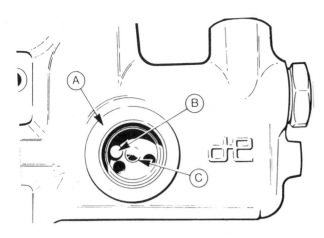

Fig. 9.21 Master cylinder (A) showing the piston stop pin (B) and secondary inlet port (C) (Sec 14)

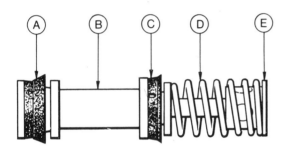

Fig. 9.22 Primary piston components – assembled position (Sec 14)

A   Seal   D   Spring
B   Piston   E   Retainer
C   Seal

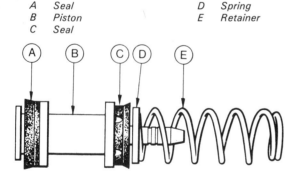

Fig. 9.23 Secondary piston components – assembled position (Sec 14)

A   Seal   D   Retainer
B   Piston   E   Spring
C   Seal

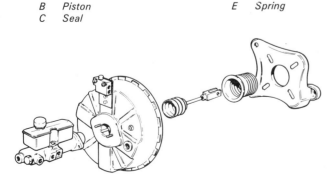

Fig. 9.24 The master cylinder and servo unit (Sec 15)

6   Dip the internal components in clean hydraulic fluid and then fit them into the master cylinder bore in the reverse order to removal, making sure that the new seals are fitted the correct way round. Refer to Figs. 9.22 and 9.23 for the correct position of the primary and secondary piston components. When handling the seals use only the fingers to manipulate them into position.

7   The remaining reassembly procedure is a reversal of the dismantling procedure. As a safety precaution, when the cylinder has been refitted to the vehicle, have an assistant depress the footbrake pedal hard for a minimum of ten seconds and observe the cylinder for signs of fluid leakage.

15 Vacuum servo unit – removal and refitting

1   The vacuum servo unit is located between the master cylinder and the engine bulkhead. First remove the master cylinder as described in Section 13.

2   Prise free and release the check valve with vacuum hose from the servo.

3   Unscrew and remove the vacuum buzzer switch (if fitted) (Fig. 9.25).

4   Unscrew and remove the brake pipes from the metering valve fitted to the servo unit.

5   Working inside the vehicle, disconnect the servo operating rod from the brake pedal by removing the spring clip and clevis pin.

6   Unscrew and remove the two nuts and one bolt retaining the servo unit to the bulkhead and withdraw the unit from the vehicle complete with its mounting bracket; the bracket and rubber dust cover can be detached by removing the four nuts and washers. Detach the metering valve by unscrewing and removing the two retaining nuts and washers.

7   Refitting the vacuum servo unit is a reversal of the removal procedure but the following additional points should be noted:

   (a)   Before tightening the mounting bracket to the bulkhead, connect the operating rod to the brake pedal and ensure that it is aligned correctly; check the operating rod movement again after tightening the bracket

   (b)   The operating rod length should be adjusted so that, with the brake pedal fully lifted, the clevis pin can be inserted without any interference; tighten the locknut when this adjustment is correct

   (c)   Bleed the braking system as described in Section 3

8   A defective servo unit must be renewed, no repair being possible. Before condemning the servo, however, make sure that the fault does not lie in the vacuum hose or check valve.

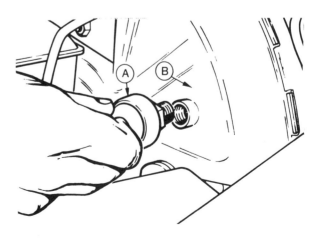

Fig. 9.25 Buzzer switch (A) location in servo unit (B) (Sec 15)

16 Load conscious brake valve – general

1   Some models are fitted with a load conscious brake valve, the purpose of which is to regulate the pressure applied to the rear brakes according to vehicle loading. This then prevents the wheels 'locking up' if the vehicle is empty or carrying a light load when heavy brake pressure is applied.
2   The valve assembly is mounted on the chassis in front of the rear axle (Fig. 9.26).
3   The only time that the valve assembly will have to be removed is (a) if the valve is defective or (b) if the rear axle is to be removed, in which case the valve assembly will not have to be completely removed but the coil spring will have to be detached at its top end. If the spring is detached at the bottom end the valve will have to be readjusted. (Refer to Chapter 8 for rear axle removal).
4   The valve will also have to be readjusted on refitting if the assembly has been removed. This requires the use of specialised equipment and reference to several graphs depending on body type fitted. Because of this factor the removal, refitting and adjustment procedure should be entrusted to a suitably equipped Ford garage.

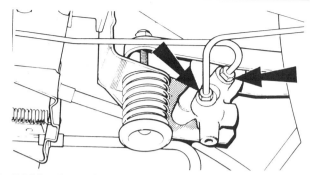

Fig. 9.26 Load conscious brake valve location and (arrowed) brake pipes (Sec 16)

17 Brake pedal – removal and refitting

The procedure is identical to that for the clutch pedal and full information will be found in Chapter 5.

18 Fault diagnosis – braking system

Symptom	Reason(s)
Pedal travels almost to floor before brakes operate	
Leaks and air bubbles in hydraulic system	Brake fluid too low
	Wheel cylinder leaking
	Master cylinder leaking (bubbles in master cylinder fluid)
	Brake flexible hose leaking
	Brake line fractured
	Brake system unions loose
Normal wear	Linings over 75% worn
Incorrect adjustment	Defective automatic adjuster mechanism
	Master cylinder pushrod out of adjustment causing too much pedal free movement
Brake pedal feels 'springy'	
Brake lining renewal	New linings not yet bedded-in
Excessive wear or damage	Brake drums badly worn and weak or cracked
	Brake discs badly worn or loose
	Master cylinder securing nuts loose
Brake pedal feels 'spongy' and 'soggy'	
Leaks or bubbles in hydraulic system	Wheel cylinder leaking
	Master cylinder leaking (bubbles in master cylinder reservoir)
	Brake pipe line or flexible hose leaking
	Unions in brake system loose
Excessive effort required to brake vehicle	
Lining type or condition	Linings or pads badly worn
	New linings recently fitted – not yet bedded-in
	Harder linings or pads fitted than standard causing increase in pedal pressure
Oil or grease leaks	Linings, brake drums or discs contaminated with oil, grease or hydraulic fluid
Servo unit defective	Leaking vacuum hose
	Servo unit worn internally
Brakes uneven and pulling to one side	
Oil or grease leaks	Linings, pads and brake drums or discs contaminated with oil, grease, or hydraulic fluid

Symptom	Reason(s)
Lack of maintenance	Tyre pressures unequal
	Radial ply tyres fitted at one end of vehicle only
	Brake backplate loose
	Brake shoes or pads fitted incorrectly
	Different type of linings fitted at each wheel
	Anchorages for front suspension or rear axle loose
	Brake drums or disc badly worn, cracked or distorted

Brakes tend to bind, drag, or lock-on

Symptom	Reason(s)
Incorrect adjustment	Faulty automatic adjuster causing brake shoes to be adjusted too tightly
	Handbrake cable over-tightened
Wear or dirt in hydraulic system or incorrect fluid	Reservoir vent hole in cap blocked with dirt
	Master cylinder trap valves restricted – brakes seize in 'on' position
	Wheel cylinder seized in 'on' position
Mechanical wear	Brake shoe pull-off springs broken, stretched or loose
Incorrect brake assembly	Brake shoe pull-off springs fitted wrong way round, omitted, or wrong type used
Neglect	Handbrake system rusted or seized in the 'on' position

Chapter 10 Electrical system

For modifications, and information applicable to later models, see Supplement at end of manual

Contents

Specifications

General

System type	12 volt, negative earth
Battery type	Lead acid
Battery capacity	38 to 68 Ah depending on model

Alternator

Make and type	Bosch K1-28A or K1-35A, or Lucas 15 or 17 ACR
Nominal output at 13.5 V and 6000 alternator rpm:	
K1-28A and 15 ACR	28 amps
K1-35A and 17 ACR	35 amps
Regulating voltage at 4000 rpm with 3 to 7 amp loading:	
Bosch	13.7 to 14.5 volts
Lucas	14.2 to 14.6 volts
Minimum brush length protruding from brush box in free position	0.197 in (5 mm)

Starter motor

Make and type (according to model)	Lucas M35J inertia, or M35J, 5M90, M50G or 2M100 pre-engaged; Bosch 0.7, 0.8 or 1.1 PS pre-engaged
Direction of rotation	Clockwise
Number of brushes	4
Minimum brush length:	
Lucas M35J and 5M90	0.3 in (8.0 mm)
Lucas M50G	0.5 in (12.0 mm)
Lucas 2M100	0.37 in (9.5 mm)
Bosch	0.39 in (10.0 mm)
Brush spring pressure:	
Lucas M50G	62 ozf (1.8 kgf)
Lucas M35J, 5M90 and 2M100	32 ozf (0.9 kgf)
Bosch	31 to 45 ozf (0.9 to 1.3 kgf)
Commutator minimum dimension:	
Thickness (Lucas)	0.08 in (2.05 mm)
Diameter (Bosch)	1.29 in (32.8 mm)
Armature endfloat (pre-engaged only):	
Lucas M35J and 5M90, and all Bosch	0.004 to 0.012 in (0.1 to 0.3 mm)
Lucas M50G	0.025 in (0.6 mm) maximum
Lucas 2M100	0.012 in (0.3 mm)

Light bulbs (typical)

	Wattage
Headlight — sealed beam (circular)	40/45
Headlight — semi-sealed, tungsten (circular)	40/45
Headlight — semi-sealed, halogen (square)	55/60
Sidelights	4
Direction indicators — front and rear	21
Tail lights	5
	21/5
Rear number plate light	4 or 5
Reversing light	21 (festoon)
Rear fog light	21
Instrument panel warning lights	1.3
Switch warning lights	1.3
Hazard flasher warning light	1.3
Brake warning light	1.3
Rear fog lamp warning light	1.3
Instrument panel lights	2.6 (standard) or 2.0 (tachograph variants)
Heater control light	2.0
Automatic transmission selector quadrant light	1.4
Clock light	2.6
Interior light	5.0
Cigarette lighter illumination light	1.4
Engine compartment light	5.0

Fuses (typical)

1	Hazard flashers/interior lights	8 amp
2	LH headlight (dip)	8 amp
3	LH headlight (main beam)	8 amp
4	LH side and rear lights/instrument panel lights	8 amp
5	RH side and rear lights	8 amp
6	RH headlight (dip)/rear fog light	8 amp
7	RH headlight (main beam)	8 amp
8	Stop-lights/direction indicators	8 amp
9	Horn/heater blower motor	8 amp
10	Windscreen wipers and washers	8 amp
11	Ignition and oil pressure warning light	8 amp
12	Headlight washers	25 amp

Note: *The reversing lights are integral with the main ignition circuit and are not directly fused*

---

1 General description

The electrical system consists of three major components; the battery, the alternator and its regulator, and the starter. In addition the remaining electrical equipment can be divided into three further groups; the lighting system, auxiliary components and instruments and warning light circuits.

The battery supplies a steady amount of current for starting, ignition, lighting, and other electrical circuits, and provides a reserve of power when the current consumed by the electrical equipment exceeds that being produced by the alternator.

The alternator generates electricity in order to maintain the battery in its optimum charged state and also to ensure that the electrical circuits are supplied with the correct current to enable the auxiliary components to function. A regulator is incorporated into the alternator circuit and effectively controls the output to match the requirements of the electrical system and battery.

The starter motor turns the engine with a pinion which engages with the flywheel ring gear, and due to the amount of current required by the starter, it is necessary to use a separate circuit direct to the battery incorporating heavy cable.

When recharging the battery it is important to disconnect the terminal leads from the battery otherwise serious damage can occur to the alternator internal diodes. In addition there may be other semi-conductor devices and accessories fitted to the vehicle which could also be damaged.

The electrical system has a negative earth and it is important to check that such items as radios, electronic ignition systems, and extra electrical items are connected correctly.

In emergencies it is in order to connect another battery with the aid of jump leads, but connect the positive terminals first followed by the negative terminals, and remove them in the reverse order.

To comply with EEC legislation, some models are fitted with a tachograph in place of the normal speedometer. Details of this instrument are given in Section 50.

2   Battery – removal and refitting

1   The battery is located on a tray in the engine compartment.
2   Disconnect the negative (earth) terminal first by unscrewing and removing the terminal bolt, then similarly disconnect the positive terminal.
3   Bend the terminal leads away from the battery, and unscrew and remove the battery clamp bolt which retains the battery to the tray.
4   Lift out the battery carefully to avoid spilling electrolyte on the body paintwork.
5   Refitting the battery is a reversal of the removal procedure, but before reconnecting the terminals, clean off any corrosion present and smear them with petroleum jelly. Do not overtighten the terminal bolts – the terminals are made of lead and are easily damaged.

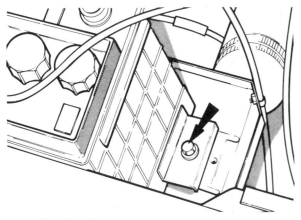

Fig. 10.1 Battery clamp bolt (arrowed) (Sec 2)

3.1 Topping up the battery

3   Battery – maintenance and inspection

1   Normal weekly battery maintenance consists of checking the electrolyte level of each cell to ensure that the separators are covered by $\frac{1}{2}$ in (13 mm) of electrolyte. If the level has fallen top up the battery using distilled water only (photo). Do not overfill. If a battery is overfilled or any electrolyte spilled, immediately wipe away the excess as electrolyte attacks and corrodes any metal it comes into contact with very rapidly.
2   As well as keeping the terminals clean and covered withh petroleum jelly, the top of the battery, and especially the top of the cells, should be kept clean and dry. This helps prevent corrosion and ensures that the battery does not become partially discharged by leakage through dampness and dirt.
3   Once every three months remove the battery and inspect the battery securing bolts, the battery clamp plate, tray, and battery leads for corrosion (white fluffy deposits on the metal which are brittle to the touch). If any corrosion is found, clean off the deposits with ammonia and paint over the clean metal with an anti-rust anti-acid paint.
4   At the same time inspect the battery case for cracks. If a crack is found, clean and plug it with one of the proprietary compounds marketed for this purpose. If leakage through the crack has been excessive then it will be necessary to refill the appropriate cell with fresh electrolyte as detailed later. Cracks are frequently caused to the top of the battery case by pouring in distilled water in the middle of winter *after* instead of *before* a run. This gives the water no chance to mix with the electrolyte and so the former freezes and splits the battery case.
5   If topping up the battery becomes excessive and the case has been inspected for cracks that could cause leakage, but none are found, the battery is being overcharged and the voltage regulator will have to be checked.
6   Every three months check the specific gravity with a hydrometer to determine the state of charge and the condition of the electrolyte. There should be very little variation between the different cells and if a variation in excess of 0.025 is present, it will be due to either:

(a) *Loss of electrolyte from the battery caused by spillage or a leak, resulting in a drop in the specific gravity of the electrolyte. The deficiency was probably made up with distilled water instead of fresh electrolyte*
(b) *An internal short-circuit caused by buckling of the plates or a similar malady pointing to the likelihood of total battery failure in the near future.*

7   The specific gravity reading of a fully charged battery should be 1.270 to 1.290 at 25°C (77°F).

4   Battery – electrolyte replenishment

1   If the battery is in a fully charged state and one of the cells maintains a specific gravity reading which is 0.025 or more lower than the others, and (if possible) a check of each cell has been made with a voltmeter to check for short-circuits (a four to seven second heavy discharge test should give a steady reading of between 1.2 to 1.8 volts), then it is likely that electrolyte has been lost from the cell which shows the low reading.
2   Top up the cell with a solution of 1 part sulphuric acid to 2.5 parts of water. If the cell is already fully topped up, draw some electrolyte out of it with a pipette.
3   When mixing the sulphuric acid and water **never add water to sulphuric acid** – always pour the acid slowly into the water in a glass container. **If water is added to sulphuric acid it will explode.**
4   Continue to top up the cell with the freshly made electrolyte and then recharge the battery and check the hydrometer readings.

5   Battery – charging

1   In winter time when heavy demand is placed upon the battery, such as when starting from cold, and much electrical equipment is continually in use, it is a good idea to occasionally have the battery fully charged from an external source at the rate of 3.5 to 4 amps.

2 Continue to charge the battery at this rate until no further rise in specific gravity is noted over a four hour period.

3 Alternatively, a trickle charger charging at a rate of 1.5 amps can safely be used overnight.

4 Specially rapid boost charges which are claimed to restore the power of the battery in 1 to 2 hours are most dangerous as they can cause serious damage to the battery plates through overheating.

5 While charging the battery, note that the temperature of the electrolyte should never exceed 100°F (37.8°C), and, if the battery is being charged in the vehicle, always disconnect the negative (earth) terminal to avoid damage to the alternator.

6 Alternator – general description

An alternator of either Lucas or Bosch manufacture is fitted. The output is controlled by an integral regulator, the maximum output being given in the Specifications.

The alternator is mounted towards the front of the engine and is driven by the V-belt which also serves to drive the water pump, the drive being taken from the crankshaft pulley.

The alternator assembly basically consists of a fixed coil winding (stator) in an aluminium housing, which incorporates the mounting lugs. Inside this stator, rotates a shaft wound coil (rotor). The shaft is supported at each end by ball race bearings which are lubricated for life.

Slip rings are used to conduct current to and from the rotor field coils via the two carbon brushes which bear against them. By keeping the mean diameter of the slip rings to a minimum, relative speed between brushes and rings, and hence wear, are also minimal.

A pressed steel fan adjacent to the drive pulley draws cooling air through the machine. This fan forms an integral part of the alternator

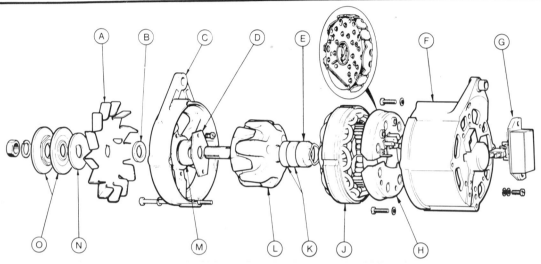

Fig. 10.2 The Bosch alternator components (Sec 6)

A	Fan	E	Slip ring end bearing	J	Stator	M	Drive end housing
B	Spacer	F	Slip ring end housing	K	Slip rings	N	Spacer
C	Drive end housing	G	Brush box and regulator	L	Rotor	O	Pulley
D	Thrust plate	H	Rectifier (diode) pack				

Fig. 10.3 The Lucas alternator components – models 15 and 17 ACR (Sec 6)

A	Regulator	E	Drive end bearing	H	Fan	L	Slip ring end housing
B	Rectifier (diode) pack	F	Drive end housing	J	Rotor	M	Surge protection diode
C	Stator	G	Pulley	K	Slip ring	N	End cover
D	Slip ring end bearing						

specification. It has been designed to provide adequate airflow with a minimum of noise, and to withstand the high stresses associated with the maximum speed. Rotation is clockwise viewed on the drive end.

The brush gear is housed in a moulding, screwed to the slip ring end bracket. This moulding thus encloses the slip ring and brush gear assembly, and together with the shielded bearing, protects the assembly against the entry of dust and moisture.

The regulator is set during manufacture and requires no further attention.

Electrical connections to external circuits are brought out to connector blades, these being grouped to accept a moulded connector socket which ensures correct connection. Detail design differences are shown in Figs. 10.2 and 10.3.

7   Alternator – maintenance

1   Every 6000 miles (10 000 km) clean the exterior of the alternator with a lint-free cloth, particularly around the slip ring and ventilating holes (opposite the fan end).
2   At the same interval adjust the drivebelt as described in Chapter 2. Only lever the alternator gently and at the front end to prevent stress in the mounting brackets.
3   The alternator brushes should be examined after about 75 000 miles (120 000 km) usage, and renewed as necessary.
4   No provision is made for lubrication of the alternator as the bearings are pre-packed with grease during manufacture.

8   Alternator – special precautions

Whenever the electrical system of the car is being attended to or external means of starting the engine are used, there are certain precautions that must be taken otherwise serious and expensive damage can result.
1   Always make sure that the negative terminal of the battery is earthed. If the terminal connections are accidentally reversed or if the battery has been reverse charged, the alternator diodes will burn out.
2   The output terminal on the alternator marked 'BAT' or B+ must never be earthed but should always be connected directly to the positive terminal of the battery.
3   Whenever the alterator is to be removed or when disconnecting the terminals of the alternator circuit, always disconnect the battery earth terminal first.
4   The alternator must never be operated without the battery to alternator cable connected.
5   Should it be necessary to use a booster charge or booster battery to start the engine, always double check that the negative cable is connected to the negative terminal and the positive cable to the positive terminal.

9   Alternator – removal and refitting

1   Open the bonnet and disconnect the battery negative terminal followed by the positive terminal.
2   Note the location of the alternator supply wires, then disconnect them from the rear cover.
3   Loosen the adjustment and pivot bolts (photo) swivel the alternator towards the engine and remove the drivebelt from the pulley.
4   Support the alternator and unscrew and remove the adjustment and pivot bolts; the alternator can then be carefully lifted from the vehicle.
5   Refitting the alternator is a reversal of the removal procedure but the following additional points should be noted:

(a)   *Connect the alternator wiring before reconnecting the battery terminals*
(b)   *Adjust the drivebelt tension as described in Chapter 2*

10   Alternator – fault finding and repair

1   Due to the specialist knowledge and equipment required to test or service an alternator it is recommended that if the performance is suspect, the car be taken to an automobile electrician who will have the facilities for such work. Because of this recommendation, information is limited to the inspection and renewal of the brushes. Should the alternator not charge or the system be suspect the following points may be checked before seeking further assistance.
2   Check the drivebelt tension, as described in Chapter 2.
3   Check the battery, as described in Section 3.
4   Check all electrical cable connections for cleanliness and security.
5   Inspect the alternator brushes (Section 11 or 12) and renew if necessary.

11   Alternator brushes (Bosch) – inspection, removal and refitting

1   If the alternator is in the vehicle, disconnect the battery.
2   Undo and remove the two screws, spring and plain washers that secure the regulator box to the rear of the end housing (see Fig. 10.4). Lift away the box.
3   Check that the carbon brushes are able to slide smoothly in their guides without any sign of binding.
4   Measure the length of the brushes protruding from the box. If they have worn beyond the specified limit, they must be renewed.
5   Hold the brush wire with a pair of engineer's pliers and unsolder it from the box. Lift away the two brushes.
6   Insert the new brushes (Fig. 10.5), and check to make sure that they are free to move in their guides. If they bind, lightly polish with a very fine file.
7   Solder the brush wire ends to the box, taking care that solder is allowed to pass to the stranded wire.
8   Whenever new brushes are fitted, new springs should be fitted.
9   Refitting is the reverse sequence to removal.

12   Alternator brushes (Lucas) – inspection, removal and refitting

1   If the alternator is in the vehicle, disconnect the battery.
2   Refer to Fig. 10.3 and undo and remove the two screws that hold on the end cover. Lift away the end cover.
3   Remove the brush retaining screws (Fig. 10.6) and withdraw the brushes from the brush box.
4   Measure the length of the brushes and if they have worn down beyond the specified limit, they must be renewed.
5   Insert the new brushes and check to make sure that they are free to move in their guides. If they bind, lightly polish with a very fine file.
6   Reassemble in the reverse order of dismantling. Make sure that leads which may have been connected to any of the screws are reconnected correctly.

9.3 Alternator pivot bolts viewed from underneath

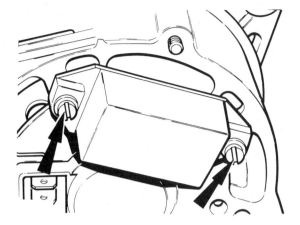

Fig. 10.4 Remove the regulator/brush box – the retaining screws are arrowed (Bosch) (Sec 11)

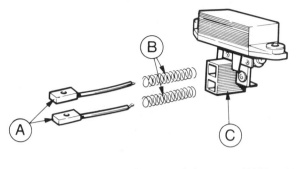

Fig. 10.5 The brushes (A); springs (B) and box (C) (Sec 11)

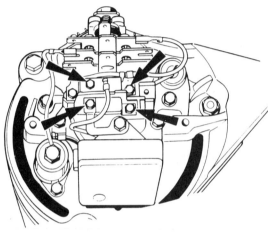

Fig. 10.6 The brush box retaining screws (arrowed) on the Lucas alternator (Sec 12)

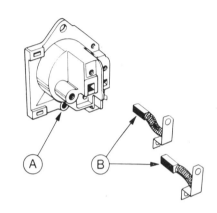

Fig. 10.7 The Lucas brush box (A) and brush assemblies (B) (Sec 12)

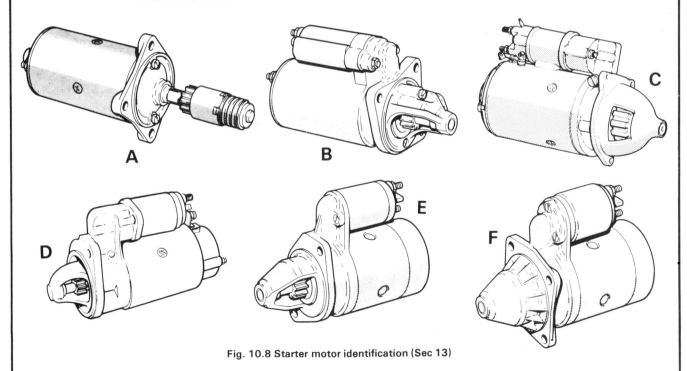

Fig. 10.8 Starter motor identification (Sec 13)

A	Lucas M35J inertia	C	Lucas M50G pre-engaged	E	Bosch 0.7 and 0.8 PS pre-engaged	F	Bosch 1.1 and 3.3 PS pre-engaged
B	Lucas M35J pre-engaged	D	Lucas 2M100 pre-engaged				

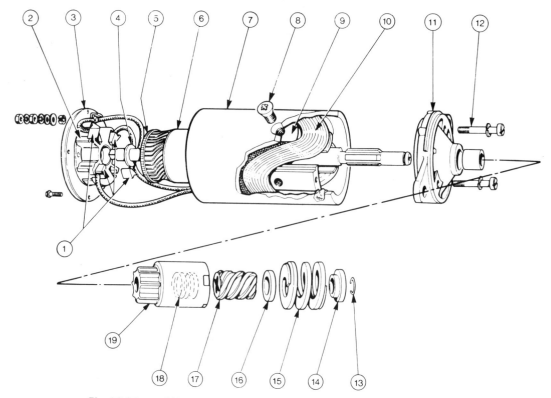

Fig. 10.9 Lucas M35J inertia starter motor components (Sec 13)

1	Brushes	6	Armature	11	Drive endplate	16	Cushion washer
2	Brush box moulding	7	Main casing (yoke)	12	Drive endplate retaining screws	17	Screwed sleeve
3	Commutator endplate	8	Pole piece retaining screw	13	C-clip	18	Anti-drift spring
4	Thrust washer	9	Pole piece	14	Spring cup	19	Drive pinion
5	Commutator	10	Field winding	15	Cushion spring		

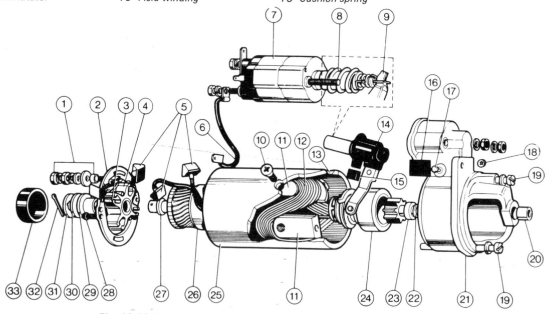

Fig. 10.10 Lucas pre-engaged starter motor components (Sec 13)

1	Terminal nuts and washers	9	Actuating lever	18	Retaining clip	27	Thrust washer
2	Commutator endplate	10	Pole screw	19	Housing retaining screws (2)	28	Commutator endplate retaining screws (2)
3	Brush housings	11	Pole shoe	20	Bearing bush	29	Bearing bush
4	Brush springs	12	Field coils	21	Drive end housing	30	Thrust plate
5	Brushes	13	Field to earth connection	22	Jump ring	31	Shim washer
6	Connector link, solenoid to starter	14	Rubber seal	23	Thrust collar	32	Split pin
7	Solenoid unit	15	Rubber dust pad	24	Drive assembly	33	Dust cover
8	Return spring	16	Rubber dust cover	25	Main casing		
		17	Pivot pin	26	Armature		

13 Starter motor – general description

The starter motor fitted is of Lucas or Bosch manufacture, and is either an inertia or pre-engaged type, depending on the model to which it is fitted.

All starter motors are series wound, four-pole, four-brush motors. Outline illustrations of the models fitted are shown in Fig. 10.8 for identification.

On the Lucas starter motor, the main case has two independently fixed endplates. The commutator endplate screws into the main body, while the drive endplate screws into the pole pieces. Access to the brushes is by removing the commutator and plate. The drive pinion

fitted to the inertia motor runs on a screwed sleeve with an internal spline (Fig. 10.9). This sleeve, the pinion and the cushion spring are retained on the shaft by a 'C' clip. The pre-engaged type of motor is fitted with a pre-engagement solenoid (Fig. 10.10).

On the Bosch starter motor, the commutator end housing and the drive end housing are attached to the main casing by common through-bolts or studs, nuts and washers (Fig. 10.11). Access to the brushes is made by removing the commutator end housing.

A roller clutch drive is incorporated into the drive pinion assembly of both the Lucas and Bosch pre-engaged type starter motors. The purpose of the roller drive is to stop the armature rotating at a very high speed should the drive remain engaged after the engine has started.

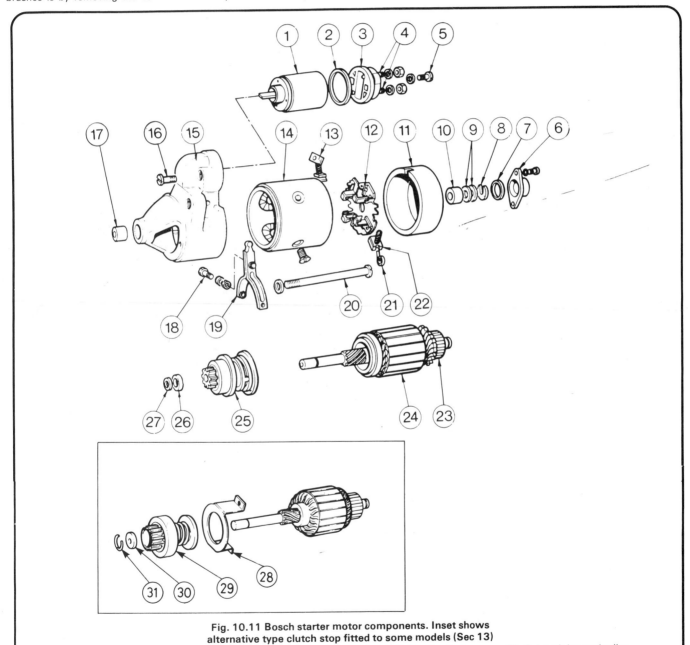

Fig. 10.11 Bosch starter motor components. Inset shows alternative type clutch stop fitted to some models (Sec 13)

1 Solenoid body	9 Shim washer	17 Bearing bush	25 Drive pinion and roller clutch assembly
2 Gasket	10 Bearing bush	18 Pivot screw	26 Bearing bush
3 Switch contacts and cover	11 Commutator end housing	19 Actuating lever	27 Thrust washer
4 Terminals (main)	12 Brushbox assembly	20 Through bolt	28 Clutch stop bracket
5 Retaining screw	13 Feed cable	21 Brush spring	29 Drive pinion and clutch unit
6 End cover	14 Main casing (yoke)	22 Brush	30 Thrust collar
7 Seal	15 Drive end housing	23 Commutator	31 C-clip
8 C-clip	16 Solenoid retaining screw	24 Armature	

The drive pinion is actuated by means of the operating lever attached to the solenoid. The operating lever is preset during manufacture and requires no further adjustment.

14 Starter motor – testing on engine

1   If the starter motor fails to operate, then check the condition of the battery by turning on the headlamps. If they glow brightly for several seconds and then gradually dim, the battery is in an uncharged condition.

2   If the headlights continue to glow brightly and it is obvious that the battery is in good condition, then check the tightness of the battery wiring connections (and in particular the earth lead from the battery terminal to its connection on the body frame). If the positive terminal on the battery becomes hot when an attempt is made to work the starter this is a sure sign of a poor connection on the battery terminal. To rectify, remove the terminal, clean the mating faces thoroughly and reconnect. Check the connections on the rear of the starter solenoid.Check the wiring with a voltmeter or test lamp for breaks or shorts.

Pre-engaged starter motors

3   Disconnect the battery earth cable, and the heavy battery and feed cables and the solenoid energising lead from the solenoid (Fig. 10.12). Connect a test lamp circuit, comprising a 12V battery, 12V 3W bulb and leads, between the starter feed terminal and the body of the solenoid. If the solenoid windings are intact, the lamp will light.

4   Substitute a higher wattage lamp (18 to 21W) in the test circuit and connect the lamp between the solenoid battery terminal and the test rig battery. Connect the other battery terminal to the solenoid feed terminal. Energise the solenoid by applying 12 volts to the spade terminal (from the terminal of the test rig battery which is connected to the test bulb). The solenoid should be heard to operate and the test lamp should light.

Inertia starter motors

5   Check the solenoid by bridging the large solenoid terminals with a heavy cable. If the starter motor then operates, the solenoid is at fault, or is not receiving current from the ignition/starter switch.

6   Ensure that the starter motor pinion has not jammed in mesh with the flywheel by engaging a gear (not automatic) and rocking the car to-and-fro. This should free the pinion if it is stuck in mesh with the flywheel teeth.

All starters

7   If the battery is fully charged, the wiring in order, and the starter/ignition switch working and the starter motor still fails to operate, then it will have to be removed from the car for examination.

15 Starter motor – removal and refitting

1   Disconnect the positive and negative terminals from the battery.

2   Make a note of the cable connections to the rear of the solenoid (photo) and detach the cable terminals from the solenoid. **Note:** *On inertia starter motors there is only one cable to remove from the motor.*

3   Undo and remove the starter motor securing nuts, bolts and spring washers and lift away the starter motor.

4   Refitting is the reverse sequence to removal.

16 Lucas pre-engaged starter motor – dismantling and reassembly

Before dismantling the starter motor for repair, check that spares are available, and compare their cost with that of an exchange starter motor. If the motor is generally worn and has seen much service, renewal of the complete unit may be more satisfactory than repair.

1   Clamp the starter motor in a vice with soft jaws and remove the plastic cap from the commutator endplate.

2   Remove the retaining clip from the end of the armature shaft and discard the clip. Remove the thrust washer.

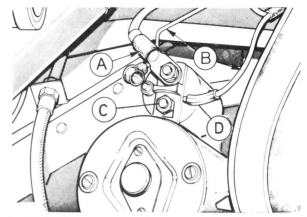

Fig. 10.12 Starter motor lead connections (pre-engaged type) (Sec 14)

A	Battery cable	C	Feed terminal
B	Loom wires	D	Spade terminal (energising lead)

15.2 Note wire connections to starter motor before detaching

3   Disconnect and remove the connecting cable from the end of the solenoid. Remove the two securing nuts and washers and guide the solenoid away from the drive end housing. Unhook the solenoid armature from the actuating lever by moving it upwards and away from the lever.

4   Remove the two drive end housing screws and guide the housing and armature assembly away from the body.

5   Remove the armature from the end housing, unhooking the actuating arm from the pinion assembly (Fig. 10.13). Remove the rubber block and sleeve from the housing.

6   Drive the pivot pin from the end housing, and remove the actuating lever. Discard the pivot pin clip, which will be distorted.

7   If it is necessary to dismantle the starter pinion drive, place the armature between soft faces in a bench vice and using a universal puller draw the jump ring from the armature.

8   Tap down the circlip retaining cover and remove the washer, circlip and cover. The pinion assembly may now be removed.

9   Draw the actuating bush towards the pinion so as to expose the circlip and remove the circlip, bush, spring and large washer. It is very important that the one-way roller clutch is not gripped in the vice at the point adjacent to the pinion whilst this is being carried out otherwise the clutch will be damaged.

10   The drive pinion and one-way clutch are serviced as a complete assembly so if one part is worn or damaged a new assembly must be obtained.

11   Remove the four commutator endplate screws and carefully tap the plate free from the body. Withdraw the plate slightly, remove the two field winding brushes and remove the plate.

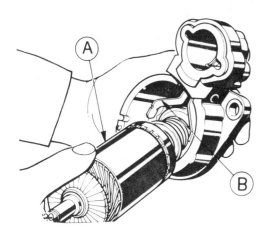

Fig. 10.13 Unhook the actuating arm (B) from the armature (A) (Sec 16)

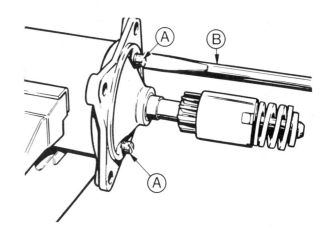

Fig. 10.14 Drive endplate removal showing retaining screws (A) and screwdriver (B) (Sec 17)

12 To renew the field winding brushes, their flexible connectors must be cut leaving 0.25 in (7 mm) attached to the field coil. Discard the old brushes. Solder new brushes to the flexible connector stubs. Check that the new brushes move freely in their holders.

13 The main terminal stub and its two brushes are available as a unit. To remove, take off the nut, washer and insulator and push the stud and second insulator through the endplate.

14 If cleaning the commutator with petrol fails to remove all the burnt areas and spots, then clean it with fine abrasive paper.

15 If the commutator is very badly worn, remove the drive gear, (if still in place on the armature), and mount the armature in a lathe. With the lathe turning at high speed take a very fine cut-out of the commutator and finish the surface by polishing with glass paper. **Do not undercut the mica insulators between the commutator segments.** The commutator thickness must not be reduced below the minimum given in the Specifications.

16 With the starter motor dismantled, test the four field coils for an open-circuit. Connect a 12 volt battery with a 12 volt bulb in one of the leads between the field terminal post and the tapping point of the field coils to which the brushes are connected. An open-circuit is proved by the bulb not lighting.

17 If the bulb lights, it does not necessarily mean that the field coils are in order, as there is a possibility that one of the coils will be earthed to the starter yoke or pole shoes. To check this, remove the lead from the brush connector and place it against a clean portion of the starter yoke. If the bulb lights, then the field coils are earthing. Replacement of the field coils calls for the use of a wheel operated screwdriver, a soldering iron, caulking and riveting operations and is beyond the scope of the majority of owners. The starter yoke should be taken to a reputable electrical engineering works for new field coils to be fitted. Alternatively purchase an exchange starter motor.

18 If the armature is damaged this will be evident after visual inspection. Look for signs of burning, discolouration, and for conductors that have lifted away from the commutator.

19 With the starter motor stripped down, check the condition of the bushes. They should be renewed when they are sufficiently worn to allow visible side movement of the armature shaft.

20 The old bushes are simply driven out with a suitable drift and the new bushes inserted by the same method. As the bushes are of the phosphor bronze type it is essential that they are allowed to stand in engine oil for at least 24 hours before fitment. If time does not allow, place the bushes in oil at 100°C (212°F) for 2 hours.

21 Reassembly is the reverse sequence to dismantling, but the following points should be noted:

  (a) When refitting the drive end housing, the peg on the housing should align with the notch in the casing

  (b) New retaining clips should be fitted to the actuating arm pivot pin and the armature shaft

  (c) When fitting the clip to the armature shaft end it should be pressed home so as to achieve the specified endfloat

17 Lucas inertia starter motor – dismantling and reassembly

1 The procedure is basically similar to that for the pre-engaged starter motor, Section 16, with the following differences.

2 There is no retaining clip at the commutator end of the armature shaft.

3 The armature, drive endplate and pinion are removed as an assembly after removing the two retaining screws (Fig. 10.14).

4 Remove the drive pinion by compressing the large cushion spring and removing the C-clip. (A small proprietary tool is available for this purpose). Remove the spring and drive pinion, then pull the drive endplate from the armature shaft.

18 Bosch starter motor – dismantling and reassembly

Refer to the note at the beginning of Section 16.

1 Firmly support the starter motor in the jaws of a vice fitted with protective jaws. Refer to Fig. 10.11.

2 Unscrew and remove the feed cable-to-solenoid retaining nut, then remove the cable from the stud.

3 On starter motors fitted to ohc models, remove the solenoid retaining screws and withdraw the solenoid from the housing. Detach the solenoid armature.

4 Remove the screws retaining the commutator end housing cap and withdraw the cap with its rubber seal. Unclip and remove the C-clip and shims from the end of the armature.

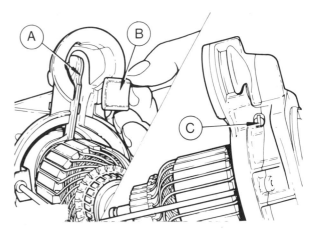

Fig. 10.15 Removing the rubber insert (B). Note the lever arm (A) and its pivot pin location (C) (Sec 18)

5   Unscrew and remove the nuts with washers from the end housing retaining studs, then pull the end housing clear. On some models, screws may retain the end housing.

6   Extract the respective brushes from the holders in the brush plate. Prise each brush spring clear before extracting the brushes. The brush plate can now be withdrawn.

7   Detach the drive end housing from the yoke by pushing the armature through whilst supporting the yoke.

8   On ohc engine starter motors, extract the rubber insert from the drive end housing (Fig. 10.15), then remove the lever arm pivot nut and slide the pivot screw from its location.

9   On starter motors fitted with studs to retain the motor components, remove the studs and release the drive pinion clutch step bracket.

10   On ohc engine starter motors, the armature and operating arm are now removed from the drive end housing, unhooking the arm from the drive pinion flange (Fig. 10.16).

11   The drive pinion is removed from the armature shaft by separating the thrust collar from the C-clip using a suitable size tube of the correct diameter as shown in Fig. 10.17. Remove the C-clip. Do not grip the one-way clutch in the vice when doing this as it may be damaged.

12   With the starter motor dismantled, clean the respective components with a lint-free cloth and lay out in order for inspection.

13   Check the brush length. If they are worn down to the specified minimum or less, they must be renewed (as a set). Cut each brush lead about halfway and resolder the new brushes into position. Check on completion that the respective soldered joints are secure, and clean each holder with a petrol-moistened rag prior to refitting. Ensure that the brushes do not stick in their holders.

14   Check and clean the armature, referring to Section 16, paragraphs 14 and 15. The commutator can be skimmed down to its minimum specified diameter.

15   Test the four field coils for an open-circuit, referring to Section 16, paragraphs 16 and 17.

16   Reassembly is a reversal of the dismantling procedure, but note the following special points:

(a)   When locating the brush plate onto the armature on 'through stud' models, position the plate so that the cutaway sections are aligned with the studs

(b)   When locating the brush plate onto the armature on models with screws to retain the drive endplate, align the plate cut-out sections with the field winding loops as shown in Fig. 10.18. The plate will then be correctly positioned to allow the screws to be fitted later

(c)   Don't forget to insert the rubber insulator into the commutator end housing (if applicable)

(d)   When the armature is fitted, check that it is fully located and fit sufficient shims to achieve the specified endfloat when the C-clip is in position (Fig. 10.19)

(e)   Smear the end of the armature shaft with some lithium-based grease before refitting the bearing cap

(f)   On ohc engine models, smear the solenoid armature hook with lithium-based grease before engaging the operating arm. Check that the solenoid armature return spring is positioned correctly and then fit the solenoid yoke over the armature, aligning the yoke with the drive end housing

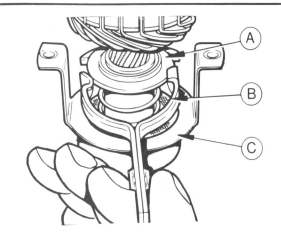

Fig. 10.16 Remove the operating arm (B). Note location flange (A) and clutch stop bracket (C) (Sec 18)

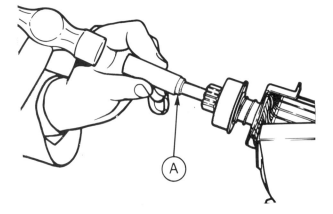

Fig. 10.17 Drive pinion removal method (Sec 18)

A   Thrust collar

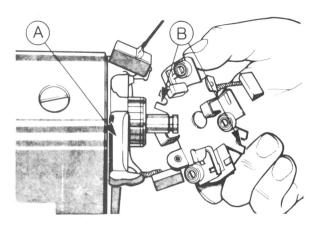

Fig. 10.18 Brush plate location – align the cut-outs (B) with the field winding loops (A)

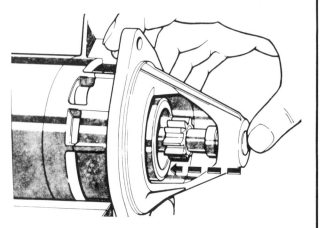

Fig. 10.19 Check the armature endfloat (Sec 18)

19 Fuses – general

1 The fuse block unit is located below the right-hand side of the dash panel. It contains eleven 8-amp and one 25-amp fuses. The fuses are numbered and the respective circuits which each protects are listed in the Specifications and shown graphically on the inside of the fuse box cover (photo).

2 Two additional fuses may be fitted, and these are;

(a) The heated rear window fuse. This is located under a plastic cap on the circuit relay unit under the facia, next to the bonnet release lever

(b) The radio fuse. This is an in-line fuse and is situated directly behind the radio

3 Whenever a fuse has blown, first check and where necessary rectify the fault in the circuit concerned which caused the fuse to blow. Then renew the fuse, being sure to use a replacement of the correct capacity.

4 Do not be tempted to bypass persistently blowing fuses with silver foil or wire, nor fit a fuse of a higher rating. Serious damage or fire may result.

20 Headlights – removal and refitting

1 Disconnect the battery earth lead.

2 Unscrew and remove the two headlamp surround retaining screws and lift the surround clear.

3 Unscrew and remove the headlight unit retaining screw(s) and extract the unit from the front (photos). On models fitted with sealed beam headlight units, also remove the bezel.

4 On models fitted with sealed beam headlights, simply disconnect the multi-plug lead connection at the rear of the unit to remove it completely.

5 On models fitted with headlight units with separate bulbs, rotate

19.1 The main fuse block with cover removed

the bulb anti-clockwise. Withdraw the bulb and holder, or release the spring clip, and extract the bulb, but do not handle it with the fingers (photos). Should the bulb be accidentally touched, the glass must be wiped clean with a soft cloth soaked in methylated spirit, then wiped dry, with a dust-free cloth. (Grease marks from your fingers will cause blackening and premature failure).

6 Unclip the sidelight bulb and its holder from the headlight unit reflector.

7 Refitting of the headlight unit and bulb(s), as applicable, is a reversal of the removal procedure. Providing the headlight adjuster screws have not been disturbed, it will not be necessary to realign the headlights on completion.

20.3a Remove the retaining screws ...

20.3b ... and withdraw the unit. Note that the adjusting screws (arrowed) have not been disturbed

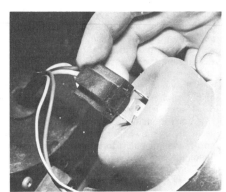

20.5a Detach wire connection from rear of headlight (non sealed beam) ...

20.5b ... remove protector ...

20.5c ... unclip the holder and ...

20.5d ... remove the holder and bulb

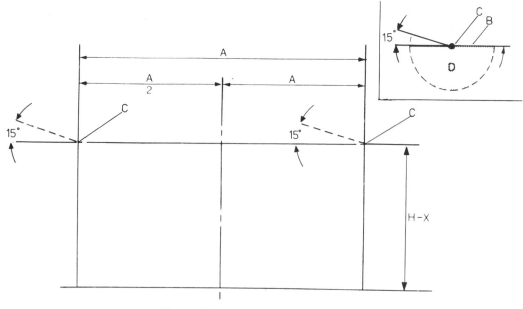

Fig. 10.20 Headlight alignment chart (Sec 21)

A	Distance between headlight centres	B	Light/dark margin	H	Ground to headlight centre distance
		C	Dipped beam centre	X	4 in (100 mm)
		D	Dipped beam pattern		

21 Headlight alignment

1   It is always advisable to have the headlamps aligned professionally on optical beam setting equipment, but failing this, the following procedure may be used.
2   The vehicle should be loaded as for normal night driving and then positioned 33 feet (10 metres) away from a dark wall or board.
3   Bounce the front of the vehicle a few times to settle the suspension, then measure the distance from the ground to the centre of the headlamps.
4   Draw a horizontal line on the wall or board at the headlight centre height, and a further line 4 in (100 mm) below it.
5   The vehicle should be at right-angles to the wall or board and a line corresponding to the centre of the vehicle should be drawn vertically on the wall or board. Further vertical lines should be marked on the wall or board to intersect the horizontal lines and indicate the headlight centre points each side – refer to Fig. 10.20.
6   Remove the headlamp surrounds and switch on the headlamp main beams. Drape a coat or piece of cardboard over one headlamp while the other unit is being adjusted.
7   Using a screwdriver turn the two headlamp adjusting screws until the brightest area of the beam coincides with the two previously made

crosses. (It may be necessary to remove the headlamp surrounds to gain access to the screws).
8   Switch off the headlamps and refit the surrounds to the front wings.

22 Sidelight bulb – renewal

1   The front sidelight bulbs are located in the headlight reflector units, and therefore access to them is only possible after removal of the headlight unit. Refer to Section 20 and withdraw the headlight unit, but do not detach it completely. Remove the bulb holder from the socket and extract the bulb from the holder (photo).
2   Fit a new bulb and reassemble the headlight unit.

23 Front direction indicator unit – removal and refitting

1   Unscrew and remove the four screws retaining the indicator unit to the front wing panel. Withdraw the unit (photo).
2   Turn the bulb holder anti-clockwise in the back of the unit to free and withdraw it (photo). The unit can be removed and the bulb extracted from its holder for renewal if required.

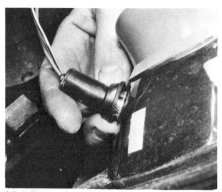

22.1 Remove the sidelight bulb and holder from the rear of the headlight reflector

23.1 Remove indicator lens screws

23.2 Indicator unit removed for access to bulb and holder

3   Refit in the reverse order and check that the indicator operates on completion.

24 Rear combination light – removal and refitting

1   To check and renew a stop/tail and/or rear indicator light bulb, unscrew and remove the lens retaining screws and remove the bulb concerned (Fig. 10.21). On some models the lens does not have to be detached to remove the bulb as it is accessible from within the inner corner panel recess. In this case simply twist free the bulb holder and remove it, with the bulb, from the rear of the unit as shown (photo).
2   Each bulb has a bayonet fitting and is removed by depressing and twisting it to release it from the holder.
3   Refitting the bulb is a reversal of the removal procedure, but the rear stop lamp double filament bulb can only be fitted in one position. Make sure that the gasket (when fitted) is located correctly to prevent the ingress of water through the lens surround.
4   Where the light unit is to be removed, detach the battery earth lead, then open the rear door or tailgate as applicable. Remove any trim panel on the side concerned at the rear corner inside to gain access to the light unit.
5   Remove the lens and gasket and then unscrew and remove the four unit retaining screws (Fig. 10.21). Withdraw the unit and detach the respective leads or bulb holders as applicable.
6   Refit in the reverse order and check the respective light for correct operation before refitting the lens and gasket.

25 Reversing light – removal and refitting

1   To remove the bulb unscrew the lens retaining screws and withdraw the lens. A festoon bulb is fitted and this is easily removed from its holders for replacement.
2   Should it be necessary to remove the unit, detach the battery earth lead, then disconnect the leads to the light unit. Remove the retaining screws and withdraw the unit (Fig. 10.22).
3   Refit in the reverse order and check the operation of the light by engaging reverse gear with the ignition switched on.

26 Rear fog light – removal and refitting

1   To check or renew the bulb, unscrew and remove the lens retaining screws and detach the lens (photo). Depress and remove the bulb from its bayonet fixing.
2   To remove the unit complete, disconnect the battery earth lead and the lead to the light unit. Unbolt and remove the unit from the chassis mounting.

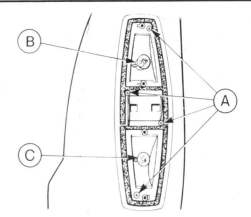

Fig. 10.21 Rear combination light with lens removed (Sec 24)

A   Unit retaining screws   C   Stop/tail light bulb
B   Indicator bulb

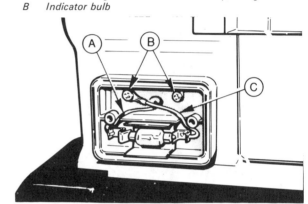

Fig. 10.22 The reversing light with the lens removed (Sec 25)

A   Feed wire   C   Earth wire
B   Retaining screws

3   Refit in the reverse order to removal and check for correct operation on completion.

27 Number plate light – removal and refitting

1   Use a suitable screwdriver and lever the lens from its aperture in the body, in which it is secured by two spring clips. With the lens and

24.1 Removing the rear light bulb and holder on later models

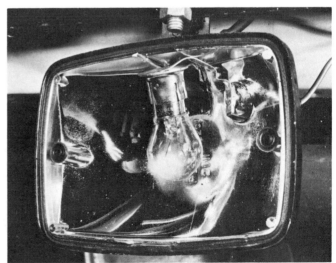

26.1 Detach rear fog light lens for access to bulb

unit removed, untwist and remove the bulb and its holder and lead (photo).

2   Refit in the reverse order to removal and check for correct operation on completion.

28 Rear reflectors – removal and refitting

1   When new reflectors are required, prise the old ones free by levering from their body location using a screwdriver. Take care not to chip or scratch the paintwork around the reflector.

2   To fit the new reflector, first ensure that it is the correct way up (it should be marked 'Top'), then locate the reflector pegs in the holes in the body and press fully home (Fig. 10.23).

29 Windscreen wiper blades – removal and refitting

1   The windscreen wiper blades should be checked every 6000 miles (10 000 km) and renewed if there are signs of deterioration or damage.

2   Hold the blade with one hand and the arm with the other hand. Position the arm and blade at 90° to each other (Fig. 10.4), depress the spring clip and then slide the blade down the arm. Slide the blade up and clear from the hook of the arm.

3   Detach the two metal inserts from within the wiper rubber and unhook the rubber from the blade.

4   Refit in the reverse sequence to removal. When assembling the new rubber to the blade, ensure when fitting the metal inserts that their cut-outs face inward as shown in Fig. 10.25.

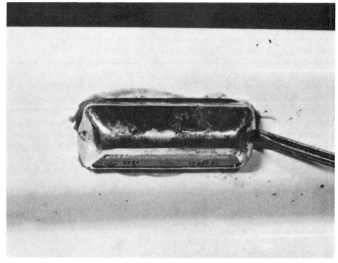

27.1a Prise free the number plate light ...

27.1b ... for access to the bulb

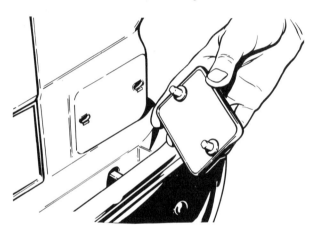

Fig. 10.23 Rear reflector showing location pegs and holes (Sec 28)

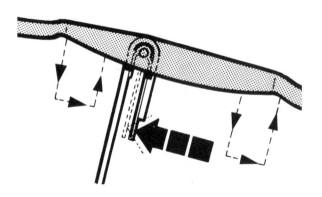

Fig. 10.24 Wiper blade removal position (Sec 29)

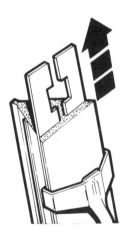

Fig. 10.25 Cut-outs face inwards

30.2 Wiper arm retaining nut

31.5a Rotate screws 90° ...

31.5b ... and lift the panel clear

30 Windscreen wiper arms – removal and refitting

1   Before removing a wiper arm, turn the windscreen wiper switch on and off to ensure that the arms are in their normal parked position parallel with the bottom of the windscreen.
2   Prise and pivot back the wiper arm retaining nut cover, then unscrew and remove the retaining nut (photo).
3   Withdraw the wiper arm from the spindle; the internal spring tends to seize the arm on the spindle and it may therefore be necessary to use a wide blade screwdriver to free the arm.
4   Refitting the windscreen wiper arm is a reversal of the removal procedure. Check for correct operation on completion.

31 Windscreen wiper motor and linkage – removal and refitting

1   Disconnect the battery earth lead.
2   Remove the wiper arms and blades as given in Section 30.
3   Unscrew and remove the nuts, spacers and seals from the wiper pivots. Now work inside the vehicle.
4   Where a radio is fitted remove the knobs (Fig. 10.26).
5   Rotate the facia panel retaining screws by 90° and withdraw the panel (photos), then remove the glovebox lid (where applicable). Remove the facia trim strip.
6   Detach the wire connections to the radio, unscrew and remove the radio mounting bracket screws and withdraw the radio from the facia. Remove the speaker unit (Fig. 10.27).
7   Detach and remove the fresh air hose on the passenger side.
8   Remove the two facia vent duct retaining screws on the passenger side and lower the duct so that it is clear of the wiper linkage.

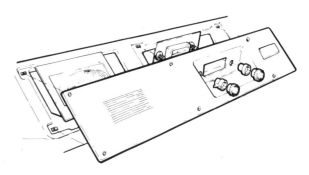

Fig. 10.26 Detach radio knobs (where fitted) and facia panel
(Sec 31)

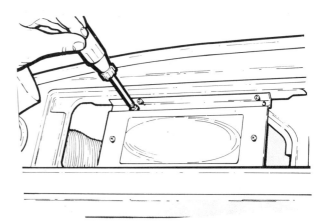

Fig. 10.27 Remove the speaker unit (where fitted) (Sec 31)

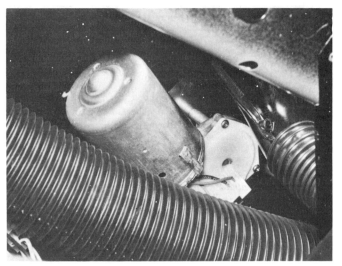

31.9 The wiper motor unit viewed from above with facia cover removed for access

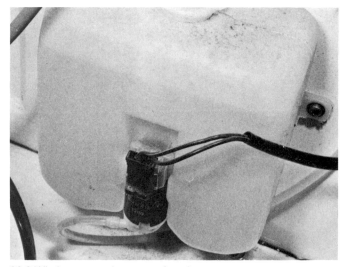

32.3 Windscreen washer reservoir and pump

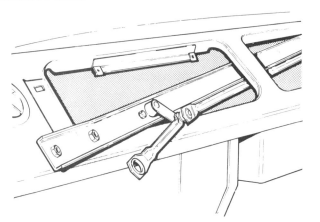

Fig. 10.28 Withdraw the wiper motor linkage (Sec 31)

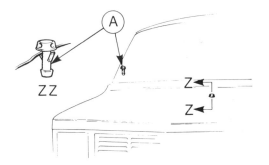

Fig. 10.29 Windscreen washer nozzle (Sec 32)

9   Detach the multi-plug connector from the wiper motor, then unscrew the motor retaining bolt and lower the motor and linkage assembly (photo).

10 Lever the linkage from the motor operating arm, then unscrew the two bolts which hold the motor and bracket to the linkage. Withdraw the motor and bracket, also the wiper linkage.

11 Remove the drive spindle nut and detach the operating arm. To separate the motor from the bracket, unscrew and remove the three retaining bolts.

12 Refit in the reverse sequence but note the following special points:

   (a) When refitting the motor operating arm ensure that the spindle groove aligns with the spline on the arm.
   (b) Do not secure the motor and linkage assembly until the rubber seals, spacers and spindle nuts are fitted
   (c) Ensure that the wiper arms and blades are refitted to their correct positions
   (d) Check the operation of the windscreen wiper, radio and fresh air vent on completion.

32 Windscreen washer pump – removal and refitting

1   Disconnect the battery earth lead.

2   Detach the respective hoses and wires from the pump unit, allowing for a small amount of fluid spillage (photo).

3   Unscrew and remove the unit retaining screws, and remove the pump and reservoir together.

4   Refit in the reverse order to removal, top up the pump reservoir and check the operation of the pump.

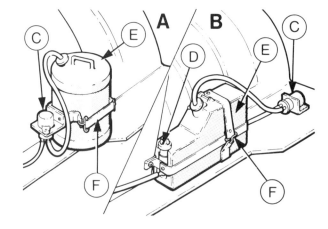

Fig. 10.30 The windscreen washer (A) and combined windscreen and headlight washer (B) assemblies (Sec 32)

C   Washer pump – windscreen   E   Reservoir
D   Washer pump – headlights   F   Retaining strap

5   If the windscreen washer nozzles are to be removed compress their retaining clips (see Fig. 10.29) and press the nozzles through the panel. Detach the hoses.

6   Refit in the reverse order and check the operation of the washer, ensuring that the nozzles are correctly adjusted for direction.

7   An alternative type of windscreen washer, and a combined windscreen and headlight installation, are shown in Fig. 10.30. The combined pump and reservoir is removed in the same manner as the ordinary windscreen washer unit.

34.2 The horn and mounting bracket

33 Headlight washer nozzles – removal and refitting

1   The washer nozzles for the headlights are located in each overrider, therefore unbolt the overrider concerned and remove it from the bumper (Fig. 10.31).
2   Unscrew the hose clip and detach the hose.

3   Unbolt and remove the washer nozzle from the inside of the overrider.
4   Refit in the reverse order and check for correct operation. When ejected, the fluid should hit the centre of the headlight lens.

34 Horn – removal and refitting

1   Disconnect the battery earth lead.
2   Detach the horn wire, unscrew and remove the horn retaining bolt and withdraw the horn (photo).
3   Refit in the reverse order and check the operation of the horn.

35 Interior light – removal and refitting

1   Disconnect the battery earth lead.
2   Prise the lamp unit carefully from its aperture, detach the wires and remove the bulb (Fig. 10.32).
3   Refit in reverse sequence and check for correct operation on completion.

36 Selector quandrant light (automatic transmission) – removal and refitting

1   Unclip the selector quandrant housing from its location in the floor and carefully lift it clear of the selector mechanism, (Fig. 10.33).
2   The bulb holder can be removed by sliding it from its location at the base of the selector lever, and the bulb extracted.
3   Refit in the reverse order and check for correct operation.

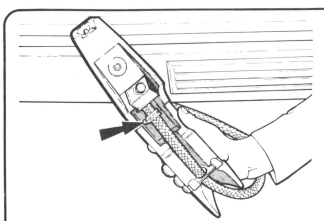

Fig. 10.31 Headlight washer and feed hose location in overrider. Hose clip is arrowed (Sec 33)

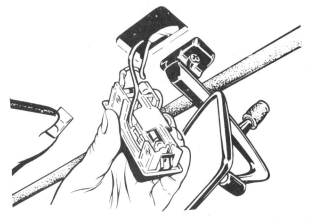

Fig. 10.32 Interior light unit removed from its aperture (Sec 35)

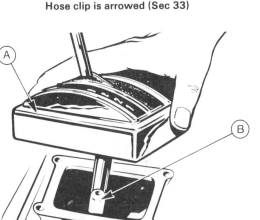

Fig. 10.33 Remove selector housing (A) for access to quadrant light (B) (Sec 36)

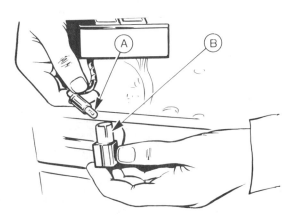

Fig. 10.34 Remove bulb (A) from its socket (B) (Sec 36)

37 Instrument panel – removal and refitting

Models without tachograph

1   Disconnect the battery earth cable.
2   Remove the steering column upper shroud. This is retained by a single retaining screw (photo).
3   Unscrew and remove the two screws retaining the instrument housing shroud in place, then lift the housing clear.
4   To separate the instrument panel from the facia panel remove the four retaining screws.
5   Detach the auxiliary switch wire connectors and where applicable, unplug the warning lights from their sockets.
6   Detach the two multi-plug connectors from the instrument cluster.
7   The speedometer drive cable is disconnected by depressing the outer sleeve to release the retaining peg.
8   The instrument cluster housing, with auxiliary switches and warning lights panel (as applicable), can now be withdrawn.

Models with tachograph

9   On models equipped with a tachograph, the following additional or alternative items will have to be disconnected before the instrument cluster can be removed:

   (a) Three wires and illumination light socket from the fuel gauge
   (b) Two wires from the voltage regulator and two wires from the temperature gauge. Remove their respective bulbs and holders

All models

10   The printed circuit can be removed from its location on the rear face of the instrument cluster by first removing the two clock illumination bulbs and holders, followed by the five warning lights (see Fig. 10.35). Now loosen but do not remove the four fuel/temperature gauge housing retaining screws, also the four screws retaining the speedometer housing. Remove the three clock nuts and washers and then carefully lift the printed circuit panel from the four location pegs. Release it from the underside of the speedometer and fuel/temperature gauge housings and withdraw the circuit (Fig. 10.36).
11   To remove the instrument cluster glass, remove the two screws retaining it to the instrument cluster upper edge and then prise free the clips from the lower edge lugs.
12   Where a clock is fitted, unscrew and remove the clock adjuster knob. Remove the glass.
13   Reassembly is a reversal of the removal procedure, but ensure that all electrical connections are secure. Check the operation of all instruments, switches and lights on completion.

38 Instrument panel switches – removal and refitting

1   The switches are removed from the instrument panel by inserting a screwdriver at their lower edge and then levering them from their locations. Use a pad of suitable material to prevent damage to the instrument panel (Fig. 10.37).

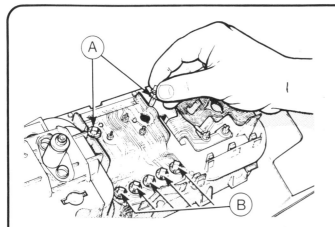

Fig. 10.35 The illumination bulb (A) and warning light (B) locations (Sec 37)

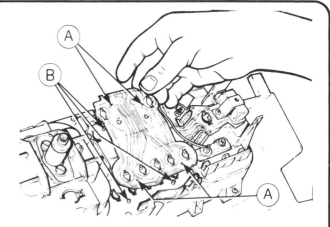

Fig. 10.36 Remove the printed circuit (Sec 37)

A   Location holes   B   Location pegs

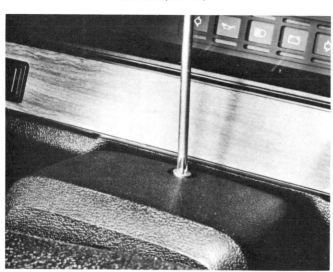

37.2 The upper column shroud retaining screw being removed

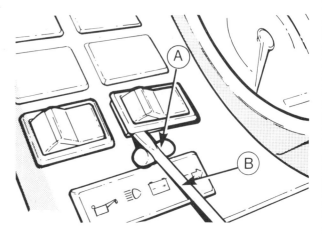

Fig. 10.37 Switch removal method using protective material (A) and screwdriver (B) as lever (Sec 38)

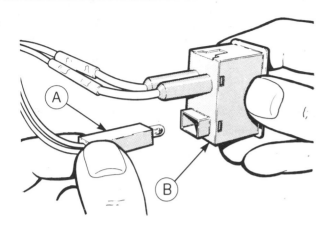

Fig. 10.38 Switch warning light holder (A) and switch (B) (Sec 38)

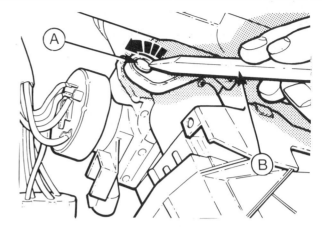

Fig. 10.39 Shear bolt (A) removal using a chisel (B) (Sec 39)

39.2 The ignition switch is exposed when the shrouds are removed

2   Withdraw the switch far enough to permit the multi-plug to be disconnected.
3   To refit the switch, connect the multi-plug and push the switch firmly into its location.
4   Where switches incorporate a warning light, the bulb can be renewed after withdrawing the holder from the rear of the switch. The bulb is then simply pulled from its holder (do not twist the bulb to remove it). Refit in the reverse order.
5   Check the operation of the switch and/or bulb on completion.

39 Ignition switch and steering lock – removal and refitting

1   Disconnect the battery earth lead.
2   Remove the upper steering column shroud (one screw) and the lower shrouds (two screws) to expose the switch (photo).
3   Unscrew the column-to-facia panel retaining bolts and lower the column.
4   Use a suitable pin punch or chisel and remove the two shear bolts which retain the ignition switch to the steering column (Fig. 10.39).
5   The switch can then be disconnected from the main wiring loom at the multi-plug and the switch removed.
6   To refit the switch, first reconnect the wiring connector to the main loom, then locate the switch onto the steering column with its lock section engaged with the column cut-out.
7   Fit the two shear bolts and before fully tightening them check that the lock is operational. Then tighten the bolts until the heads shear off.
8   Relocate the steering column to the facia and tighten the two retaining bolts.
9   Refit the upper and lower shrouds and recheck that the switch operation is satisfactory to complete.

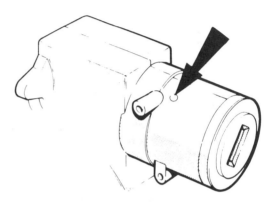

Fig. 10.40 Leaf spring access hole (arrowed) (Sec 40)

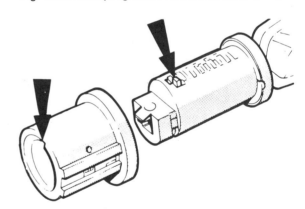

Fig. 10.41 Align barrel and cylinder as shown (Sec 40)

40 Ignition switch lock barrel – removal and refitting

1   Disconnect the battery earth lead.
2   Remove the retaining screws and detach the upper and lower steering column shrouds.
3   Turn the ignition key to the I (accessory) position, then use a scriber or similar implement to depress the cylinder leaf spring through the access hole (shown in Fig. 10.40) whilst simultaneously pulling on the key to withdraw the cylinder and lock barrel. It may be necessary to turn the key slightly in each direction to assist withdrawal.
4   On removal insert the key fully into its barrel and detach the circlip. Take care not to damage the clip location on the barrel, or difficulty could be experienced when refitting.
5   Withdraw the key about 0.2 in (5 mm) and extract the barrel from the cylinder.

6   Reassemble in the reverse sequence, noting the following special points:

(a) When fitting the barrel to the cylinder, align as shown in Fig. 10.41. When fitted ensure that the key can be turned fully through all positions, then return the key to position I and fit the circlip with its open section towards the cylinder keyway

(b) When the cylinder is refitted into its housing, check that the leaf spring engages in the housing slot

(c) Before refitting the upper and lower shrouds recheck that the key actuation is satisfactory in all positions

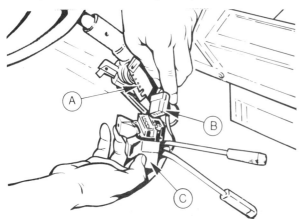

Fig. 10.42 Disconnecting the column switches (Sec 41)

A   Wiper switch multi-plug   C   Switch
B   Light switch multi-plug

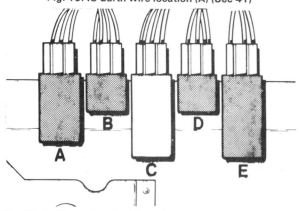

Fig. 10.43 Earth wire location (A) (Sec 41)

Fig. 10.45 The main relay block showing the respective units (Sec 42)

A   Intermittent windscreen wiper   D   Heated rear screen relay
      relay   E   Direction indicator/hazard
B   Headlight wash relay   flasher relay
C   Headlight washer circuit control
      relay

41 Steering column switches – removal and refitting

1   Disconnect the battery earth lead.
2   Remove the retaining screws and withdraw the upper and lower column shrouds.
3   Remove the two switch retaining screws and separate the switches from the column. Detach the wiring multi-connector to the main loom from the switch concerned and withdraw the switch (Fig. 10.42).
4   Refit in the reverse order, ensuring the correct location of the switch(es). Make sure that the earth wires are connected to the lower screw before it is fully tightened (Fig. 10.43).
5   Note also that the indicator switch must be relocated with its peg engaged in the hole in the steering column as shown in Fig. 10.44.
6   Check all switch functions on completion.

42 Relays – general

1   Some circuits have relay units fitted, and those are located in two places in the vehicle. The automatic transmission starter inhibitor relay is attached to the battery tray, whilst the remaining circuit relays are found under the facia panel next to the bonnet release.
2   The main relays clip into position. Their positions are shown in Fig. 10.45. The starter inhibitor relay on automatic transmission models is retained by a single screw as shown in Fig. 10.46.
3   The relays are electrically-operated switches. If a circuit served by a relay fails to operate, remember that the cause could be a faulty relay. Renewal is the only solution, no repair being possible.

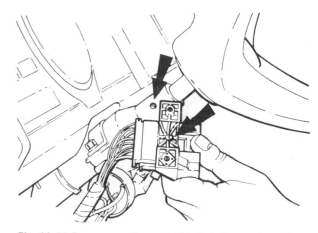

Fig. 10.44 Engage peg (in switch) in hole in steering column (Sec 41)

Fig. 10.46 The starter inhibitor relay is retained by a single screw (arrowed) (Sec 42)

43 Speedometer unit – removal and refitting

1   Refer to Section 37 and remove the instrument panel. (Owners with tachograph equipped models should also refer to Section 50 before proceeding).
2   Unscrew and remove the four screws which retain the speedometer and housing in position on the instrument panel.
3   Detach and withdraw the two speedometer illumination bulbs with their holders.
4   Unclip the wiring loom as shown in Fig. 10.47 from the rear of the speedometer housing.
5   Unscrew the two retaining screws and withdraw the speedometer, gasket and two grommets (Fig. 10.48).
6   Refitting is a reversal of the removal procedure. Ensure that all electrical connections are secure.

44 Speedometer cable – removal and refitting

1   Refer to Section 37 and remove the instrument panel. (Owners with tachograph equipped models should refer to Section 50 before proceeding).
2   Jack up the front of the vehicle and support it on axle stands.
3   Disconnect the cable from the gearbox, referring to Chapter 6, Section 10. Pull the cable through the bulkhead when detached and extract it upwards through the engine compartment.
4   Refit in the reverse order to removal, ensuring that the cable is correctly engaged at both the gearbox and speedometer end. When fitted the cable must have no sharp bends in it, nor be stretched or distorted in any way.

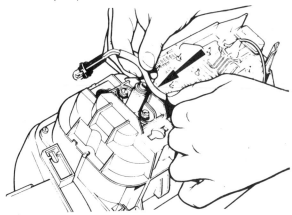

Fig. 10.47 Unclip the wiring loom (arrowed) (Sec 43)

45 Clock – removal and refitting

1   Refer to Section 37 and remove the instrument panel.
2   From the rear of the panel, extract the three illumination bulbs and their sockets.
3   Unscrew and remove the clock adjuster knob retaining screw and remove the knob.
4   Remove the speedometer housing and fuel/temperature gauge housing head by unscrewing their retaining screws.
5   Remove the four retaining screws from the clock and warning light plate and withdraw the assembly. To remove the clock from the plate, unscrew the three nuts and remove with washers.
6   Refitting is a reversal of the removal procedure. Ensure that all electrical connections are secure before refitting the instrument panel.

46 Cigarette lighter – removal and refitting

1   Disconnect the battery earth lead.
2   Release the six screw clips and withdraw the facia panel. Where a radio is fitted, remove the control knobs and withdraw its surround bezel.
3   Remove the light unit by withdrawing the element, detaching the earth wire and feed wire at the rear and also extracting the illumination bulb. Press the collar and twist anti-clockwise to withdraw the unit.
4   Refit in the reverse order to removal. Ensure that the wire connections are secure and correctly made (Fig. 10.49).

47 Door courtesy light switch – removal and refitting

1   Disconnect the battery earth lead.
2   The switch is enclosed in the door pillar and is easily removed by unscrewing the retaining screw, withdrawing the switch and detaching the wire connections.
3   Refit in the reverse order, ensuring that the wire connections are secure.

48 Reversing light switch – removal and refitting

1   The reversing light switch is located in the gearbox selector housing and is removed from underneath the vehicle. Jack up the front of the vehicle and support with axle stands.
2   Detach the wiring from the switch unit and unscrew the switch to remove it.
3   Refit in the reverse order. When the wires are reattached, ensure that they are clear of the exhaust system.

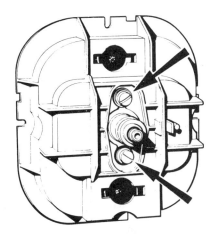

Fig. 10.48 Speedometer unit housing retaining screw positions (arrowed) (Sec 43)

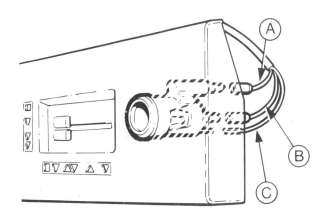

Fig. 10.49 The cigarette lighter wiring (Sec 46)

A   Illumination light wire   C   Earth wire (brown)
B   Main feed (red)

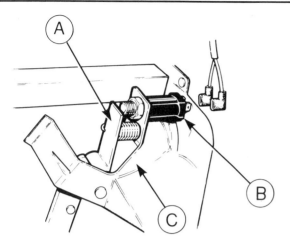

Fig. 10.50 Stop-light switch (B), brake pedal (A) and pedal box (C)
(Sec 49)

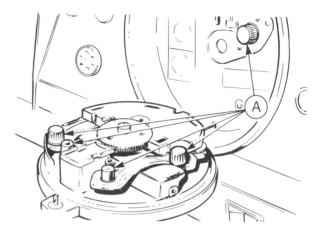

Fig. 10.51 Tachograph bulb holder locations (arrowed) (Sec 50)

49 Stop-light switch – removal and refitting

1   Disconnect the battery earth lead.
2   The stop-light switch is attached to the brake pedal bracket.
Disconnect the wires from the switch, then remove the locknut
retaining the switch to the bracket and withdraw the switch (Fig.
10.50).
3   Refit the switch in the reverse order to removal. Adjust the switch
position so that it is actuated within the first inch of pedal travel, then
tighten the locknut.
4   Check the operation of the brake lights on completion.

50 Tachograph – general description and precautions

1   The Bus, Crewbus and Kombi models with a minimum seating
capacity of nine (including the driver) are fitted with a tachograph to
comply with EEC legislation.
2   The tachograph comprises a speedometer, odometer, time clock
and a device for recording vehicle journeys. Single or dual tachographs
are fitted as applicable, the dual model having two record chart
facilities (one for each driver). The instrument also contains speed and
stylus error warning lights.
3   The tachograph is a sealed unit and therefore apart from changing
the record charts and resetting them according to the manufacturer's
instructions, they must not be dismantled in any way should a fault
occur.
4   Tachograph faults will be due to one of four main reasons, these
being:

   (a) Broken or defective drive cable
   (b) Defective tachograph unit
   (c) Defective calibration unit
   (d) Defective drive unit in the gearbox

5   As the tachograph unit and the cable are sealed, any jobs which
require the seals to be broken must be left to your Ford dealer; or the
broken seals must be resealed on job completion, again by your Ford
dealer.
6   The tachograph illumination light bulb can easily be renewed by
opening the front of the tachograph, twisting the bulb anti-clockwise
and withdrawing it. On dual tachograph models, lift the bulb contact
first. Refit in the reverse order. Refer to Fig. 10.51 for the bulb holder
locations.
7   Note that the tachograph should only ever be opened when the
vehicle is stationary, or damage will result.
8   If a vehicle is fitted with a tachograph which is not to be used, the
normal paper chart should be replaced by a 'blind' chart to prevent
damage to the instrument stylus (and eventually the unit itself). Do not
leave the original paper chart in position indefinitely. Similar damage
can also result where the vehicle is off the road for an extended period
with the battery connected.

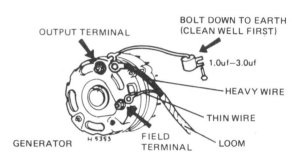

Fig. 10.52 The correct way of fitting a capacitor to the generator
(Sec 52)

51 Radios and tape players – installation

A radio or tape player is an expensive item to buy, and will only
give its best performance if fitted properly. It is useless to expect
concert hall performance from a unit that is suspended from the
dashpanel by string with its speaker resting on the floor! If you do not
wish to do the installation yourself, there are many in-car entertain-
ment specialists who will do the fitting for you.
Make sure the unit purchased is of the same polarity as the vehicle
(ie negative earth). Ensure that units with adjustable polarity are
correctly set before commencing installation.
It is difficult to give specific information with regard to fitting, as
final positioning of the radio/tape player, speakers and aerial is largely
a matter of personal preference. However, the following paragraphs
give guidelines which are relevant to all installations. The points below
should be considered:

   (a) The unit must be within easy reach of the driver wearing a
        seat belt
   (b) The unit must not be mounted in close proximity to a
        tachometer, the ignition switch and its wiring, or the flasher
        unit and associated wiring
   (c) The unit must be mounted within reach of the aerial lead, and
        in such a place that the aerial lead will not have to be routed
        near the components detailed in the preceding paragraph
   (d) The unit should not be positioned in a place where it might
        cause injury to the car occupants in an accident; for in-
        stance,under the dashpanel above the driver's or passenger's
        legs
   (e) The unit must be fitted really securely

Radios

Some radios will have mounting brackets provided, together with
instructions; others will need to be fitted using drilled and slotted
metal strips, bent to form mounting brackets. These strips are available
from most accessory shops. The unit must be properly earthed by
fitting a separate lead between the casing of the radio and the vehicle
frame.
Use the radio manufacturers' instructions when wiring the radio

into the vehicle's electrical system. If no instructions are available, refer to the relevant wiring diagram to find the location of the radio feed connection in the vehicle's wiring circuit. A 1 to 2 amp 'in-line' fuse must be fitted in the radio's feed wire; a choke may also be necessary (see next Section).

The type of aerial used and its fitted position, is a matter of personal preference. In general, the taller the aerial, the better the reception. It is best to fit a fully retractable aerial; especially if a mechanical car-wash is used or if you live in an area where vehicles tend to be vandalised. In this respect, electric aerials which are raised and lowered automatically when switching the radio on or off are convenient, but are more likely to give trouble than the manual type.

When choosing a site for the aerial, the following points should be considered:

(a) *The aerial lead should be as short as possible; this means that the aerial should be mounted at the front of the vehicle*

(b) *The aerial must be mounted as far away from the distributor and HT leads as possible*

(c) *The part of the aerial which protrudes beneath the mounting point must not foul the roadwheels, or anything else*

(d) *If possible, the aerial should be positioned so that the coaxial lead does not have to be routed through the engine compartment*

(e) *The plane of the panel on which the aerial is mounted should not be so steeply angled that the aerial cannot be mounted vertically (in relation to the end-on aspect of the vehicle). Most aerials have a small amount of adjustment available*

Having decided on a mounting position, a relatively large hole will have to be made in the panel. The exact size of the hole will depend upon the specific aerial being fitted, although generally, the hole required is of $\frac{3}{4}$ in diameter. A tank-cutter of the relevant diameter is the best tool to use for making the hole. This tool needs a small diameter pilot hole drilled through the panel, through which the tool clamping bolt is inserted. When the hole has been made the raw edges should be de-burred with a file and then painted to prevent corrosion.

Fit the aerial according to the manufacturer's instructions. If the aerial is very tall, or if it protrudes beneath the mounting panel for a considerable distance, it is a good idea to fit a stay beneath the aerial and the vehicle frame. This stay can be manufactured from the slotted and drilled metal strips previously mentioned. The stay should be securely screwed or bolted in place. For best reception, it is advisable to fit an earth lead between the aerial and the vehicle frame.

It will probably be necessary to drill one or two holes through bodywork panels in order to feed the aerial lead into the interior of the cab. Where this is the case, ensure that the holes are fitted with rubber grommets to protect the cable and to stop possible entry of water.

Positioning and fitting of the speaker depends mainly on its type and personal preference. Wherever it is fitted it must be correctly located and care taken not to damage the speaker diaphragm. It is a good idea to fit a 'gasket' beneath the speaker frame and the mounting panel, in order to prevent vibration; some speakers will already have such a gasket fitted.

Further information on speaker installation is given in the tape player sub-section.

When connecting a rear-mounted speaker to the radio, the wires should be routed through the vehicle beneath the carpets or floor mats, preferably through the middle, or along the side of the floorpan, where they will not be trodden on by passengers. Make the relevant connections as directed by the radio manufacturer.

By now you will have several yards of additional wiring in the vehicle. Use PVC tape to secure this wiring out of harm's way. Do not leave electrical leads dangling. Ensure that all new electrical connections are properly made (wires twisted together will not do) and completely secure.

If you experience poor reception or where a new radio has been installed, you will have to 'trim' the radio to the aerial. Follow the radio manufacturer's instructions regarding this adjustment.

Tape players

Fitting instructions for both cartridge and cassette stereo tape players are the same, and in general the same rules apply as when fitting a radio. Tape players are not usually prone to electrical interference like radios – although it can occur – so positioning is not so critical. If possible, the player should be mounted on an even keel.

Also, it must be possible for a driver wearing a seat belt to reach the unit in order to change, or turn over, tapes.

For the best results from speakers designed to be recessed into a panel, mount them so that the back of the speaker protrudes into an enclosed chamber within the vehicle, the most obvious location for a single speaker being behind the facia grille panel. Twin speakers are sometimes fitted into the doors.

To fit recessed type speakers in the front doors, first check that there is sufficient room to mount the speaker in each door without it fouling the latch or window winding mechanism. Hold the speaker against the skin of the door and draw a line around the periphery of the speaker. With the speaker removed, draw a second cutting line within the first to allow enough room for the entry of the speaker back, but at the same time providing a broad seat for the speaker flange. When you are sure that the cutting-line is correct, drill a series of holes around its periphery. Pass a hacksaw blade through one of the holes and then cut through the metal between the holes until the centre section of the panel falls out.

De-burr the edges of the hole and then paint the raw metal to prevent corrosion. Cut a corresponding hole in the door trim panel, ensuring that it will be completely covered by the speaker grille. Now drill a hole in the door edge and a corresponding hole in the door surround. These holes are to feed the speaker leads through, so fit grommets. Pass the speaker leads through the door trim, door skin and out through the holes in the side of the door and door surround. Refit the door trim panel and then secure the speaker to the door using self-tapping screws. If the speaker is fitted with a shield to prevent water dripping on it, ensure that this shield is at the top.

52 Radios and tape players – suppression of interference (general)

To eliminate buzzes and other unwanted noises costs very little and is not as difficult as sometimes thought. With a modicum of common sense and patience and following the instructions in the following paragraphs, interference can be virtually eliminated.

The first cause for concern is the generator. The noise this makes over the radio is like an electric mixer and the noise speeds up when the engine is revved. (To prove the point, remove the fanbelt and try it). The remedy for this is simple; connect a 1.0 to 3.0 mf capacitor between earth, probably the bolt that holds down the generator base and the *output* terminal on the alternator. This is most important, for if it is connected to the small terminal, it will probably damage the generator permanently (see Fig. 10.52).

A second common cause of electrical interference is the ignition system. Here a 1.0 mf capacitor must be connected between earth and the SW or + terminal on the coil (see Fig. 10.53). This may stop the tick-tick sound that comes over the speaker. Next comes the spark itself.

There are several ways of curing interference from the ignition HT system. One is the use of carbon-cored HT leads as original equipment. Where copper-cable is substituted then you must use resistive

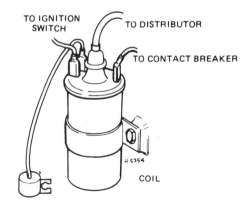

TO IGNITION SWITCH

TO DISTRIBUTOR

TO CONTACT BREAKER

COIL

Fig. 10.53 Capacitor must connect to ignition switch side of coil (Sec 52)

spark plug caps (see Fig. 10.54). These should be of about 10 000 to 15 000 ohms resistance. If, due to lack of room, these cannot be used, an alternative is to use in-line suppressors. If the interference is not too bad, it may be possible to get away with only one suppressor in the coil to distributor line. If the intererence does continue (a clacking noise), then modify all HT leads.

At this stage it is advisable to check that the radio is well earthed, also the aerial, and to see that the aerial plug is pushed well into the set and that the radio is properly trimmed (see preceding Section). In addition, check that the wire which supplies the power to the set is as short as possible and does not wander all over the car. It is a good idea to check that the fuse is of the correct rating. For most sets this will be about 1 to 2 amps.

At this point, the more usual causes of interference have been suppressed. If the problem still exists, a look at the cause of interference may help to pinpoint the component generating the stray electrical discharges.

The radio picks up electromagnetic waves in the air. Some are made by regular broadcasters and some, which we do not want, are made by the vehicle itself. The home made signals are produced by stray electrical discharges floating around in the vehicle. Common producers of these signals are electrical motors, ie the windscreen wipers, electric screen washers, heater fan or an electric aerial if fitted. Other sources of interference are flashing turn signals and instruments. The remedy for these cases is shown in Fig. 10.55 for an electric motor whose interference is not too bad and Fig. 10.56 for instrument

suppression. Turn signals are not normally suppressed. In recent years, radio manufacturers have included in the line (live) of the radio, in addition to the fuse, an in-line choke. If your circuit lacks one of these, put one in as shown in Fig. 10.57.

All the foregoing components are available from radio stores or accessory stores. If you have an electric clock fitted this should be suppressed by connecting a 0.5 mf capacitor directly across it as shown for a motor in Fig. 10.55.

If, after all this, you are still experiencing radio interference, first assess how bad it is, for the human ear can filter out unobtrusive unwanted noises quite easily. But if you are still adamant about eradicating the noise, then continue.

As a first step, a few 'experts' seem to favour a screen between the radio and the engine. This is OK as far as it goes – literally! – for the whole set is screened anyway and if interference can get past that then a small piece of aluminium is not going to stop it.

A more sensible way of screening is to discover if interference is coming down the wires. First, take the live lead; interference can get between the set and the choke (hence the reason for keeping the wires short). One remedy here is to screen the wire and this is done by buying screened wire and fitting that. The loudspeaker lead could be screened also to prevent pick-up getting back to the radio although this is unlikely.

Without doubt, the worst source of radio interference comes from the ignition HT leads, even if they have been suppressed. The ideal way of suppressing these is to slide screening tubes over the leads

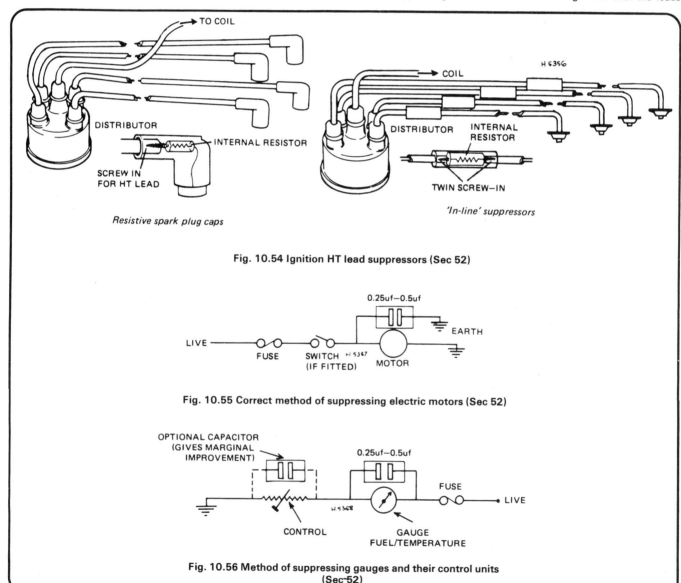

Fig. 10.54 Ignition HT lead suppressors (Sec 52)

Fig. 10.55 Correct method of suppressing electric motors (Sec 52)

Fig. 10.56 Method of suppressing gauges and their control units
(Sec 52)

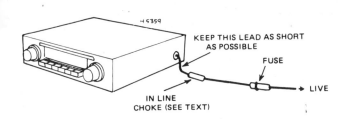

Fig. 10.57 An in-line choke should be fitted into the live supply lead as close to the unit as possible (Sec 52)

themselves. As this is impractical, we can place an aluminium shield over the majority of the lead areas.

Now for the really impossible cases, here are a few tips to try out. Where metal comes into contact with metal, an electrical disturbance is caused which is why good clean connections are essential. To remove interference due to overlapping or butting panels, you must bridge the join with a wide braided earth strap (like that from the frame to the engine/transmission). The most common moving parts that could create noise and should be strapped are, in order of importance:

(a) Silencer to frame
(b) Exhaust pipe to engine block and frame
(c) Air cleaner to frame
(d) Front and rear bumpers to frame
(e) Steering column to frame
(f) Bonnet to frame

These faults are most pronounced when (1) the engine is idling or (2) labouring under load. Although the moving parts are already connected with nuts, bolts, etc, these do tend to rust and corrode, this creating a high resistance interference source.

If you have a 'ragged' sounding pulse when mobile, this could be wheel or tyre static. This can be cured by buying some anti-static powder and sprinkling inside the tyres.

If the interference takes the shape of a high pitched screeching noise that changes its note when the vehicle is in motion and only comes now and then, this could be related to the aerial, especially if it is of the telescopic or whip type. This source can be cured quite simply by pushing a small rubber ball on top of the aerial as this breaks the electric field before it can form; but it would be much better to buy yourself a new aerial of a reputable brand. If, on the other hand, you are getting a loud rushing sound every time you brake, then this is brake static. This effect is most prominent on hot dry days and is cured only by fitting a special kit, which is quite expensive.

In conclusion, it is pointed out that it is relatively easy and therefore cheap, to eliminate 95 per cent of all noise, but to eliminate the final 5 per cent is time and money consuming. It is up to the individual to decide if it is worth it. Please remember also, that you cannot get a concert hall performance out of a cheap radio.

Finally, players and eight track players are not usually affected by vehicle noise but in a very bad case, the best remedies are the first three suggestions plus using a 3 to 5 amp choke in the live line and in incurable cases screening the live and speaker wires.

Note: *If your vehicle is fitted with electronic ignition, then it is not recommended that either the spark plug resistors or the ignition coil capacitor be fitted as these may damage the system. Most electronic ignition units have built in suppression and should, therefore, not cause interference.*

53 Fault diagnosis – electrical system

Symptom	Reason(s)
Starter motor fails to turn engine	Battery discharged Battery defective internally Battery terminal leads loose or earth lead not securely attached to body Loose or broken connections in starter motor circuit Starter motor switch or solenoid faulty Starter brushes badly worn, sticking, or brush wires loose Commutator dirty, worn or burnt Starter motor armature faulty Field coils earthed
Starter motor turns engine very slowly	Battery in discharged condition Starter brushes badly worn, sticking, or brush wires loose Loose wires in starter motor circuit
Starter motor operates without turning engine	Starter motor pinion sticking on the screwed sleeve (inertia starter) Pinion or flywheel gear teeth broken or worn
Starter motor noisy or excessively rough engagement	Pinion or flywheel gear teeth broken or worn Starter motor retaining bolts loose
Battery will not hold charge for more than a few days	Battery defective internally Electrolyte level too low or electrolyte too weak due to leakage Plate separators no longer fully effective Battery plates severely sulphated Alternator drivebelt slipping Battery terminal connections loose or corroded Alternator not charging properly Short in lighting circuit causing continual battery drain
Ignition light fails to go out, battery runs flat in a few days	Drivebelt loose and slipping or broken Alternator faulty
Fuel gauge gives no reading	Fuel tank empty! Electric cable between tank sender unit and gauge earthed or loose Fuel gauge case not earthed Fuel gauge supply cable interrupted Fuel gauge unit broken

Symptom	Reason(s)
Fuel gauge registers full all the time	Electric cable between tank unit and gauge broken or disconnected
Horn operates all the time	Horn push either earthed or stuck down Horn cable to horn push earthed
Horn fails to operate	Blown fuse Cable or cable connection loose, broken or disconnected Horn has an internal fault
Horn emits intermittent or unsatisfactory noise	Cable connections loose
Lights do not come on	Blown fuse If engine not running, battery discharged Light bulb filament burnt out or bulbs broken Wire connections loose, disconnected or broken Light switch shorting or otherwise faulty
Lights come on but fade out	If engine not running, battery discharged
Lights give very poor illumination	Lamp glasses dirty Reflector tarnished or dirty Lamps badly out of adjustment Incorrect bulb with too low wattage fitted Existing bulbs old and badly discoloured Electrical wiring too thin not allowing full current to pass
Lights work erratically – flashing on and off, especially over bumps	Battery terminals or earth connection loose Lights not earthing properly Contacts in light switch faulty
Wiper motor fails to work	Blown fuse Wire connections loose, disconnected or broken Brushes badly worn Armature worn or faulty
Wiper motor works very slowly and takes excessive current	Commutator dirty, greasy or burnt Drive to wheelboxes bent or unlubricated Wheelbox spindle binding or damaged Armature bearings dry or unaligned Armature badly worn or faulty
Wiper motor works slowly and takes little current	Brushes badly worn Commutator dirty, greasy or burnt Armature badly worn or faulty
Wiper motor works but wiper blades remain static	Wheelbox gear and spindle damaged or worn Wiper motor gearbox parts badly worn

Wiring diagrams commence overleaf
All models up to 1984

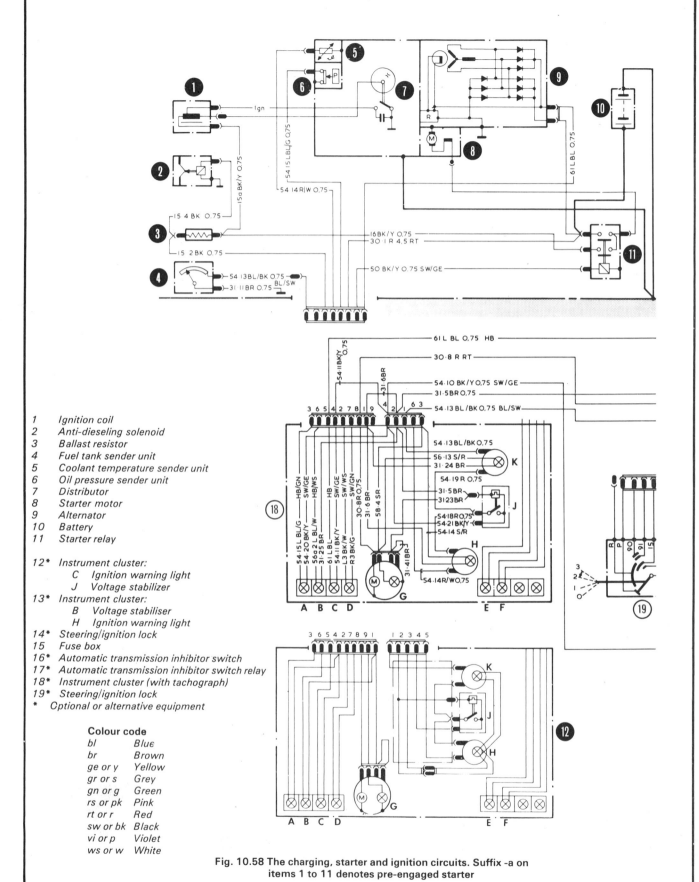

1   Ignition coil
2   Anti-dieseling solenoid
3   Ballast resistor
4   Fuel tank sender unit
5   Coolant temperature sender unit
6   Oil pressure sender unit
7   Distributor
8   Starter motor
9   Alternator
10   Battery
11   Starter relay

12*   Instrument cluster:
       C   Ignition warning light
       J   Voltage stabilizer
13*   Instrument cluster:
       B   Voltage stabiliser
       H   Ignition warning light
14*   Steering/ignition lock
15   Fuse box
16*   Automatic transmission inhibitor switch
17*   Automatic transmission inhibitor switch relay
18*   Instrument cluster (with tachograph)
19*   Steering/ignition lock
*   Optional or alternative equipment

Colour code
bl	Blue
br	Brown
ge or y	Yellow
gr or s	Grey
gn or g	Green
rs or pk	Pink
rt or r	Red
sw or bk	Black
vi or p	Violet
ws or w	White

Fig. 10.58 The charging, starter and ignition circuits. Suffix -a on
items 1 to 11 denotes pre-engaged starter

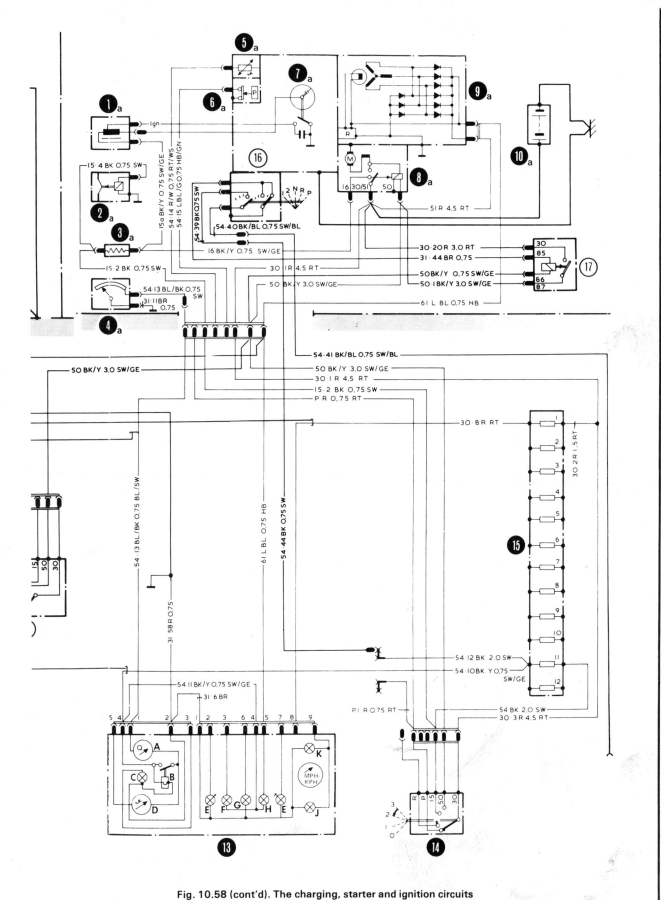

Fig. 10.58 (cont'd). The charging, starter and ignition circuits

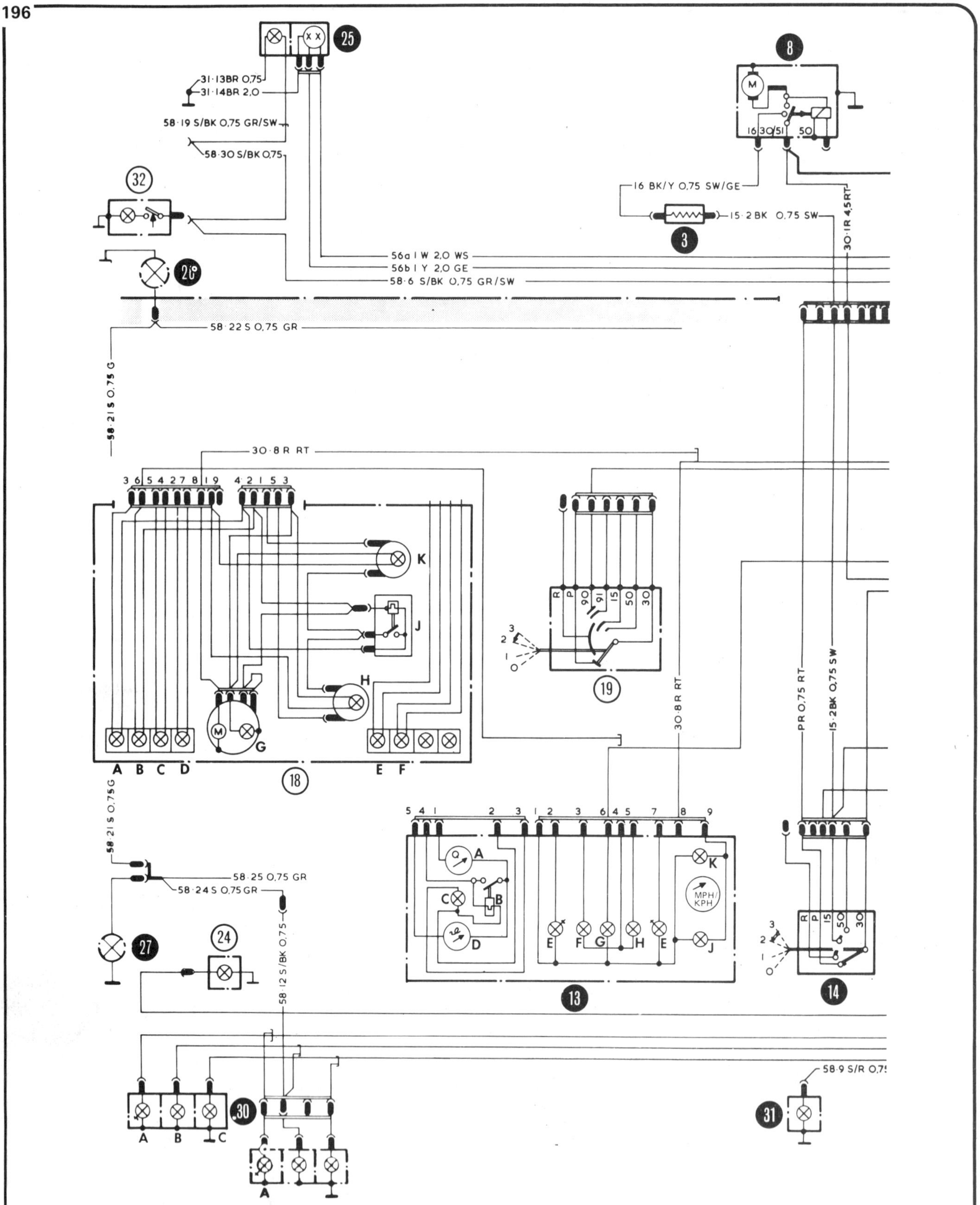

Fig. 10.59 Exterior lighting circuits. For colour code see Fig. 10.58

3	Series resistance	14	Steering/ignition lock	24*	Reversing light	30	Combination rear lights
8	Starter motor	15	Fuse box	25	Headlights and sidelights	31	Number plate lights
10	Battery	18*	Instrument cluster:	26*	Side marker lights (front)	32*	Engine compartment light
13*	Instrument cluster:		B Main beam warning	27*	Side marker lights (rear)	33*	Headlight sensing relay
	G Main beam warning		light	28	Multi-function switch	*	Optional or alternative
	light	19*	Instrument cluster (with	29	Lighting/wiper switch		equipment
			tachograph)				

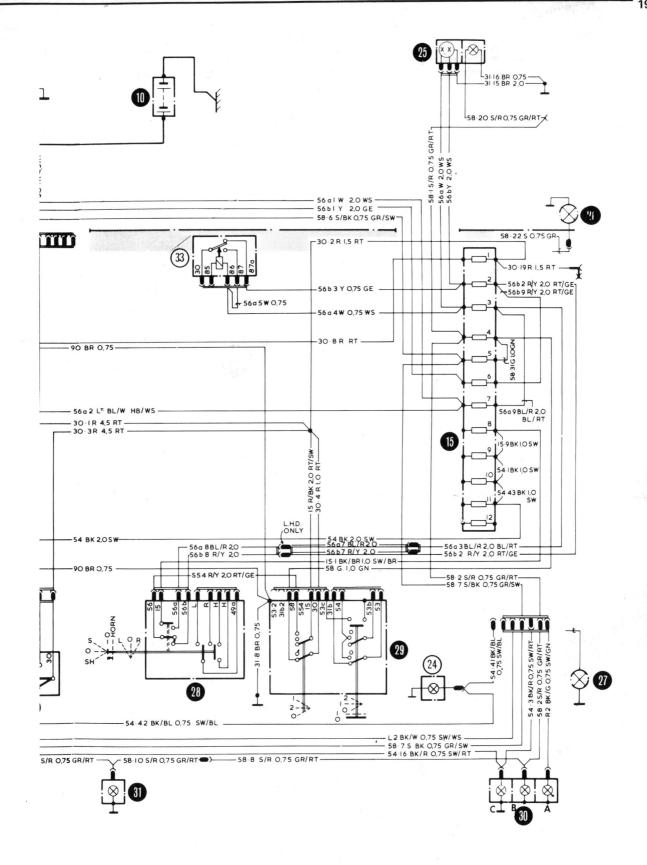

Fig. 10.59 (cont'd). Exterior lighting circuits

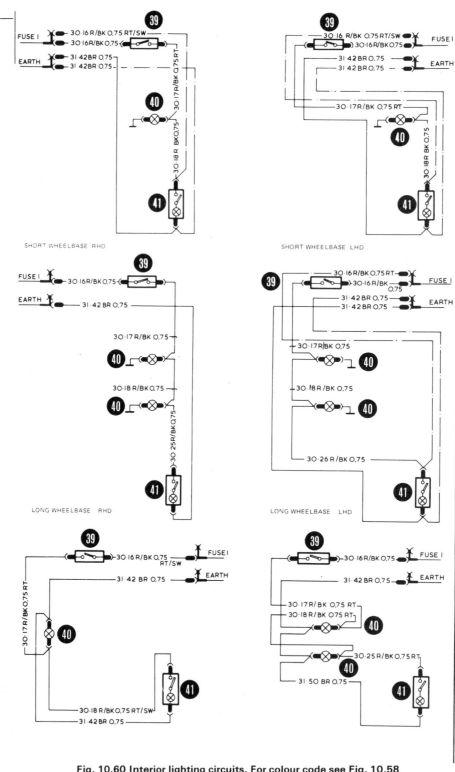

Fig. 10.60 Interior lighting circuits. For colour code see Fig. 10.58

3	Series resistance	G	Tachograph light
8	Starter motor	H	Coolant temperature gauge light
10	Battery	K	Fuel gauge light
13*	Instrument cluster:	19*	Steering/ignition lock
	C Water temperature/oil pressure light	39	Interior light switch
	K Speedometer light	40	Interior lights
	J Speedometer light	41	Courtesy lights
14*	Steering/ignition lock	42	Courtesy light switch
15	Fuse box	43*	Cigarette lighter light
18*	Instrument cluster:	*	Optional or alternative equipment

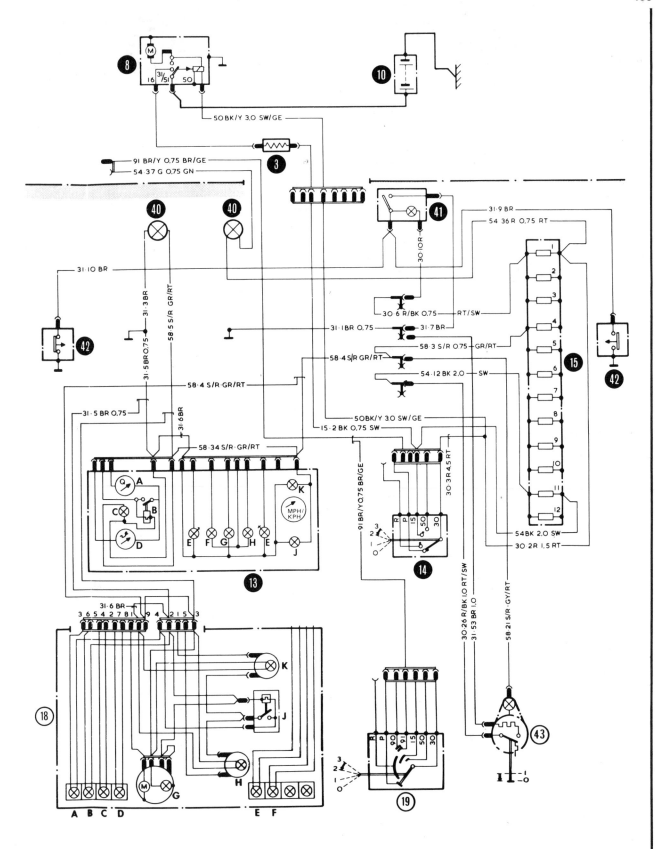

Fig. 10.60 (cont'd). Interior lighting circuits

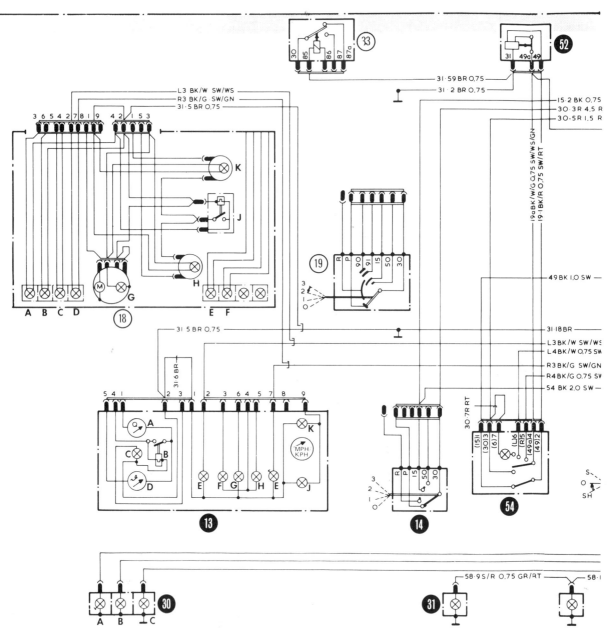

Fig. 10.61 Horn, indicator and hazard light circuits. For colour code see Fig. 10.58

3	Series resistance	19*	Steering/ignition lock	52	Flasher unit
8	Starter motor	26*	Side marker lights – front	53	Stop-light switch
10	Battery	27*	Side marker lights – rear	54	Hazard flasher switch
13*	Instrument cluster:	30	Combination rear lights	55*	Rear fog light switch
	E Direction indicator light	33*	Headlight washer sensing relay	56*	Rear fog light
14*	Steering/ignition lock	50	Direction indicator lights	67*	Direction indicator side repeaters
15	Fuses	51	Horn	*	Optional or alternative equipment
18*	Instrument cluster:				
	D Direction indicator light				

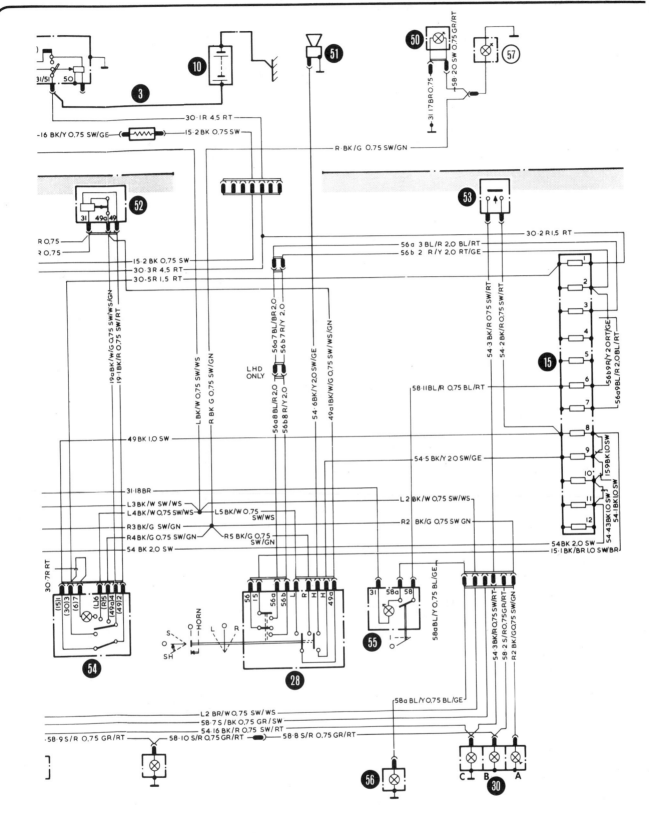

Fig. 10.61 (cont'd). Horn, indicator and hazard light circuits

202

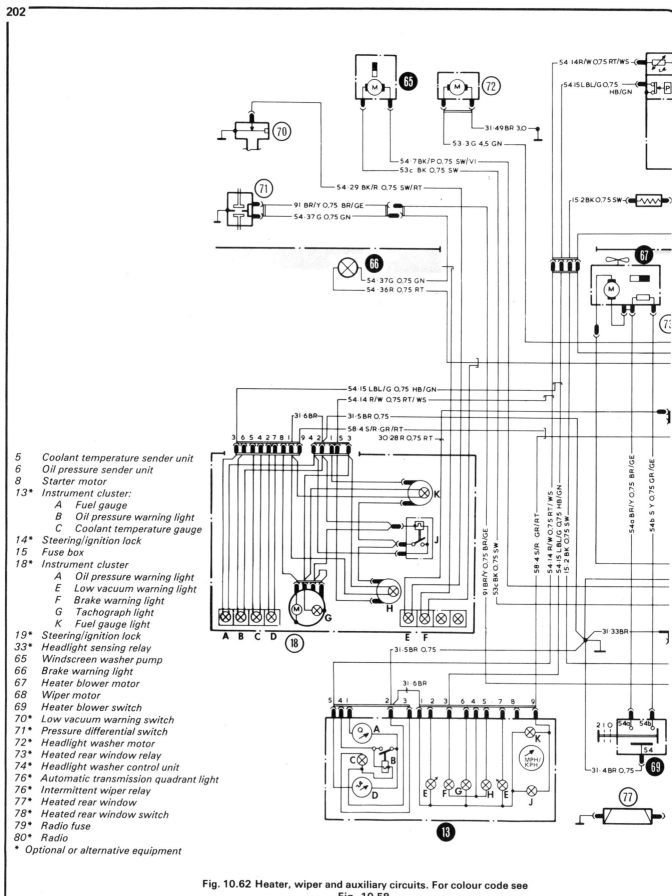

5   Coolant temperature sender unit
6   Oil pressure sender unit
8   Starter motor
13* Instrument cluster:
     A   Fuel gauge
     B   Oil pressure warning light
     C   Coolant temperature gauge
14* Steering/ignition lock
15   Fuse box
18* Instrument cluster
     A   Oil pressure warning light
     E   Low vacuum warning light
     F   Brake warning light
     G   Tachograph light
     K   Fuel gauge light
19* Steering/ignition lock
33* Headlight sensing relay
65   Windscreen washer pump
66   Brake warning light
67   Heater blower motor
68   Wiper motor
69   Heater blower switch
70* Low vacuum warning switch
71* Pressure differential switch
72* Headlight washer motor
73* Heated rear window relay
74* Headlight washer control unit
76* Automatic transmission quadrant light
76* Intermittent wiper relay
77* Heated rear window
78* Heated rear window switch
79* Radio fuse
80* Radio
*   Optional or alternative equipment

Fig. 10.62 Heater, wiper and auxiliary circuits. For colour code see
Fig. 10.58

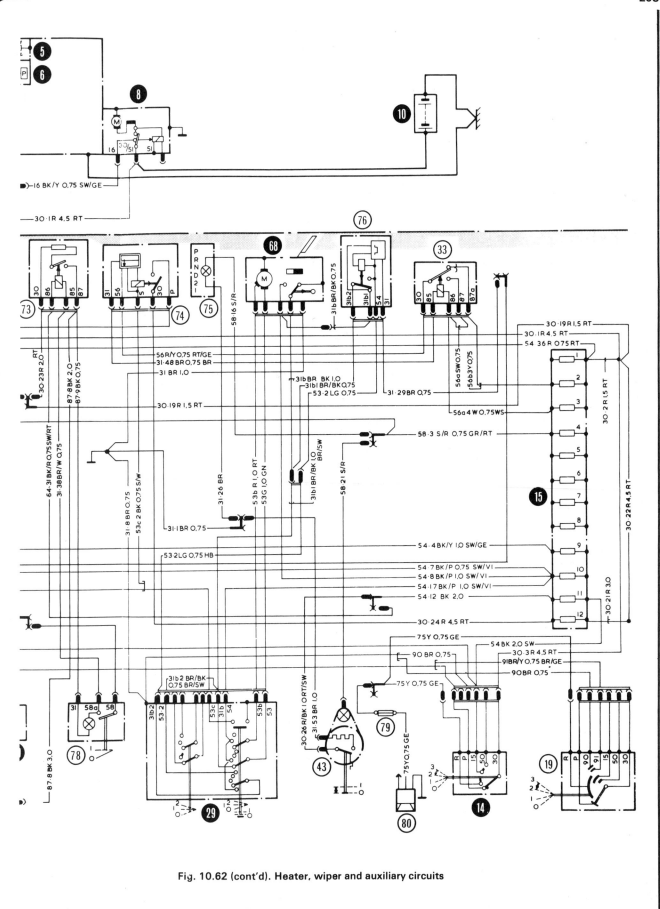

Fig. 10.62 (cont'd). Heater, wiper and auxiliary circuits

Chapter 11 Suspension and steering

For modifications, and information applicable to later models, see Supplement at end of manual

Contents

Specifications

Front suspension

Type	Beam axle with semi-elliptic springs and telescopic shock absorbers
Kingpin inclination	5° ± 10'
Toe-in – crossply tyres	0.094 to 0.156 in (2.38 to 3.97 mm)
Toe-in – radial ply tyres	0.00 to 0.063 in (0.00 to 1.60 mm)
Camber	0° to 1°
Castor:	
75 and 115 models	5°45' (max) to 3°15' (min)
130 and 190 models	6° (max) to 4° (min)
Stub axle body to axle beam clearance	0.001 to 0.004 in (0.025 to 0.1 mm)
Wheel bearing endfloat	0.001 to 0.005 in (0.025 to 0.13 mm)

Steering

Type	Worm and nut (recirculating ball)
Lubricant type	Steering gear grease (SLM 1C 9110-A)
Lubricant capacity	0.7 lb (0.32 kg)
Ratio	19.88 to 1
Wormshaft preload	3.5 to 6.0 lbf in (4.0 to 7.0 kgf m)
Total preload (wormshaft preload plus mesh load)	39 lbf in (45 kgf cm)
Adjusting screw shim thicknesses	Various, between 0.062 and 0.069 in (1.57 and 1.75 mm)

Rear suspension

Type	Rigid rear axle suspended from semi-elliptic leaf springs with telescopic shock absorbers

Wheels

LCX 80 to 120 and 100L variants	14 x 5½J (5-stud fixing)
LCY 130 and 190 variants	14 x 5½J (6-stud fixing)

Tyres

Tyre type and size	Various, according to model
Tyres fitted	185 x SR Reinforced-radial; 195 x R14C (6PR) – radial, 205 x R14C (6PR) – radial; 7.50 x 14 (6PR) crossply

Tyre pressures (cold)

Tyre size/model type:	lbf/in²		Bar	
	Front	Rear	Front	Rear
185 x SR14R/80	36	42	2.4	2.9
195 x R14C/100 & /115	30	45	2.0	3.1
205 x R14C/120	24	42	1.6	2.9
185 x SR14R/130	30	30	2.0	2.0
185 x SR14R/160	30	36	2.0	2.4
185 x SR14R/175	42	42	2.9	2.9
185 x 14C/190	33	46	2.2	3.2
195 x R14C/190	30	37	2.0	2.6
7.50 x 14/80/130 & /160	30	30	2.0	2.0
7.50 x 14/100 & /115	30	45	2.0	3.1
7.50 x 14/190	30	37	2.0	2.6

Torque wrench settings

	lbf ft	kgf m
Wheels		
5-stud wheel nuts	55 to 70	7.5 to 9.5
6-stud wheel nuts	114 to 132	15.5 to 18.0
Front axle and steering		
Drop arm locknut	110 to 130	15.2 to 18.0
Drag link to drop arm	33 to 37	4.6 to 5.2
Rocker arm side cover	14 to 17	1.9 to 2.3
Steering box side cover	16 to 19	2.4 to 2.8
Steering shaft adjuster locknut	22 to 29	3.0 to 4.0
Wormshaft endplate bolts	15 to 18	2.1 to 2.5
Steering column tube lower clamp pinch-bolt	15 to 18	2.0 to 2.5
Steering column tube upper clamp	30 to 35	4.2 to 4.9
Steering wheel locknut	20 to 25	2.8 to 3.4
Steering arm to stub axle	43 to 50	5.8 to 6.9
Drag link to steering arm	51 to 66	7.0 to 9.0
Track rod to steering arm	51 to 66	7.0 to 9.0
Steering box to chassis	40 to 47	5.4 to 6.4
Front axle/suspension		
Disc to hub	37 to 44	4.8 to 6.2
Brake caliper to mounting bracket	66 to 81	9.0 to 11.0
Shock absorber mounting bolts	51 to 66	7.0 to 9.0
Spring U-bolts:		
1st stage	15 to 18	2.0 to 2.5
2nd stage	30 to 33	4.0 to 4.5
3rd stage	40 to 45	5.4 to 6.1
Rear axle		
Spring U-bolts:		
F axle	63 to 74	8.6 to 10.2
G axle	96 to 104	13.2 to 14.3
H axle	63 to 74	8.6 to 10.2
Rear spring to front shackle	116 to 146	16.0 to 20.1
Rear spring to rear shackle:		
F axle	44 to 52	6.0 to 7.1
G axle (120 model)	44 to 52	6.0 to 7.1
G axle (other variants)	116 to 146	16.0 to 20.1
H axle (100L model)	116 to 146	16.0 to 20.1
H axle (other variants)	44 to 52	6.0 to 7.1
Spring centre nut	25 to 30	3.5 to 4.0

1 General description

The front axle is of solid forged steel construction, with spindle bodies mounted at each end which pivot on spindle shafts (kingpins). Bronze bushes are pressed into the spindle body bosses and thrust washers located beneath the axle beam support the weight of the vehicle.

Steering is provided by a worm and nut steering gear with recirculating ball action which is connected to the side steering arm by a drop arm and drag link. The right- and left-hand steering arms are linked by a track rod which is adjustable to accommodate the front wheel alignment.

The front suspension consists of semi-elliptic single leaf springs with hydraulically damped shock absorbers, and all mountings are rubber bushed.

The rear suspension consists of semi-elliptic multi-leaf springs with hydraulically damped telescopic shock absorbers. All mountings are rubber bushed.

All models are fitted with 14 in (35.6 cm) diameter pressed steel wheels, the short wheelbase vehicles having single wheels front and rear, and certain long wheelbases having single front wheels and twin rear wheels.

The front hubs are of two tapered roller bearing type and are adjustable for endfloat. The rear hubs, according to model, are of three-quarter floating type with a single non-adjustable ball bearing, or are fully floating and mounted on tapered roller bearings which are adjustable for endfloat. Refer to Chapter 8 for details.

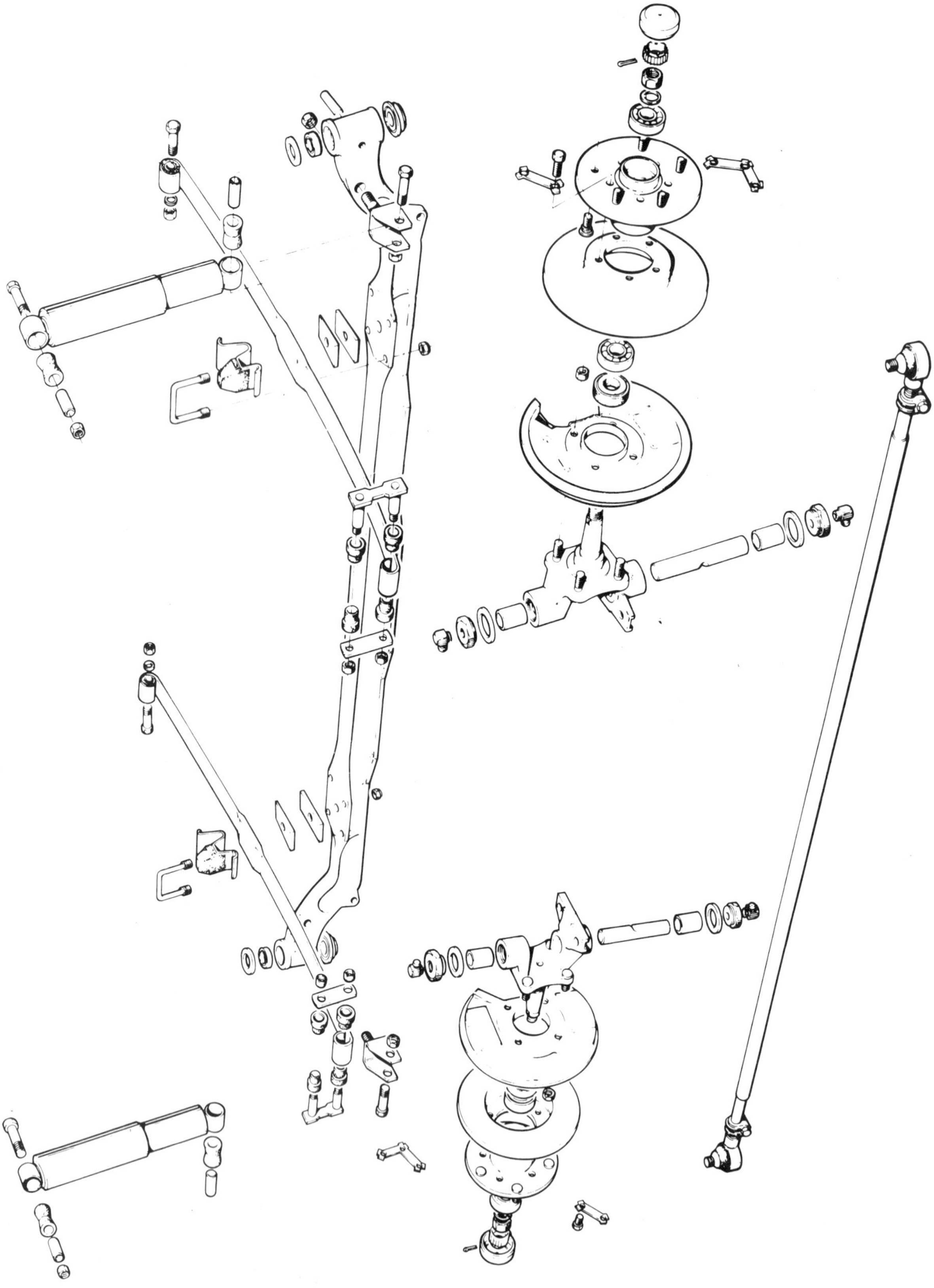

Fig. 11.1 Front axle and suspension components (Sec 1)

Fig. 11.2 Check the U-bolt nuts (arrowed) for tightness (Sec 2)

2 Suspension and steering – maintenance and inspection

1 A regular routine inspection and service of the steering and suspension is essential, particularly where the vehicle operates in arduous conditions with regular maximum capacity loading.

2 Carry out the following at least every 6000 miles (10 000 km):

(a) Lubricate the steering spindle pins (kingpins)
(b) Inspect the steering and suspension components for signs of wear and possibly damage
(c) Check the tyre pressures and tightness of wheel nuts
(d) Check and if necessary tighten the spring U-bolt nuts

3 The steering gear sector shaft preload should be adjusted at the first 6000 mile (10 000 km) and 18 000 mile (30 000 km) intervals and thereafter at 24 000 mile (40 000 km) intervals.

3 Front wheel bearings – lubrication and adjustment

1 Remove the wheel trim (where fitted) apply the handbrake, and jack up the front of the vehicle, supporting it adequately on stands.

2 Using a screwdriver or similar tool, carefully ease the wheel bearing dust cap from the hub (photo), extract the split pin and remove the retainer.

3 If the wheel bearings are to be lubricated, slacken the wheel nuts and remove the roadwheel, otherwise adjust them as described in paragraphs 13 to 18 inclusive.

4 Unscrew and remove the brake caliper mounting bolts to detach the caliper unit. On models fitted with a vertically split brake system, the caliper hydraulic hose can be left attached whilst the caliper is supported and suspended clear of the hub by a suitable piece of wire or cord. This avoids having to bleed the hydraulic system on re-assembly. On models fitted with a horizontally split brake system, the hydraulic fluid line must be disconnected and plugged, and the caliper removed. Refer to Chapter 9 for full details.

5 Unscrew and remove the hub adjusting nut and withdraw the washer and outer cone and rollers (Fig. 11.3).

6 Lift the hub assembly away from the stub axle and, using a suitable metal or wooden drift, drive out the inner cone and rollers together with the grease retainer.

7 Scrape out the bearing grease from the hub and wash the hub and bearings with paraffin.

8 Examine the bearing surfaces for wear and pitting; if new bearings need to be fitted, refer to Section 4 of this Chapter. If the bearings are serviceable, repack the rollers with fresh grease but leave the hub body empty.

9 Check that each bearing is a push fit onto the stub axle and if excessive clearance is noticed, renew both bearings and stub axle spindle.

10 Install the inner cone and rollers, then, using a suitable diameter tube, carefully drive the grease retainer squarely into the hub with the sealing lip facing into the hub.

11 Wipe clean the stub axle spindle and sealing surface, then fit the hub assembly.

3.2 Remove the front wheel bearing dust cap

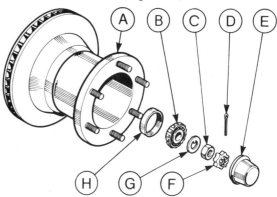

Fig. 11.3 Front hub and disc components (Sec 3)

A Hub and disc	E Cap
B Bearing cone (outer)	F Retainer
C Nut	G Washer
D Split pin	H Bearing cup (outer)

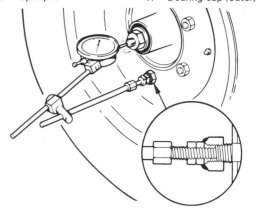

Fig. 11.4 Hub endfloat check, using dial gauge and adaptor to attach onto wheel stud (Sec 3)

12 Install the outer cone and rollers followed by the washer and adjusting nut.

13 Using a torque wrench, tighten the adjusting nut to 17 lbf ft (2.3 kgf m) whilst rotating the wheel in order to settle the bearings.

14 Loose the adjusting nut by four flats or two thirds of a turn, then vigorously rock the hub to reposition the bearings.

15 Using a dial gauge, check that the bearing endfloat is within the limits given in the Specifications and make a final adjustment as necessary. It is advantageous to refit the wheel during the bearing adjustment to assist settling the bearings.

16 Locate the retainer on the hub nut and secure it with a new split pin, then carefully tap the dust cap onto the hub.

17 Refit the brake caliper as described in Chapter 9. On horizontally split braking system models, bleed the brakes, also as given in Chapter 9.

18 Refit the roadwheel and tighten the wheel nuts, then lower the vehicle to the ground and finally tighten the wheel nuts to the specified torque. Refit the hub cap (if applicable).

4 Front hub bearings and wheel studs – removal and refitting

1 Refer to Section 3 and remove the front wheel hub bearing rollers, and grease retainer.

2 Bend straight the locktabs and remove the hub-to-brake disc retaining bolts. Before separating the hub from the disc check the alignment marks as shown in Fig. 9.13 (Chapter 9).

3 Using a soft metal drift, drive the bearing cups out of the hub, making sure that they remain square during removal to prevent seizure.

4 Extract the wheel studs by using a tube as a distance piece and pressing the studs out in a vice.

5 Refitting the front hub bearings and wheel studs is a reversal of the removal procedure, with reference to paragraphs 7 to 18 of Section 3. Remember to tighten the wheel nuts to the specified torque.

5 Front axle beam – removal and refitting

1 The front axle beam can be removed in a fully assembled state or partially dismantled; if the spindle shafts (kingpins) are seized it will be advantageous to remove the axle beam first and press them out with a hydraulic press.

2 Apply the handbrake, chock the rear wheels and jack up the front of the vehicle (unladen) supporting it with stands placed beneath the chassis members. Support the axle beam with a trolley jack and stands.

3 If necessary, remove the stub axles as described in Section 6.

4 Unscrew and remove the nuts and bolts retaining each shock absorber to the axle beam, noting that the bolts are entered from the rear of the axle beam at the top mounting. The lower bolts are inserted from the outside to the inside.

5 If the stub axles are still in position detach the steering arms by extracting the split pins and unscrewing and removing the retaining nuts and bolts; tie the track rod and steering arms away from the axle beam. Also remove the hub assemblies as described in Section 3 and detach the disc splash shields as described in paragraph 4 of Section 6.

6 With the trolley jack supporting the axle beam, unscrew and remove the eight U-bolt nuts which retain the axle beam to the springs, and withdraw the U-bolts and the bump stop/spacer.

7 Lower the axle beam from the vehicle and recover the wedges fitted between the springs and beam.

8 If distortion of the axle beam is suspected it should be checked by a suitably equipped garage and renewed if necessary.

9 Refitting the front axle beam is a reversal of the removal procedure but the following additional points should be noted:

(a) Fit the wedges between the springs and axle beam with their thicker ends to the rear as shown in Fig. 11.5

(b) Tighten all nuts and bolts to the correct torque wrench settings and tighten the U-bolt nuts again with the full laden weight of the vehicle on the axle beam

(c) Adjust the wheel alignment as described in Section 15

6 Stub axle – removal, overhaul and refitting

1 Remove the front hub assembly as described in paragraphs 1, 2, 4 and 5 of Section 3, but support the front of the vehicle beneath the chassis members after making sure that the vehicle is unladen.

2 Straighten and remove the split pins from the steering arm retaining nuts, unscrew and remove the nuts and detach the arm from the spindle body; extract the retaining bolts.

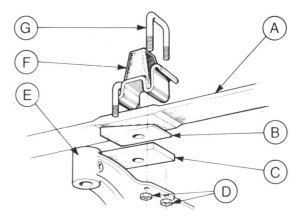

Fig. 11.5 Front spring to axle attachment (Sec 5)

A　Spring　　　　　　E　Axle
B　Wedge　　　　　　F　Bump stop
C　Spacer plate　　　G　U-bolt
D　U-bolt nuts

6.3 Steering swivel pin lower grease nipple

3 Unscrew and remove the kingpin upper and lower grease nipples (photo).

4 Unscrew and remove the four nuts retaining the brake disc splash shield to the knuckle and detach the shield.

5 Unscrew and remove the kingpin nut at the top and remove it together with the copper shim(s).

6 Drive out the cotter pin and remove the kingpin. You may have to use a suitable press or drift to extract the pin, which may in turn entail removal of the axle beam.

7 Remove the stub axle and upper shim.

8 Thoroughly clean the stub axle and axle beam with paraffin and dry them with a lint-free cloth. Examine the stub axle and axle beam for signs of distortion or damage. If in doubt regarding the condition of the axle beam or stub axle, have your Ford dealer make an inspection and renew as necessary.

9 Assuming that the kingpin is to be renewed, the stub axle pivot bushes will also have to be renewed. As the bush removal and refitting procedure requires the use of specialised equipment, their replacement is best entrusted to your Ford dealer who will also ream the newly fitted bushes to suit the kingpin.

10 With the new bushes fitted, locate the stub axle unit to the axle beam and then select and insert new shims of the required thickness between the top face of the stub axle and the lower face of the upper hole in the axle beam. Select the shims as necessary to give the specified clearance. Measure the clearance using a feeler gauge (with the bearing fitted – Fig. 11.7).

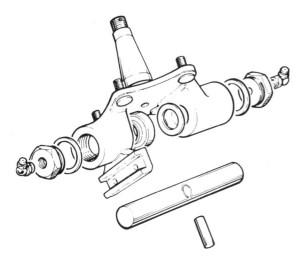

Fig. 11.6 Stub axle and kingpin components (Sec 6)

Fig. 11.7 Select shim(s) to give correct clearance between the stub axle and axle beam (Sec 6)

11 Lightly smear the kingpin with grease and check that the stub axle and shims are exactly aligned with the holes in the axle beam. Insert the kingpin so that its cutaway section is aligned with the cotter pin hole in the axle beam.
12 With the kingpin in position insert the new cotter pin to secure, using a suitable drift.
13 Relocate the nuts and copper washers to each end of the kingpin. Refit the grease nipples and then lubricate the stub axle assembly until grease emerges from the joint faces. Check that the stub axle pivots freely without binding or excessive play.
14 Refit the disc shield and retain with four self-locking nuts.
15 Refit the steering arm to the stub axle and retain with the two nuts and bolts.
16 The remaining refitting procedure is a reversal of the removal procedure but the following additional points should be noted:

   (a) Tighten all nuts and bolts to the correct torque wrench settings
   (b) Adjust the front wheel bearings as described in Section 3

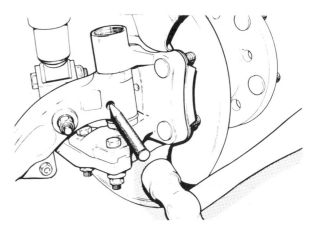

Fig. 11.8 Drive in a new cotter pin (Sec 6)

7 Steering arm – removal and refitting

1 Remove the hub cap (where fitted), loosen the wheel nuts, and jack up the front of the vehicle, supporting it adequately with axle stands. Remove the wheel.
2 Straighten and remove the split pin on the drag link to steering arm ballpin retaining nut, unscrew and remove the nut, then separate the joint using a universal balljoint separator. Similarly separate the track rod from the steering arm.
3 Straighten and remove the split pins from the steering arm to stub axle spindle body retaining nuts, unscrew and remove the nuts and tap the steering arm from its locating slot and retaining bolts.
4 Examine the steering arm for distortion through impact, fractures and deterioration. Renew the arm if it is faulty. Do not attempt to straighten it.
5 Refitting the steering arm is a reversal of the removal procedure but the following additional points should be noted:

   (a) Make sure that the mating surfaces of the steering arm, spindle body, and ballpin tapers are clean
   (b) Tighten the retaining nuts to the correct torque wrench settings and retain them with new split pins
   (c) Adjust the front wheel alignment as described in Section 15.

8 Drag link assembly – removal and refitting

1 Straighten and extract the split pins from the ballpin nuts at each end of the drag link, then unscrew and remove the nuts.
2 Using a universal balljoint separator, free the ballpins and withdraw the drag link.

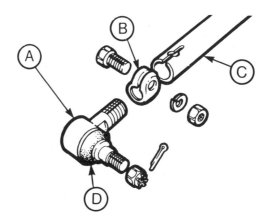

Fig. 11.9 Drag link end components (Sec 8)

   A Drag link end   C Drag link
   B Clamp   D Rubber cap

3 To remove the drag link ends, loosen the clamp bolts and unscrew the ends, noting that they have left- and right-hand threads.
4 Screw the new ends onto the drag link an equal number of threads so that the ballpin centres are 18 in (45.7 cm) apart.
5 Refit the drag link, tighten the ballpin nuts and fit new split pins.
6 With the wheels in the straight-ahead position, the steering gear must be at the centre of its travel; adjust the drag link accordingly and then tighten the clamp bolts.

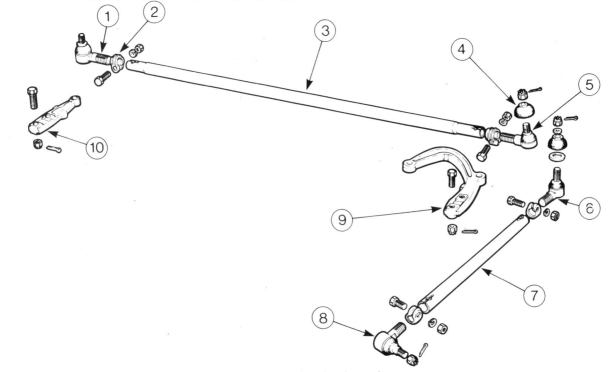

Fig. 11.10 The steering track rod and associate components
(Sec 9)

1	LH track rod end (RH thread)	4	Dust seal
2	Clamp	5	RH track rod end (LH thread)
3	Track rod	6	Drag link end (LH thread)
		7	Drag link
		8	Drag link end (RH thread)
		9	Steering arm (RH side)
		10	Steering arm (LH side)

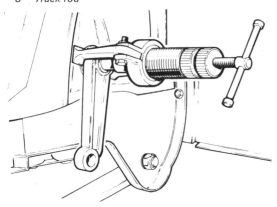

Fig. 11.11 Drop arm removal using Ford puller No 14008 (Sec 10)

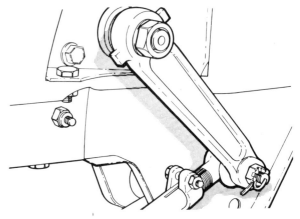

Fig. 11.12 Drop arm fully located (Sec 10)

Fig. 11.13 Steering column to dash panel clamp. Securing nut arrowed (Sec 11)

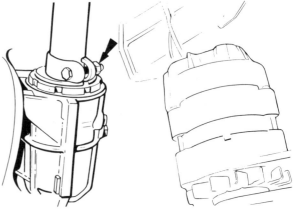

Fig. 11.14 Steering column tube to box clamp. Pinch-bolt arrowed (Sec 11)

9.1 Track rod end to steering arm joint

11.2 Central cap prised free for access to steering wheel nut

9 Track rod – removal and refitting

1   Straighten and remove the split pins from the ballpin nuts at each end of the track rod, then unscrew and remove the nuts (photo).
2   Using a universal balljoint separator, free the ballpins and withdraw the track rod.
3   To remove the track rod ends, loosen the clamp bolts and unscrew the ends, noting that they have left- and right-hand threads.
4   Screw the new ends onto the track rod an equal number of threads.
5   Refit the track rod, tighten the ballpin nuts, and fit new split pins.
6   Adjust the front wheel alignment as described in Section 15 and finally tighten the clamp bolts.

10 Steering drop arm – removal and refitting

1   Raise the vehicle at the front end and support with axle stands. Remove the right-hand roadwheel.
2   Working under the wheel arch, unscrew and remove the nut and spring washer retaining the drop arm to the sector shaft. Use a suitable universal puller and withdraw the drop arm from the sector shaft (Fig. 11.11).
3   Extract the split pin and unscrew the locknut from the drag link to drop arm balljoint. Use a universal balljoint separator and detach the arm from the link.
4   To refit, centralise the steering and locate the drop arm onto the sector shaft – it only fits in one position. Fit and tighten the retaining nut to the specified torque setting.
5   Reattach the drag link, tighten the balljoint locknut to the specified torque and insert a new split pin.
6   Refit the roadwheel and lower the vehicle. Check that the steering action is satisfactory.

11 Steering gear – removal and refitting

1   Disconnect the battery earth lead.
2   Prise free the central pad from the steering wheel (photo) and using a box or socket spanner, unscrew and remove the steering wheel locknut. Note the steering wheel location on the shaft and withdraw it.
3   Unscrew and remove the steering column upper and lower shroud retaining screws and detach the shrouds.
4   Unscrew the column switch and bracket retaining screws and remove the switches from the column. Detach the wiring loom connector from the steering lock.
5   Unscrew and remove the two nuts and their washers retaining the column at its top mounting (Fig. 11.13).
6   In the engine compartment, loosen the pinch-bolt at the steering column tube lower end (Fig. 11.14).

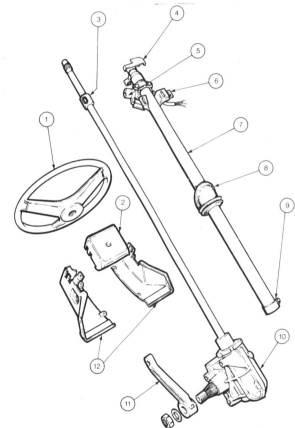

Fig. 11.15 Steering column and associated components (Sec 11)

1	Steering wheel	7	Column tube
2	Upper shroud	8	Grommet (bulkhead)
3	Steering shaft	9	Clamp
4	Multi-switch bracket	10	Steering box
5	Ignition switch	11	Drop arm
6	Column retaining bracket	12	Lower shrouds

7   Disconnect the steering drop arm from the steering sector shaft as described in Section 10.
8   Unscrew and remove the three steering box-to-body retaining bolts.
9   The steering column tube can now be withdrawn upwards and separated from its dash panel location, simultaneously detaching its grommet in the bulkhead (Fig. 11.15).

10 Withdraw the steering box unit with steering shaft from its location and lower it through the front of the vehicle for removal.

11 To refit the steering box unit, relocate the grommet into the sector aperture in the body and reposition the steering box, passing it up through the front of the vehicle. Retain the box in position by loosely fitting the three securing bolts with washers.

12 Refit the steering column tube down through the bulkhead to engage with the steering box. Relocate the bulkhead grommet and loosely refit the column mounting-to-dash nuts with washers.

13 Tighten the pinch-bolt at the lower end of the column tube to the specified torque.

14 Tighten the three steering box-to-body retaining bolts to the specified torque.

15 Relocate the steering drop arm onto the sector shaft and tighten the retaining nut to the specified torque.

16 Fully tighten the steering column tube-to-dash mounting nuts to the specified torque.

17 Reconnect the steering lock wire connector.

18 Relocate and secure the combination switches to the column (see Chapter 10) and refit the upper and lower column shrouds.

19 Refit the steering wheel to its original position on the shaft. If this was not noted when removing, centralise the roadwheels to the straight-ahead position, centralise the steering wheel and fit it to the shaft. Tighten the retaining nut to the specified torque.

20 Reconnect the battery and check the functions of the combination switches and the steering lock/ignition switch.

21 Finally check the steering for satisfactory action.

12 Steering gear – dismantling, overhaul and reassembly

1 Clean the exterior of the steering gear with paraffin and thoroughly dry it.

2 Loosen the locknut which secures the rocker shaft adjuster screw, then unscrew and remove the three bolts which retain the rocker shaft housing side cover in position. Remove the side cover and gasket and withdraw the rocker shaft assembly (Fig. 11.17).

3 Remove the adjustment locknut and unscrew the side cover from the adjusting screw, then slide the adjusting screw and spacer out of the rocker shaft location.

4 Straighten the tabs of the lockwasher retaining the upper bearing housing lockring and unscrew and remove the lockring; a special C-spanner is required to do this and should be borrowed from a tool agent.

5 Unscrew and remove the upper bearing housing and carefully withdraw the steering shaft together with the upper and lower bearings.

6 Using a suitable drift, drive the upper and lower bearing cups out of the upper housing and steering box.

7 Hold the wormshaft in a soft-jawed vice and detach the transfer tubes and balls from the nut by unscrewing and removing the clamp retaining screws.

8 Slide off the nut assembly together with the 62 steel balls.

9 Prise the oil seal from the drop arm end of the steering box.

10 Thoroughly wash all components in paraffin and dry them with a lint-free cloth.

11 Examine all the components for damage, fractures, and excessive wear. Fit the rocker shaft temporarily in the steering box bush and check that there is no excessive clearance, then inspect the teeth of the sector and nut assembly for wear. Check the bearing races and balls for pitting and signs of wear and inspect the bush in the side cover for wear. New bushes should be drifted into position where necessary, but if the rocker and steering shafts need renewal it will probably be more economical to obtain a reconditioned steering gear.

12 Obtain a new oil seal, side cover gasket and bearing housing lockwasher.

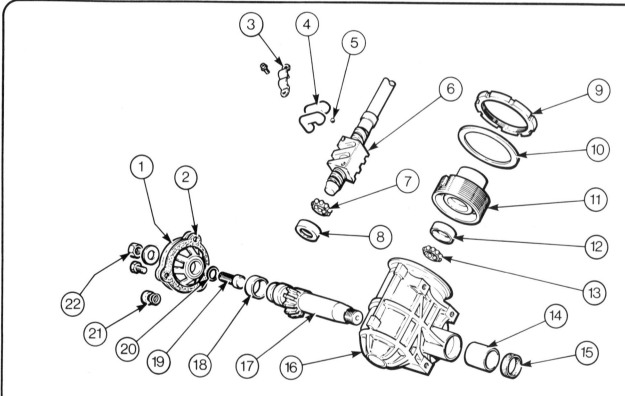

Fig. 11.16 The steering gearbox components (Sec 12)

1 Housing end cover	7 Lower bearing	13 Upper bearing	18 Cover bush
2 Cover gasket	8 Lower bearing cup	14 Bush	19 Adjusting screw
3 Balljoint clamp	9 Locking ring	15 Oil seal	20 Spacer (shim)
4 Transfer tubes	10 Locking washer	16 Housing	21 Filler plug
5 One of (62) balls	11 Adjuster	17 Rocker shaft	22 Locknut
6 Nut and shaft	12 Upper bearing cup		

13 To reassemble the steering gear first drive the oil seal and lower bearing cup into the steering box making sure that they are fitted squarely. Similarly, using suitable diameter tubing, drive the upper bearing cup into the upper housing.

14 Smear the worm, nut and transfer tubes with the specified grease and press the steel balls into the transfer tubes.

15 Slide the nut onto the worm and press the steel balls into each of the four holes until all 62 are in position; it will be necessary to shake the assembly to settle the balls in their grooves.

16 Refit the transfer tubes, align the transfer holes and tighten the retaining screws.

17 Grease the caged ball races and position them in the bearing cups, then screw the upper bearing housing onto the wormshaft and tighten to achieve the specified pre-load. (Use a spring balance and some string around the shaft to measure this.)

18 Refit the lockwasher and lockring and tighten it with the special tool. Bend one tab into the lockring slot and the remaining tab over the housing (Fig. 11.18).

19 Fit the adjuster screw to the rocker shaft and select a spacer to give the adjuster screw 0.002 in (0.05 mm) clearance in the slot. Remove the screw, fit the spacer, and refit the screw.

20 Screw on the side cover and locknut and position the new joint on the side cover with grease.

21 Insert the rocker shaft and side cover, making sure that the centre teeth of both shaft and nut are engaged, then tighten the three side cover retaining bolts.

22 Adjust the steering gear as described in Section 13.

23 Fill the steering box with the correct amount of grease as given in the Specifications.

13 Steering gear – adjustment

1 Drain the cooling system as described in Chapter 2 and remove the bottom radiator hose.

2 With the front wheels in the straight-ahead position, loosen the adjustment locknut on the side of the steering gearbox (photo) and tighten the adjusting screw to 3 lbf ft (45 kgf cm).

3 Back off the adjusting screw a quarter of a turn (90°), then tighten the locknut.

4 Refit the radiator bottom hose and fill the cooling system as described in Chapter 2.

14 Steering column upper bearing – removal and refitting

1 Refer to Section 11 and detach and remove the steering column tube as given in paragraphs 1 to 6. Withdraw the tube upwards to remove it.

2 The bearing can then be removed from its location in the top of the column tube using a suitable extractor.

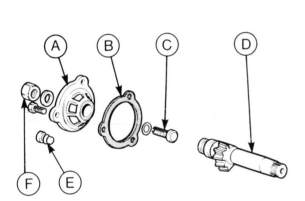

Fig. 11.17 The end cover components (Sec 12)

A   End cover
B   Gasket
C   Adjuster screw
D   Rocker shaft
E   Filler plug
F   Adjuster screw locknut

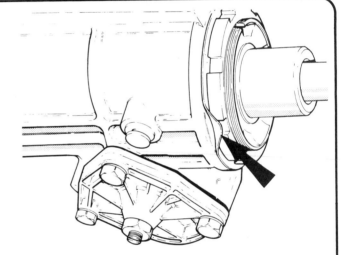

Fig. 11.18 Bend lockwasher tab (arrowed) to secure lockring (Sec 12)

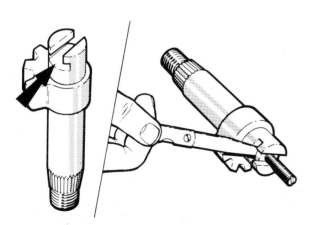

Fig. 11.19 Check the screw head to rocker shaft clearance at point indicated (Sec 12)

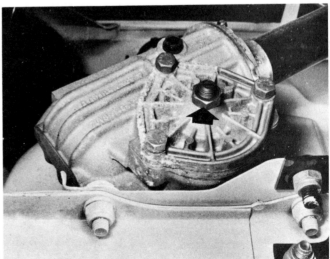

13.2 Steering gearbox adjusting screw and locknut (arrowed)

Fig. 11.20 Bearing location (arrowed) in the top of the steering column tube (Sec 14)

3   Carefully insert the new bearing into the column tube (Fig. 11.20).
4   Refit the steering column in the reverse order to removal. Loosely fit the column clamp and mounting nuts and bolts initially, then when the column is in position tighten the fastenings to the specified torque wrench settings.

15 Front wheel alignment

1   Accurate front wheel alignment is essential to provide good

steering and slow tyre wear. The camber and kingpin inclination angles are built into the spindle bodies and axle beam and are not adjustable. The castor angle is set by the wedges fitted between the springs and the axle beam and, provided these are fitted correctly with the wedge to the rear, the castor angle will be correct.
2   Checking of all wheel alignment angles and adjustments is best carried out by a suitably equipped garage, but the toe-in can be checked by the home mechanic by obtaining or making an adjustable tracking gauge. The gauge should have two pointers, one adjustable which can be positioned between the inner or outer faces of the wheels.
3   Before making any adjustments check that the following are within limits:

  (a) Tyre pressures
  (b) Wheel run-out
  (c) Front wheel bearing adjustment
  (d) Front axle bushes
  (e) Steering balljoints

4   Using the gauge, measure the distance between the wheel rims at the hub height at the rear of the wheel and mark the tyre with chalk to indicate where the measurement was taken.
5   Roll the vehicle forwards so that the chalk mark is now at the front of the wheel and measure the distance between the wheel rims again at hub height and on the same measuring points; the latter measurement should be less than the original by the amount of toe-in given in the Specifications.
6   To adjust the toe-in dimension, loosen the nut and bolt at each end of the track rod, turn the rod as required, then tighten the clamp bolts and check the adjustment again.

16 Front spring – removal and refitting

1   Apply the handbrake firmly and jack up the front of the vehicle (unladen), supporting it adequately with stands beneath the chassis members. Support the axle beam on a trolley jack.
2   Unscrew and remove the U-bolt nuts and detach the U-bolts, bump stop, and wedge (photo).
3   Unscrew and remove the self-locking nuts from the spring shackle and withdraw the side plate, then, using a soft metal drift, drive out the remaining shackle pins and plate and extract the rubber bushes (photo).
4   Unscrew and remove the front mounting nut and washer, and drive out the bolt whilst supporting the spring.
5   Lift the spring away from the axle and mountings.
6   Examine the front and rear mounting bushes and the condition of the shackle, U-bolts and bump stop, and renew any faulty components.

16.2 Front spring to axle location showing U-bolts, bump stop and wedge (between spring and axle)

16.3 Front spring rear shackle location

7   Refitting the front spring is a reversal of the removal procedure, but the following additional points should be noted:

(a) *The wedge between the axle beam and spring must be positioned with the thicker end to the rear*
(b) *Insert the bolt and shackle pins from the outer facing side of the mountings*
(c) *Do not fully tighten the retaining nuts until the vehicle is free standing. Refer to the Specifications for the respective torque wrench settings*

17   Front shock absorber – removal and refitting

1   Apply the handbrake and jack up the front of the vehicle, supporting it adequately with stands.
2   Remove the roadwheel, then unscrew and remove the upper and lower shock absorber mounting self-locking nuts, and drive out the mounting bolts using a suitable diameter drift (photo).
3   Withdraw the shock absorber from the axle and underframe mountings together with mounting rubbers and plain washers.
4   Refitting the front shock absorber is a reversal of the removal procedure. Tighten the nuts to the torque wrench settings given in the Specifications.

18   Rear shock absorber – removal and refitting

The procedure is identical to that given for front shock absorber removal and refitting in the previous Section, but note that the upper bolt retains the handbrake cable bracket on some models.

19   Rear spring – removal and refitting

1   Chock the front wheels and jack up the rear of the vehicle (unladen), supporting it adequately with stands placed beneath the chassis members. Remove the roadwheel(s).
2   Place a jack beneath the rear axle, and raise to support it.
3   Unscrew and remove the spring shackle retaining nuts and withdraw the plate, shackle pins, and rubber bushes using a soft metal drift as necessary.
4   Unscrew and remove the front mounting retaining nut and washer and drive out the mounting bolt with a soft metal drift (photo).
5   Unscrew and remove the U-bolt nuts and detach the U-bolts together with the clamp plate; the rear spring can now be lifted from the rear axle and withdrawn from beneath the vehicle.
6   Examine the front and rear (where fitted) mounting bushes and the condition of the shackle and rebound pin (where fitted), U-bolts, and bump stop, and renew any faulty components.
7   Refitting the rear spring is a reversal of the removal procedure but the following additional points should be noted:

(a) *Insert the mounting bolt and shackle pins from the outer facing side of the mountings*
(b) *Insert shims in the slipper bracket to eliminate any side clearance; a maximum of four shims may be fitted on each spring*
(c) *Make sure that the spring centre bolt registers with the hole provided in the axle mounting*
(d) *Tighten all nuts and bolts to the correct torque wrench settings and recheck the torque of the U-bolts with the laden weight of the vehicle on the rear axle*

20   Rear spring assembly – overhaul

1   Before dismantling the rear spring, check whether individual parts are available and consider whether the purchase of a reconditioned unit would be more economical.
2   Using a vice and suitable tubing, press out the rubber bush from the spring front eye.
3   Prise the leaf clamps away from the spring using a screwdriver or cold chisel, and then mount the spring in a vice near the centre bolt and compress the leaves.

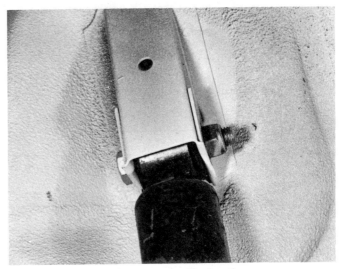

17.2 Front shock absorber upper mounting location

19.4 Rear spring forward location

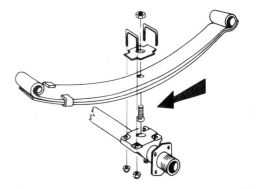

Fig. 11.21 Rear spring to axle location bolt and U-bolts (Sec 19)

4   Unscrew and remove the centre bolt, then slowly release the vice whilst supporting the spring leaves.
5   Clean the leaves with a wire brush and carefully examine them for damage and fractures; similarly examine the front bush for wear. Where plastic interleaves are fitted, check them for wear. Any unserviceable components must be removed.
6   To reassemble the rear spring mount the leaves and plastic interleaves in their correct order on a suitable length of dowel rod the

same diameter as the centre bolt, then compress the leaves in a vice near the centre and remove the rod.

7   Insert the centre bolt from the bottom of the spring and tighten the retaining nut to the specified torque; stake the end of the bolt with a centre punch to lock the nut.

8   Hold the spring clamps in a vice and bend their ends over the top of the spring.

9   Press the rubber bush into the spring front eye using a vice and suitable tubing.

21 Rear wheel hub – overhaul

The overhaul procedures of the rear wheel hub are given in Chapter 8.

22 Wheels and tyres – general

1   Correct tyre pressures are important, both to ensure safe handling of the vehicle and to give maximum tyre life. Pressures should be checked with the tyres cold, ie at least one hour after an extended journey, as the heat generated whilst the vehicle is in motion may give a falsely high pressure reading.

2   Check the tightness of the wheel nuts periodically. Remember that on vehicles having 6-stud wheel fixings, the left-hand studs have a *left-hand thread*. At the same time, inspect the tyres for wear and damage.

3   Uneven wear of the front tyres may be due to incorrect toe-in, or to other steering or suspension damage. Over- or under-inflation will give rise to premature wear at the centre or edges of the tread respectively. Worn shock absorbers or grabbing brakes can cause patchy wear of front or rear tyres. Consult a tyre specialist if in doubt.

4   Rotation of the tyres may be worthwhile if it is wished to even out wear, so long as the wheels have been balanced off the vehicle. Radial tyres should only be moved from front to rear, or vice versa, not from side to side.

5   Tyres must be renewed when the tread wear is approaching the legal minimum. Most modern tyres have built-in tread wear indicators, which show up as solid bars across the tread when its depth is reduced to 1.6 mm (0.06 in) or thereabouts.

6   When refitting twin rear wheels, make sure that the mating faces of the wheels are clean.

23 Fault diagnosis – suspension and steering

Before diagnosing faults from the following chart, check that any irregularities are not caused by:
(a) Binding brakes
(b) Incorrect 'mix' of radial and crossply tyres
(c) Incorrect tyre pressures
(d) Misalignment of the bodyframe

Symptom	Reason(s)
Steering feels vague, vehicle wanders and floats at speed	Tyre pressures uneven Shock absorbers worn Spring U-bolts broken Steering balljoints badly worn Suspension geometry incorrect Steering gear adjustment incorrect Chassis underframe out of alignment Vehicle overladen
Stiff and heavy steering	Tyre pressures too low Kingpins need greasing Steering gear needs topping up or is incorrectly adjusted Steering balljoints seizing Wheel alignment incorrect Steering column misaligned Suspension geometry incorrect
Wheel wobble and vibration	Wheel nuts loose Front wheels and tyres out of balance Steering balljoints badly worn Hub bearings badly worn Steering gear free play excessive Front springs loose, weak or broken Front shock absorbers worn
Excessive pitching and rolling on corners and during braking	Shock absorbers worn Spring leaf broken Vehicle overladen

Chapter 12 Bodywork and fittings

For modifications, and information applicable to later models, see Supplement at end of manual

Contents

1 General description

The body and chassis frame is of integral monocoque construction on van, bus and Kombi versions; on chassis cab and chassis windscreen versions a ladder type chassis frame is fitted.

The cab and body is of an all-steel construction with ribbed floor steel panels. The larger 130 to 190 models have the same integral construction for the vans, buses and Kombis but a cruciform type chassis frame is fitted on the chassis cab and chassis windscreen model. All other specifications are similar to the smaller models.

Due to the large number of specialist applications of this vehicle range, information contained in this Chapter is given on parts found to be common on the popular factory produced version. No information is given on special body versions.

2 Maintenance – bodywork and underframe

1 The general condition of a vehicle's bodywork is the thing that significantly affects its value. Maintenance is easy but needs to be regular. Neglect, particularly after minor damage, can lead quickly to further deterioration and costly repair bills. It is important also to keep watch on those parts of the vehicle not immediately visible, for instance the underside, inside all the wheel arches and the lower part of the engine compartment.

2 The basic maintenance routine for the bodywork is washing – preferably with a lot of water, from a hose. This will remove all the loose solids which may have stuck to the vehicle. It is important to flush these off in such a way as to prevent grit from scratching the finish. The wheel arches and underframe need washing in the same way to remove any accumulated mud which will retain moisture and tend to encourage rust. Paradoxically enough, the best time to clean the underframe and wheel arches is in wet weather when the mud is thoroughly wet and soft. In very wet weather the underframe is usually cleaned of large accumulations automatically and this is a good time for inspection.

3 Periodically, it is a good idea to have the whole of the underframe of the vehicle steam cleaned, engine compartment included, so that a thorough inspection can be carried out to see what minor repairs and renovations are necessary. Steam cleaning is available at many garages and is necessary for removal of the accumulation of oily grime which sometimes is allowed to become thick in certain areas. If steam cleaning facilities are not available, there are one or two excellent grease solvents available which can be brush applied. The dirt can then be simply hosed off.

4 After washing paintwork, wipe off with a chamois leather to give an unspotted clear finish. A coat of clear protective wax polish will give added protection against chemical pollutants in the air. If the paintwork sheen has dulled or oxidised, use a cleaner/polisher combination to restore the brilliance of the shine. This requires a little effort, but such dulling is usually caused because regular washing has

been neglected. Always check that the door and ventilator opening drain holes and pipes are completely clear so that water can be drained out (photos). Bright work should be treated in the same way as paintwork. Windscreens and windows can be kept clear of the smeary film which often appears, by adding a little ammonia to the water. If they are scratched, a good rub with a proprietary metal polish will often clear them. Never use any form of wax or other body or chromium polish on glass.

---

3   Maintenance – upholstery and carpets

1   Mats and carpets should be brushed or vacuum cleaned regularly to keep them free of grit. If they are badly stained remove them from the vehicle for scrubbing or sponging and make quite sure they are dry before refitting. Seats and interior trim panels can be kept clean by a wipe over with a damp cloth. If they do become stained (which can be more apparent on light coloured upholstery) use a little liquid detergent and a soft nail brush to scour the grime out of the grain of the material. Do not forget to keep the head lining clean in the same way as the upholstery. When using liquid cleaners inside the vehicle do not over-wet the surfaces being cleaned. Excessive damp could get into the seams and padded interior causing stains, offensive odours or even rot. If the inside of the vehicle gets wet accidentally it is worthwhile taking some trouble to dry it out properly, particularly where carpets are involved. *Do not leave oil or electric heaters inside the vehicle for this purpose.*

---

4   Minor body damage – repair

The photographic sequences on pages 222 and 223 illustrate the operations detailed in the following sub-sections.

Repair of minor scratches in the vehicle's bodywork

If the scratch is very superficial, and does not penetrate to the metal of the bodywork, repair is very simple. Lightly rub the area of the scratch with a paintwork renovator, or a very fine cutting paste, to remove loose paint from the scratch and to clear the surrounding bodywork of wax polish. Rinse the area with clean water.

Apply touch-up paint to the scratch using a thin paint brush; continue to apply thin layers of paint until the surface of the paint in the scratch is level with the surrounding paintwork. Allow the new paint at least two weeks to harden: then blend it into the surrounding paintwork by rubbing the paintwork, in the scratch area, with a paintwork renovator or a very fine cutting paste. Finally, apply wax polish.

Where the scratch has penetrated right through to the metal of the bodywork, causing the metal to rust, a different repair technique is required. Remove any loose rust from the bottom of the scratch with a penknife, then apply rust inhibiting paint to prevent the formation of rust in the future. Using a rubber or nylon applicator fill the scratch with bodystopper paste. If required, this paste can be mixed with cellulose thinners to provide a very thin paste which is ideal for filling narrow scratches. Before the stopper-paste in the scratch hardens,

wrap a piece of smooth cotton rag around the top of a finger. Dip the finger in cellulose thinners and then quickly sweep it across the surface of the stopper-paste in the scratch; this will ensure that the surface of the stopper-paste is slightly hollowed. The scratch can now be painted over as described earlier in this Section.

Repair of dents in the vehicle's bodywork

When deep denting of the vehicle's bodywork has taken place, the first task is to pull the dent out, until the affected bodywork almost attains its original shape. There is little point in trying to restore the original shape completely, as the metal in the damaged area will have stretched on impact and cannot be reshaped fully to its original contour. It is better to bring the level of the dent up to a point which is about $\frac{1}{8}$ in (3 mm) below the level of the surrounding bodywork. In cases where the dent is very shallow anyway, it is not worth trying to pull it out at all. If the underside of the dent is accessible, it can be hammered out gently from behind, using a mallet with a wooden or plastic head. Whilst doing this, hold a suitable block of wood firmly against the outside of the panel to absorb the impact from the hammer blows and thus prevent a large area of the bodywork from being 'belled-out'.

Should the dent be in a section of the bodywork which has double skin or some other factor making it inaccessible from behind, a different technique is called for. Drill several small holes through the metal inside the area – particularly in the deeper section. Then screw long self-tapping screws into the holes just sufficiently for them to gain a good purchase in the metal. Now the dent can be pulled out by pulling on the protruding heads of the screws with a pair of pliers.

The next stage of the repair is the removal of the paint from the damaged area, and from an inch or so of the surrounding 'sound' bodywork. This is accomplished most easily by using a wire brush or abrasive pad on a power drill, although it can be done just as effectively by hand using sheets of abrasive paper. To complete the preparation for filling, score the surface of the bare metal with a screwdriver or the tang of a file, or alternatively, drill small holes in the affected area. This will provide a really good 'key' for the filler paste.

To complete the repair see the Section on filling and re-spraying.

Repair of rust holes or gashes in the vehicle's bodywork

Remove all paint from the affected area and from an inch or so of the surrounding 'sound' bodywork, using an abrasive pad or a wire brush on a power drill. If these are not available a few sheets of abrasive paper will do the job just as effectively. With the paint removed you will be able to gauge the severity of the corrosion and therefore decide whether to renew the whole panel (if this is possible) or to repair the affected area. New body panels are not as expensive as most people think and it is often quicker and more satisfactory to fit a new panel than to attempt to repair large areas of corrosion.

Remove all fittings from the affected area except those which will act as a guide to the original shape of the damaged bodywork (eg headlamp shells etc). Then, using tin snips or a hacksaw blade, remove all loose metal and any other metal badly affected by corrosion. Hammer the edges of the hole inwards in order to create a slight depression for the filler paste.

Wire brush the affected area to remove the powdery rust from the

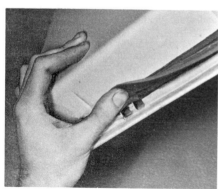
2.4a Check the door drain holes

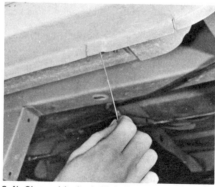
2.4b Clear a blocked sill drain hole with a piece of wire

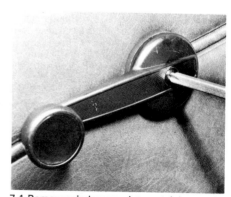
7.1 Remove window regulator retaining screw

surface of the remaining metal. Paint the affected area with rust inhibiting paint; if the back of the rusted area is accessible treat this also.

Before filling can take place it will be necessary to block the hole in some way. This can be achieved by the use of aluminium or plastic mesh, or aluminium tape.

Aluminium or plastic mesh is probably the best material to use for a large hole. Cut a piece to the approximate size and shape of the hole to be filled, then position it in the hole so that its edges are below the level of the surrounding bodywork. It can be retained in position by several blobs of filler paste around its periphery.

Aluminium tape should be used for small or very narrow holes. Pull a piece off the roll and trim it to the approximate size and shape required, then pull off the backing paper (if used) and stick the tape over the hole; it can be overlapped if the thickness of one piece is insufficient. Burnish down the edges of the tape with the handle of a screwdriver or similar, to ensure that the tape is securely attached to the metal underneath.

Bodywork repairs – filling and re-spraying

Before using this Section, see the Sections on dent, deep scratch, rust holes and gash repairs.

Many types of bodyfiller are available, but generally speaking those proprietary kits which contain a tin of filler paste and a tube of resin hardener are best for this type of repair. A wide, flexible plastic or nylon applicator will be found invaluable for imparting a smooth and well contoured finish to the surface of the filler.

Mix up a little filler on a clean piece of card or board – measure the hardener carefully (follow the maker's instructions on the pack) otherwise the filler will set too rapidly or too slowly.

Using the applicator apply the filler paste to the prepared area; draw the applicator across the surface of the filler to achieve the correct contour and to level the filler surface. As soon as a contour that approximates the correct one is achieved, stop working the paste – if you carry on too long the paste will become sticky and begin to 'pick up' on the applicator. Continue to add thin layers of filler paste at twenty-minute intervals until the level of the filler is just proud of the surrounding bodywork.

Once the filler has hardened, excess can be removed using a metal plane or file. From then on, progressively finer grades of sandpaper should be used, starting with a 40 grade production paper and finishing with 400 grade wet-and-dry paper. Always wrap the abrasive paper around a flat rubber, cork, or wooden block – otherwise the surface of the filler will not be completely flat. During the smoothing of the filler surface the wet-and-dry paper should be periodically rinsed in water. This will ensure that a very smooth finish is imparted to the filler at the final stage.

At this stage the dent should be surrounded by a ring of bare metal, which in turn should be encircled by the finely 'feathered' edge of the good paintwork. Rinse the repair area with clean water, until all of the dust produced by the rubbing-down operation has gone.

Spray the whole repair area with a light coat of primer – this will show up any imperfections in the surface of the filler. Repair these imperfections with fresh filler paste or bodystopper, and once more smooth the surface with abrasive paper. If bodystopper is used, it can be mixed with cellulose thinners to form a really thin paste which is ideal for filling small holes. Repeat this spray and repair procedure until you are satisfied that the surface of the filler, and the feathered edge of the paintwork are perfect. Clean the repair area with clean water and allow to dry fully.

The repair area is now ready for final spraying. Paint spraying must be carried out in warm, dry, windless and dust free atmosphere. This condition can be created artificially if you have access to a large indoor working area, but if you are forced to work in the open, you will have to pick your day very carefully. If you are working indoors, dousing the floor in the work area with water will help to settle the dust which would otherwise be in the atmosphere. If the repair area is confined to one body panel, mask off the surrounding panels; this will help to minimise the effects of a slight mis-match in paint colours. Bodywork fittings (eg chrome strips, door handles etc) will also need to be masked off. Use genuine masking tape and several thicknesses of newspaper for the masking operations.

Before commencing to spray, agitate the aerosol can thoroughly, then spray a test area (an old tin, or similar) until the technique is mastered. Cover the repair area with a thick coat of primer; the thickness should be built up using several thin layers of paint rather than one thick one. Using 400 grade wet-and-dry paper, rub down the surface of the primer until it is really smooth. While doing this, the work area should be thoroughly doused with water, and the wet-and-dry paper periodically rinsed in water. Allow to dry before spraying on more paint.

Spray on the top coat, again building up the thickness by using several thin layers of paint. Start spraying in the centre of the repair area and then, using a circular motion, work outwards until the whole repair area and about 2 inches of the surrounding original paintwork is covered. Remove all masking material 10 to 15 minutes after spraying on the final coat of paint.

Allow the new paint at least two weeks to harden, then, using a paintwork renovator or a very fine cutting paste, blend the edges of the paint into the existing paintwork. Finally, apply wax polish.

---

5 Major body damage – repair

1 With the exception of chassis cab versions, the chassis members are spot welded to the underbody, and in this respect can be termed of monocoque or unit construction. Major damage repairs to this type of body combination must of necessity be carried out by body shops equipped with welding and hydraulic straightening facilities.

2 Extensive damage to the body may distort the chassis and result in unstable and dangerous handling as well as excessive wear to tyres and suspension or steering components. It is recommended that checking of the chassis alignment be entrusted to a Ford agent with specialist checking jigs.

---

6 Maintenance – hinges and locks

1 Every six months or 6000 miles (9600 km), the bonnet catch, door locks, door hinges, door check straps, sliding door, and sliding step (where fitted), should be oiled with a few drops of engine oil from an oil can.

2 At the same interval the door striker plates should be given a thin smear of grease.

---

7 Door trim panel – removal and refitting

1 First remove the interior door handle by noting its position and unscrewing the retaining screw, then withdrawing the handle from the control shaft. Similarly remove the window regulator handle from its control shaft when fitted (photo).

2 Remove the two retaining screws and withdraw the armrest (where fitted).

3 Using a wide blade screwdriver, carefully prise the trim panel away from the door frame at the retaining clip points, being careful not to tear the trim base.

4 Refitting the door trim panel is a reversal of the removal procedure.

---

8 Front door exterior handle (hinged door) – removal and refitting

1 Fully close the window and remove the trim panel as described in Section 7.

2 Peel off the plastic sealing sheet, and then unscrew and remove the three door lock retaining screws and shakeproof washers.

3 Through the two upper apertures unscrew and remove the two door handle retaining screws and washers and recover the two rubber joints.

4 Detach the short control rod, then separate the long control rod from the nylon bush; the door handle can then be extracted from the outside by lifting it vertically and pivoting it so that the control rods can be removed.

5 Refitting is a reversal of the removal procedure.

---

9 Front door lock (hinged door) – removal and refitting

1 Remove the door exterior handle as described in Section 8.

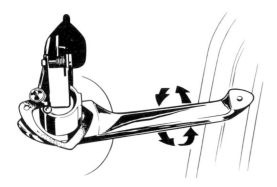

Fig. 12.1 Twist the door handle towards the front (Sec 8)

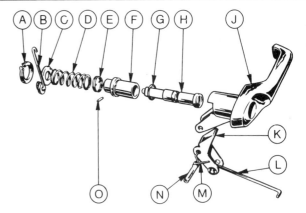

Fig. 12.2 Door handle and lock components (Sec 9)

A	Circlip	H	Lock barrel
B	Control rod	J	Handle
C	Lockplate	K	Crankarm
D	Spring	L	Control rod
E	Lock return spring	M	Spring
F	Lock barrel housing	N	Pin
G	Seal	O	Pin

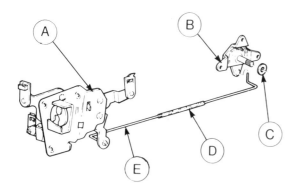

Fig. 12.3 Door lock and remote control assembly (Sec 10)

A	Lock	D	Anti-rattle pad
B	Remote control	E	Connecting rod
C	Seat washer		

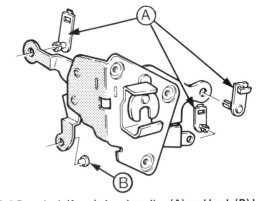

Fig. 12.4 Door lock (front) showing clips (A) and bush (B) locations (Sec 10)

2   Using a suitable pin punch, drive the crankarm pivot pin out whilst steadying the return spring, then remove the crankarm.

3   Extract the circlip from the handle and withdraw the lock barrel, lockplate, spring, and housing together.

4   Remove the spacer washers from the housing and prise the return spring from the barrel.

5   Extract the lock housing rubber joint, drive out the barrel retaining pin, and remove the barrel from the housing; the lock is now fully dismantled.

6   Refitting the front door lock is a reversal of the removal procedure, but the following additional points should be noted:

(a) Make sure that the lock return spring tangs are located in the same housing and lock barrel slot

(b) The retaining circlip must be fully entered in its locating groove

10 Front door remote control mechanism and lock (hinged door) – removal and refitting

1   Fully close the window and remove the trim panel as described in Section 7.

2   Carefully peel off the plastic sealing sheet, then detach the remote control mechanism from the door inner panel by unscrewing and removing the three cross-head retaining screws, spring and cup washers (photo). Let the remote control mechanism hang down within the shell.

3   Unclip the lock and exterior handle rods from the lock levers and then remove the lock-to-door edge retaining screws to withdraw the lock and remote control unit from the door.

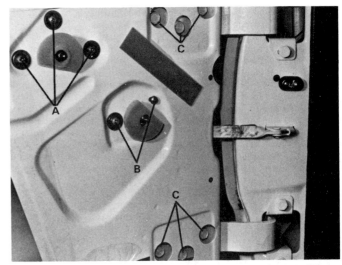

10.2 Inner door panel showing the three remote control screws (A), the regulator unit screws (B) and door hinge bolts (C)

4   Detach the remote control rod link from the lock.

5   Refitting the remote control mechanism and lock unit is a reversal of the removal procedure. When in position ensure that the anti-rattle pad (Fig. 12.3) is located correctly on its rod and also that the sealing washer is fitted to the remote handle shaft. The bush and clip locations on the lock are shown in Fig. 12.4.

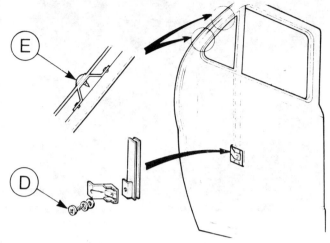

Fig. 12.5 Fixed quarter window frame fixing (E) and inner panel fixing (D) (Sec 12)

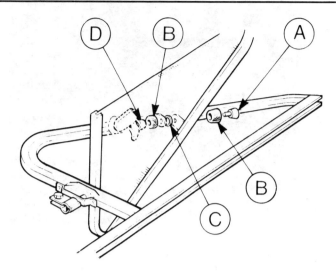

Fig. 12.6 Hinged quarter window assembly (Sec 13)

A *Shouldered rivet*	C *Spacer*
B *Cover*	D *Insert*

11 Front door alignment and lock adjustment (hinged door)

1   Check that the door weatherseal is intact in the vicinity of the door lock, and then close the door slowly, at the same time observing whether the door moves relative to the body aperture.
2   If the action of the striker plate alters the position of the door, temporarily loosen its retaining screws.
3   To adjust the position of the door within the body aperture, slightly loosen the door hinge retaining bolts, re-locate the door, and then tighten the retaining bolts. The door hinge bolts are accessible after removal of the interior trim panel as given in Section 7. The hinge bolt positions are shown in photo 10.2.
4   Using a pencil, mark the body pillar at the same height as the upper edge of the striker, then loosen the striker plate retaining screws and set the upper edge of the striker plate to the pencil mark, tightening the retaining screws to 7 to 9 lbf ft (0.97 to 1.24 kgf m).
5   Check that, when closing the door, two distinct clicks are heard indicating that the safety and fully closed positions have been engaged; also check that the door is flush with the body.
6   If the lock safety position only is engaged, it will be necessary to move the striker plate out a little.

12 Front door quarter window (fixed) – removal and refitting

1   Fully open the window and remove the trim panel as described in Section 7.
2   Carefully peel off the plastic sealing strip and also the weatherstrip from the quarter window channelling. Remove the door belt weatherstrips (internal and external).
3   Unscrew and remove the quarter window channel-to-door inner panel retaining screw with flat washer. Also remove the two screws, lockwashers and flat washers retaining the quarter window to the door frame. The quarter window and frame can then be withdrawn from the door shell (Fig. 12.5).
4   To remove the glass from its frame, drill out the two pop rivets retaining the frame top section and the two tubular rivets which secure the frame lower end to the division bar. Separate the frame and glass from the bar and then the glass from the frame.
5   Refitting is a reversal of the removal process. If the frame weatherstrip was removed its installation will be eased by coating it with a soapy solution. Tap the glass into position using a rubber mallet. Rivet the frame together and refit to the door, and restick the weatherstrip firmly into position.

13 Front door quarter window (hinged) – removal and refitting

1   Remove the window and frame assembly as given in the previous Section.

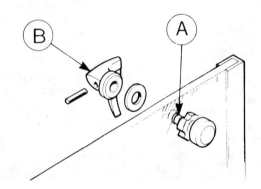

Fig. 12.7 Hinged quarter window handle components (Sec 13)

A *Shaft*	B *Handle*

2   Loosen and remove the screw retaining the clip on the lower pivot.
3   Drill out the end of the shouldered rivet (Fig. 12.6) which retains the glass frame to the upper pivot. Take care when drilling. Extract the rivet, cover, spacer and insert.
4   The glass and its frame can now be carefully removed from the lower pivot.
5   Remove the screw retaining the clip to the lower pivot and remove the clip.
6   Drill out (taking care) the rivets retaining the weatherstrip to the division bar and separate the bar from the frame.
7   Support the glass and frame and carefully tap out the pin from the handle, then pull the handle and its washer from the shaft (Fig. 12.7).
8   Unscrew the shaft nut and detach the shaft, nut and washer.
9   To fit a new glass into the frame, first ensure that all old sealant is removed from the frame channel. Insert a strip of suitable glazing mastic sealer into the channel and fit the glass, tapping into position with a rubber mallet. Clean excess sealant from the glass.
10 The quarter window refitting procedure is a reversal of removal, but when fitting the handle, ensure that the lock face is parallel to the glass face. Grease the pivots and do not forget to insert the spacer.

14 Front door window glass (hinged door) – removal and refitting

1   Fully open the window and remove the trim panel and quarter window as described in Sections 7 and 12 or 13 respectively of this Chapter.

This sequence of photographs deals with the repair of the dent and paintwork damage shown in this photo. The procedure will be similar for the repair of a hole. It should be noted that the procedures given here are simplified – more explicit instructions will be found in the text

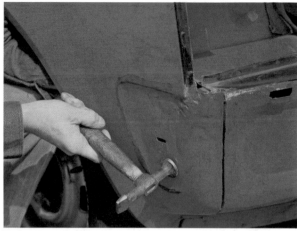

In the case of a dent the first job – after removing surrounding trim – is to hammer out the dent where access is possible. This will minimise filling. Here, the large dent having been hammered out, the damaged area is being made slightly concave

Now all paint must be removed from the damaged area, by rubbing with coarse abrasive paper. Alternatively, a wire brush or abrasive pad can be used in a power drill. Where the repair area meets good paintwork, the edge of the paintwork should be 'feathered', using a finer grade of abrasive paper

In the case of a hole caused by rusting, all damaged sheet-metal should be cut away before proceeding to this stage. Here, the damaged area is being treated with rust remover and inhibitor before being filled

Mix the body filler according to its manufacturer's instructions. In the case of corrosion damage, it will be necessary to block off any large holes before filling – this can be done with aluminium or plastic mesh, or aluminium tape. Make sure the area is absolutely clean before ...

... applying the filler. Filler should be applied with a flexible applicator, as shown, for best results; the wooden spatula being used for confined areas. Apply thin layers of filler at 20-minute intervals, until the surface of the filler is slightly proud of the surrounding bodywork

Initial shaping can be done with a Surform plane or Dreadnought file. Then, using progressively finer grades of wet-and-dry paper, wrapped around a sanding block, and copious amounts of clean water, rub down the filler until really smooth and flat. Again, feather the edges of adjoining paintwork

The whole repair area can now be sprayed or brush-painted with primer. If spraying, ensure adjoining areas are protected from over-spray. Note that at least one inch of the surrounding sound paintwork should be coated with primer. Primer has a 'thick' consistency, so will find small imperfections

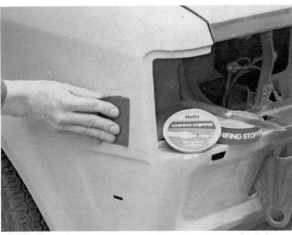

Again, using plenty of water, rub down the primer with a fine grade wet-and-dry paper (400 grade is probably best) until it is really smooth and well blended into the surrounding paintwork. Any remaining imperfections can now be filled by carefully applied knifing stopper paste

When the stopper has hardened, rub down the repair area again before applying the final coat of primer. Before rubbing down this last coat of primer, ensure the repair area is blemish-free – use more stopper if necessary. To ensure that the surface of the primer is really smooth use some finishing compound

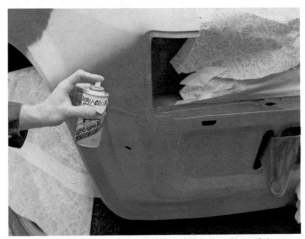

The top coat can now be applied. When working out of doors, pick a dry, warm and wind-free day. Ensure surrounding areas are protected from over-spray. Agitate the aerosol thoroughly, then spray the centre of the repair area, working outwards with a circular motion. Apply the paint as several thin coats

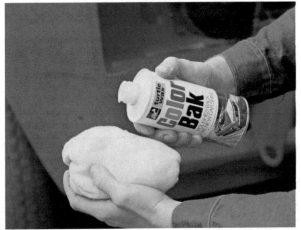

After a period of about two weeks, which the paint needs to harden fully, the surface of the repaired area can be 'cut' with a mild cutting compound prior to wax polishing. When carrying out bodywork repairs, remember that the quality of the finished job is proportional to the time and effort expended

14.3 Front door window lower channel and regulator plate

2   Pull the weatherstrip from the inner and outer lower edges of the window aperture.
3   Wind the window up halfway by temporarily refitting the winder handle, then detach the lower channel from the regulator plate by removing the two retaining screws and washers; it will be necessary to support the glass during this operation (photo).
4   Lift and tilt the window glass as shown in Fig. 12.8 and withdraw it from the door.
5   Refitting the front door window glass is a reversal of the removal procedure.

15 Front door window regulator (hinged door) – removal and refitting

1   Remove the trim panel as described in Section 7, then peel the plastic sealing sheet from the door inner panel.
2   Temporarily refit the window regulator handle and lower the window to expose the lower channel, and remove the two screws and washers retaining the channel to the regulator plate; it will be necessary to support the window during this operation.
3   Carefully lower the window to the bottom stop.
4   Withdraw the window regulator handle and unscrew and remove the remote control mechanism retaining screws and washers.
5   Detach the flexible guide tube assembly from the door inner panel by unscrewing and removing the three cross-head retaining screws and washers.
6   Unbolt the lower end of the quarter window dividing channel, then lower the complete regulator assembly and withdraw it through the door inner panel aperture.
7   Refitting the front door window regulator is a reversal of the removal procedure.

16 Front door handles (sliding door) – removal and refitting

1   Remove the door trim panel and then unscrew and remove the six screws and washers retaining the lockplate and inner handle to the door. Detach the lockplate and handle from the door.
2   Unscrew and remove the three screws with washers retaining the exterior handle to the door. Withdraw the handle and mounting pads.
3   Refit the exterior and interior door handles in the reverse order to removal.

17 Front door lock (sliding door) – removal and refitting

1   Refer to the previous Section and remove the interior handle and lockplate unit.
2   Refer to Fig. 12.10. Prise free the circlip from the lock lever pivot and detach the release rod.

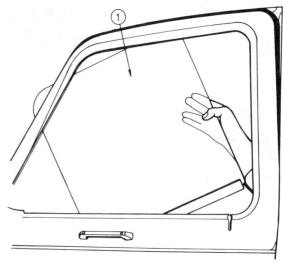

Fig. 12.8 Removing front door window glass (1) (hinged door) (Sec 14)

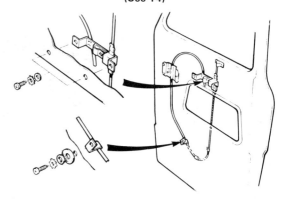

Fig. 12.9 Upper and lower regulator retaining brackets (Sec 15)

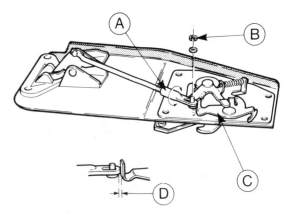

Fig. 12.10 Sliding door lock, lever and release rod assembly shown in locked position (Sec 17)

A   Adjuster   C   Lock lever
B   Circlip   D   0.040 in (1.0 mm)

3   Carefully drill out the rivets and remove the retaining lock unit from the lockplate. Detach the lock.
4   Refitting the front door lock is a reversal of the removal procedure. It will be necessary to pop rivet the lock to the lockplate with a special tool.
5   Lock the lever by means of the private (interior) lock and then adjust the length of the lock release rod so that a clearance of 0.040 in (1.0 mm) exists between the lever end and the rod (Fig. 12.10). The rod can then be refitted onto its pivot and secured with the flat washer and circlip.

18 Front door striker plates (sliding door) – removal and refitting

1 To remove the front striker plate, first unscrew and remove the three plastic cover retaining screws and withdraw the cover from the mounting bracket. Mark around the plate to facilitate refitting.
2 Unscrew and remove the two cross-head screws retaining the striker plate and remove the plate and spring washers from the bracket.
3 Detach the mounting bracket from the front pillar by unscrewing and removing the four cross-head screws.
4 To remove the rear striker plate, first mark around the plate. Unscrew and remove the three retaining screws and washers and withdraw the plate from the rear pillar.
5 Refitting the striker plates is a reversal of the removal procedure. Align the plates using the marks made before removal.

19 Front door (sliding) – removal and refitting

1 Working beneath the door, unscrew and remove the nuts and washers retaining the two guide brackets.
2 Unscrew and remove the upper internal brush seal-to-body screws and detach the strip.
3 Unscrew and remove the retainer and packing strip retaining screws from under the front roller. Loosen the front roller-to-door nut and belt assemblies.
4 Loosen the upper rear roller bracket and cover-to-door retaining bolts, and remove the single screw to withdraw the cover. Loosen off the remainder of the bolts retaining the bracket to the door.

5 Carefully lift the complete door upwards and outwards to release the door runners from the guide channel.
6 Refitting the front door is a reversal of the removal procedure.

20 Door guide rollers (sliding door) – removal and refitting

1 Remove the support from the front 'B' pillar by unscrewing the two retaining screws (Fig. 12.13).
2 Carefully drill out the upper guide rail shroud retaining rivets and remove the shroud and cap.
3 Remove the shroud from the upper guide arm, having removed the retaining screw and washer. Open the door and then prise free the circlip and remove the washer from the central roller arm spindle (Fig. 12.14).
4 Shut the door and then remove the guide arm from the upper guide rail by prising free, having removed the upper screw and washer and loosened the lower screw.
5 Loosen the lower guide arm screws, then lift the door from the central roller spindle and guide the roller from the guide rail.
6 Refitting is a reversal of the removal procedure.

21 Door glass and frame (sliding window) – removal and refitting

1 Use a suitable lipped tool and carefully push the weatherstrip lip under the top and sides of the opening flange.
2 Working from within the cab, push the weatherstrip, frame and glass as a unit outwards to remove. An assistant will be required on the outside to catch the unit as it is pushed free.

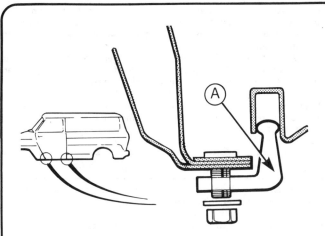

Fig. 12.11 Sliding door lower guide (A) and locations (Sec 19)

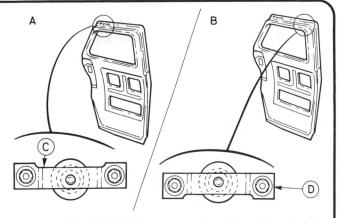

Fig. 12.12 Sliding door rollers (Sec 19)

A   Front roller   C   Front roller cut-out at top
B   Rear roller   D   Rear roller cut-out at bottom

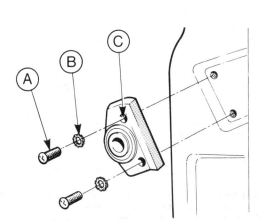

Fig. 12.13 'B' pillar support, showing screw (A), shakeproof washer (B) and support (C) (Sec 20)

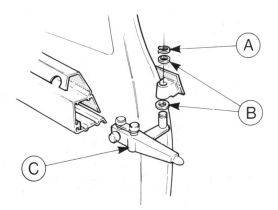

Fig. 12.14 Central roller arm spindle showing circlip (A), washer (B) and roller arm (C) (Sec 20)

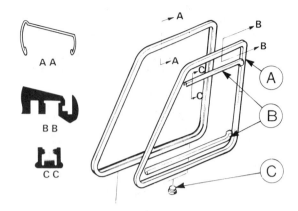

Fig. 12.15 Sliding window frame and weatherstrip components (Sec 21)

A Weatherstrip   C Buffers
B Glass runs

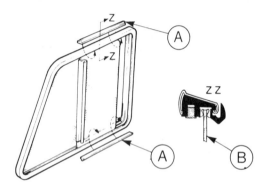

Fig. 12.16 Filler (A) location in glass (B) (Sec 21)

3   To remove the glass from the frame, carefully prise out the fillers from the top and bottom weatherstrip sections and at the rear of the fixed glass. The sliding glass and handle can now be prised carefully from the frame and weatherstrip.

4   Remove the fixed glass in a similar manner.

5   The weatherstrip can be removed by pulling free the glass runs from the upper and lower horizontal sections of weatherstrip. Then pull free the weatherstrip from the frame.

6   Refitting is a reversal of removal, but note the following points:

(a) When fitting a new fixed glass, apply a soapy solution to the rear vertical edge of the glass and tap it into position using a rubber mallet

(b) When fitting a sliding glass, a suitable length of sealant and glazing strip should be applied to the channel and then the glass carefully tapped into position using a rubber mallet. Trim excess glazing strip when glass is fitted

(c) Before refitting the weatherstrip into the channel, ensure that the rubber buffers are in position (Fig. 12.15)

(d) When fitting the fixed glass channel fillers use a suitable adhesive, Ford GES M2G 4502A, or similar (Fig. 12.16)

(e) When the glass and weatherstrip are assembled they are fitted to the frame using a suitable length of cord around the periphery of the weatherstrip so that as it is pressed into the frame (from the outside) the cord can be pulled to locate the seal lip. A more detailed explanation of this fitting method is given in Section 22

22 Windscreen – removal and refitting

1   If you are unfortunate enough to have a windscreen shatter or should you wish to renew your present windscreen, fitting a replacement is one of the few jobs which the average owner is advised to leave to a professional. For the owner who wishes to do the job himself the following instructions are given.

2   Cover the bonnet, wings, and facia with a blanket or cloth to prevent accidental damage, then remove the windscreen wiper blades and arms as described in Chapter 10.

3   If the screen has shattered, knock the crystals out of the rubber weatherstrip surround and remove it. Clean the glass channel free of sealer and crystals and renew it if it is cut or hardened.

4   If the screen is intact, sitting inside the vehicle, and starting at one corner of the screen, use a blunt-ended lever to push the weatherstrip lip under the weatherstrip aperture flange, at the same time pushing the glass forwards to fully disengage the glass and rubber from the flange. Continue the process, working in small lengths at a time, around the periphery of the screen until the glass and weatherstrip assembly is completely out of the screen aperture.

5   Check the windscreen aperture in the vehicle to ensure that the flange is free from buckles and distortion and that all traces of hardened sealer are removed from both sides of the flange.

6   Using a suitable sealer fill the weatherstrip inner groove and assemble the weatherstrip to the glass.

7   Place a length of cord in the weatherstrip outer groove so that both ends emerge at the bottom centre with about six inches free, then apply a suitable non-hardening sealer or PVC foam tape to the section of the weatherstrip which contacts the body aperture.

8   Ensure the weatherstrip remains correctly positioned to the glass by sticking lengths of masking tape to the inner and outer edges.

9   Lubricate the body aperture and weatherstrip inner lip with soapy water, then, with the help of an assistant, position the windscreen centrally in the aperture with the cord free ends inside the vehicle.

10   Locate the lower edge of the weatherstrip on the aperture flange and, with an assistant pressing from outside, pull one cord end towards the centre of the glass at the same time removing the masking tape.

11   When one half of the weatherstrip has been fitted and the cord has reached the top centre, repeat the operation for the remaining half, and finally press the weatherstrip and glass to make sure they are fully seated.

12   Wipe away any surplus sealer from the windscreen, weatherstrip, and body aperture, and refit the wiper arms and blades as described in Chapter 10.

23 Hinged type side window – removal and refitting

1   Detach the window catch from the body by unscrewing and removing the two retaining screws, then open the window.

2   Prise the window frame from the two rubber inserts with a screwdriver covered with a soft cloth, and withdraw the assembly from the body aperture.

3   Carefully extract the weatherstrip from the body aperture and examine it for perishing and deterioration; obtain a new weatherstrip if necessary.

4   To refit the side window first apply a suitable non-hardening sealer to the weatherstrip groove and press it firmly into position in the body aperture.

5   Locate the window frame lugs to the pillar rubber inserts and tap the assembly into position with the palm of the hand.

6   Close the window and secure the window catch to the body with the two screws.

24 Rear door and fixed side window glass – removal and refitting

1   Using a smooth-ended lever, carefully push the inner lip of the weatherstrip over the aperture flange from the inside of the vehicle, working gradually around the glass.

2   When about two-thirds of the weatherstrip has been released from the flange, have an assistant support the glass from the outside, and carefully push the glass and weatherstrip out of the aperture.

3   Separate the weatherstrip from the glass, and check it for signs of perishing and deterioration; obtain a new weatherstrip if necessary.

4   To refit the glass, first fill the weatherstrip inner groove with suitable sealer and carefully fit the glass into position.

5   Place a length of cord in the weatherstrip outer groove so that

both ends emerge at the bottom centre with about six inches free, then apply a suitable non-hardening sealer to the section of the weatherstrip which contacts the body aperture.

6   Ensure the weatherstrip remains correctly positioned to the glass by sticking lengths of masking tape to the inner and outer edges, then, with the help of an assistant, position the glass assembly centrally on the outer face of the aperture with the cord free ends inside the vehicle.

7   Locate the lower edge of the weatherstrip on the aperture flange and pull the cord towards the centre of the glass until one side of the weatherstrip is fitted and the cord has reached the top centre.

8   Repeat the operation with the remaining half of the cord and finally press the weatherstrip and glass to make sure they are fully seated.

9   Wipe away any surplus sealer from the glass, weatherstrip, and body aperture, together with the masking tape.

25 Side loading door (hinged) – general

The internal components of the side loading door are similar to those of the front hinged door, and therefore the removal and refitting procedures are identical; reference should be made to the relevant earlier Sections.

26 Side door lock – removal and refitting

1   Remove the trim panel from the door.

2   Unscrew and remove the three screws retaining the remote control plate to the door inner panel, then lower the plate (in the cavity) and detach the remote control rod from the lock lever.

3   Detach the external handle rods from their lock levers, remove the three lock-to-door retaining screws (with shakeproof washers) and withdraw the lock.

4   Refit in the reverse order to removal. Do not fully tighten the

remote control plate screws until the remote control rod is attached to the lock lever (Fig. 12.18).

27 Rear door – removal and refitting

1   Unscrew and remove the shroud retaining screws and withdraw the shrouds from the hinges of the door to be removed.

2   Prise free the door trim panel and disconnect the door check strap.

3   Mark around the hinge locations on the door with a pencil or similar to show the hinge outlines for realignment on refitting.

4   Remove the hinge retaining screws and lift the door clear.

5   Refit in the reverse order. Do not fully tighten the hinge-to-door retaining screws until the door is correctly aligned.

28 Rear door handles and lock – removal and refitting

1   To remove the interior handle (where fitted), unscrew and withdraw the handle retaining screw. Pull the handle and escutcheon or washers (as applicable) free.

2   The external handle is removed by first turning it to the open position. Remove the handle retaining screws and withdraw the handle.

3   The lock can now be removed from the external handle by unclipping the C-clip and withdrawing the spring and spacer washers and escutcheon from the handle. Use a small drift to drive out the pin which retains the rod. Withdraw the rod, then tap out the lock barrel-to-handle retaining pin in a similar fashion. Extract the lock barrel.

4   Refitting is a reversal of the removal process but note the following:

(a)   When the barrel is inserted into the handle, check that the operating pin on the barrel nose engages with the handle boss locking peg slot

(b)   Check the lock operation before refitting to the door

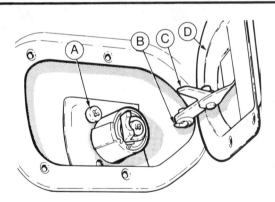

Fig. 12.17 Side door lock unit (Sec 25)

A   Retaining screw   C   Actuating arm
B   Lock rod   D   Control plate

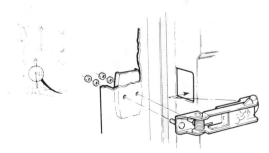

Fig. 12.19 Rear door check strap location (Sec 27)

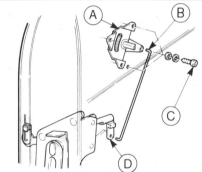

Fig. 12.18 Side door remote control unit (Sec 26)

A   Control unit   C   Screw
B   Connecting rod   D   Lock lever

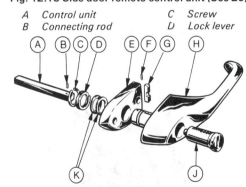

Fig. 12.20 Rear door handle (exterior) and lock components (Sec 28)

A   Rod   F   Pin
B   Pin   G   Locking peg
C   Circlip   H   Exterior handle
D   Spring washer   J   Lock barrel
E   Escutcheon   K   Spacers

29 Tailgate – removal and refitting

1   Open and support the tailgate and mark around the hinge edges to ensure correct alignment of the hinge position on refitting.
2   Get an assistant to support the tailgate whilst you unscrew the hinge retaining bolts. When the hinges are free, lift the tailgate clear.
3   Refit the tailgate in the reverse order to removal and check alignment when in the closed position. If necessary adjust alignment by loosening off the bumper screws on the tailgate and on the tailgate aperture pillars. Loosen the tailgate striker retaining screws and also the hinge screws.
4   Close and align the tailgate to give a uniform clearance around its periphery, retain in this position whilst raising it and retighten the hinge bolts. Close the tailgate again and adjust the position of the striker to suit so that the tailgate lower edges are aligned with the back panel. Tighten the striker screws when satisfactory.
5   Check the bumper alignments. If necessary, add or subtract pads to alter the bumper to body pillar contact as required, and then retighten the bumper screws to secure (Fig. 12.21).

30 Tailgate lock and barrel – removal and refitting

1   Open and support the tailgate. Remove the trim panel on the inside of the tailgate.

2   Unscrew the lever-to-lock barrel retaining screw and remove the lever.
3   Remove the three handle-to-tailgate retaining screws and detach the handle and pad. Unclip the circlip and withdraw the lock barrel from the handle.
4   To remove the lock unit, unscrew and remove the bolt and spacer retaining the lock release lever to the tailgate. Unscrew and remove the four lock-to-inner panel retaining screws and detach the lock unit (Fig. 12.23).
5   Refit in the reverse order, and check operation before closing the tailgate.

31 Tailgate torsion bar – removal and refitting

1   Remove the trim panel from the torsion bar location.
2   Detach the T-retainer and counterplate by unscrewing and removing the securing nuts.
3   A special tool is required to release the torsion bar and is shown in Fig. 12.24; it should be obtained from a tool hire agent if possible.
4   Fit the tool to the U-shaped end of the torsion bar and, with the tailgate open, push the tool lever forwards and unhook the torsion bar from the hinge plate.
5   Working on the opposite hinge, detach the torsion bar from its retaining sleeve, then release the U-shaped end of the torsion bar from the hinge lug.

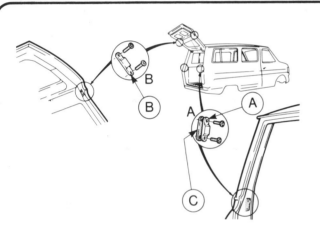

Fig. 12.21 Tailgate 'bumpers' and locations (Sec 29)

    A   Bumper to body   C   Pads
    B   Bumper to tailgate

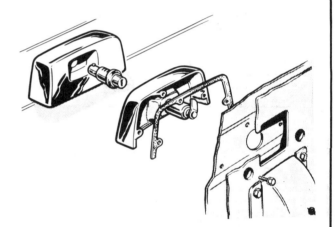

Fig. 12.22 Tailgate lock, barrel and handle (Sec 30)

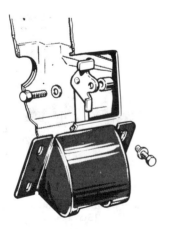

Fig. 12.23 Tailgate lock unit (Sec 30)

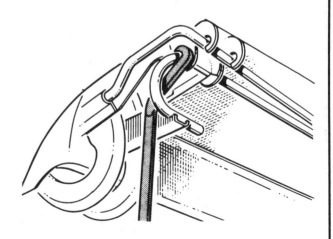

Fig. 12.24 Rear tailgate torsion bar removal tool (Sec 31)

6   Refitting the rear tailgate torsion bar is a reversal of the removal procedure, but to ensure quiet operation, smear the T-retainer and torsion bar contact faces with a little grease before assembling them.

32 Front and rear bumprs – removal and refitting

Front

1   Prise and pull free the bumper end caps at each end, disengaging them from their retaining clips (Fig. 12.25).
2   From inside the engine compartment, unscrew and remove the two nuts and washers securing the bumper boss to the side-member brackets.
3   Withdraw the bumper from the front body panel. On some models the headlight washer feed tubes to the washer nozzles housed in the overriders will have to be detached also. To remove the mounting brackets, unscrew the four retaining bolts.
4   Refit in the reverse order to removal, aligning the bumper correctly before finally tightening the retaining bolts.

Rear

5   Prise and pull free the bumper end caps at each side panel location, then pull the caps from the ends of the bumper.
6   Working underneath the rear of the vehicle, unbolt the bumper mounting bars from the body. Note that the left-hand mounting also retains the tow hook (if fitted). Remove the bumper.

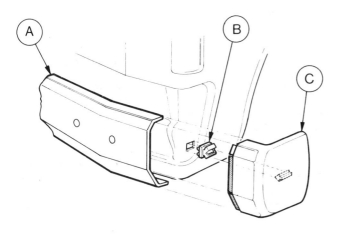

Fig. 12.25 Front bumper (A), retainer (B) and end clip (C) (Sec 32)

7   Where applicable, detach the foglight bracket and light lead.
8   Refit in the reverse order to removal and check alignment. Ensure that the end caps are secure when refitted.

33 Front panel – removal and refitting

1   The radiator is attached to the inside of the front panel. If it is to be removed with the panel, detach the bottom hose and drain the coolant. Detach the top hose from the radiator.
2   To separate the radiator from the panel, remove the four retaining bolts. If the radiator is to remain in the vehicle, support it so that the hoses are not strained.
3   Remove the retaining screws and detach the headlight surround panels. Refer to Chapter 10 and remove the headlights.
4   Disconnect the bonnet catch release cable.
5   Unscrew and remove the six upper retaining bolts from the front panel (along its top face).
6   Refer to Section 32 and remove the front bumper.
7   Remove the nine bolts from the lower edge of the panel and carefully withdraw it.
8   Refit in the reverse order to removal. Insert all lower and upper panel retaining bolts before tightening them. Top up the coolant on refitting the radiator and check for leaks.
9   Check the headlights for correct operation and alignment.

34 Bonnet – removal, refitting and adjustment

1   Open the bonnet and support it with its stay rod.
2   Detach the windscreen washer tubes and the engine compartment light lead.
3   Mark around the bonnet hinges to show the outline of their fitted positions for correct realignment on assembly.
4   Get an assistant to support the bonnet whilst you unscrew and remove the hinge retaining bolts. Then lift the bonnet clear.
5   Refit in reverse sequence and only tighten the hinge bolts fully when bonnet alignment is satisfactory.
6   Further adjustment of the bonnet fit is available by loosening the hinges and the locknuts of the bump stops on the front crossmember. The bonnet can now be adjusted to give an even clearance between its outer edges and the surrounding panels. Adjust the front bump stops to align the edges of the bonnet with the front wing panels, then retighten the locknuts and hinge bolts.
7   When correctly fitted the bonnet to front panel crossmember clearance should be 0.3 in (7.5 mm) as shown in Fig. 12.27. The bonnet lock striker can be adjusted if necessary by loosening the striker locknut and then screwing the striker in or out as required. Retighten the locknut to complete.

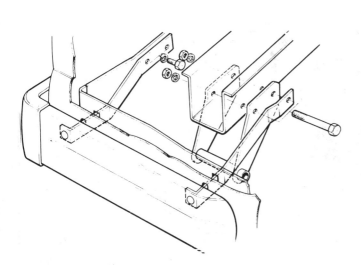

Fig. 12.26 Rear bumper mounting and tow hook location (Sec 32)

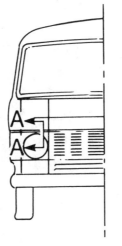

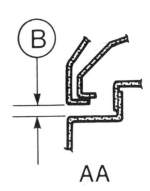

Fig. 12.27 Bonnet setting when closed, showing bonnet to front panel crossmember clearance (B) (Sec 34)

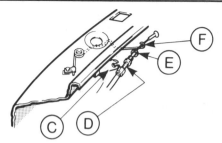

Fig. 12.28 Bonnet release cable to catch spring attachment
(Sec 35)

C   Adjuster location bracket   E   Locknut
D   Adjuster   F   Spring

35 Bonnet release cable – removal, refitting and adjustment

1   Open the bonnet, support it with the stay and disconnect the
battery earth lead.
2   Loosen the bonnet release cable and adjustment locknuts (Fig.
12.28). Unclip the outer cable from the inner wing and crossmember.
3   Detach the inner cable from the release spring and manoeuvre it
through the adjuster bracket slot.
4   Working in the cab, detach the release cable handle pivot pin
circlip and withdraw the handle and cable from the bracket. Withdraw
the cable, pulling it through into the cab.
5   Refit the cable in the reverse order to removal.
6   To adjust the cable, pull it so that the bonnet lock spring contacts
the front face of the bonnet lock sleeve as shown in Fig. 12.29. Retain
the cable in this position and then tighten the adjustment screws.
Check that the spring setting is still satisfactory by closing the bonnet
and pulling the release cable. The bonnet should open to the safety
catch position.

36 Heater unit – removal and refitting

1   Disconnect the battery earth lead.
2   Refer to Chapter 2 and drain the cooling system of approximately
7 pints (4.0 litres) of coolant.
3   Working under the bonnet, disconnect the two hoses from the
heater unit. Take great care doing this or the soldered pipe stubs may
be torn out of the heater matrix.

Fig. 12.29 Bonnet catch release spring position – adjust so that it
contacts front face of sleeve (arrowed) (Sec 35)

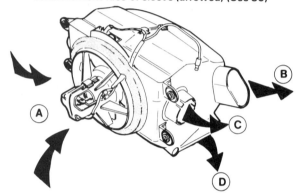

Fig. 12.30 Heater/blower unit showing airflow (Sec 36)

A   Air inlet   C   Airflow to demister nozzles
B   Airflow to vents   D   Airflow to footwell

4   Remove the four retaining screws and detach the cover plate from
the bulkhead (Fig. 12.32).
5   Make a note of the electrical connections at the rear of the heater
and disconnect them at the connectors.
6   Unscrew and remove the four retaining bolts, spring and plain
washers which secure the heater to its mounting brackets; there are
two bolts each side of the unit.

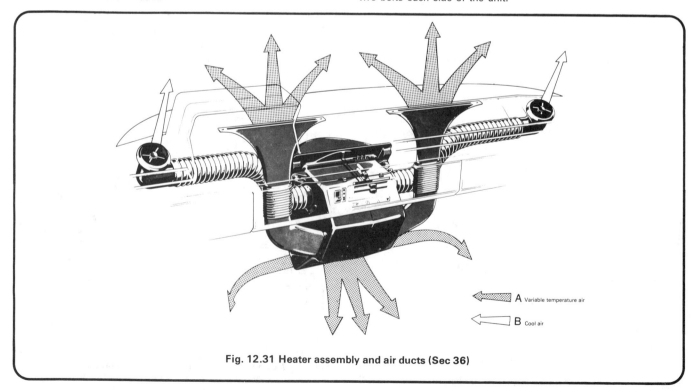

A   Variable temperature air

B   Cool air

Fig. 12.31 Heater assembly and air ducts (Sec 36)

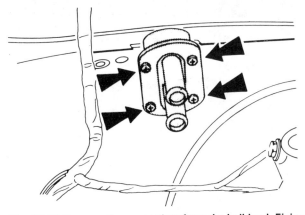

Fig. 12.32 Remove the cover plate from the bulkload. Fixing screws arrowed (Sec 36)

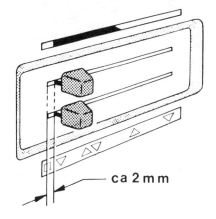

Fig. 12.33 Control lever adjustment position (Sec 36)

7   Carefully lower the heater unit, at the same time disconnecting the demister hoses from the top tube extensions, the airflow duct hoses and the respective control cables, noting their locations. Withdraw the heater from the vehicle, tilting it to prevent water spilling onto the cab floor.

8   Refitting the heater unit is a reversal of the removal procedure, but it will be necessary to fill the cooling system in accordance with the instructions given in Chapter 2.

9   When reconnecting the control cables to the air flap levers, adjust by moving the appropriate flap valve to its end location. The cable outer sleeve is then clipped into position on the heater housing. The control lever must be about 0.08 in (2 mm) from the end of its travel slot (Fig. 12.33).

37 Heater unit – dismantling and reassembly

1   With the unit removed, tip the unit to empty out any remaining coolant from the heater unit radiator.

2   Detach the foam gasket (with care) from the blower flange and then disconnect the ten clips to separate the unit housing half sections.

3   Withdraw the blower motor and air flap valves from the housings, followed by the heater radiator.

4   Reassembly is a reversal of the dismantling process. Renew the foam gaskets if necessary and ensure that the housing retaining clips are securely fitted.

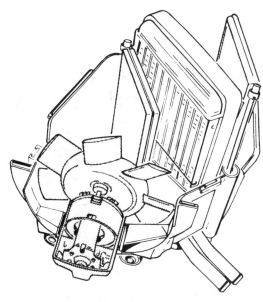

Fig. 12.34 Blower motor and flap valves removal from housings (Sec 37)

Chapter 13 Supplement:
Revisions and information on later models

Contents

1 Introduction

This Supplement contains information which is additional to, or a revision of, material in the first twelve Chapters. The Sections in the Supplement follow the same order as the Chapters to which they relate (although there may be more than one Section per Chapter). The

Specifications are grouped together for convenience, but they too follow Chapter order.

It is recommended that before any particular operation is undertaken, reference be made to the appropriate Section(s) of the Supplement. In this way any change in procedures or components can be noted before referring to the main Chapters.

2 Specifications

Engine
Torque wrench settings

	lbf ft	kgf m
Rocker arm ball stud locknut:		
Early type (7.0 mm thick)	33 to 37	4.5 to 5.0
Later type (8.0 mm thick)	37 to 41	5.0 to 5.5

Cooling system
Torque wrench settings

	lbf ft	kgf m
Viscous type fan blades to clutch hub	17	2.3

Fuel system
Ford VV carburettor

Application	All models from September 1981
Choke pull-down setting	0.16 in (4.0 mm)
Choke gauging	0.13 in (3.4 mm)
Idle speed	750 to 850 rpm
CO at idle	0.5 to 1.5%

Ignition system (breakerless)
Distributor

Type	Bosch
Rotor rotation	Clockwise
Static initial advance:	
1.6 litre ohc	6° BTDC
2.0 litre ohc	6° BTDC

Ignition coil

Type	Bosch, Femsa or Polmot high output
Output	25 kV minimum
Primary resistance	0.72 to 0.88 ohm
Secondary resistance	4500 to 7000 ohm

Spark plugs

Type:	
1.6 litre ohc	Motorcraft BF 22X, BRF 22X
2.0 litre ohc	Motorcraft BF 32X, BRF 32X
Electrode gap	0.75 mm (0.030 in)
Firing order	1-3-4-2 (No 1 at crankshaft pulley end)

Rear axle
Torque wrench setting

	lbf ft	kgf m
Crownwheel bolts (Type H rear axle; Dec 15th 1980 and later)	63	8.5

Electrical system
Alternator

Type	Motorola
Rated output	28A, 35A or 45A according to model
Regulator voltage at 4000 rpm and 3 to 7A load	13.7 to 14.6 volts
Minimum length of brushes	4.0 mm (0.16 in)
Drivebelt deflection at centre of longest run	10.0 mm (0.39 in)

Bulbs (1984 on) – exterior lamps

Lamp	Type	Wattage
Headlamp	H4	55/60
Front parking lamps	T8/4	4
Direction indicators	P25-1	21
Stop-lamps (Chassis cab)	P25-1	21
Tail lamps (Chassis cab)	R19/5	5
Stop/tail lamps (Van, Bus, Kombi)	P25-2	21/5
Reverse lamp (Chassis cab)	P25-1	21
Reverse lamp (Van, Bus, Kombi)	P25-1	21
Rear fog lamp (Chassis cab)	P25-1	21
Rear fog lamp (Van, Bus, Kombi)	P25-1	21
Rear number plate lamp (Chassis cab)	R19/10	10
Rear number plate lamp (Van, Bus, Kombi)	T8/4	4

Suspension and steering
Burman heavy duty steering

Lubricant:	
Type/specification	Hypoid gear oil, viscosity SAE 80EP, to Ford spec. SQM-2C9008-A (Duckhams Hypoid 80)
Capacity	0.74 pint (0.42 litre)

Tyre pressures (cold)

Vehicle	Tyre size	lbf/in²		Bar	
		Front	Rear	Front	Rear
80 Van and Kombi	185 x SR 14 R	36	42	2.5	2.9
130 Van and Kombi	185 x SR 14 R	30	30	2.0	2.0
130 Van, all 160 models	185 x SR 14 R	30	36	2.0	2.5
All 175 models	185 x SR 14 R	42	42	2.9	2.9
All 190 models	185 x 14 C	33	46	2.2	3.2
All 100 models except Bus	195 x SR 14 C	30	45	2.0	3.1
100 Bus	195 x SR 14 C	30	36	2.0	2.5
All 120 models	205 x R 14 C	24	42	1.6	2.9

Torque wrench settings

	lbf ft	kgf m
Burman steering system:		
Bearing retainer bolts	15 to 18	2.1 to 2.5
Side cover bolts	15 to 18	2.1 to 2.5
Anti-roll bar link to bracket	57 to 65	7.7 to 8.8
Anti-roll bar link to bar	57 to 65	7.7 to 8.8
Anti-roll bar U-bolt nuts	27 to 32	3.6 to 4.4
Anti-roll bar mounting bracket	30 to 38	4.0 to 5.1

Bodywork and underframe
Torque wrench setting

	lbf ft	kgf m
Wheelbase extension bolts	59 to 63	8.0 to 8.5

3 Engine

Rocker arm ballstud locknuts

1   In order to eliminate loosening of the rocker arm ballstud locknuts in service, the locknuts on 1984 and later models have been increased in thickness from 7.0 to 8.0 mm.
2   The torque wrench settings given in the Specifications for early and later type locknuts should be matched approximately if a suitable torque wrench adaptor (Tool No 21-004A) is not available.

Camshaft cover

3   After September 1983 the camshaft cover mating flanges have been increased in width using modified gaskets, seals and reinforcing plates.
4   A leaking early type camshaft cover can be repaired by straightening the flange and fitting reinforcement plates under the screw heads instead of the original spring washers. Use oil seals on the screws. All the parts required are available individually.

Engine oil – revised specification

5   As an aid to lower fuel consumption and to prevent unduly low fast idle speed at cold start on later models with the VV carburettor a lighter engine oil (SAE 10W-30) is now recommended for all year round use where temperatures are between -20 and $+30°C$.

4 Cooling system

Thermo viscous fan

1   This type of radiator cooling fan was fitted to ohc engined vehicles equipped with a VV carburettor.
2   To remove this type of fan, open the bonnet and disconnect the battery.
3   A cranked 32.0 mm (1¼ in AF) open-ended spanner will be required to unscrew the fan/clutch from the hub of the coolant pump. The thread is *left-handed* and the pump hub must be held against rotation while unscrewing the fan.
4   The fan may be disconnected from the clutch after removing the four connecting bolts.
5   When reconnecting the fan and clutch, tighten the bolts to the torque given in the Specifications at the beginning of this Supplement.
6   Refitting the fan/clutch to the coolant pump is a reversal of removal.

5 Fuel system

Accelerator cable – routing

1   It is important that the accelerator cable is routed over the heater and brake servo hoses as shown in Fig. 13.3.
2   Failure to observe this condition can cause binding of the cable and damage.

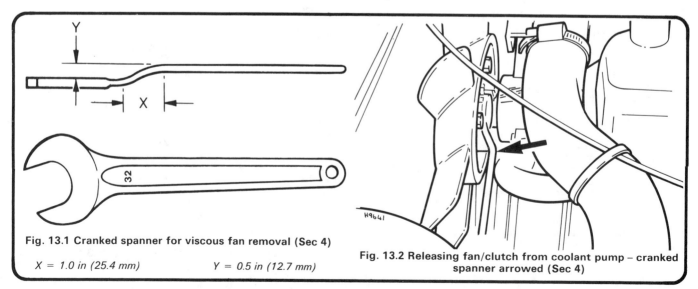

Fig. 13.1 Cranked spanner for viscous fan removal (Sec 4)

X = 1.0 in (25.4 mm)   *Y = 0.5 in (12.7 mm)*

Fig. 13.2 Releasing fan/clutch from coolant pump – cranked spanner arrowed (Sec 4)

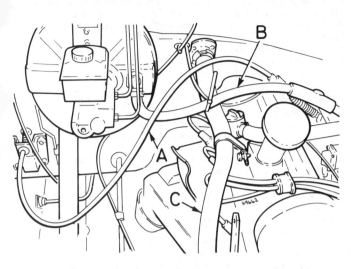

Fig. 13.3 Accelerator cable routing (air cleaner removed)
(Sec 5)

A   Accelerator cable   C   Heater hose
B   Brake servo hose

Ford VV carburettor – general description

3   The Ford variable venturi carburettor is theoretically more efficient than fixed jet types due mainly to the improved fuel atomisation especially at low engine speeds and loads. The carburettor operates as follows.

4   Fuel is supplied to the carburettor via a needle valve which is actuated by the float. When the fuel level is low in the float chamber in the carburettor, the float drops and opens the needle valve. When the correct fuel level is reached the float will close the valve and shut off the fuel supply.

5   The float level on this type of carburettor is not adjustable since minor variations in the fuel level do not affect the performance of the carburettor. The valve needle is prevented from vibrating by means of a ball and light spring and to further ensure that the needle seats correctly it is coated in a rubber-like coating of Viton.

6   The float chamber is vented internally via the main jet body and carburettor air inlet, thus avoiding the possibility of petrol vapour escaping into the atmosphere.

7   The air/fuel mixture is controlled by the air valve which is opened or closed according to the operating demands of the engine. The valve is actuated by a diaphragm which opens or closes according to the vacuum supplied through the venturi between the air valve and the throttle butterfly. As the air valve and diaphragm are connected they open or close correspondingly.

8   When the engine is idling the air intake requirement is low and therefore the valve is closed, causing a high air speed over the main jet exit. However, as the throttle plate is opened, the control vacuum (depression within the venturi) increases and is channelled to the diaphragm which then opens the air valve to balance the control spring and control vacuum.

9   When the throttle is opened further this equality of balance is maintained as the air valve is progressively opened to equalise the control spring and control vacuum forces throughout the speed range.

10 Fuel from the float chamber is drawn up the pick-up tube and then regulated through two jets and the tapered needle into the engine. The vacuum within the venturi draws the fuel. This is shown in Fig. 13.5. At low engine speeds the needle taper enters the main jet to restrict the fuel demand. On acceleration and at high speeds the needle is withdrawn through the main jet by the action of the air valve to which it is attached. As the needle is tapered, the amount by which it is moved regulates the amount of fuel passing through the main jet.

11 The sonic idle system as used on other Ford fixed jet carburettors is also employed in the VV type, with 70% of the idle fuel mixture supplied via the sonic idle system and 30% from the main system. When idling, fuel is drawn through the main pick-up tube (Fig. 13.6)

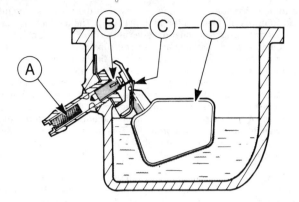

Fig. 13.4 Sectional view of VV carburettor float chamber
(Sec 5)

A   Filter   C   Pivot
B   Needle valve   D   Float

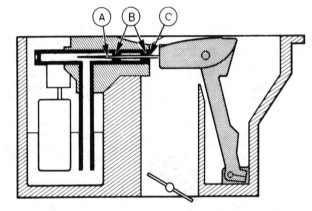

Fig. 13.5 VV carburettor jet arrangement (Sec 5)

A   Tapered metering rod   C   Main fuel outlets
B   Main and secondary jets

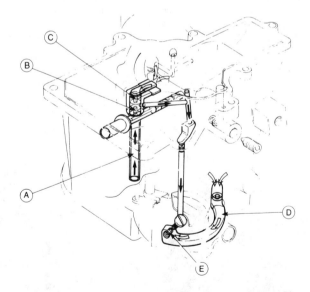

Fig. 13.6 VV carburettor sonic idle system (Sec 5)

A   Main pick-up tube   D   Bypass gallery
B   Idle fuel jet   E   Sonic discharge tube
C   Idle air jet

passes through the idle jet and then mixes with the air stream being supplied from the air bleed in the main jet body. The air/fuel mixture then passes on through the inner galleries at the mixture control screw which regulates the fuel supply at idle. This mixture then mixes with the air from the by-pass idle channel and finally enters the inlet manifold via the sonic discharge tube at an accelerated rate of flow.

12 Throttle actuation is via a progressive linkage which has a cam and roller mechanism. The advantage of this system is that a large initial throttle movement allows only a small throttle plate opening. As the throttle is opened up and approaches its maximum travel the throttle plate movement accelerates accordingly. This system aids economy, gives a good engine response through the range on smaller engines, and enables the same size of carburettor to be employed on other models in the range.

13 To counterbalance the drop in vacuum when initially accelerating, a restrictor is fitted into the air passage located between the control vacuum areas and the control diaphragm. This restrictor causes the valve to open slowly when an increase in air flow is made which, in turn, causes a higher vacuum for a brief moment in the main jet, caused by the increase in air velocity. This increase in vacuum causes the fuel flow to increase thus preventing a 'flat spot'. The large amounts of fuel required under heavy acceleration are supplied by the accelerator pump.

14 The accelerator pump injects fuel into the venturi direct when acceleration causes a drop in manifold vacuum. This richening of the mixture prevents engine hesitation under heavy acceleration. The accelerator pump is a diaphragm type and is actuated from vacuum obtained from under the throttle plate. During acceleration the vacuum under the throttle plate drops, the diaphragm return spring pushes the diaphragm and the fuel in the pump is fed via the inner galleries through the one-way valve and into the venturi. The system incorporates a back bleeder and vacuum break air hole. Briefly explained, the back bleed allows any excess fuel vapour to return to the float chamber when prolonged idling causes the carburettor temperature to rise and the fuel in the accelerator pump reservoir to become overheated. The vacuum break air hole allows air into the pump outlet pipe to reduce the vacuum at the accelerator pump jet at high speed. Fuel would otherwise be drawn out of the accelerator pump system.

15 A fully automatic choke system is fitted incorporating a coolant operated bi-metallic spring. According to the temperature of the coolant, the spring in the unit opens or closes. This in turn actuates the choke mechanism, which consists of a variable needle jet and a variable supply of air. Fuel to the choke jet is fed from the main pick-up tube via the internal galleries within the main jet body. When the bi-metal spring is contracted (engine cold), it pulls the tapered needle from the jet to increase the fuel delivery rate. The spring expands as the engine warms up and the needle reduces the fuel supply as it re-enters the jet. The choke air supply is supplied via the venturi just above the throttle plate. The fuel mixes with the air in the choke air valve and is then delivered to the engine.

16 A choke pull-down system is employed whereby if the engine is under choke but is only cruising, ie, not under heavy loading, the choke is released. This is operated by the vacuum piston which is connected to the choke spindle by levers.

17 Last but not least, an anti-dieselling valve is fitted on the outside of the body of the carburettor. This valve shuts off the fuel supply to the idle system when the engine is turned off and so prevents the engine running on or 'dieselling'. The solenoid valve is actuated electrically. When the ignition is turned off, it allows a plunger to enter and block the sonic discharge tube to stop the supply of fuel into the idle system. When the ignition is switched on the solenoid is actuated and the plunger is withdrawn from the tube.

Ford VV carburettor – slow running and mixture adjustment

18 Run the engine to normal operating temperature then stop it.

19 Connect a tachometer and, if available, an exhaust gas analyser to the engine.

20 Run the engine at 3000 rpm for 30 seconds, then allow it to idle and note the idle speed and CO content.

21 Adjust the idle speed screw to give the specified idle speed.

22 Adjustment of the CO content (mixture) is not normally required during routine maintenance, but if the reading noted in paragraph 20 is not as given in the Specifications first remove the tamperproof plug. On the VV carburettor use a thin screwdriver.

23 Run the engine at 3000 rpm for 30 seconds then allow it to idle. Adjust the mixture screw within 10 to 30 seconds. If more time is required run the engine at 3000 rpm again for 30 seconds.

24 Adjust the idle speed if necessary and recheck the CO content.

25 Fit new tamperproof plugs. Note that it is not possible to adjust the idling mixture accurately without an exhaust gas analyser.

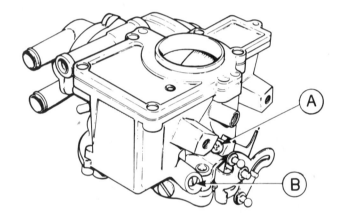

Fig. 13.7 VV carburettor adjusting screws (Sec 5)

A Idle speed   *B Idle mixture*

Ford VV carburettor – overhaul

Note: *Before attempting to overhaul a well worn carburettor, ensure that spares are available. It may be both quicker and cheaper to obtain a complete carburettor on an exchange basis.*

26 Before dismantling the carburettor clean it off externally and

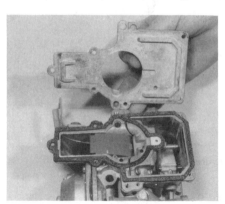

5.27 Removing VV carburettor cover

5.30A Main jet body screws on VV carburettor

5.30B Removing main jet body from VV carburettor

prepare a suitable work space on the bench to lay out the respective components in order of appearance.

27 Unscrew and remove the seven carburettor cover retaining screws. Carefully lift the cover clear trying not to break the gasket. Remove the gasket (photo).

28 Drain any remaining fuel from the float chamber.

29 If the variable choke metering rod (or needle) is to be removed, prise the tamperproof plug from the body and insert a suitable screwdriver through the hole. Unscrew the metering rod and withdraw it. However, note that the manufacturers do not recommend removing the rod. If the rod is damaged, the carburettor should be renewed.

30 To remove the main jet body, unscrew the four retaining screws (photo) and carefully lift the body clear, noting gasket. If the metering rod is still in position, retract it as far as possible from the jet, press the

float down and carefully pull the jet body clear of the metering rod (photo). Great care must be taken here not to bend or distort the rod in any way.

31 The accelerator pump outlet one-way valve ball and weight can now be extracted by inverting the carburettor body.

32 Withdraw the float pivot pin followed by the float and needle valve (photo).

33 Unscrew and remove the four screws retaining the control diaphragm housing. Carefully detach the housing, spring, and seat, taking care not to split or distort the diaphragm. Fold back the diaphragm rubber from the flange. Using a small screwdriver, prise free the retaining clip to release the diaphragm. Put the clip in a safe place to prevent it getting lost before reassembly (photos).

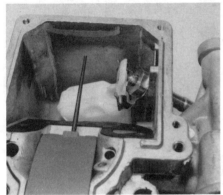

5.32 Float and needle valve on VV carburettor

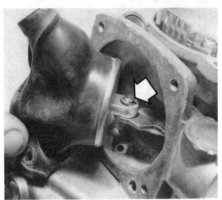

5.33A Diaphragm pivot pin circlip (arrowed) on VV carburettor

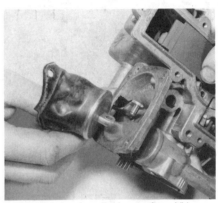

5.33B Withdrawing diaphragm from VV carburettor

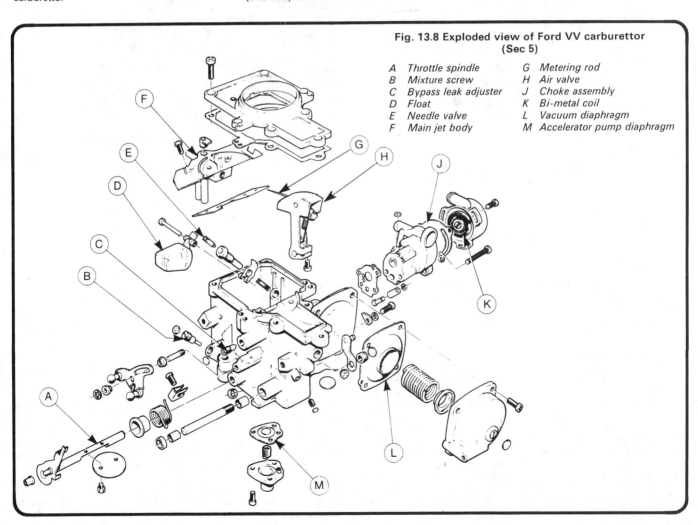

Fig. 13.8 Exploded view of Ford VV carburettor (Sec 5)

A Throttle spindle
B Mixture screw
C Bypass leak adjuster
D Float
E Needle valve
F Main jet body
G Metering rod
H Air valve
J Choke assembly
K Bi-metal coil
L Vacuum diaphragm
M Accelerator pump diaphragm

5.35A Choke housing alignment marks on VV carburettor

5.35B Removing automatic choke housing from VV carburettor

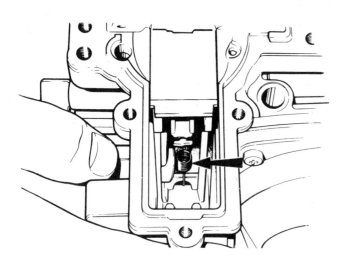

Fig. 13.9 VV carburettor metering rod spring correctly located (Sec 5)

VACUUM HOLE

5.39 Diaphragm with twin corner holes correctly aligned on VV carburettor

34 Now remove the accelerator pump by unscrewing the three retaining screws. Remove the housing, spring and diaphragm.

35 To remove the choke housing, note its positional markings, unscrew the retaining screws and carefully withdraw the housing (photos). Unscrew the solenoid unit.

36 The carburettor is now dismantled and the various components can be cleaned and inspected.

37 Check the body and components for signs of excessive wear and/or defects and renew as necessary. In particular inspect the main jet in the body. Excessive wear is present if the body is oval. Also pay particular attention to the air valve and linkage, the throttle plate (butterfly), its spindle and the throttle linkages for wear. The diaphragm rubber must be in good condition and not split or perished. Check also that the metering rod spring is correctly fitted to the air valve (Fig. 13.9). Renew all gaskets and seals during assembly and ensure that the mating surfaces are perfectly clean.

38 Commence assembly by refitting the accelerator pump. Locate the gasket face of the diaphragm towards the pump cover and when in position it must not be distorted at all. Fit the spring and cover and tighten the screws evenly.

39 Reconnect the diaphragm to the control linkage and retain by fitting the circlip. This is fiddly and requires a steady hand and a little patience. Check that the clip is fully engaged when in position. As the diaphragm is fitted ensure that the double holes on one corner align with the corresponding holes in the carburettor body (photo). With the diaphragm in position, relocate the housing and spring and insert the retaining screws to secure. Take care not to distort the diaphragm as the housing is tightened.

40 If removed, refit the mixture adjustment screw, but don't relocate the tamperproof plug yet as the mixture must be adjusted when the engine is restarted. Do not overtighten the screw! Back off the screw three full turns.

41 Insert the float needle, the float and the pivot pin. When installing the needle valve the spring-loaded ball must face towards the float.

42 Locate the accelerator pump ball and weight into the discharge gallery, fit a new gasket into position and then refit the main jet body (photo). If the metering rod is already in position, retract and raise it to re-engage the main jet housing over the rod and then lower it into position. Do not force or bend the rod in any way during this operation. Tighten the jet body retaining screws. If the metering rod is still to be fitted, do not fully tighten the jet body retaining screws until after the jet is fitted and known to be centralised. If still to be fitted, slide the

5.42 Main jet body gasket on VV carburettor

5.44 Choke operating lever slots on VV carburettor

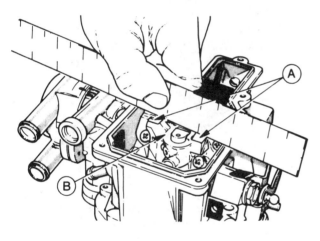

Fig. 13.10 Checking alignment of VV carburettor main jet
body (Sec 5)

A   Alignment flanges   B   Main jet body

metering rod into position and screw it in until the rod shoulder aligns
with the main body vertical face. Do not overtighten the rod. Should it
bend during assembly, try re-centralising the main jet body, then
tighten the retaining screws. Using a straight edge check that the main
jet body alignment flanges are flush with the top face of the
carburettor. Where applicable fit the plug to the metering rod
extraction hole in the carburettor body.
43 Position the new top cover gasket in position and refit the top
cover. Tighten the retaining screws progressively and evenly.
44 The auto choke housing can be refitted to complete assembly.
Ensure that the body alignment marks correspond and as it is fitted
engage the bi-metal coil with the middle choke lever slot (photo). Use
a new gasket. Refit the three retaining screws and before tightening
check that the body alignment markings correspond.

Air cleaner (temperature-controlled type) – description and maintenance

45 Used in conjunction with the Ford VV carburettor, this type of air
cleaner incorporates a heat sensor and a vacuum diaphragm unit in
order to blend the intake air to the carburettor as a means of
maintaining the optimum temperature under all engine conditions.

46 Renewal of the element is as described in Chapter 3.
Removal and refitting
47 Disconnect the vacuum and breather hoses from the air cleaner
casing.
48 Extract the securing screws and lift the air cleaner with hot air
intake hose from the carburettor.
49 When refitting the air cleaner, always renew the sealing ring
between it and the carburettor.

6 Ignition system

Breakerless type ignition – warning and description

1   When working on the electronic ignition system remember that the
high tension voltage can be considerably higher than on a conventional system and in certain circumstances could prove fatal.
Depending on the position of the distributor trigger components it is
also possible for a single high tension spark to be generated simply by
knocking the distributor with the ignition switched on. It is therefore
important to keep the ignition system clean and dry at all times, and to
make sure that the ignition switch is off when working on the engine.
2   As from 1984, ohc models are equipped with a breakerless type
ignition system. The system incorporates the following components:
an ignition coil mounted on the left-hand side of the battery tray
support, a TFI (thick film ignition) module mounted on the engine
compartment rear bulkhead and a breakerless distributor.

Maintenance

3   Maintenance is minimal and consists of checking the wiring
connections and keeping the external surfaces of the components
clean.
4   As there are no contact breaker points, checking the dwell angle is
not required.
5   The distributor position is set during production to ensure precise
timing and the unit should not be removed unless essential.
6   Service the spark plugs in the normal way and periodically check
the carbon brush in the centre of the distributor cap for wear. If worn,
renew the cap.

Distributor – removal and refitting

7   Disconnect the battery negative terminal.
8   Disconnect the HT lead from the coil and the LT lead multi-plug.
9   Release the distributor cap and move it aside.
10 Disconnect the distributor vacuum pipe.
11 Turn the crankshaft by means of the pulley bolt until the contact
end of the rotor is aligned with the mark on the rim of the distributor

body – Fig. 13.12 (Number 1 piston is at its static advance firing position).

12 Mark the distributor mounting flange in relation to the crankcase.

13 Unscrew the clamp bolt and withdraw the distributor.

14 Before refitting the distributor, check that Number 1 piston is still at its static advance setting.

15 Turn the rotor until its contact end is in alignment with the body cut-out nearest the vacuum unit (Fig. 13.13).

16 Insert the distributor into its hole with the flange mark in alignment with the one on the crankcase. As the gears mesh, the rotor will turn to align with the mark on the distributor body rim.

17 Turn the distributor body if necessary to align the stator and trigger wheel arms exactly (Fig. 13.14).

18 Screw in and tighten the clamp bolt, fit the distributor cap and re-make all electrical connections.

19 Check the ignition timing, as described in Chapter 4, using a stroboscope and with the distributor vacuum pipe disconnected.

Amplifier module – removal and refitting

20 Disconnect the battery negative terminal.

21 Disconnect the multi-plug from the module. Grip the plug not the wires to do this.

22 Unscrew the module fixing screws and remove it.

23 Refitting is a reversal of removal.

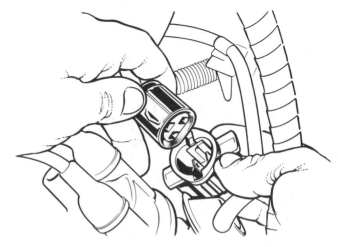

Fig. 13.11 Distributor LT lead multi-plug (Sec 6)

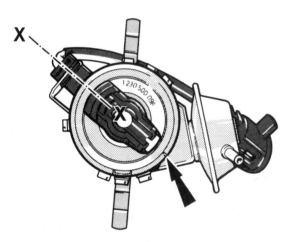

Fig. 13.12 Distributor rotor alignment mark – arrowed (Sec 6)

X–X   90° to centre line of crankshaft

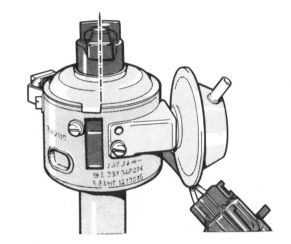

Fig. 13.13 Distributor rotor aligned with body cut-out prior to distributor installation (Sec 6)

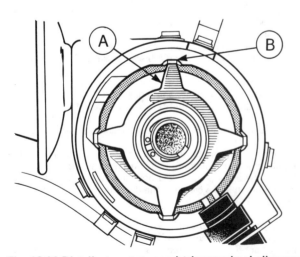

Fig. 13.14 Distributor stator and trigger wheel alignment (Sec 6)

A   Trigger wheel arm   B   Stator arm

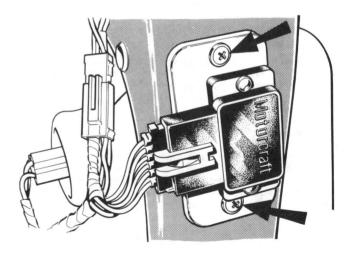

Fig. 13.15 Ignition amplifier module retaining screws – arrowed (Sec 6)

Spark plugs (all ignition systems) – ohc engines
24 The distributor cap incorporates a dimple next to the No 1 spark plug lead socket. Connect the leads in their correct firing order (see Fig. 13.16) remembering that the rotor rotational direction is clockwise.

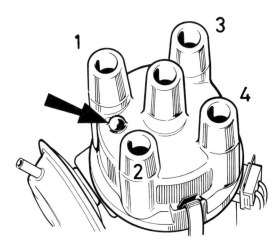

Fig. 13.16 Distributor cap HT lead connecting sequence (Sec 6)

No 1 mark arrowed

Breakerless ignition system – testing
25 Should a fault occur in the breakerless ignition system, the following checks can be carried out if the engine cranks but will not start. Remember that the voltages produced by this system are very high.
26 Check all plugs and terminals for security.
27 Remove a spark plug, rest it on the engine and, with the engine being cranked, check for a spark at the electrode. If there is a spark, check the fuel system.
28 If there is no spark at the plug, check the coil HT output by removing the distributor cap central lead and holding it, with a well-insulated tool, near the engine block. Crank the engine with the starter and check for a spark. If there is a spark, check and renew the rotor, distributor cap or HT leads as necessary.
29 If there is no spark from the end of the coil HT lead, change it for a known good lead and repeat the test.
30 If a spark is still not available, use a voltmeter to check the coil supply voltage; this should be the same as the battery voltage. If not, check the battery and its wiring for condition, also the ignition switch.
31 If the coil supply voltage is correct, disconnect both LT wires from the coil. Connect a test bulb between them and crank the engine. If the bulb flashes while cranking the engine, then the ignition coil is faulty. If the bulb does not flash then the coil is satisfactory and proceed to the next test.
32 With the test bulb still connected between the coil LT terminals, connect the ignition module multi-plug to a substitute module and crank the engine. The test bulb should flash, which indicates that the original module is faulty.

---

7   Manual transmission

Gearbox – lubricant
1 The gearbox is filled for life during production.
2 At the specified service intervals, remove the filler/level plug and top up if necessary to the bottom of the plug hole with oil of the specified type. Refit the plug.
3 A drain plug is provided if the oil has to be drained for overhaul.

---

8   Automatic transmission

Automatic transmission fluid
1 As from October 1980, a new fluid was introduced for use in C3

automatic transmissions.
2 The old and new fluids **must not** be mixed (see *Recommended lubricants and fluids*).
3 To avoid confusion when topping-up or at fluid changing, transmissions with a black dipstick must use the earlier type fluid (SQM-2C-9007-AA) while those with a red dipstick must use fluid SQM-2C-9010-A.
4 If a replacement transmission is being fitted but the original torque converter is retained, make sure that the converter, fluid cooler and pipelines are flushed through with paraffin and drained before filling with the later type of fluid.

Inhibitor switch relay
5 If the inhibitor switch relay on models equipped with automatic transmission is removed for any reason, always make sure that it is refitted to the battery tray with its terminals pointing downwards.

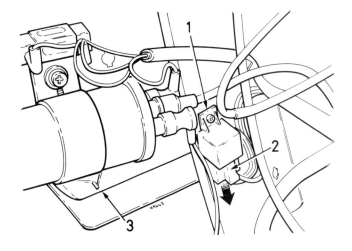

Fig. 13.17 Automatic transmission inhibitor switch relay (Sec 8)

1   *Inhibitor switch relay*   3   *Battery tray*
2   *Relay terminals*

Modified kickdown cable link
6 As from January 1981, a one piece link is fitted to the kickdown (downshift) cable on vehicles equipped with automatic transmission.
7 The following adjustment procedure should be carried out on vehicles with this type of link.
8 Refer to (A) Fig. 13.18 and turn the cable adjuster to give a clearance between the cable ferrule and the end of the adjuster of between 0.020 and 0.060 in (0.5 and 1.5 mm).
9 Open the throttle fully and check that the kickdown cable passes the detent position (hard spot) and then has a further 0.12 in (3.0 mm) of free travel.
10 The kickdown cable must not be taut when the throttle is fully open.
11 When the accelerator pedal is depressed from idle to full throttle, the kickdown cable movement should be between 1.75 and 1.81 in (44.5 and 46.0 mm).
12 Any deviation from these tolerances can be corrected by adjusting the length of rod (G) and turning the screw (3).

Front brake band – adjustment
13 Unhook the kickdown cable from the lever on the side of the transmission.
14 Release and unscrew the brake band adjuster screw locknut a few turns.
15 Screw in the adjuster screw to 10 lbf ft (1.4 kgf m), then unscrew it by exactly 1$\frac{1}{2}$ turns.
16 Without moving the position of the screw, tighten the locknut. Reconnect the kickdown cable.

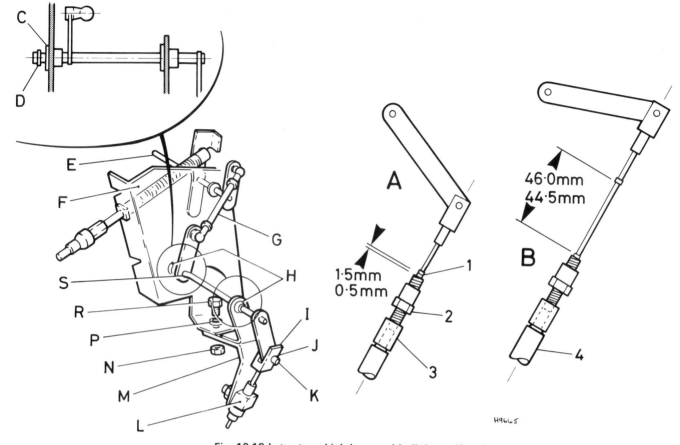

Fig. 13.18 Later type kickdown cable linkage (Sec 8)

A	Idle position	F	Front bracket	L	Trunnion
B	Full throttle position	G	Connecting rod	M	Rear bracket
C	Bush	H	Plastic bushes	N	Washers
D	Circlip	I	Clevis fork	P	Lockwashers
E	Throttle operating shaft	J	Lock pin	R	Bolts
		K	Clevis pin	S	Shaft

1	Kickdown cable
2	Locknut
3	Adjusting sleeve
4	Outer cable (conduit)

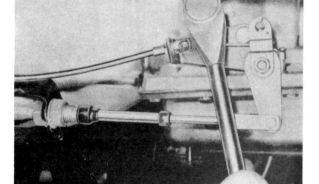

Fig. 13.19 Adjusting front brake band (Sec 8)

9 Propeller shaft

Propeller shaft universal joints

1 On LCX and 100L models built after May 1980, the propeller shaft universal joints are repairable. The staked type joints previously used

have been superseded by conventional circlip type assemblies.

2 To remove a later type joint, first remove the propeller shaft from the vehicle, as described in Chapter 7.

3 Clean away external dirt from the joint which is to be repaired.

4 Extract and discard the circlips from the bearing cups.

5 Using a sharp knife, cut through the oil seals and discard them.

6 Locate the universal joint on two blocks of wood so that one bearing cup is facing upward and the opposite one has space to be ejected between the blocks in a downward direction.

7 Using a hammer and flat-ended bar, drive the upper bearing cup downward until the lower cup protrudes far enough to be gripped in the jaws of a vice and twisted out of the yoke.

8 Turn the propeller shaft through 180° so that the bearing cup to which the drift was applied is at the bottom.

9 Drive the spider downwards to eject the lower bearing cup. Remove it using the vice, as previously described.

10 Repeat the removal operations on the remaining two bearing cups.

11 Discard the bearing cups and spider, clean out the yoke bores and circlip grooves.

12 Using the repair kit supplied specifically for your type of vehicle, withdraw the bearing cups from the spider; taking care not to dislodge the needle rollers which should be held in position by the grease. Do not remove the oil seals.

13 Locate the spider in the propeller shaft yoke. Make sure that the nylon thrust pads are in position in their recesses in the ends of the spider.

14 Smear the bearing cups with grease and fit them into the yoke bores. Do this by squeezing two opposing cups gently in the jaws of a vice or by tapping them home with a copper-faced hammer or drift. As this operation proceeds, check that the needle rollers do not become

displaced or trapped. Make sure that the bearing cups are pushed sufficiently far into the yoke to expose the circlip grooves.
15 Fit the new circlips.
16 Some joints incorporate a grease nipple; in which case apply the grease gun (wheel bearing grease) to it.

10 Rear axle

Crownwheel bolts

1 Although it is not recommended (see Chapter 8) that the differential be dismantled, should any overhaul be undertaken the following must be noted.
2 On H type rear axles built before December 15th 1980, the crownwheel retaining bolts must have thread locking fluid applied to their threads and the bolts tightened to the torque given in the Specifications Section of Chapter 8.
3 On H type rear axles built after December 15th 1980, self-locking crown wheel bolts are used and their threads should not be coated with locking fluid.
4 Tighten the bolts to the torque given at the beginning of this Supplement.
5 The earlier and later type bolts are not interchangeable.

Rear axle lubricant

6 The rear axle is filled for life during production.
7 At the specified service intervals, remove the filler/level plug and top up if necessary to the bottom of the plug hole with oil of recommended type. Refit the plug.
8 If for any reason the oil must be drained, then the axle casing cover must be unbolted and lifted away from the casing, as a drain plug is not fitted.

11 Electrical system

Rear fog warning lamp

1 As from October 1979, rear fog lamps were fitted in production. Such lamps may be fitted to earlier models provided the following conditions are complied with.
2 The lamps must not be wired up so that they operate in conjunction with the brake stop-lamps.
3 The lamps must not be positioned closer than 100.0 mm (3.94 in) to either of the brake stop-lamps.
4 A warning lamp must be incorporated in the wiring circuit to indicate to the driver that the lamps are switched on.
5 The lamps should be fixed to the rear of the vehicle so that they are not more than 1000.0 mm (39.4 in) above the ground, nor less than 250.0 mm (9.8 in).
6 One or two rear foglamps may be fitted. A single lamp should be located on the right-hand side or if two are fitted then they must be located symmetrically.
7 The wiring to the lamps must be so connected that they can only be illuminated if the headlamps, or front foglamps have been switched on.

Instrument panel warning lamps

8 On vehicles built after October 1981, the instrument panel warning lamps have combined bulb and holder assemblies, from which the bulb can be removed from its holder.
9 These one-piece assemblies are coloured blue to identify them and are interchangeable with the separate bulb and holder type.

Alternator – Motorola type

10 This type of alternator is fitted to some models as an alternative to the Bosch or Lucas units described in Chapter 10.
11 Note that a multi-plug connector is used at the rear of the alternator and the belt tension should be 10.0 mm (0.39 in) deflection at the centre of the longest run of the belt. Otherwise removal and refitting operations are as for the Bosch and Lucas alternators.

Motorola alternator – brush renewal

12 Brush renewal should be regarded as the limit of overhaul. Where further dismantling is required, a new or factory rebuilt unit should be obtained, as the cost of individual components needed to fully overhaul a well worn alternator will not make it an economic proposition.

13 Although brush renewal can be carried out without having to remove the alternator, it is recommended that it is removed from the engine and external dirt cleaned away.
14 Remove the voltage regulator and connecting wires.
15 Extract the brush box fixing screw and withdraw the brush box very gently.
16 Unsolder the brush connections and remove the brushes.
17 With the brush box withdrawn, clean the slip rings with a fuel-moistened cloth or, if badly discoloured, fine glass paper.
18 Solder the new brushes into position and reassemble the components by reversing the dismantling operation.

Fig. 13.20 Self-locking type crownwheel bolts (Sec 10)

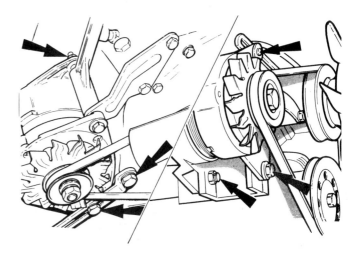

Fig. 13.21 Motorola alternator mounting and adjuster link bolts – arrowed (Sec 11)

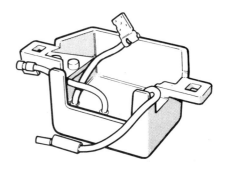

Fig. 13.22 Voltage regulator and leads (Sec 11)

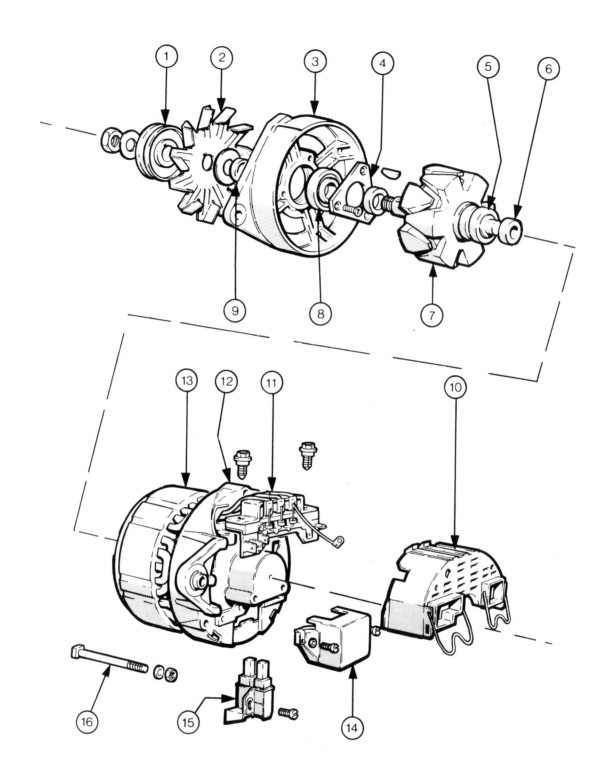

Fig. 13.23 Components of the Motorola alternator (Sec 11)

1	Pulley	5	Slip ring	9	Spacer	13	Stator
2	Fan	6	Slip ring and bearing	10	End cover	14	Voltage regulator
3	Drive end housing	7	Rotor	11	Diode bridge	15	Brush box
4	Drive end bearing retaining plate	8	Drive end bearing	12	Slip ring end housing	16	Tie-bolt

Headlamp washer system
19 A headlamp washer system is fitted to certain models.
20 The components of the system include an electric pump and jets built into the headlamp surround. Wash fluid is obtained from the windscreen fluid reservoir.

Headlamp (1984 on) – removal and refitting
21 Extract the eight grille fixing screws and withdraw the radiator grille. If headlamp washers are fitted, disconnect the washer pipes as the grille is withdrawn.
22 From the rear of the headlamp, pull off the multi-plug and rubber cover.
23 Disconnect the parking lamp bulb and holder from the rear of the headlamp.

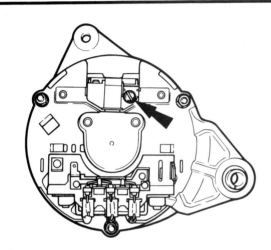

Fig. 13.24 Brush box fixing screw – arrowed (Sec 11)

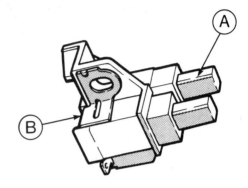

Fig. 13.25 Brushes (A) and soldered connection (B) (Sec 11)

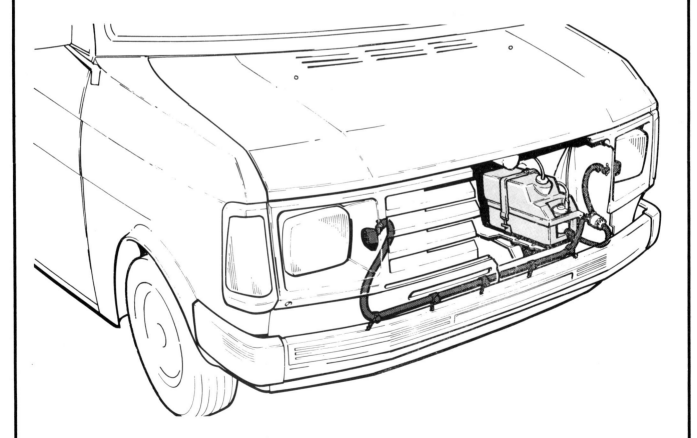

Fig. 13.26 Headlamp washer system (Sec 11)

24 Release the spring clip and remove the bulb/holder. Avoid touching the bulb glass with the fingers.
25 Release the headlamp upper stud by pushing out the locking arm (A) – Fig. 13.28 – and twisting the retaining stud until it will pass through the shaped hole in the panel.
26 Pull the headlamp off the remaining two studs by giving it a sharp jerk.
27 Refitting is a reversal of removal.
28 Adjust the headlamp beam using the two screws (B) – Fig. 13.29.

Front direction indicator lamp unit – removal and refitting
29 The procedure is similar to that described in Chapter 10, Section 23 except that the grille fixing screws adjacent to the lamp should be slackened before work begins.

Rear combination lamp – removal and refitting
30 Extract the three fixing screws (Fig. 13.30) and withdraw the complete lamp assembly until the multi-plugs can be disconnected.
31 The bulb carriers and bulbs are now accessible.
32 On Van variants, the bulb carriers and bulbs are accessible from inside the vehicle.
33 Refitting is a reversal of removal.

Battery – maintenance-free type
34 On later models, a maintenance-free type battery is used. The electrolyte in these batteries should not require topping-up throughout their normal service life.
35 When charging this type of battery from a mains charger, if the electrolyte starts to effervesce, switch off the charger until it ceases.

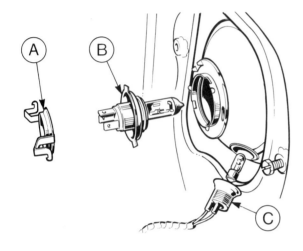

Fig. 13.27 Rear view of later type headlamp (Sec 11)

A   Clip
B   Headlamp bulb

C   Parking bulb and holder

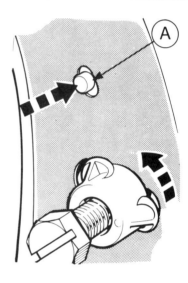

Fig. 13.28 Headlamp fixing stud locking arm (A) (Sec 11)

Push in locking arm and rotate stud

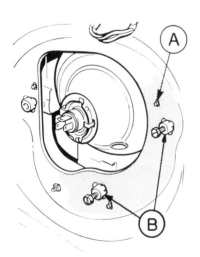

Fig. 13.29 Headlamp beam adjusting screws (Sec 11)

A   Fixing stud   B   Beam adjusting screws

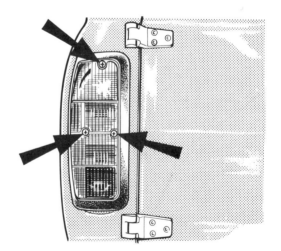

Fig. 13.30 Rear lamp fixing screws (Sec 11)

Key to Fig. 13.31: Wiring diagram for all models 1984 on

1 Anti-dieseling solenoid
2 Water temperature sender
3 Oil pressure switch
4 Alternator
5 Ignition coil
6 Ignition module
7 Starter motor
8 Fuel tank sender
9 Battery
10 Fusebox
11 Instrument cluster
12 Ignition switch/steering lock
13 Automatic transmission inhibitor switch
14 Automatic transmission relay
15 Instrument cluster (with tachometer)
16 Ignition switch/steering lock

17 Headlights
18 Reversing light switch
19 Stop-lamp switch/brake light switch
20 Rear foglamp switch
21 Flasher switch/horn and indicator switch
22 Light switch and wiper motor switch
23 Rear lights/rear light cluster
24 Number plate lights
25 Engine compartment light
28 Interior light switch
29 Interior light
30 Courtesy light
31 Courtesy light switch
32 Cigar lighter
33 Heater control illumination

34 Heater blower switch
38 Flasher lamp/front indicator lights
39 Horn
40 Flasher unit
41 Hazard flasher switch
42 Side repeater lights
46 Windscreen washer bottle
47 Heater resistor
48 Heater blower motor
49 Wiper motor
50 Headlight jet wash motor
51 Low vacuum warning switch
52 Low brake fluid
53 Trailer indicator warning light
54 Heavy duty flasher unit

55 Automatic transmission illumination
56 Intermittent wipe relay
57 Heated rear window relay
58 Headlamp/light jet wash timer
59 Daytime running light relay
60 Light and wiper motor switch
61 Intermittent wipe delay
62 Heated rear window switch
63 Heated rear window

Not all items are fitted to all models

Colour code

BK	Black (SW)
BL	Blue (HB)
BR	Brown
G	Green (GN)
GR	Grey (S)
LBL	Light blue
LG	Light green
P	Pink (PK or RS)
R	Red (RT)
VI	Violet (P)
W	White (WS)
Y	Yellow (GE)

Wire identification

eg 58-4 S/R 0.75
58-4 Wire number
S Main colour
R Secondary colour
0.75 Wire cross-section (mm²)

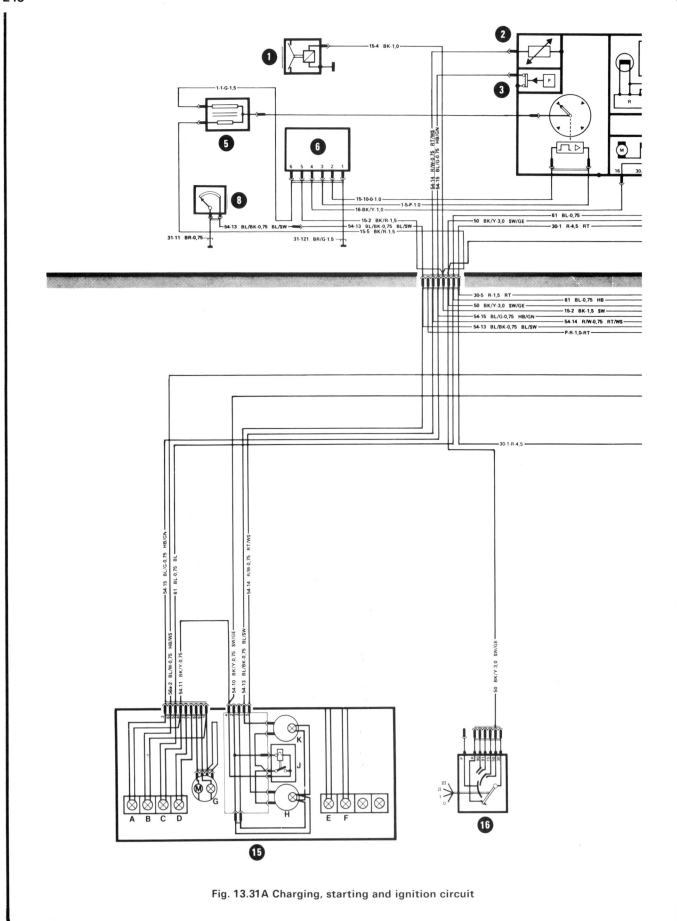

Fig. 13.31A Charging, starting and ignition circuit

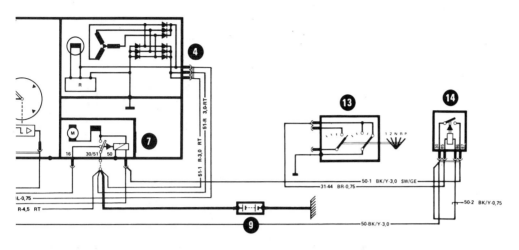

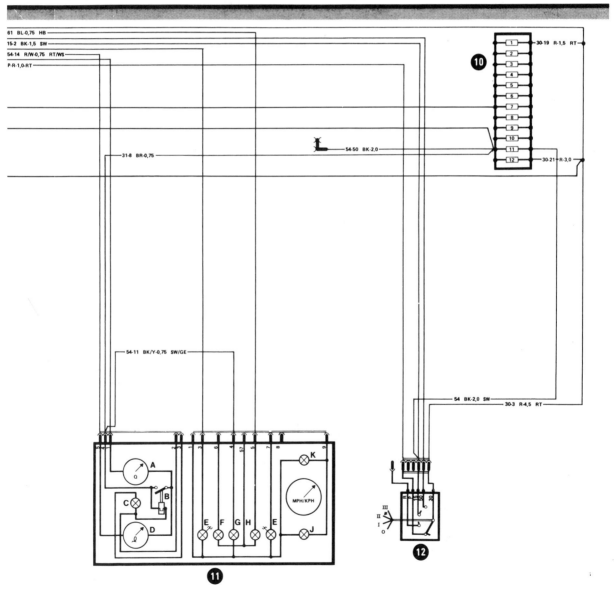

Fig. 13.31A Charging, starting and ignition circuit (continued)

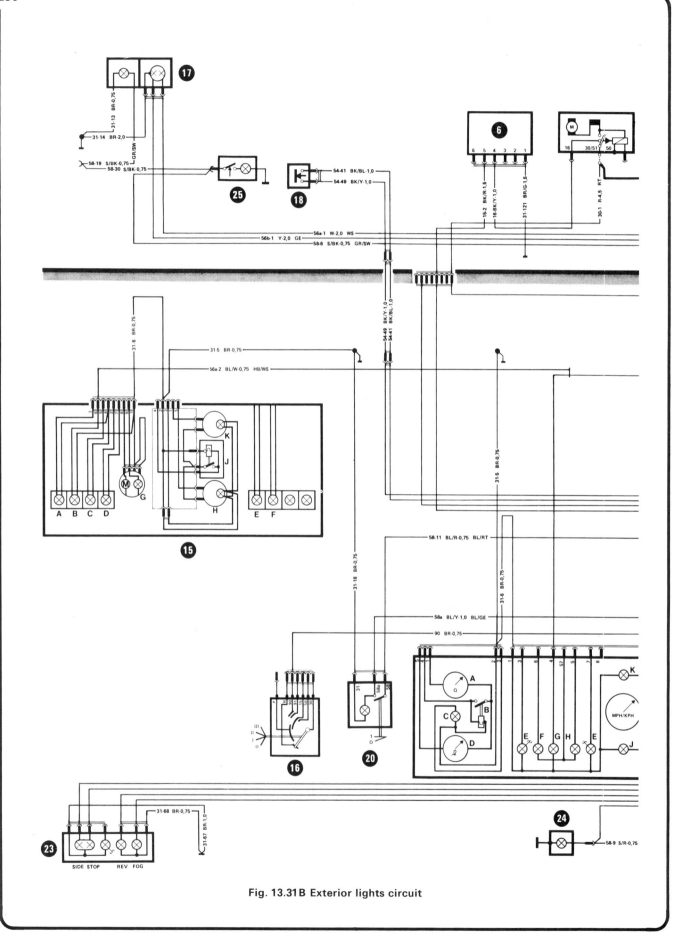

Fig. 13.31 B Exterior lights circuit

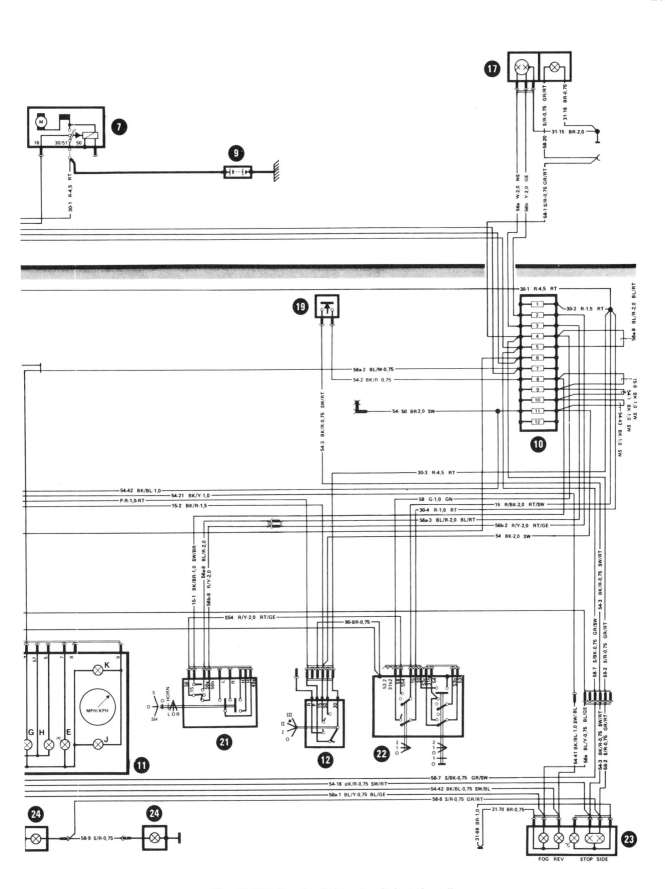

Fig. 13.31B Exterior lights circuit (continued)

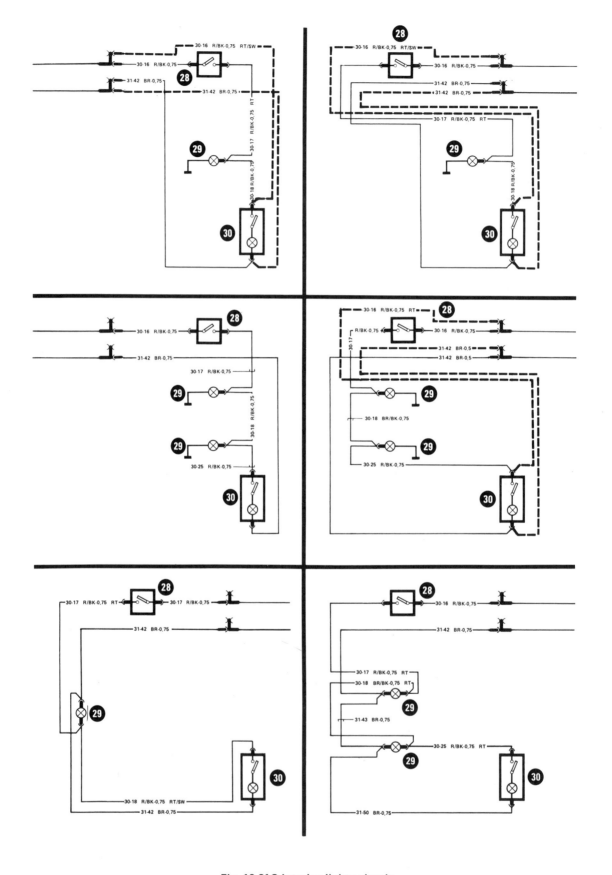

Fig. 13.31C Interior lights circuit

Alternative arrangements shown

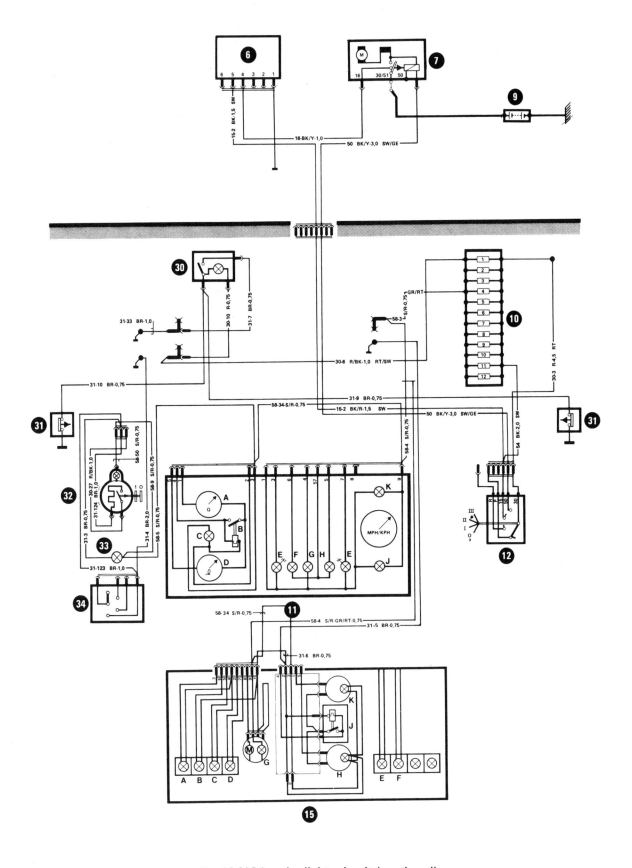

Fig. 13.31C Interior lights circuit (continued)

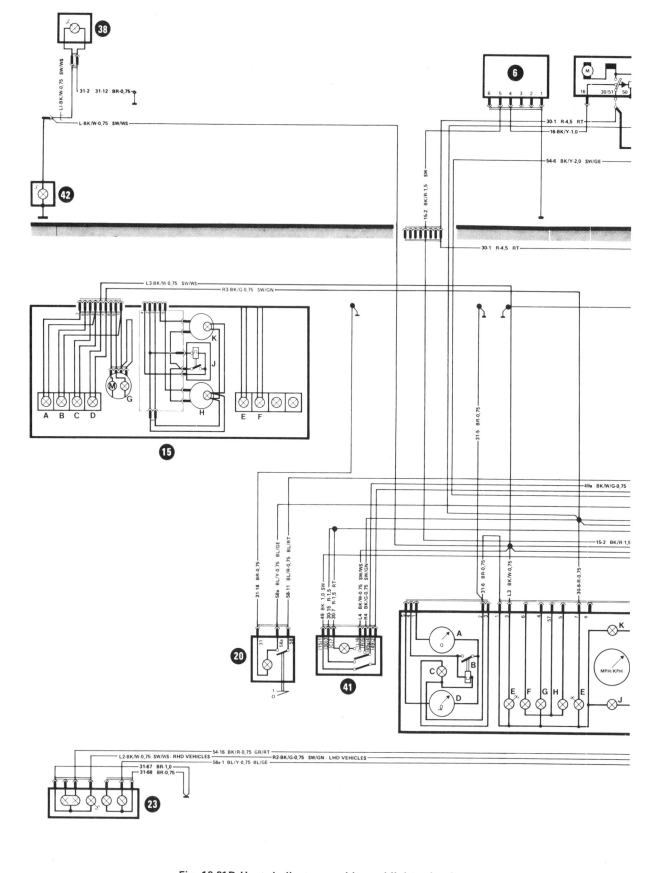

Fig. 13.31D Horn, indicators and hazard lights circuit

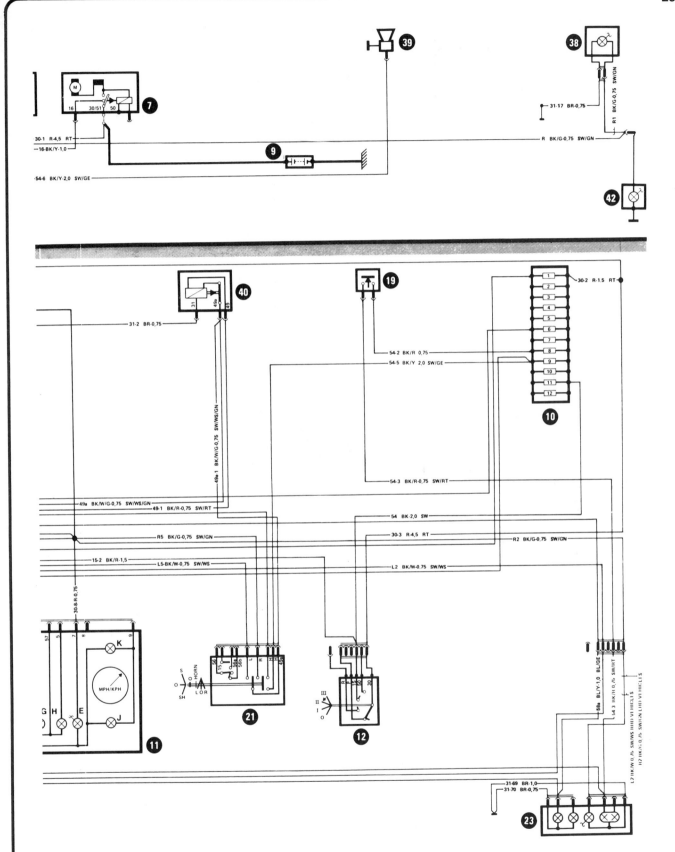

Fig. 13.31D Horn, indicators and hazard lights circuit (continued)

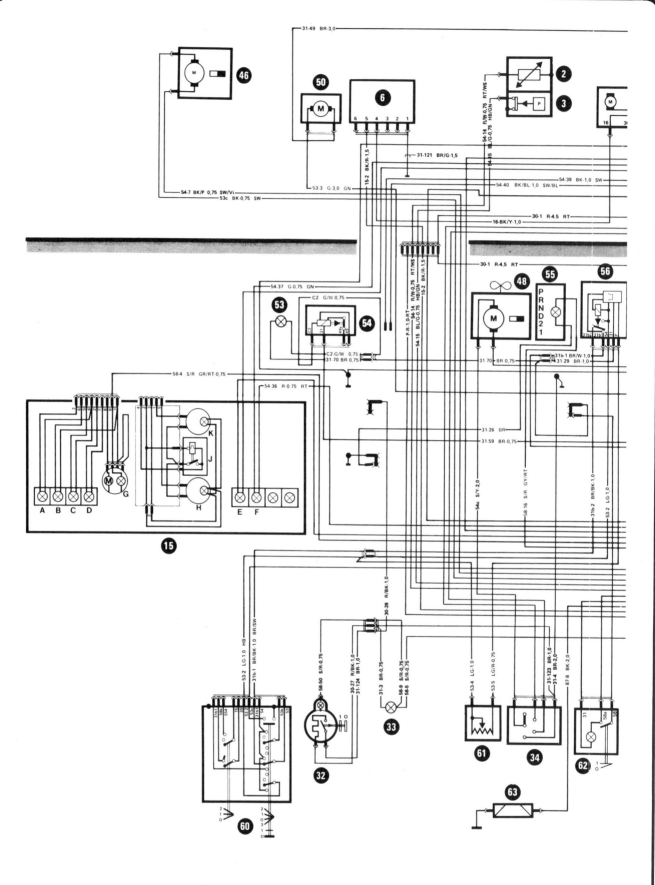

Fig. 13.31E Heater, wiper and exterior lights circuit

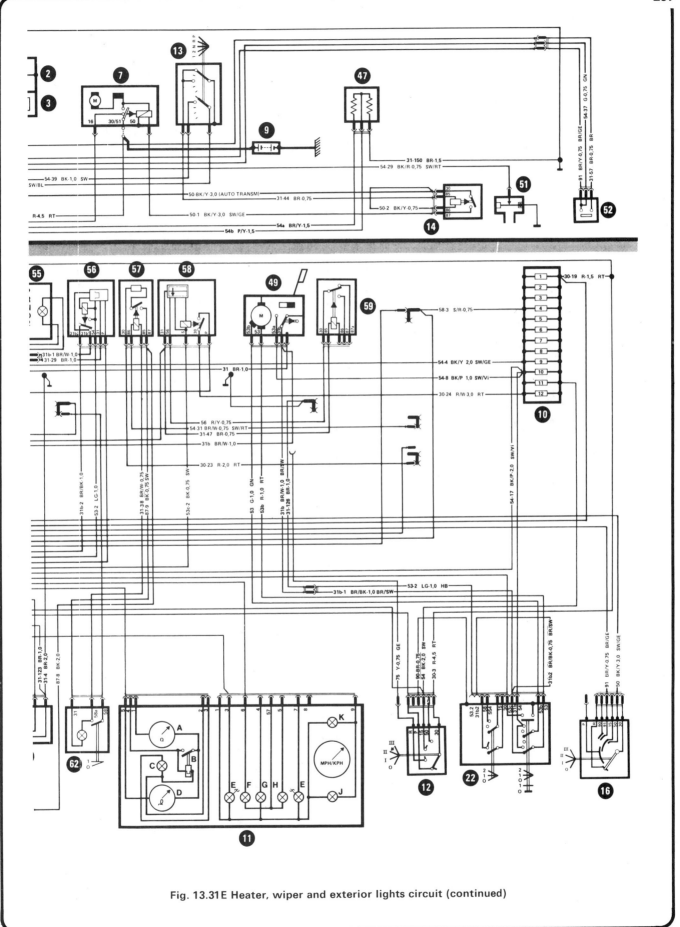

Fig. 13.31E Heater, wiper and exterior lights circuit (continued)

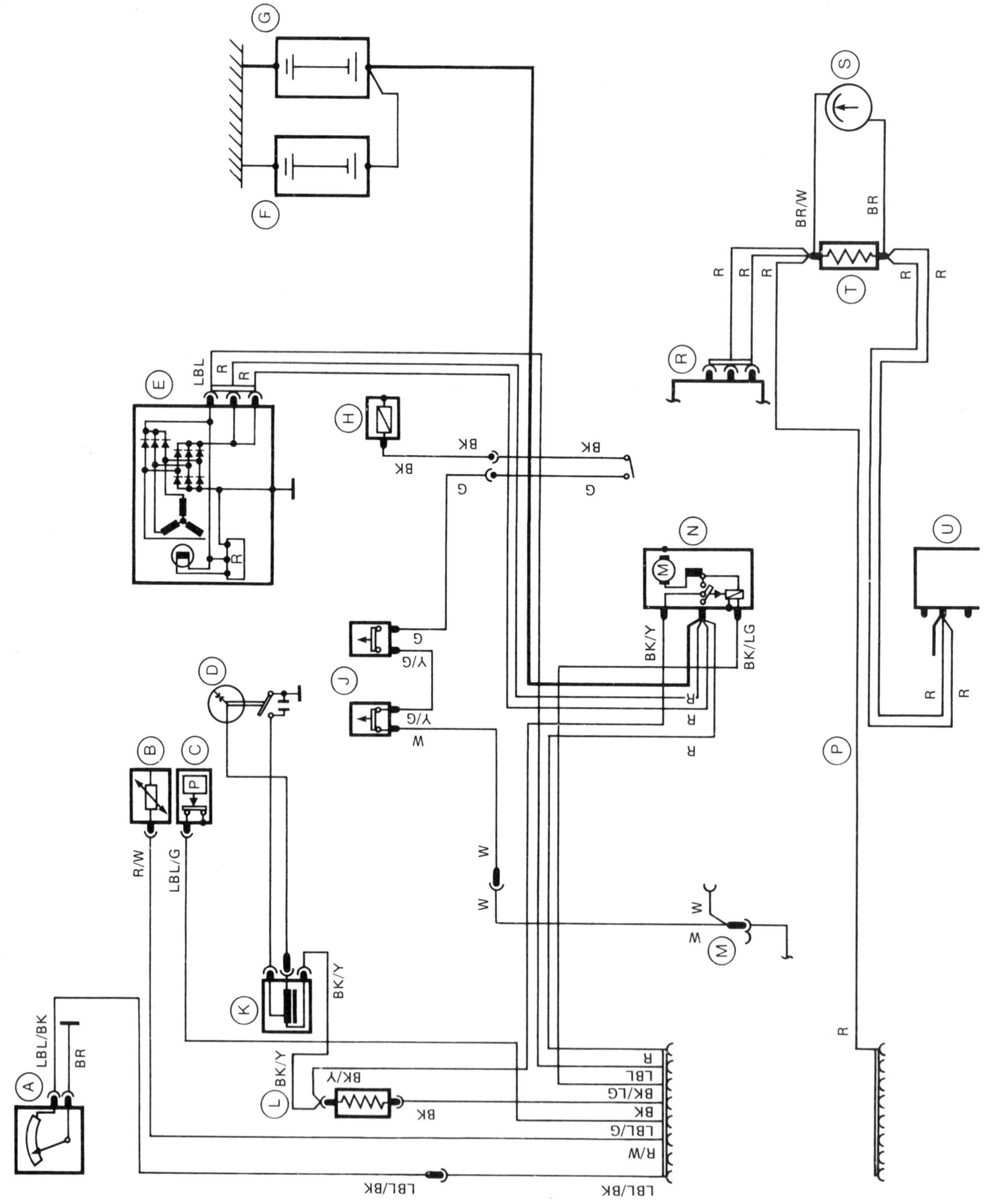

Fig. 13.32 Wiring diagram: overdrive – all models

Key to Fig. 13.32 Wiring diagram: overdrive – all models

A Fuel tank sender unit
B Coolant temperature sender unit
C Oil pressure switch
D Distributor
E Alternator
F Dual battery (if fitted)
G Battery

H Overdrive solenoid
J Transmission inhibitor switches
K Ignition coil
L Ballast resistor
M Wiring from fuse number 11
N Starter motor
P Alternative wiring when ammeter fitted

R Alternator
S Ammeter
T Ammeter shunt
U Starter motor

For colour code see key to Fig. 13.31

Colour code

BK Black (SW)
BL Blue (HB)
BR Brown

G   Green (GN)
GR Grey (S)
LBL Light blue
LG Light green
P   Pink (PK or RS)
R   Red (RT)
VI Violet (P)
W   White (WS)
Y   Yellow (GE)

Wire identification

eg 58-4 S/R 0.75
58-4 Wire number
S   Main colour
R   Secondary colour
0.75 Wire cross-section (mm²)

12 Suspension and steering

Steering gear (heavy duty type) – overhaul

1   Burman heavy duty steering gear is fitted to certain models including the Transit Ambulance. It should be overhauled in the following way.

2   With the steering gear removed from the vehicle, as previously described in Chapter 11, clean away external dirt.

3   Remove the filler plug and drain the oil.

4   Unscrew the securing bolts and remove the side cover (E) – Fig. 13.33 – and its gasket.

5   Remove the adjuster (F) and its locknut.

6   Withdraw the rocker shaft (D) and the sliding pivot (G).

7   Unbolt the upper bearing retainer (K) and withdraw the retainer, gasket and shims from the shaft (L).

8   Withdraw the steering shaft carefully until the upper thrust bearing track is clear of the housing (A). Retrieve the balls, thirteen from the upper bearing and ten from the lower bearing.

9   Remove the steering shaft and nut assembly through the side aperture of the housing and then remove the lower bearing track.

10 Secure the steering nut in the jaws of a vice fitted with jaw protectors, then remove the clamp from the transfer tube (B). Withdraw the tube; taking care not to lose any of the balls.

11 Take the steering nut and shaft from the vice and release the remaining balls by slowly unscrewing the shaft from the nut. A total of 27 balls is used in the steering assembly.

12 Check the rocker shaft bush for wear. To renew the bush, relieve the staking at the rocker shaft bore and discard the retainer and seal.

13 Extract the bush by screwing in a $^7/_8$ in BSP tap and then press out the bush and tap.

14 Press the new rocker shaft bush into the housing so that the open end of the oil groove faces the inside of the housing. Ream the bush to a diameter of between 1.124 and 1.125 in (28.550 and 28.575 mm). Remove the swarf.

15 Fit a new seal and retainer, and stake the housing to secure them.

16 If, on inspection, the rocker shaft bush was found to be in good condition, then only the retainer O-ring seal need be renewed.

17 If the steering worm or nut are worn then they must be renewed as an assembly.

Reassembly

18 Commence reassembly by feeding as many steel balls as possible into the nut and transfer tube. These balls are larger than those used in the two bearings.

19 In order to make room for the balls, fit the transfer tube and turn the nut on the shaft. Remove the tube and repeat the process until all the balls have been accommodated, then finally fit the transfer tube.

20 Clamp the transfer tube and lock the clamp bolts by bending up the ends of the clamp.

21 Fit the lower bearing track.

22 Pass the shaft and nut through the side aperture and position the nut so that the transfer tube is furthest from the aperture.

23 Stick the balls in the upper and lower bearing cups using thick grease and locate the steering shaft in the lower bearing.

24 Pass the upper bearing over the steering shaft and locate it in the housing.

25 Fit the original shims, a new gasket and the upper bearing retainer over the steering shaft.

26 Screw in the bearing retainer bolts and gradually tighten to a torque of between 15 and 18 lbf ft (2.1 and 2.5 kgf m) while turning the steering shaft. If the shaft binds or if, on completion of bolt tightening, any shaft endfloat is evident, adjust the number of shims to eliminate either condition.

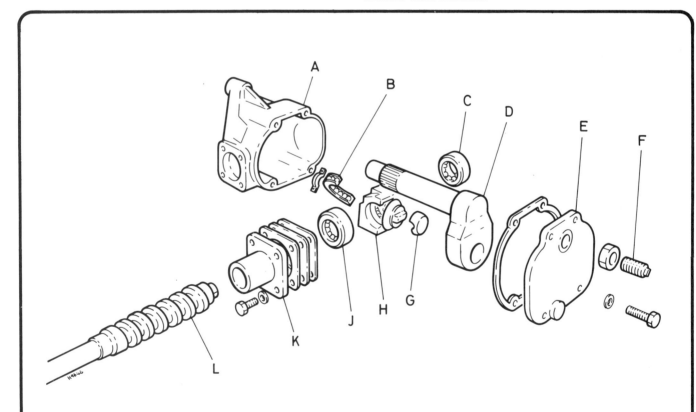

Fig. 13.33 Exploded view of Burman heavy duty steering gear (Sec 12)

A Housing	E Side cover	J Upper thrust bearing
B Transfer tube	F Adjusting screw	K Upper bearing retainer
C Lower thrust bearing	G Sliding pivot	L Steering shaft
D Rocker shaft	H Steering nut	

27 Finally, remove one shim (0.002 to 0.003 in (0.051 to 0.076 mm) in thickness) which will introduce the required bearing preload. Before finally tightening the bearing retainer bolts, smear their threads with sealant (jointing compound).

28 Turn the steering shaft so that the nut is centrally positioned, then fit the sliding pivot.

29 Locate the rocker shaft in the housing so that it engages with the steering nut.

30 Fit the side cover and gasket. Screw in the bolts, making sure that the two shorter ones which go into the holes which break through into the housing have sealant applied to their threads. Tighten the bolts to a torque of between 15 and 18 lbf ft (2.1 and 2.5 kgf m).

31 Screw in the rocker shaft adjusting screw until it just contacts the shaft and any endfloat in the shaft is eliminated. Without moving the screw, fit and tighten the locknut.

32 Fill the steering box after the steering gear has been refitted to the vehicle. Pour in the specified gear oil until it is level with the bottom of the filler plug hole. Refit the plug.

Steering balljoints – wear check

33 The track rod end and drag link balljoints may be regarded as serviceable if socket movement does not exceed 0.12 in (3.0 mm) when a load of 220 lb (100 kg) is applied at the adjacent rod or link. Should any movement be evident under hand pressure then the balljoint must be renewed.

Front anti-roll bar – fitting

34 A front anti-roll bar kit is now available for fitting to all Transit versions. This is of particular benefit on models such as motor home conversions having a high centre of gravity, in order to reduce body roll during cornering.

35 Fitting is carried out in the following way.

36 Jack up the front of the vehicle and support it securely on axle stands.

37 Inspect the front springs for the inclusion of castor wedge spacers (Fig. 13.34). If spacers are not evident then they must be fitted and secured with longer U-bolts. Make sure that the thickest end of the wedge is towards the rear of the vehicle. Tighten the U-bolt nuts to the specified torque (Chapter 11).

38 Remove the bolts from either the left or right-hand engine mounting, having adequately supported the engine, and fit the anti-roll bar mounting bracket, as shown in Fig. 13.35. Tighten the bolts to the specified torque.

39 Fit the anti-roll bar mounting bracket to the opposite side of the vehicle.

40 Partially assemble the anti-roll bar, setting the bushes on the bar as shown in Fig. 13.36.

41 Locate the bush clamps, U-bolts and support plates.

42 Fit a connecting link to either the left or right-hand anti-roll bar mounting bracket (Fig. 13.37).

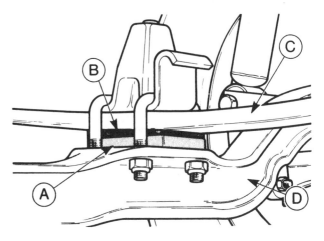

Fig. 13.34 Front spring attachment (Sec 12)

A Spacer
B Castor wedge
C Roadspring
D Axle beam

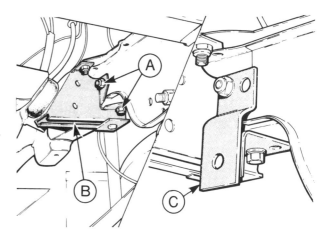

Fig. 13.35 Front anti-roll bar mounting bracket (Sec 12)

A Fixing nuts
B Engine mounting
C Anti-roll bar bracket

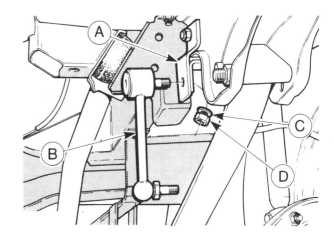

Fig. 13.37 Front anti-roll bar end link (Sec 12)

A Mounting bracket
B Link
C Washer
D Nut

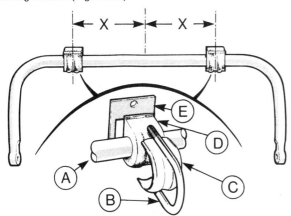

Fig. 13.36 Front anti-roll bar mounting clamps (Sec 12)

A Anti-roll bar
B U-Bolt
C Clamp
D Bush
E Support plate

X = 9.9 to 10.2 in
(250.0 to 260.0 mm)

43 Offer up the anti-roll bar to the axle, making sure that the recess in the bracket is towards the axle. Tighten the U-bolt nuts finger tight.
44 Fit the remaining link and connect both links to the anti-roll bar.
45 Lower the vehicle to the ground and tighten all nuts to the torque wrench settings given in the Specifications.

Roadwheels – high load capacity type

46 As from December 1983, high load capacity roadwheels have been fitted to LCX and 100L models.
47 The wheels are identified by a blue paint spot and the letter H stamped onto the front face of the wheel.
48 It is imperative that low load capacity wheels are not fitted to the models referred to in paragraph 46.

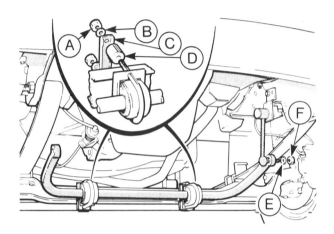

Fig. 13.38 Front anti-roll bar clamp components (Sec 12)

A   Nut
B   Washer
C   Clamp rear bracket

D   Plastic spacer
E   Washer
F   Nut

13 Bodywork

Wheelbase extension

1 On Chassis Cab versions which have an extended wheelbase, the extension fixing bolts should be tightened to the torque wrench settings given in Specifications at the beginning of this Supplement.
2 Check the tightness of these bolts at 12 000 mile (20 000 km) service intervals.

Window regulator (hinged door)

3 As from December 1983, the window regulators have been changed from cable operated type to arm and quadrant design.
4 Fitting the later type regulator as a replacement may be carried out in the following way.
5 Remove the door trim panel and waterproof sheet, as described in Chapter 12.
6 Remove the inner and outer weatherstrips from the door waist.
7 Remove and retain the anti-rattle pad from the regulator plate (original assembly).
8 Extract the fixing screws and remove the quarter window, frame and divider from the door.
9 Raise the window until the regulator-to-glass fixing screws are accessible, then remove them and withdraw the glass upwards and out of the door.
10 Unscrew the regulator fixing bolts and remove the regulator from the door.
11 Using a block of wood, tap the channel from the lower edge of the glass.
12 Fit the new rubber strip and channel to the glass, locating it as shown in Fig. 13.42. Fit the glass to the door.
13 Fit the anti-rattle pad to the regulator arm and then insert the regulator through the aperture into the door. Engage the regulator arm with the roller guide (E).
14 Align the regulator holes, drilling new ones as necessary (Fig. 13.43), then rivet the regulator in place.
15 Refit the door waist weatherstrips, waterproof sheet and trim panel.

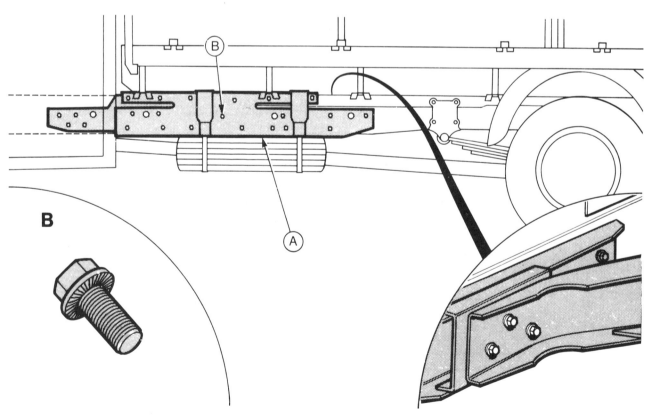

Fig. 13.39 Wheelbase extension (A) and special locking bolts (B) (Sec 13)

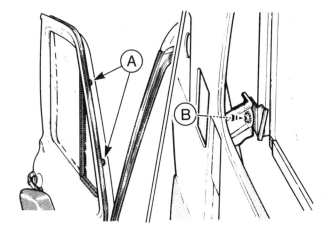

Fig. 13.40 Quarter window screws (A) and glass guide
screw (B) (Sec 13)

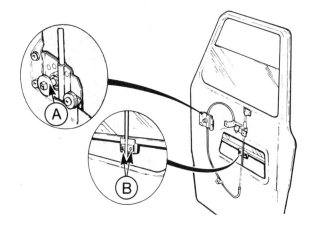

Fig. 13.41 Cable type window regulator (Sec 13)

A   Anti-rattle pad   B   Regulator fixing screws

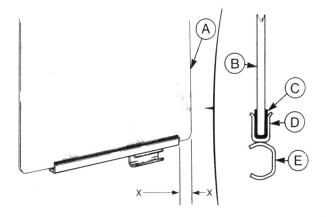

Fig. 13.42 Glass channel position (quadrant type regulator)
(Sec 13)

A   Rear edge of glass   D   Channel
B   Glass   E   Roller guide
C   Weatherstrip   X = 1.18 in (30.0 mm)

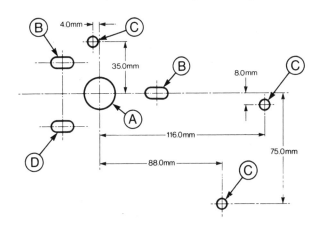

Fig. 13.43 Quadrant type regulator fixing holes (Sec 13)

A   Regulator shaft aperture   C   0.28 in (7.0 mm) diameter
B   Existing slots   holes to be drilled
                               D   Existing slot

Heater – warm air seepage

16 If warm air still tends to seep into the car even though the heater
controls are correctly adjusted and fully off, the under-bonnet coolant
valve should be turned off.

17 This valve is fitted to all manual choke versions but only to
automatic choke versions with a VV carburettor.

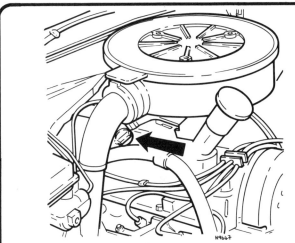

Fig. 13.44 Heater valve (arrowed) on manual choke
VV carburettor (Sec 13)

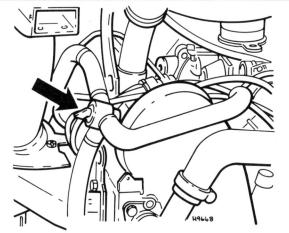

Fig. 13.45 Heater valve (arrowed) on automatic choke
VV carburettor (Sec 13)

Radiator grille – removal and refitting

18 Open the bonnet and support it securely.

19 Unscrew the eight grille fixing screws and lift the grille from the vehicle.

20 If a headlamp washer system is fitted, disconnect the washer pipes as the grille is withdrawn.

21 Refitting is a reversal of removal.

Radiator grille emblem – removal and refitting

22 Work a length of small diameter nylon cord back and forth behind the emblem to release it.

23 Clean old adhesive from the grille using methylated spirit.

24 Warm the new badge, peel off the protective backing and press it into place.

Exterior rear view mirror – removal and refitting

25 Push in the centre pins of the two plastic rivets which hold the mirror stem trim. Remove the trim.

26 Extract the two screws now exposed and lift away the mirror and gasket. Recover the plastic rivet centre pins.

27 Refitting is a reversal of removal, fit the trim fixing rivets and then push in the centre pins.

Door mirror glass – renewal

28 Protect the eyes and then prise the mirror glass and retainer from the mirror body using a flat blade.

29 Separate the glass from the retainer.

30 Fit the new glass by reversing the removal operations.

Fig. 13.46 Radiator grille securing screws – arrowed (Sec 13)

Fig. 13.47 Removing emblem with nylon cord (Sec 13)

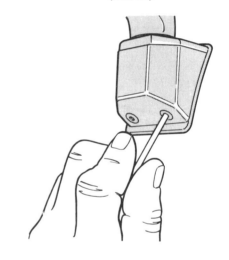

Fig. 13.48 Removing mirror trim rivet centre pins (Sec 13)

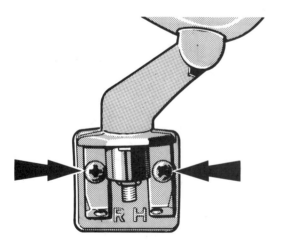

Fig. 13.49 Exterior mirror fixing screws – arrowed (Sec 13)

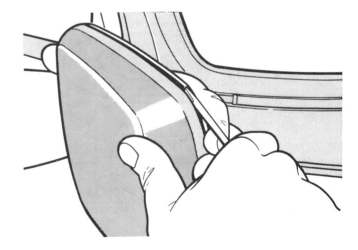

Fig. 13.50 Removing door mirror glass retainer (Sec 13)

Rear door lettering – removal

31 These can be removed if the area is heated using a hot air blower or high intensity lamp. The letters will peel off once a reasonable temperature is reached.

Front bumper – removal and refitting

32 Grip one plastic quarter bumper and pull it sharply to disengage it from its body clips.

33 Release the clip which retains the quarter bumper to the bumper bar.

34 Remove the opposite quarter bumper in a similar way.

35 Working behind the bumper, unscrew the four nuts and remove the bumper bar from the support brackets.

36 The bumper bar trim can be removed using a pair of pliers as shown in Fig. 13.53.

37 Refitting is a reversal of removal.

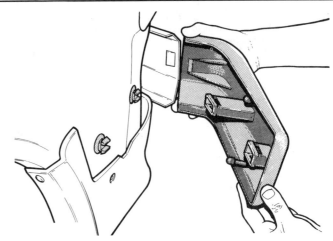

Fig. 13.51 Releasing front quarter bumper (Sec 13)

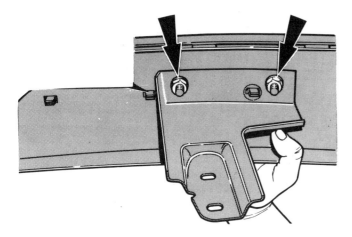

Fig. 13.52 Front bumper bar fixing nuts – arrowed (Sec 13)

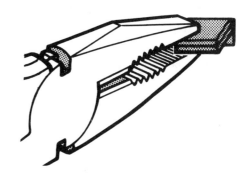

Fig. 13.53 Removing bumper bar trim (Sec 13)

Rear bumper – removal and refitting

38 Grip one quarter bumper and pull it sharply to disengage it from its body clips.

39 Unclip the opposite quarter bumper in a similar way.

40 Release both quarter bumpers from the bumper bar.

41 Unbolt the bumper bars from their mounting irons.

42 Refit by reversing the removal operations.

Front air dam – removal and refitting

43 From below the bumper remove the air dam section joint clip.

44 Extract the six screws which hold the half air dam to the front panel.

45 Remove the other air dam section in a similar way.

46 Refitting is a reversal of removal but only fit the screws finger tight until the two sections are precisely aligned.

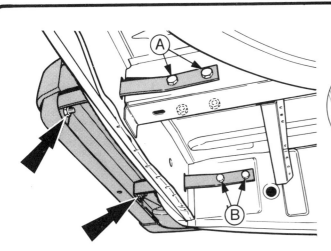

Fig. 13.54 Rear bumper section fixing nuts – arrowed (Sec 13)

A Bolts through chassis   B Bolts into captive nuts

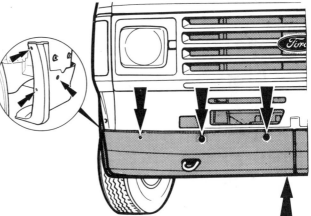

Fig. 13.55 Air dam half section fixing screws – arrowed (Sec 13)

Interior rear view mirror – removal and refitting

47 Pull off the mirror trim to expose the fixing screws. Extract the screws and remove the mirror.

48 When refitting the mirror, adjust the stem so that the rubber bump rubber just rests on the windscreen.

Facia crash padding – removal and refitting

49 Turn the twist fasteners which hold the facia panel cover and remove the cover.

50 Remove the instrument cluster, as described in Chapter 10.

51 Extract the now exposed crash padding screws and withdraw the crash padding.

52 Refitting is a reversal of removal.

Glove compartment lid – removal and refitting

53 Open the lid and, using a large screwdriver, prise off the hinge pin clips.

54 Push the pins through their holes and remove the lid.

55 Refitting is a reversal of removal.

Front seat – removal and refitting

56 Unbolt the seat slides from the floor and lift the seat from the cab.

57 If necessary, the slides can be unbolted and removed from the seat frame.

58 Refitting is a reversal of removal.

Panel partition – removal and refitting

59 Remove the bump rubber (Fig. 13.60).

60 Remove the screws which secure the two support tubes to the

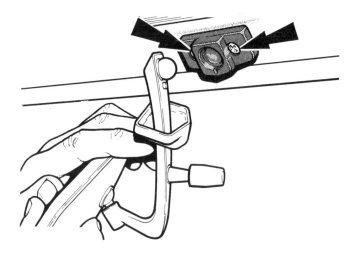

Fig. 13.56 Interior rear view mirror fixing screws – arrowed (Sec 13)

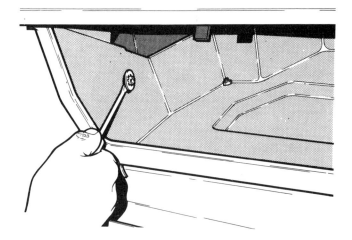

Fig. 13.58 Prising off a glovebox hinge pin clip (Sec 13)

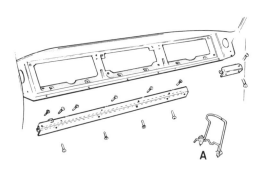

Fig. 13.57 Facia crash pad fixing screws (Sec 13)

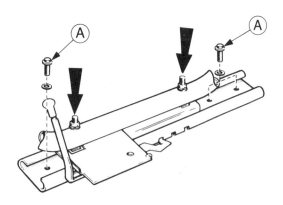

Fig. 13.59 Front seat slide nuts – arrowed (Sec 13)

A   Slide-to-floorpan bolts

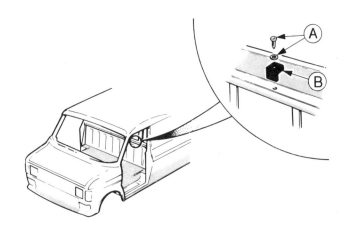

Fig. 13.60 Partition bump rubber (Sec 13)

A   Screw and washer   B   Bump rubber

partition and the body side (Fig. 13.61). Remove the support tubes.

61 Remove the screw which holds the lower partition flange to the floorpan.

62 Remove the screws which hold the outer brackets to the floorpan (Fig. 13.62).

63 Extract the top corner screws which hold the partition retainer to the side retainers.

64 Extract the six screws which hold the reinforcement plates to the upper bulkhead (Fig. 13.63).

65 Extract the screws and remove the reinforcement plates.

66 Remove the front seats and safety belts.

67 Withdraw the partition panel from the vehicle.

68 Refitting is a reversal of removal, but check the condition of the sealing strips and renew if necessary.

69 Make sure that the special nuts in the side and upper retainers are correctly located.

Half panel – removal and refitting

70 Remove the seat and safety belt.

71 Drill out the two pop rivets which hold the lower end of the partition rail to the floorpan (Fig. 13.66).

72 Extract the five screws which secure the partition panel lower flange to the floorpan.

73 Extract the two screws which hold the partition panel rail to the roof bow bracket (Fig. 13.67).

74 Extract the seven screws which hold the half panel to the body side retainer.

75 Withdraw the half panel.

76 Refitting is a reversal of removal, renew the panel seal if necessary.

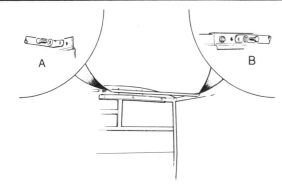

Fig. 13.61 Partition support tubes (Sec 13)

A   Fixing at partition   B   Fixing at body

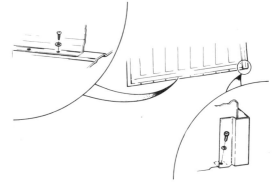

Fig. 13.62 Partition flange-to-floorpan fixing (Sec 13)

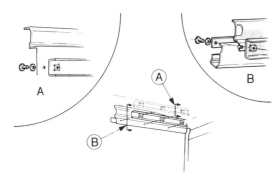

Fig. 13.63 Partition reinforcement plates to upper bulkhead (Sec 13)

A   LCY variants   B   LCX variants

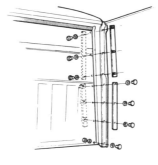

Fig. 13.64 Partition upper and lower side reinforcements (Sec 13)

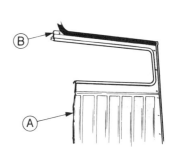

Fig. 13.65 Partition sealing strip (Sec 13)

A   Panel   B   Sealing strip

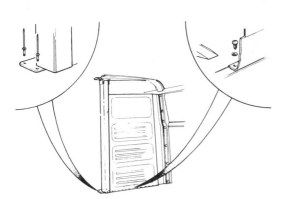

Fig. 13.66 Partition rail and lower flange fixings (Sec 13)

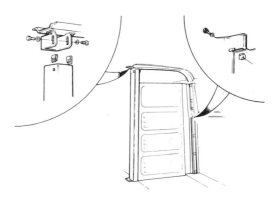

Fig. 13.67 Partition rail and panel to roof bow bracket and bodyside retainer (Sec 13)

General repair procedures

Whenever servicing, repair or overhaul work is carried out on the car or its components, it is necessary to observe the following procedures and instructions. This will assist in carrying out the operation efficiently and to a professional standard of workmanship.

Joint mating faces and gaskets

Where a gasket is used between the mating faces of two components, ensure that it is renewed on reassembly, and fit it dry unless otherwise stated in the repair procedure. Make sure that the mating faces are clean and dry with all traces of old gasket removed. When cleaning a joint face, use a tool which is not likely to score or damage the face, and remove any burrs or nicks with an oilstone or fine file.

Make sure that tapped holes are cleaned with a pipe cleaner, and keep them free of jointing compound if this is being used unless specifically instructed otherwise.

Ensure that all orifices, channels or pipes are clear and blow through them, preferably using compressed air.

Oil seals

Whenever an oil seal is removed from its working location, either individually or as part of an assembly, it should be renewed.

The very fine sealing lip of the seal is easily damaged and will not seal if the surface it contacts is not completely clean and free from scratches, nicks or grooves. If the original sealing surface of the component cannot be restored, the component should be renewed.

Protect the lips of the seal from any surface which may damage them in the course of fitting. Use tape or a conical sleeve where possible. Lubricate the seal lips with oil before fitting and, on dual lipped seals, fill the space between the lips with grease.

Unless otherwise stated, oil seals must be fitted with their sealing lips toward the lubricant to be sealed.

Use a tubular drift or block of wood of the appropriate size to install the seal and, if the seal housing is shouldered, drive the seal down to the shoulder. If the seal housing is unshouldered, the seal should be fitted with its face flush with the housing top face.

Screw threads and fastenings

Always ensure that a blind tapped hole is completely free from oil, grease, water or other fluid before installing the bolt or stud. Failure to do this could cause the housing to crack due to the hydraulic action of the bolt or stud as it is screwed in.

When tightening a castellated nut to accept a split pin, tighten the nut to the specified torque, where applicable, and then tighten further to the next split pin hole. Never slacken the nut to align a split pin hole unless stated in the repair procedure.

When checking or retightening a nut or bolt to a specified torque setting, slacken the nut or bolt by a quarter of a turn, and then retighten to the specified setting.

Locknuts, locktabs and washers

Any fastening which will rotate against a component or housing in the course of tightening should always have a washer between it and the relevant component or housing.

Spring or split washers should always be renewed when they are used to lock a critical component such as a big-end bearing retaining nut or bolt.

Locktabs which are folded over to retain a nut or bolt should always be renewed.

Self-locking nuts can be reused in non-critical areas, providing resistance can be felt when the locking portion passes over the bolt or stud thread.

Split pins must always be replaced with new ones of the correct size for the hole.

Special tools

Some repair procedures in this manual entail the use of special tools such as a press, two or three-legged pullers, spring compressors etc. Wherever possible, suitable readily available alternatives to the manufacturer's special tools are described, and are shown in use. In some instances, where no alternative is possible, it has been necessary to resort to the use of a manufacturer's tool and this has been done for reasons of safety as well as the efficient completion of the repair operation. Unless you are highly skilled and have a thorough understanding of the procedure described, never attempt to bypass the use of any special tool when the procedure described specifies its use. Not only is there a very great risk of personal injury, but expensive damage could be caused to the components involved.

Conversion factors

Length (distance)

Inches (in)	X	25.4	= Millimetres (mm)	X	0.0394	= Inches (in)
Feet (ft)	X	0.305	= Metres (m)	X	3.281	= Feet (ft)
Miles	X	1.609	= Kilometres (km)	X	0.621	= Miles

Volume (capacity)

Cubic inches (cu in; in^3)	X	16.387	= Cubic centimetres (cc; cm^3)	X	0.061	= Cubic inches (cu in; in^3)
Imperial pints (Imp pt)	X	0.568	= Litres (l)	X	1.76	= Imperial pints (Imp pt)
Imperial quarts (Imp qt)	X	1.137	= Litres (l)	X	0.88	= Imperial quarts (Imp qt)
Imperial quarts (Imp qt)	X	1.201	= US quarts (US qt)	X	0.833	= Imperial quarts (Imp qt)
US quarts (US qt)	X	0.946	= Litres (l)	X	1.057	= US quarts (US qt)
Imperial gallons (Imp gal)	X	4.546	= Litres (l)	X	0.22	= Imperial gallons (Imp gal)
Imperial gallons (Imp gal)	X	1.201	= US gallons (US gal)	X	0.833	= Imperial gallons (Imp gal)
US gallons (US gal)	X	3.785	= Litres (l)	X	0.264	= US gallons (US gal)

Mass (weight)

Ounces (oz)	X	28.35	= Grams (g)	X	0.035	= Ounces (oz)
Pounds (lb)	X	0.454	= Kilograms (kg)	X	2.205	= Pounds (lb)

Force

Ounces-force (ozf; oz)	X	0.278	= Newtons (N)	X	3.6	= Ounces-force (ozf; oz)
Pounds-force (lbf; lb)	X	4.448	= Newtons (N)	X	0.225	= Pounds-force (lbf; lb)
Newtons (N)	X	0.1	= Kilograms-force (kgf; kg)	X	9.81	= Newtons (N)

Pressure

Pounds-force per square inch (psi; lbf/in^2; lb/in^2)	X	0.070	= Kilograms-force per square centimetre (kgf/cm²; kg/cm²)	X	14.223	= Pounds-force per square inch (psi; lbf/in^2; lb/in^2)
Pounds-force per square inch (psi; lbf/in^2; lb/in^2)	X	0.068	= Atmospheres (atm)	X	14.696	= Pounds-force per square inch (psi; lbf/in^2; lb/in^2)
Pounds-force per square inch (psi; lbf/in^2; lb/in^2)	X	0.069	= Bars	X	14.5	= Pounds-force per square inch (psi; lbf/in^2; lb/in^2)
Pounds-force per square inch (psi; lbf/in^2; lb/in^2)	X	6.895	= Kilopascals (kPa)	X	0.145	= Pounds-force per square inch (psi; lbf/in^2; lb/in^2)
Kilopascals (kPa)	X	0.01	= Kilograms-force per square centimetre (kgf/cm²; kg/cm²)	X	98.1	= Kilopascals (kPa)

Torque (moment of force)

Pounds-force inches (lbf in; lb in)	X	1.152	= Kilograms-force centimetre (kgf cm; kg cm)	X	0.868	= Pounds-force inches (lbf in; lb in)
Pounds-force inches (lbf in; lb in)	X	0.113	= Newton metres (Nm)	X	8.85	= Pounds-force inches (lbf in; lb in)
Pounds-force inches (lbf in; lb in)	X	0.083	= Pounds-force feet (lbf ft; lb ft)	X	12	= Pounds-force inches (lbf in; lb in)
Pounds-force feet (lbf ft; lb ft)	X	0.138	= Kilograms-force metres (kgf m; kg m)	X	7.233	= Pounds-force feet (lbf ft; lb ft)
Pounds-force feet (lbf ft; lb ft)	X	1.356	= Newton metres (Nm)	X	0.738	= Pounds-force feet (lbf ft; lb ft)
Newton metres (Nm)	X	0.102	= Kilograms-force metres (kgf m; kg m)	X	9.804	= Newton metres (Nm)

Power

Horsepower (hp)	X	745.7	= Watts (W)	X	0.0013	= Horsepower (hp)

Velocity (speed)

Miles per hour (miles/hr; mph)	X	1.609	= Kilometres per hour (km/hr; kph)	X	0.621	= Miles per hour (miles/hr; mph)

Fuel consumption*

Miles per gallon, Imperial (mpg)	X	0.354	= Kilometres per litre (km/l)	X	2.825	= Miles per gallon, Imperial (mpg)
Miles per gallon, US (mpg)	X	0.425	= Kilometres per litre (km/l)	X	2.352	= Miles per gallon, US (mpg)

Temperature

Degrees Fahrenheit = (°C x 1.8) + 32

Degrees Celsius (Degrees Centigrade; °C) = (°F - 32) x 0.56

*It is common practice to convert from miles per gallon (mpg) to litres/100 kilometres (l/100km),
where mpg (Imperial) x l/100 km = 282 and mpg (US) x l/100 km = 235

Index

Printed by
J H Haynes & Co Ltd
Sparkford Nr Yeovil
Somerset BA22 7JJ England